**Jezyk jest tłumaczem rozumu i wiedzy,
Poznaj wartość jasnego języka, który opromienia człowieka.**

**The tongue is the interpreter to intellect and wisdom.
Know that an eloquent tongue causes a man to shine.**

**Für Verstand und Weisheit ist die Zunge der Dolmetscher.
Wisse, dass klare Rede die Erde erleuchtet.**

**Anlayış ve bilgiye tercüman olan dildir;
İnsanı aydınlatan açık dilin kıymetini bil.**

**Język wzbogaca człowieka i przynosi mu szczęście,
Język może go poniżyć i pozbawić życia.**

**It is the tongue that brings a man esteem, so that he finds fortune,
and it is the tongue that brings a man dishonour, so that he loses his head.**

**Dem Menschen verleiht die Zunge Ehre, mit ihr findet er Glück,
Die Zunge erniedrigt ihn, durch sie geht er unter.**

**Kişiyi dil kıymetlendirir ve kişi onunla mutluluk bulur;
Kişiyi dil kıymetten düşürür ve kişinin dil yüzünden başı gider.**

**Język jest jak lew, co wyleguje się na progu,
O, gospodarzu, strzeż się, by nie odgryzł ci głowy.**

**The tongue is a lion crouching on the threshold – householder,
take care, or it will bite off your head!**

**Die Zunge ist ein Löwe, sieh, sie liegt an der Tür,
Oh Weib, Schwatzhaftigkeit kostet Dich den Kopf!**

**Dil arslandır, bak, eşikte yatar;
Ey ev sahibi, dikkat et, senin başını yer.**

**Posłuchaj, co mówi ten, co ucierpiał przez język!
Postępuj wedle jego słów i miej to zawsze w pamięci!**

**Listen to a man who has suffered because of his tongue,
make his speech your companion, and apply it to your own affairs.**

**Höre, wie der von seiner Zunge geplagte Mann spricht!
Handle nach diesem Wort und beruhige Deinen Sinn!**

**Dilinden eziyet çeken adam ne der, işit;
Bu söze göre hareket et, bunu daima aklında tut.**

**Mój język sprawia mi wiele trosk,
Prędzej niechaj utną mi język niż głowę!**

**Let me cut out my tongue – it is what ruined me –
only let them not cut off my head!**

**Mich plagt meine Zunge, meine scharfe Zunge,
Dass sie mir das Haupt nicht abschneide, will ich die Zunge abschneiden!**

**Dilim bana pek çok eziyet çektiriyor;
Başımı kesmesinler de ben dilimi keseyim.**

**Zważaj na swe słowa, byś nie stracił głowy,
Trzymaj język swój na wodzy, byś nie stracił zębów.**

**Guard your speech lest you lose your head,
and guard your tongue lest you break your teeth.**

**Hüte Deine Worte, damit Du den Kopf nicht verlierst!
Hüte Deine Zunge, damit Deine Zähne nicht brechen!**

**Sözüne dikkat et ki başın gitmesin;
Dilini tut ki dişin kırılmasın.**

Lektor (*speculum linguarum*), a multichannel audio work, features a selection from the eleventh-century Turkic mirror for princes *Kutadgu Bilig* (*Wisdom of Royal Glory*), in its original Uighur with several voice-overs. The delivery of a near-monotonous, matter-of-fact voice-over stems from a translation practice called Gavrilov translation, often used in Poland and Russia. The original language is kept audible, almost equally so, to the destination language. Specifically, the excerpts extracted from *Kutadgu Bilig* offer advice pertaining to speech and tongues – tongues that bring fortune and bad luck, profit and loss – and what it means to loosen the tongue, to hold it or stick it out.

In each venue, the selection of translations for the voice-over or dub traces the itinerary of the piece through the languages of its exhibition history. Across the margins of this volume's pages are five translations, in addition to the original Uighur: Turkish, German, Polish, English and Arabic. The simultaneous playback of distinct audio tracks makes for a disruptive experience, touching on issues of legibility and authenticity – elsewhere in the world, voice-over translations are often used for news segments and documentaries – not to mention language as a form of hospitality.

pp. 1–192

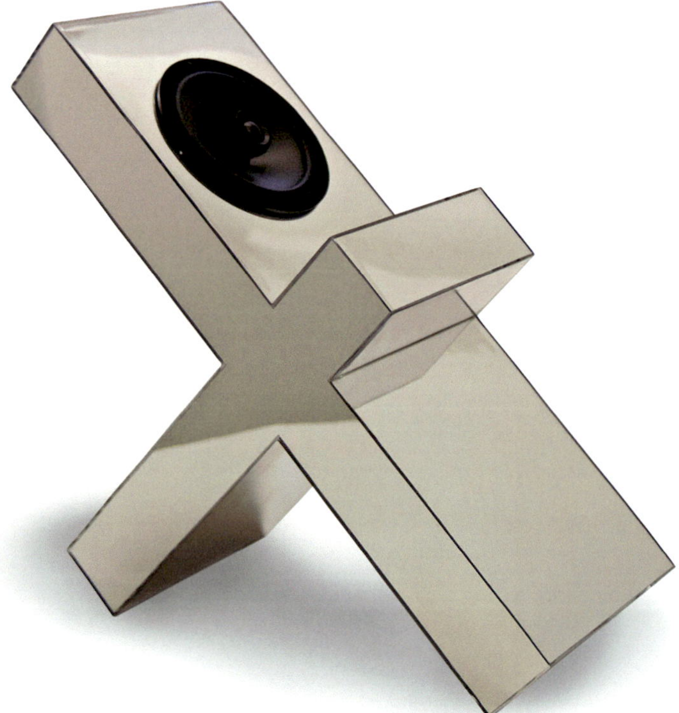

Lektor (detail),
mirrored plexiglass, speakers,
47 × 22 × 49 cm, 2014. Photo by
Lars Bergmann, GfZK Leipzig.

Table of Contents

قال أحد الحكماء في حق اللسان: رقيب رأسك يا صاحب اللسان.

Bilgili kişi dil için özlü bir söz söyledi; Başını gözet, ey dil sahibi.

The sage has laid down for the tongue these ripe words of wisdom, so guard your head, you who have a tongue!

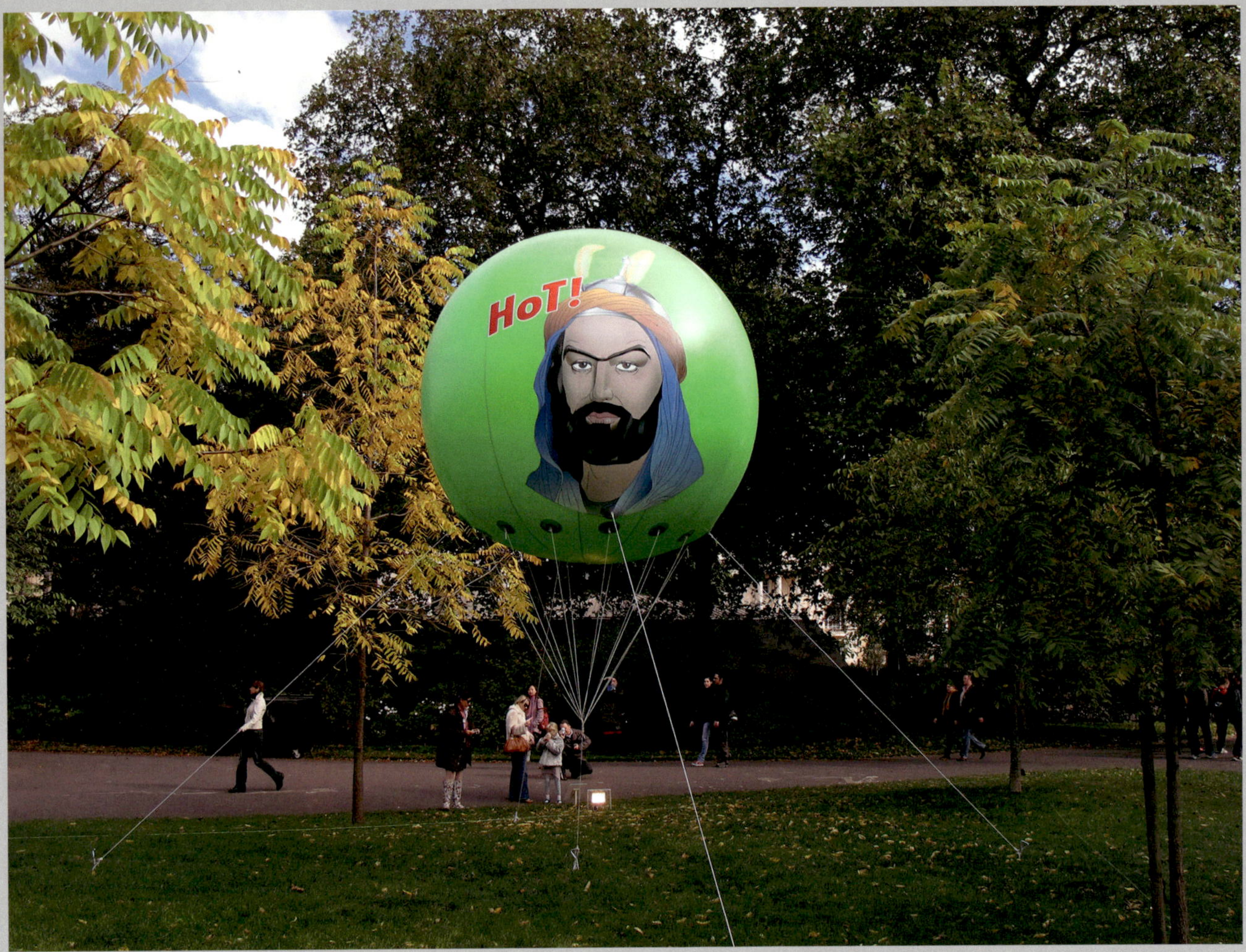

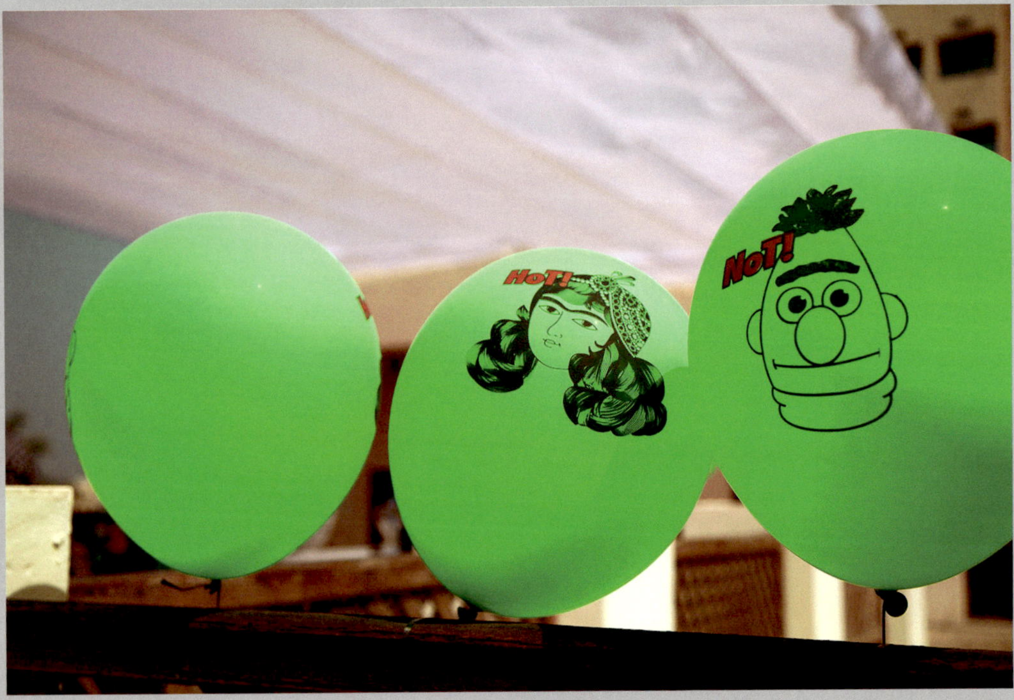

Monobrow Manifesto,
PVC, print, helium, 300 cm Ø,
2011. Frieze Sculpture Park,
London. *(top)*

Monobrow Manifesto,
rubber, screen-print, 2011.
Sharjah Biennial 10. *(left)*

CURATOR'S PROLOGUE

Maya Allison

I have been following the work of the art collective Slavs and Tatars since 2010, when I encountered their installation *Monobrow Manifesto* (2010). At the time I was preparing to relocate to Abu Dhabi, and particularly attentive to works engaged with some notion of the Middle East. *Monobrow Manifesto* is an unlikely pairing of two visual references to the 'monobrow', one identified as *hot* (Qajar, a Persian prince), one *not* (the Muppet Bert). It made me uncomfortable even as I laughed at the pairing. Ultimately, I felt invited to reflect on the underlying cultural references, and to question the source of my discomfort. The work was a gift to me as a viewer and as a curator.

I tell this story to introduce the generosity of Slavs and Tatars' art practice. Since that first encounter, I have watched their work evolve and deepen, never losing the giftlike layering of pleasure and heightened cultural awareness at work in *Monobrow Manifesto*.

These artists produce series of works that they refer to as 'cycles'. Each cycle averages several years. A cycle begins with research into a topic: the artists delve into archives, attend conferences and conduct field research in far-flung locales. They 'translate' the fruit of their research into sculptures, installations, performances and publications. Rather than touring one exhibition of work to multiple museum and gallery venues, they use each new exhibition space as a unique tour through one aspect of the cycle.

A key element in each is the production of a book, not in the sense of a traditional 'artist's book' or museum catalogue, but through commissioning scholarly essays and translations around a given cycle's research topic.

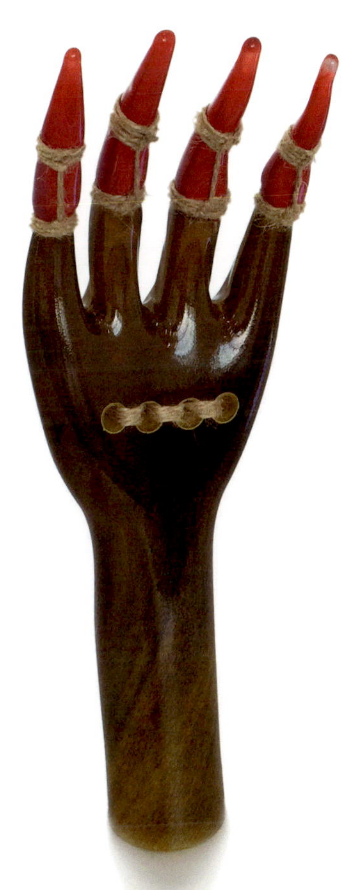

Javanfemme,
handblown glass, string,
25 × 10 × 8 cm, 2014.

The book you hold in your hands is one such publication, commissioned for Slavs and Tatars current cycle of work, *Mirrors for Princes*. The title refers to a genre of medieval statecraft that appeared in both Islamic and Christian cultures. Presented as gifts to rulers to prepare their heirs, these texts imparted advice on comportment, grooming and political leadership, always layered with praise, encouragement and celebration.

For this book the artists have commissioned essays from academics and artists on the topic of mirrors for princes. The resulting book is a gift in its own right, to the scholarship on the topic, to the audience of each exhibition, and to the larger conversation in which it engages. Like all gifts, the process of making this book created new connections, among communities (artistic and academic) and among ideas (statecraft and self-help), whether academic or artistic, regional or international.

Ultimately, Slavs and Tatars' practice aligns with the mission of the NYU Abu Dhabi Art Gallery in remarkable ways. It links the production of physical art objects to scholarly research and creative rethinking of cultural history and the cultures of the present day. It has a cultural curiosity at once omnivorous and focused. For example, the artists often describe themselves as 'devoted to an area … east of the former Berlin Wall and west of the Great Wall of China'. This formulation un-divides the regions in between, and invites one to reconsider the standard map. More subtly, it includes multiple societies that identify as 'Islamic', without conflating Islam with one location.

At the time of this writing, I am looking forward to Slav and Tatars residency at NYU Abu Dhabi in the months preceding their exhibition. Their presence contributes to the dialogue within NYU Abu Dhabi, a liberal arts university with a fundamentally cross-cultural curriculum and a student body of unprecedented international composition. NYU Abu Dhabi's curricular mandate responds in part to the university's location in the Gulf, an historical and still-evolving cultural crossroads.

This book represents collaboration among many parties. It is published by the NYUAD Art Gallery with JRP|Ringier on the occasion of the exhibition at NYU Abu Dhabi. It would not be possible without our editorial partners at Ibraaz, particularly this book's editor, Anthony Downey, and project manager Nour K Sacranie. The four other venues on the *Mirrors for Princes* cycle offered support of many kinds; they are: the Kunsthalle Zürich; the Institute of Modern Art, Brisbane; the Collective Gallery, Edinburgh; and the Blaffer Art Gallery at the University of Houston.

I am honoured that Slavs and Tatars will be the subject of the inaugural solo exhibition at the NYU Abu Dhabi Art Gallery. It is our great pleasure to participate in this cycle of gifts from Slavs and Tatars.

Maya Allison
Director and Chief Curator
New York University
Abu Dhabi Art Gallery
www.nyuad-artgallery.org

EDITOR'S INTRODUCTION

Anthony Downey

'When a man speaks knowledgeably, his words are counted as wisdom, while the words of the ignorant devour his own head.'

Yusūf Khāss Hājib, *Kutadgu Bilig*, ca. 1069-70 AD.

'The tongue is the best masseur of furrowed brows.'

Anwar-i-Suhaili (Lights of Canopus), early 16th century.

'I went to a bookstore and asked the saleswoman, "Where's the self-help section?" She said if she told me, it would defeat the purpose.'

George Carlin

Anyone who has frequented a bookshop or passed through an airport in the last decade will find the self-help book a ubiquitous sight. Founded by the aptly named Samuel Smiles, the genre invariably employs the tools of popular psychology, while promising fast-track solutions to everyday issues, be they romantic, economic, personal, sexual or psychological. Published in 1859, Smiles' *Self-Help* was concerned with elevating individuals from poverty and ignorance to relative positions of wealth and social eminence. This elevation, in true Victorian fashion, could be acquired through hard work and rigorous self-discipline, but the ultimate key was self-education. Knowledge, Smiles proposed, is of itself the highest enjoyment, better than fortune and superior to the manifold forms of sensual enjoyment that seemed destined to distract and lead otherwise virtuous men astray.

Smiles' volume was often considered to be a modern forerunner of the self-help books we encounter today; however, the genre's antecedents can be found in antiquity. In the third century BC, the propositional logic of the Stoics offered an ethos of living that promoted wisdom, courage, justice and temperance as the virtues of *eudaimonia*: the conditions, that is, for individual well-being and the communal welfare necessary to ensure 'human flourishing'. During the same period, the *Arthaśāstra*, a book written in Sanskrit and traditionally attributed to Cānakya (ca. 350–283 BCE), proposed that the guiding principles of the state and the common good of the people are one and the same. The *Arthaśāstra*, notably for its time, discussed the duties and obligations of rulers to maintain the welfare that binds a society into a collective whole that nurtures, rather than subjugates, its people.

This emphasis on statecraft and concomitant wisdom found its apogee in the 'mirror for princes' genre in the early Middle Ages and Renaissance. Concerned with good governance in an age of faith, mirrors for princes were written to groom rulers so that their spiritual obligations and right to rule would be fulfilled. With counterparts in Latin (*specula principum*) and German (*Fürstenspiegel*) traditions, the most commonly known example of this genre is Niccolò Machiavelli's political treatise, *The Prince*. Published five years after his death in 1532, *The Prince* was riveted together with a strain of steely political realism that predates the calculated pragmatism of modern political philosophies. Today, somewhat prescriptively, Machiavelli's advice is often boiled down to the suggestion that the end – the maintenance and application of power – justifies the means, no matter how pitiless the latter turns out to be in reality. This dictum nevertheless tends to overlook the book's underlying principles: that truth is ultimately more important than any abstract ideal, and anyone intent on absolute and effective rule would be well served to consider the day-to-day reality of maintaining virtue and prudence.

Writing in the eleventh century for the then prince of Kashgar (a prominent trading city on the Silk Road between China, the Middle East and Europe), Yusūf Khāss Hājib promoted a different, more egalitarian form of instruction. The *Kutadgu Bilig*, or 'Wisdom of Royal Glory', is republished in part here in English, Turkish, German, Polish, Arabic and Uighur, the latter a Turkic language spoken primarily by the people of the Xinjiang Uyghur Autonomous Region of Western China. The Persian and Arabic languages also influenced Uighur, with more recent linguistic pollination coming from Russian and Mandarin

Chinese, making it a multilingual medium of communication among people from different faiths and backgrounds. The origins of the *Kutadgu Bilig* draw on three extant manuscripts found in, respectively, Herat (Afghanistan) in 1439, a Mamluk library in Cairo in 1897, and Namangan, a city in Uzbekistan, in 1943. The most remarkable thing about this book, apart from its ontology, is the fact that the advice it offers – on matters of justice, fortune, wisdom and contentment – is intended for all citizens and not just for rulers or kings. Although written for a prince, the *Kutadgu Bilig* does not contain any specific historical names. Rather, its characters are intended to encapsulate an everyman of sorts, an individual in search of knowledge on that most pressing of questions: How do we attain contentment through wisdom and self-knowledge?

Largely concerned with the elevation of statecraft to both the secular realm of men and the divine sphere of faith and religion, an ambition that renders it both an example of the mirrors for princes genre and yet something more, the eloquence of the poetic *Kutadgu Bilig* – written in rhyming couplets (*masnavi*)   today stands in stark contrast to the self-help genres that populate our bookstores. Moreover, the advice it once offered to sovereigns has metastasized, in our time, into party political point scoring and spin. We are currently confronted with a surfeit of combative political commentators and summary commentary on our erstwhile and current rulers, leaving us increasingly bereft of intelligent, insightful and honest discourse on the importance of wisdom, not to mention the role of faith or the immaterial, in modern-day life and governance.

Although there is a pedagogical, if not didactic, element to the source texts that inform Slavs and Tatars' *Mirrors for Princes*, the work in question is neither pedagogical nor didactic. In their exploration of the modern-day notions of self-help, wisdom, advice and good counsel, against the backdrop of more recondite treatises on the subject, the artists reanimate the ideals in question and propose, in turn, an expanded field of research within which to understand the genre of mirrors for princes. For audiences who encounter these works, the relatively esoteric objectives of instructive tomes such as the *Kutadgu Bilig* are given over to a permissive linguistic, formal and conceptual practice that promotes the volume's relevance for

Von vielen Worten habe ich keinen grosser Nutzen gesehen,
Und an wiederholten Reden keinen Geschmack gefunden.

Z mówienia wielu słów korzyści nie ma,
Lecz nie mówić nie jest też korzystnie.

a modern-day audience. In her contribution to this volume, Neguin Yavari observes that 'mirrors rely on past exemplars, semiotic codes and moral teachings to edify rulers and to educate them in the taming of their innate inclination to injustice, tyranny and abuse of power.'[1] To this end, the *Kutadgu Bilig* is indeed an instructional 'self-help' book of sorts where the issues of reason, prudence, liberality, decisiveness and vigilance are not only promoted but also proposed as the predicates for stable, long-term rule. Virtue and statecraft go hand in hand in the *Kutadgu Bilig* and the juxtaposition of fate and governance, respectively, is an all-too-prominent fixture of premodern historical writing on the subject of kings and their rule. Yavari further notes that while the emergence of secularism is often considered to herald the separation of religion and politics, books such as the *Kutadgu Bilig* raise straightforward questions about whether piety, or faith, does indeed render inevitable the subordination of politics to religion. This question pervades the mirrors for princes genre, and is of manifest concern in our present milieu, where the agonistic struggle between secularism and so-called extremism across regions such as the 'Middle East' and the Caucasus would appear to be caught up in an all-too-deadly embrace.

Inasmuch as the mirrors for princes genre was used to groom future leaders, the topic of actual grooming is a coextensive factor in any ascendancy to power. Lloyd Ridgeon's extended essay, republished here, examines the significance of hair in the Islamic tradition with reference to the sacred sources (the Qurān *Ḥadīth* and biographies of the Prophet). In religious terms, followers are frequently identified by the way their hair has been groomed, cut, shaved, coloured or left untouched. Observing that treatises dealing with aspects of the barbers' trade (from the practice of shaving to the razor, whetstone and mirrors employed in the process) were also associated with issues of sexuality, asceticism and celibacy, Ridgeon's thesis in 'Shaggy or Shaved' alerts us to the ethical and moral instructiveness of actual mirrors when it comes to the relationship between grooming and governing. This focus on self-grooming, throughout *Mirrors for Princes* and elsewhere, is all the more apparent in Slavs and Tatars' emphasis on formal self-presentation. Governing, in the sense of sovereign rule and statecraft, is conjugated with an emphasis on caring for the self and attention to self-appearance, while the expansive context of the original genre of mirrors for princes, its universalist and yet esoteric import, is distilled

1
For a fuller genealogy of mirrors for princes, see: Neguin Yavari, *Advice for the Sultan: Prophetic Voices and Secular Politics in Medieval Islam* (New York: Oxford University Press, 2012), 7–44.

into a number of objects that suggest potential forms of self-grooming. In an echo of the civilising contexts of mirrors for princes, this micro-level of investigation into self-care foregrounds the civilizing function of contemporary grooming. The requirement to titivate or embellish the self before entering the public arena, so as to counter the perceived unruliness of bodily hair, reveals an idealised subject that, when projected into the public sphere, also reveals an ethos of being – a disposition or fundamental attribute – that is attentive to negotiating the mores and values of its specific historical moment.

In these expansive frameworks, the oversized combs in *Mirrors for Princes* allude to a formal excess in the contemporary investment in appearance over substance, a care of the self that reveals the predominance of mass media and its production of subjects on a cosmetic rather than substantive level. Which is not to say that the contemporary subject (be it a politician or otherwise) is a cypher, betraying an authentic and lost form of selfhood that we must search for; nor is it to suggest the possibility that the self can reveal an inner authenticity free from affectation. The subject is the locus of multiple affinities, of reason and unreason, experience and desire, delusion and aspiration. It is a syntactical, discursive construct that is dependent on normative and normalizing discourses that are, in turn, subject to historical shifts in meaning and substance over time. To observe as much is to allude, of course, to Michel Foucault's overarching insight: the subject is the product of the operation of political technologies on, through and within the social body. And the mirrors for princes genre is an all too a pertinent example of that process in action.

The once-sacral elements of grooming that applied to sovereign power, as related through Ridgeon's essay, have been secularised over time and, in this process, have become more irreverent if not irrelevant. However, the micro-level of political intercourse and behaviour reveals the extent to which, to quote the artists, a form of 'infra-politics' is always at work in the exercise of power. Apart from the numerous image consultants on the payroll of governments worldwide, the ascendancy of the 'spin doctor' is an obvious modern-day example of an infra-politics at work in contemporary forms of governance. The *sine qua non* of modern-day political intrigue and prime purveyor of Machiavellian advice, the figure of the spin doctor has spawned its own distinct characters that can be traced back to Squealer in George Orwell's *Animal Farm* (1945) and up to, more recently, the egregious Malcolm Tucker, portrayed by Peter Capaldi, in the British television series and political satire *The Thick of It* (2005).[2] Conversely, the self-preening and self-importance of contemporary politicians, with their willingness to listen to advice when it suits their agendas, has been captured in many (good and bad) films, including *A Perfect Candidate* (1996), *Primary Colours* (1998), *The Deal* (2003), *Fahrenheit 9/11* (2004), *So Goes the Nation* (2006), *W* (2008), *In the Loop* (2009) and *The Special Relationship* (2010). In fact and fiction alike, rumour and malicious whispering, partisanship and ideology, rather than good counsel and wisdom, tend to win out over truth. Tongues get twisted, throats are frequently cleared in anticipation of speech, and lip service is paid to questionable ideologies, but sound, objective advice seems not only harder to come by, but increasingly perverted into political doublespeak and the exigencies of 'spin'.

The 'infra' nature of politics, with its beneath-the-stairs rumours, whispers in the corridor and behind-the-scenes gossiping, was succinctly captured in Ryszard Kapuściński's unparallelled account of the downfall of Haile Selassie, the self-styled 'King of Kings', who was deposed in 1974.[3] In *The Emperor: Downfall of an Autocrat* (1978), Kapuściński, who had unprecedented access to Selassie's flunkies and low-level officials, detailed the end of a dynasty whose descent was prefigured by a solipsistic delusion that left the 'King of Kings' isolated and waited upon by only one remaining, ancient retainer. The combustible intrigue and infra-politics of Selassie's court, populated by various factions described as either 'Jailers', 'Talkers' or 'Floaters', was further enkindled by the fact that the 'King of Kings' preferred inept ministers (who offered no threat to his power), refused to read any printed documents (for reasons of security), and insisted on receiving all information by word of mouth. Needless to say, in a realm defined by pathological mistrust, no one's word is taken for wisdom and the double-voiced, the so-called 'Talkers', are concurrently listened to and dismissed (and in some instances done away with altogether). If lip service to the emperor is the order of the day, and good news the only news allowed, it is a foolish person indeed who brings bad news.

In David Crowley's 'Echo Translation' we are introduced to another peculiar form of the 'double voice' encapsulated by the term

2

The character of Squealer is key to the trajectory of Orwell's novel, plotting as he does the presentation of insignificant untruths, uttered at the beginning, until they become the propagandist lies of a totalitarian regime. The character was based on Joseph Stalin's protégée and head of Communist propaganda, one Vyacheslav Mikhailovich Molotov (1890–1986). At the level of 'infra-politics', mention too should be made of François Leclerc du Tremblay, the powerful behind-the-scenes decision maker and advisor to Cardinal Richelieu. Widely referred to as the 'power behind the throne', or '*éminence grise*', a reference to du Tremblay's grey sacral robes, this figure found a modern-day incarnation, for some commentators, in Vice President Dick Cheney, whose aggressive foreign policy and attempts to accrue power saw him become more powerful in terms of influence than the then-incumbent president, George W. Bush.

3

I am grateful to the artists for drawing my attention to this account. In 1982, Ryszard Kapuściński published another book on the end of another dynasty, *Shah of Shahs* (1982), a perspicacious analysis of the reasons behind the decline, fall and exile of Mohammad Reza Pahlavi, the last Shah of Iran.

acousmêtre, the latter concept being first coined by Michel Chion in his 1984 volume, *La Voix au Cinéma*. The phrase was deployed by Chion to describe a character who is not seen on screen but whose voice can be heard. Crowley notes that Alfred Hitchcock's *Psycho* (1960) provides Chion with numerous examples of how the uncanny and haunting qualities of the *acousmêtre* can be used to produce dramatic effects. One of Crowley's more notable examples of the use of this disembodied voice concerns the little-known technique (or practice) of Gavrilov translation, whereby audiences in Poland would often see films, such as Hitchcock's *Psycho*, with a simultaneous voice-over translation that was imposed onto (while retaining) the original film soundtrack. Polish audiences, upon hearing this dual soundtrack, began referring to the voice of the translator as the *Lektor Filmowy* (film reader) or *Szeptanka* (whisperer). The source language, being simultaneous and audible with the destination language, created a form of voice contest that produced disruption and confusion as much as it did clarity and sense. The effect of this disembodied voice, as noted by Crowley, highlights a concern not only with legibility but also with authenticity and authority: Who is speaking and in what capacity?

These questions are explored in Slavs and Tatars' audio piece *Lektor* (2014), for which excerpts from the *Kutadgu Bilig* were recorded in the original Uighur with various voice-overs. The language of the voice-over is dependent on the venue of exhibition: Turkish in Istanbul, Polish in Białystok, German in Zurich, Arabic in Abu Dhabi, and Scottish Gaelic in Edinburgh. The written word is actualised and made material by way of the voice, with that voice, in turn, being doubled in an effect that directly references the uncanny elements of Gavrilov translation. The geographical distance from the original Uighur language is rendered propinquitous in *Lektor*, becoming a matter of kinship rather than distance and remoteness. At first this combination may seem, to quote the artists, 'antithetical or incommensurate', but it is precisely this 'collision of registers', with their 'different voices, different worlds and different logics' that allows the viewer to engage with these voices and to locate the ideas – on topics as varied as statecraft, wisdom and nascent forms of self-help – firmly within the concerns of the present. To paraphrase the artists, the excerpts extracted from the *Kutadgu Bilig* offer advice pertaining to speech and tongues and what it means, ultimately, to loosen the tongue, to hold it or to irreverently stick it out. We encounter here, as we do across Slavs and Tatars' wider practice, a degree of disembodied recurrence whereby apparently dissimilar entities – including metaphysical texts, sacral artifacts and political treatises from different eras – are resuscitated and brought together in a cross-temporal and cross-cultural dialogue.

Focusing on the historical teledrama *Chanakya*, which debuted in 1991 in India, Manan Ahmed Asif offers further context here in his presentation of the life story of philosopher Cānakya. Also known as Kauṭilya and Vishnugupta, Cānakya was found in obscurity in the third century BC and later became counsellor to Chandragupta (340–293 BCE), the first emperor who was to unify most of greater India into one state. Ahmed Asif notes how *Chanakya*'s director Chandraprakash Dwivedi relied on a heavily Sanskritised text, the *Arthaśāstra* (*The Science of Wealth and Governance*, attributed to the author Cānakya), to not only define the relationship between the philosopher and the conquering king, but to also promote the political usage of 'ancient' Indian texts in the form of *avant la lettre* anticolonial and proto-nationalist treatises. Tracing the promiscuous genealogies of these texts reveals both the influence of Sanskrit, Arabic and Persian languages and offers a geographic purview that includes the so-called West, the regions of the Middle East and South Asia. Again, propinquity, rather than distance and a resistance to transliteration, becomes a guiding principle in effective forms of statecraft.

In Anna Della Subin's 'Mirror for Princesses', the gendered elements of the genre are reinterpreted to consider how such advice literature could be proposed for princesses. The individual's obligation to the state is understood here through the role of women as mothers and wives alongside the implications of faith in relation to governance and duty. Law, governance, morality, religion and knowledge all contain normative discourses of prohibition and prescription that Subin's essay throws further light upon, questioning the extent to which gender has defined both the public and private roles that are assumed by husbands and wives in their everyday lives, not to mention the gender bias of advice literature throughout the ages. Just as the *Kutadgu Bilig* was intended to position a Turkic tradition of governance and literature on a similar footing to Arabic and Persian counterparts, Slavs and Tatars'

Mirrors for Princes holds up a modern-day mirror so as to countenance the simultaneity and radical import of past concerns about statecraft and advice literature. Integral to both their work and this volume is an implicit engagement with how words and ideas, drawn from the mirrors for princes genre, can produce objects or soundscapes in our time. In this process, words and ideas display a degree of conceptual flexibility and cognitive permissiveness that seems to be increasingly elided in our present-day obsession with the so-called 'sound bite', another reference to the tongue and the mechanics of enunciation. The slippages that occur from one state of utterance to another produce further meanings, some of which are unintended, and the objects produced by Slavs and Tatars often effect this slippage and are, conversely, affected by it. The processes at work in *Mirrors for Princes*, furthermore, involve approaching a word or idea from 'beneath or behind', so as to catch it off-guard, so to speak, and thereafter estrange the normative, historical structures that ossify and conceptually reduce certain terms and cognitive structures.

On both a performative and reciprocal level, *Mirrors for Princes* is concerned with reviving concepts shared by Christians and Muslims alike, and thereafter imbricating them within a present-day social and linguistic order so that we can re-engage with their critical import and ongoing importance as texts and ideas. The practices presented here are, finally, as much about transliterating the literal into the visual and seeing what happens or, indeed, what deviates. The processes are about the moments when – for a variety of historical, ideological and conceptual reasons – the practice of translating across forms is frustrated and yet reified in the present. These processes of reinvigoration produce a vertiginous closeness to concerns that could, based on a cursory glance, seem remote; but we would be well minded to consider the extent to which the political discourses that define our time have been reduced to base forms of hypocritical piety, cheap jibes, opportunistic asides and ideological spin – the very forms of sophistry and casuistry, in sum, that mirrors for princes warned against in the pursuit of individual wisdom and good governance for all.

Anthony Downey
Editor-in-Chief
Ibraaz
www.ibraaz.org

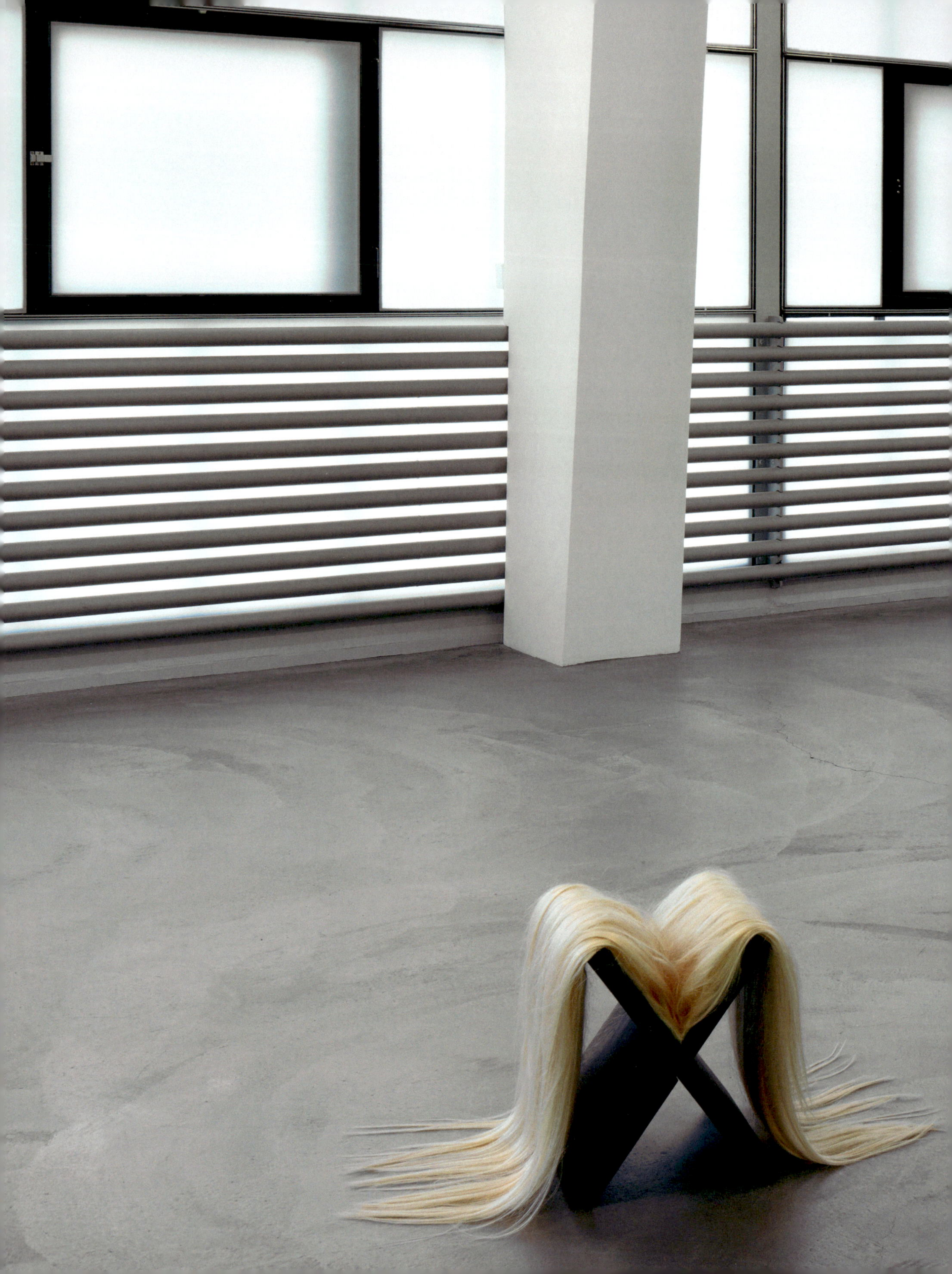

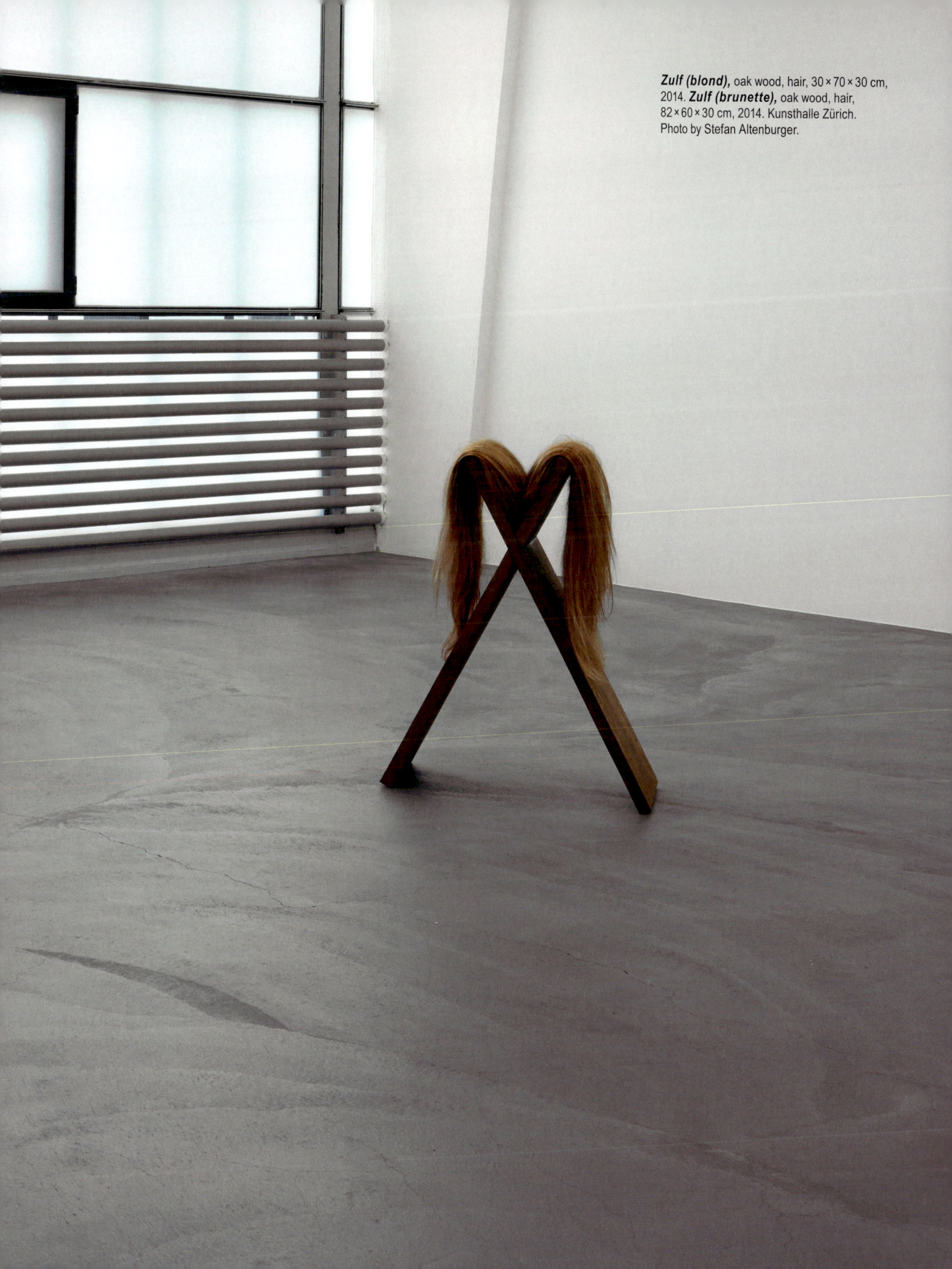

Zulf (blond), oak wood, hair, 30 × 70 × 30 cm, 2014. *Zulf (brunette),* oak wood, hair, 82 × 60 × 30 cm, 2014. Kunsthalle Zürich. Photo by Stefan Altenburger.

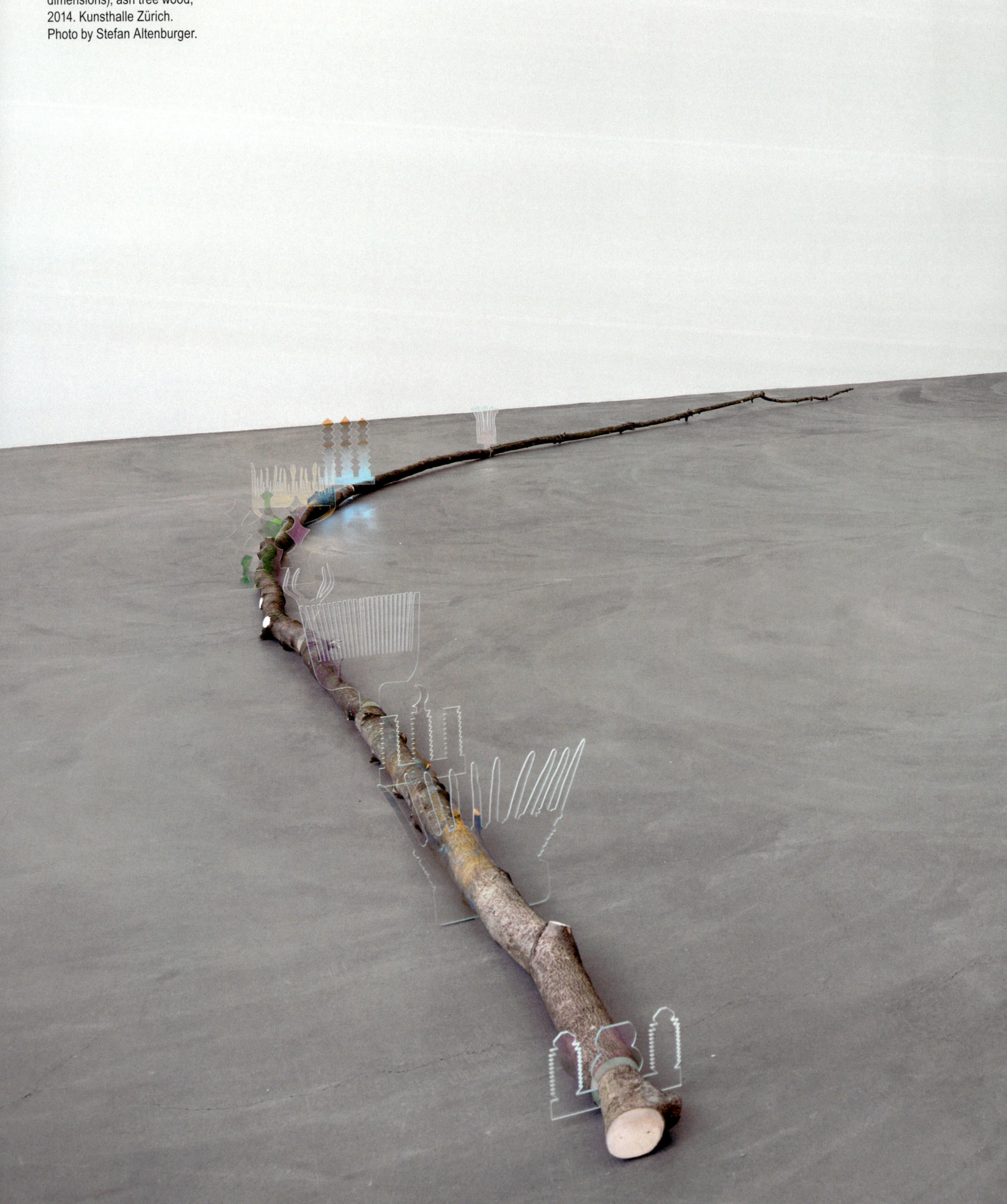

Bazm u Razm **(installation view),** dichroic glass (various dimensions), ash tree wood, 2014. Kunsthalle Zürich. Photo by Stefan Altenburger.

A CONVERSATION WITH SLAVS AND TATARS

Anthony Downey   **Beatrix Ruf**

Slavs and Tatars

If I understand correctly, the genre of mirrors for princes (*specula principum* or *Fürstenspiegel*) involves a form of political writing or advisory literature for future rulers on matters both secular and spiritual. The genre was shared by Christian and Muslim lands, in particular during the Middle Ages, with Machiavelli's *The Prince* (1532) being the most well-known, if later, example. Could you talk about this as an idea and how it manifests itself in the context of current work being produced by Slavs and Tatars?

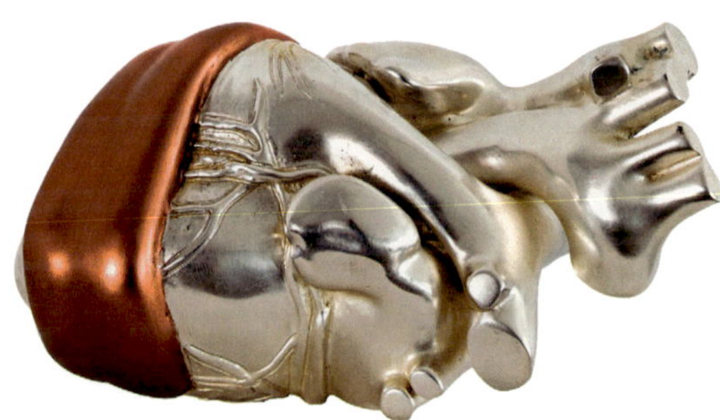

Dil be Del, silver-plated brass, metallic acrylic paint, 10 × 12 × 9 cm, 2014.

1
New Approaches to the History of Political Thought: Mirrors for Princes Reconsidered (Interdisciplinary Conference, Freie Universität, Berlin, 2–3 November, 2012).

We were first (as often is the case) seduced by the name mirrors for princes itself – we first heard it in the context of a conference at the Freie Universität in Berlin in 2012.[1] Little did we know that it was actually a genre of advice literature. We thought, what would a mirror for a prince be today? That kind of first-degree interest, coupled with a layered, complex one, is something we try to maintain in the work.

Over the span of the conference we learned that mirrors for princes were among the first forms of secular

Çok konuşana 'gevezelik etti' der bilgi;
Ama söylemezse de ona 'dilsiz' der.

تَقُولُ المَعرِفة لِمَن يَتَكَلَّمُ كَثيرًا إنَّه ثَرثار، لَكِنَّها تَقُولُ للصَّامِتِ أبْكَم!

If he talks too much, wisdom says that he chatters,
but if he talks not at all, it says that he is tongue-tied.

Anthony Downey   **Beatrix Ruf**   Slavs and Tatars

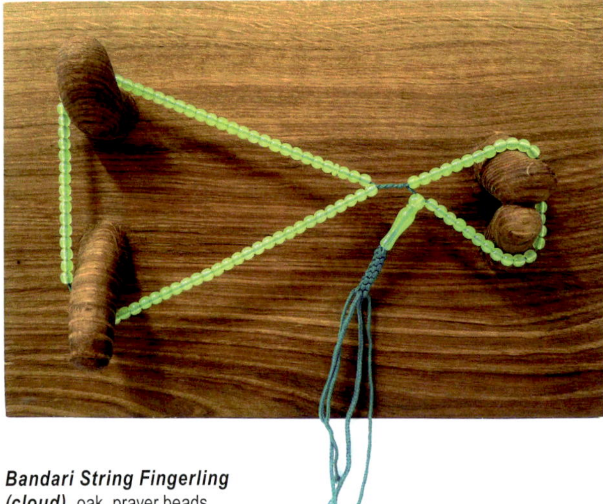

Bandari String Fingerling (cloud), oak, prayer beads, 20 × 30 × 7.5 cm, 2014.

scholarship, an attempt to put such study on the level of religious scholarship in the Middle Ages. What immediately struck us was how the pendulum has swung to the other extreme in today's political discourse. We find that there are airport bookshops full of books and CNN reporters and Twitter columnists – meaning everybody who has a political view, in sum – but there's an unspoken moratorium on intellectual or erudite scholarship on the role of faith in public life in the twenty-first or even the late-twentieth century. The more we dug into the material, the more it became clear that these books are amalgams; they're mash-ups of all different kinds of genres in one volume. So you have astrology, etiquette, military strategy, literary tropes, folklore and ethics all under this one rubric of a mirror for a prince. That spoke to us because our books also attempt to straddle those disciplines: they're not really journalism but they have journalistic elements; they're not academic scholarship but they're critical and analytical; they're not memoirs but they're intimate – it's this flattening of genres that we're interested in.

And there are further specific examples because, again, if I understand correctly, a book like

Anthony Downey   **Beatrix Ruf**   Slavs and Tatars

the *Kutadgu Bilig*, which roughly means 'the wisdom which brings happiness', has the same kind of resonance that *Beowulf* or *The Iliad* has for Western readers; it's a critically important volume with a good deal of moral instruction contained within its pages. You have chosen to look at the *Kutadgu Bilig* specifically in relation to this idea of 'wisdom', a form of wisdom that comes in a combination of secular and faith-based statecraft. Can you talk a little more about how you came across the *Kutadgu Bilig*, and the importance of it, because although it is a historical text, first published in the eleventh century, it appears to have a direct resonance in the present.

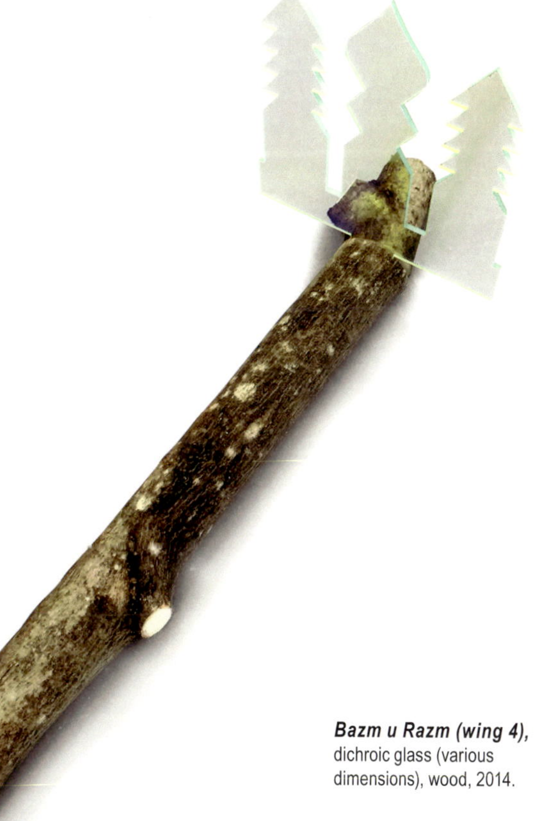

Bazm u Razm (wing 4),
dichroic glass (various dimensions), wood, 2014.

Even the notion of the word *wisdom* is problematic today. In the deconstructed world we live in, there is no such thing as an authoritative or univocal notion of what wisdom means; there are several traditions and discourses. Then to imagine that, since the advent of modernity, we have suddenly become a new species, with contrapostal thumbs for our iPhones, and that the accretion of tradition is no longer relevant, strikes us as almost comical. As Matt Mullican once said, if you want people to head as fast as possible for the exit, start using the words *faith* and *religion*.

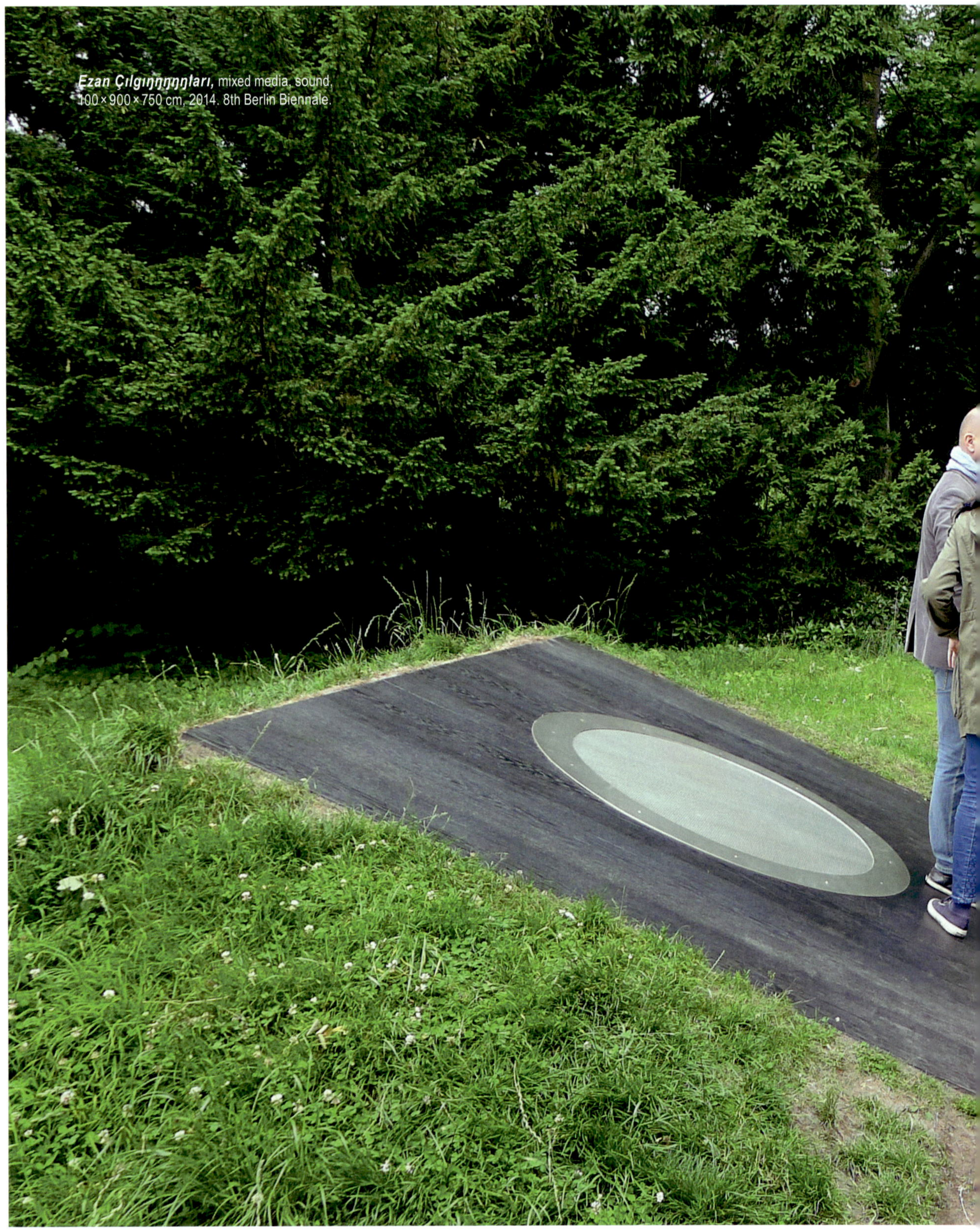

Hüte Deine Zunge! So behütest Du Dein Haupt,
Verkürze das Wort, so verlängerst Du Dein Leben.

Dobrze zważaj na swój język, byś zachował głowę,
Skracaj mowę, a żył będziesz długo.

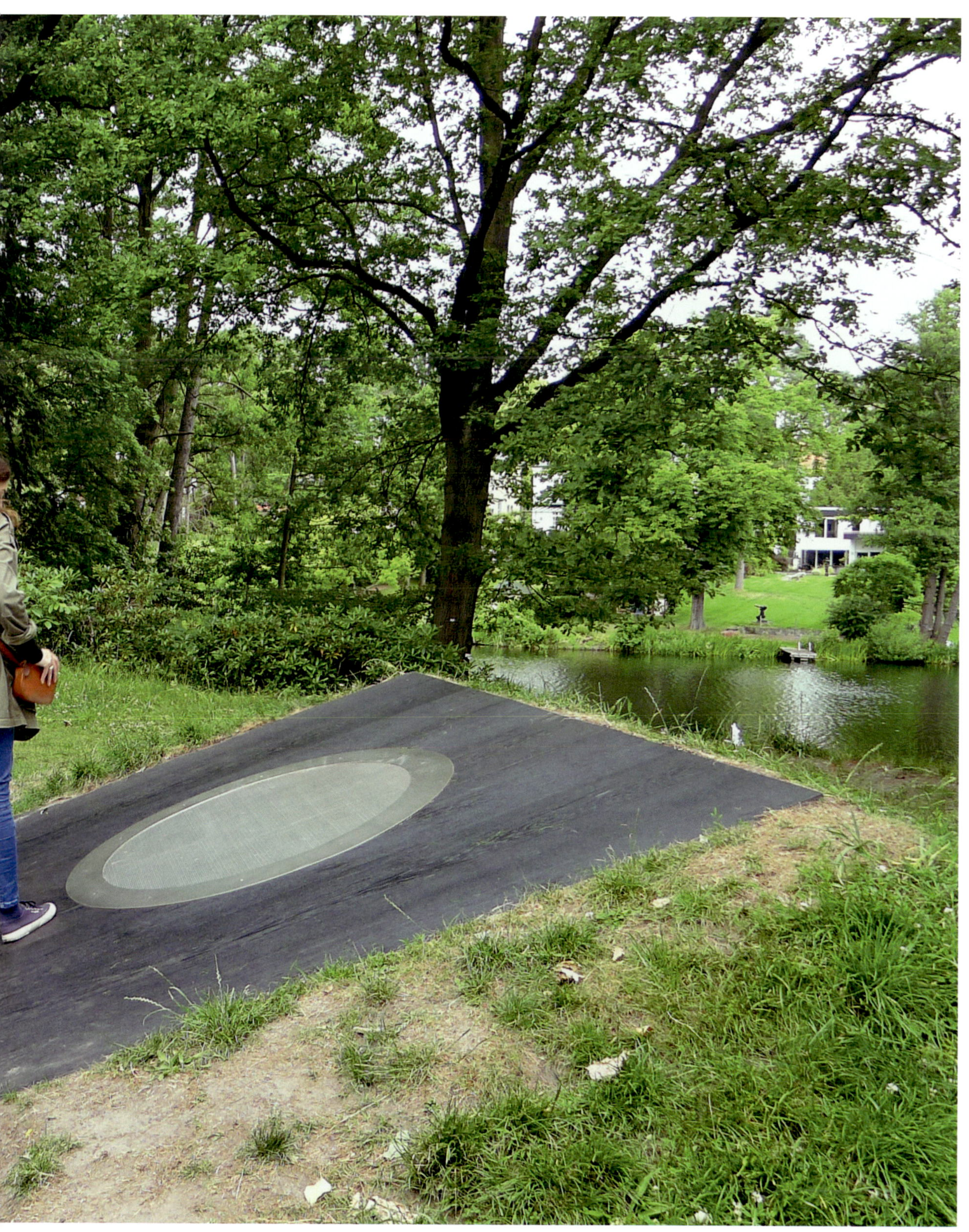

Dili iyi gözet, başın gözetilmiş olur;
Sözünü kısa kes, ömrün uzun olur.

احفظ لسانك يُحفظ رأسك.
وقصّر القول تطل بطول العمر.

Hold your tongue and you will hold on to your head.
Shorten your speech and you will lengthen your life.

Anthony Downey   **Beatrix Ruf**   Slavs and Tatars

Because both have become too politicised and yet too generalised at one and the same time?

We were recently at NYU Abu Dhabi for a site visit in advance of the residency and found it refreshing that there was a range of scholars, a self-selecting faculty that thinks rather differently from their counterparts at other elite universities. There are great things about having hundreds of years of history at Oxford and Cambridge and Heidelberg and Yale and Harvard to draw from, but there's sometimes a sclerosis and provincialism as well. If you're a transversal thinker working in the history department, you're going to have a hard time selling research that entails work in other departments, say theology or music, to the entrenched interests there. So this is our task – to think differently and to ask those questions that are not asked, including those around wisdom and faith.

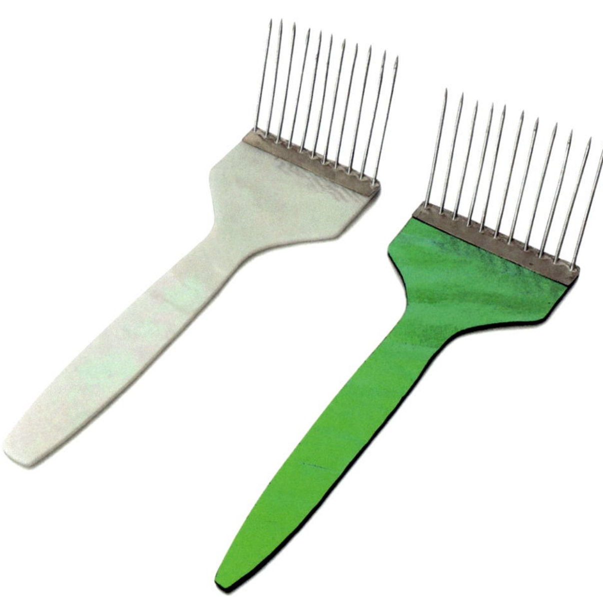

Hirsute happily with hairless, dichroic glass, tinned copper, 8 × 22 × 25 cm, 2014.

Thinking differently obviously has a visual manifestation because this way of thinking remains relatively literary until you put on a show like *Mirrors for Princes* at the Kunstalle Zürich – perhaps Beatrix wants to comment on that – and now at the NYU Art Gallery in Abu Dhabi. A lot of this seems to

Anthony Downey   **Beatrix Ruf**   Slavs and Tatars

**have translation at its core, and
the realm of transliteration, or
something copied from one medium
to another.**

**Yes, I am particularly interested in
the way a lot of your work deals with
or is primarily about translation: its
failure, how tradition translates and
gets misguided, or, in the process
of many interpretations, turns
into something different. For me,
there's an interesting, almost literal
tautology in this translation process.
Things are being translated as if
they would function as language.
When you think, objects come from
the information of language and
not, strictly speaking, of aesthetics.
Your objects do not come from the
translation process of thought into
art as we know it, so to speak, and
I would like to hear from you more
about this because I think that your
objects actually produce language,
and don't just show how language
is failing.**

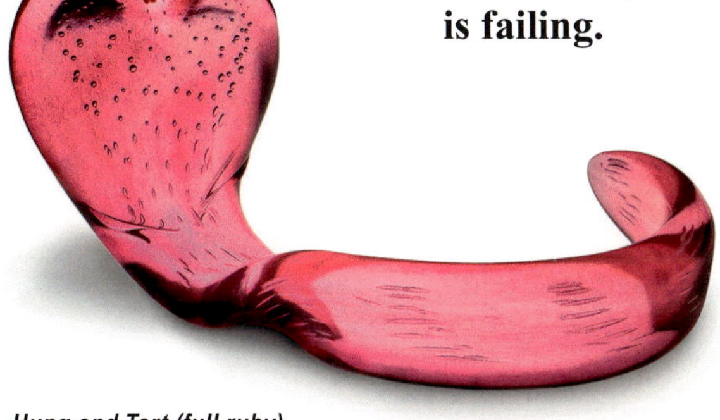

Hung and Tart (full ruby),
handblown glass,
15 × 35 × 25 cm, 2014.

It's funny you should mention that:
just recently we were thinking about
the fact that we produce most of our
work in Poland and these are the
stronger works because, as we work
with craftsmen not art technicians, they
are a form of translation in themselves.
There's a wilful loss of control or an

Anthony Downey   **Beatrix Ruf**   Slavs and Tatars

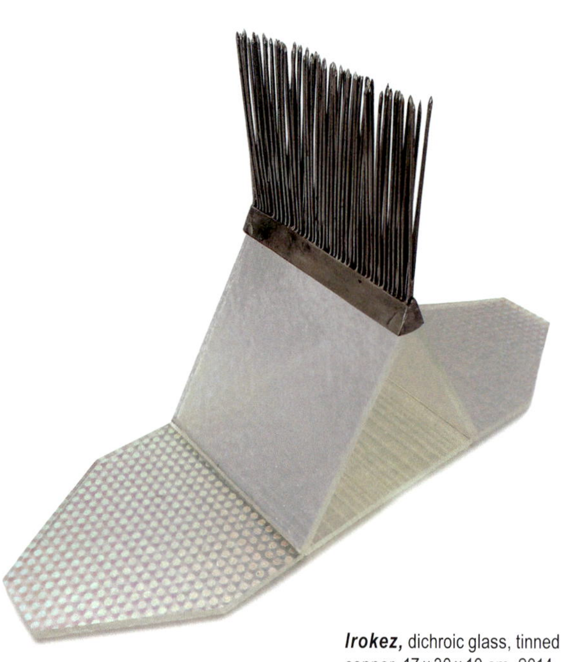

Irokez, dichroic glass, tinned copper, 17 × 30 × 10 cm, 2014.

abstraction of some sort that happens when you're working with someone who's not in any way versed in the language of art. Because of course in places like London, Berlin and elsewhere there are whole industries that produce artwork for artists.

That translation also happens first and foremost through the actual conception of the works as a discussion between ourselves, because it's two very different minds that are thinking about the same concept, and that happens through language. But we never thought about the works themselves as enabling – sorry, let me just understand it again: the works talk about the failures of language, but as objects, you said that they were –

Let's say that the translation process of thought into art is the common expectation of art as we know it, even to show the artist using language, especially when we're starting that relationship in a very constructive way. But this seems to be about the failure of language, the space between or the nonverbal – the preverbal, so to speak. Your pieces have the structure of language, are directly produced out of language and this produces the logic of language. In your objects language seems to be the natural partner or the logic or structure – or even the grammar of it.

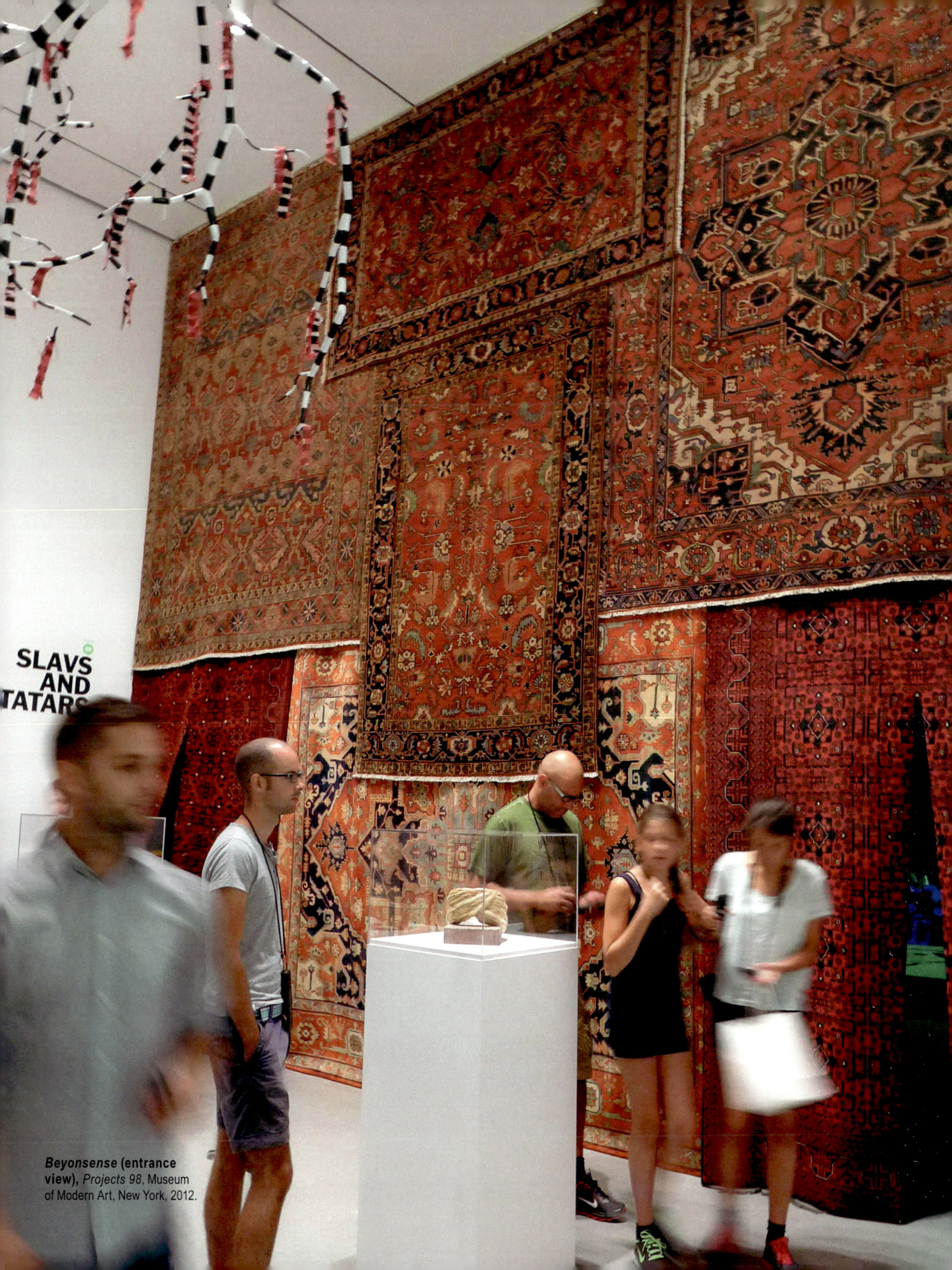

Beyonsense **(entrance view),** *Projects 98*, Museum of Modern Art, New York, 2012.

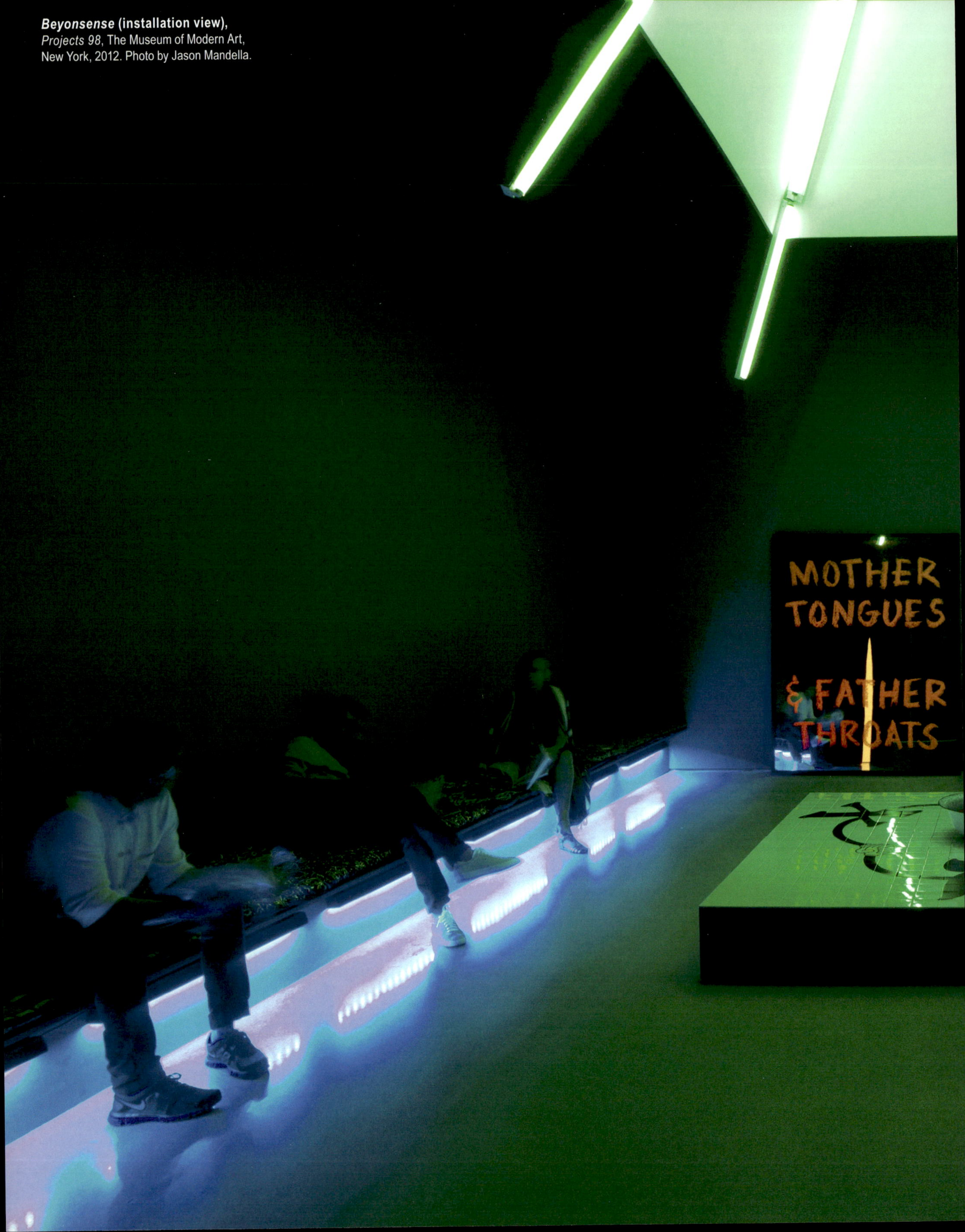

Beyonsense (installation view),
Projects 98, The Museum of Modern Art,
New York, 2012. Photo by Jason Mandella.

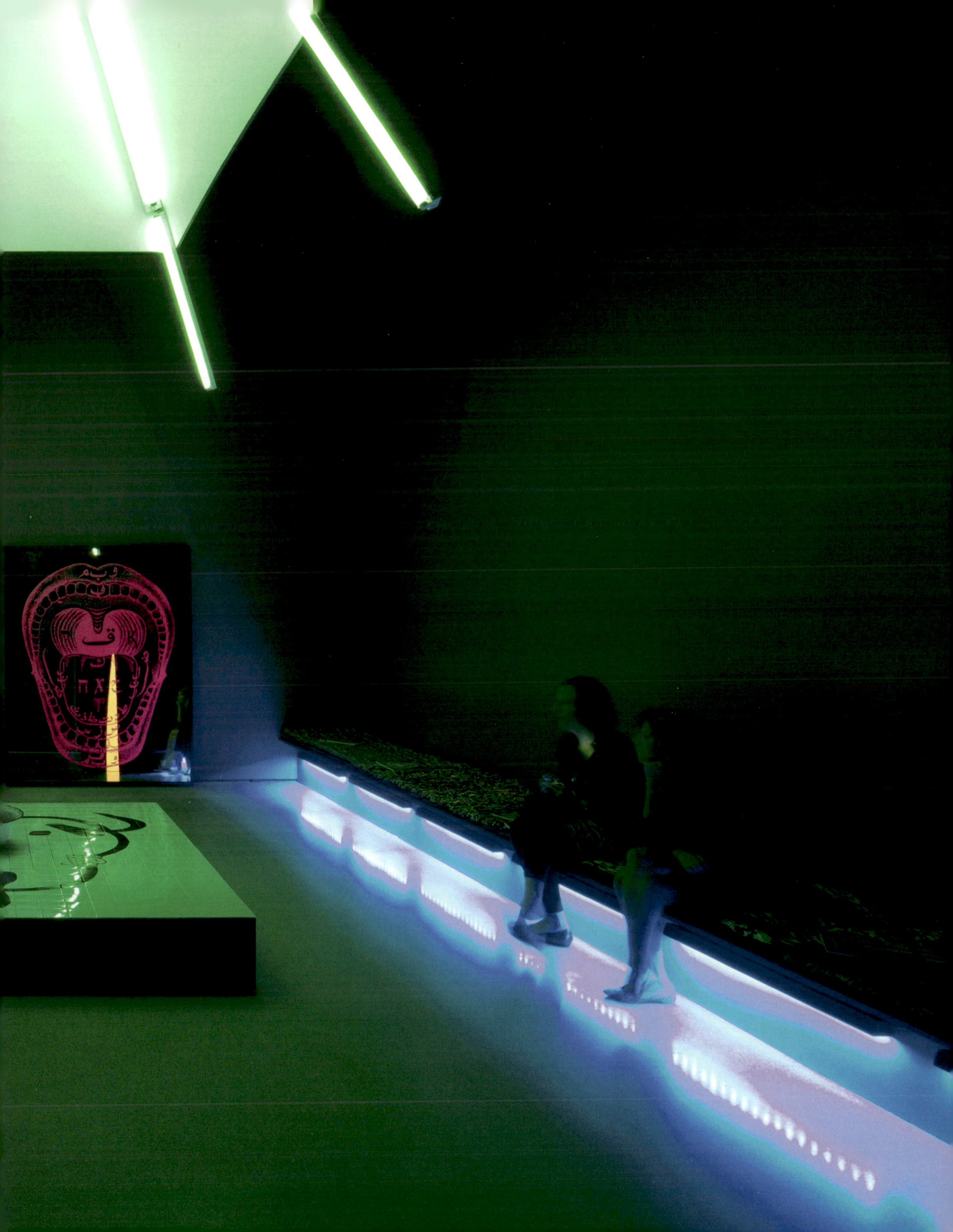

Anthony Downey   **Beatrix Ruf**   Slavs and Tatars

When we come across ideas, we really do reify them as words; we try to create three-dimensional words out of the things that we're thinking about. It's like the autistic, oral version of concrete poetry, trying to make something that is completely abstract and esoteric, primarily visible.

Like the work *Tongue Twist Her* (2013), perhaps, where the object is tongue-twisted around a dance pole?

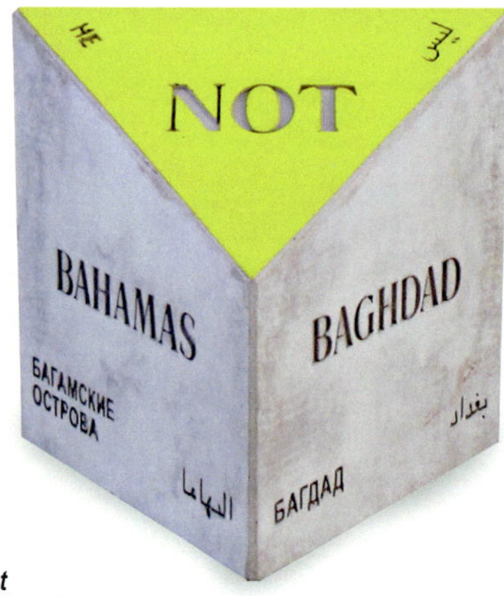

Triangulation (Not Bahamas Not Baghdad),
concrete, paint,
24 × 27 × 23 cm, 2011.

But really even just the idea – when thinking about the name *Mirrors for Princes* – we chant, like the process of *dhikr* in Sufism where you ecstatically chant, repeating words so many times that at some point *princes* starts to sound like *princesses*. We often think of this practice as going behind the word. The idea of going behind something is very threatening, not only in terms posing a threat to the normativity of heterosexuality, like 'from behind', but it also has this connotation of 'through the back door' – what does it mean to go behind the concept and sneak up on it? Perhaps this returns us to one of the functions of translation.

The physical materialisation of the word itself, you appear to be suggesting, seems to be a process of looking through the word, through language – does that make sense?

Anthony Downey **Beatrix Ruf**

Slavs and Tatars

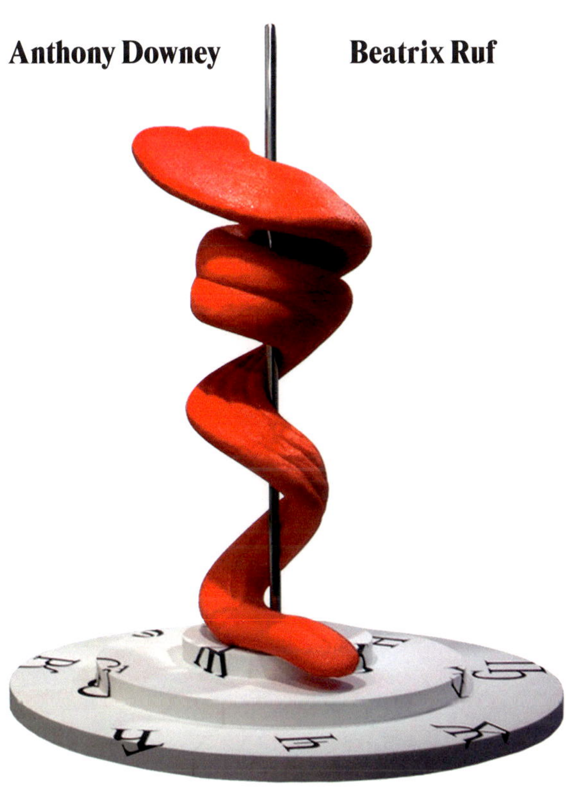

Tongue Twist Her,
silicon, polystyrene, metal
pole, MDF, acrylic paint,
300 × 245 × 245 cm, 2013.

In the genre of mirrors for princes, which do have a didactic context, and accepting that the process of production creates different ends to what are expected, do your objects retain a didactic context, or do you think it's more about opening up a permissive context, a kind of engagement that is more about a tolerance of words, or with the experience of words?

Perhaps, because the editing process is a ping-pong of sending words back and forth, back and forth, and eventually, like a process of transmogrification, that word becomes an object. There's a kind of wilful letting go, of not controlling what that aftereffect looks like.

This is what the *Mirrors for Princes* show is – when you work on something for two or three years and you don't understand it, that's the ideal situation. If you don't know where you stand on such polemical issues, whether it's questions of seclusion versus the state, faith versus secularism, occupation versus withdrawal, then the object can add a talismanic quality – that's the hope.

The question of didacticism in pedagogy is a difficult one for us because there has been a pedagogical turn, and often we're wrapped up

Der Unwissende ist blind, das ist offenbar,
Geh, Unwissender, nimm Deinen Anteil vom Wissen.

Człowiek wiedzy pozbawiony jest jak ślepy,
Nuże głupcze, czerp wiedzę od mędrca.

Anthony Downey   **Beatrix Ruf**   Slavs and Tatars

Bilgisiz insan, şüphesiz kördür;
Yürü, ey bilgisiz, bilgiden payını al.

فالجاهل بلا شك أعمى، فامضْ أيها الجاهل وخذ من العلم حظاك.

The blind, that is the ignorant.
Go then, fool, and get a share of knowledge from the wise!

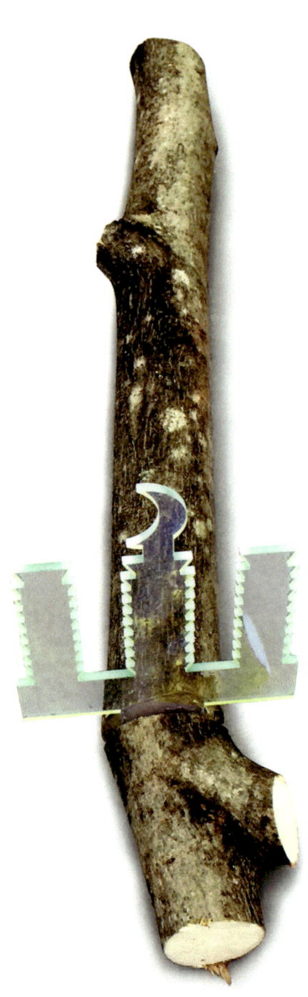

2
Calvin Tomkins, 'Profiles: Open, Available, Useful', *The New Yorker*, 19 March 1990: 48–72; reprinted in *Siah Armajani: An Ingenious World*, Parasol Unit, London, 2013.

Bazm u Razm (wing 3),
dichroic glass (various dimensions), wood, 2014.

into this. We always come back to the origin of Slavs and Tatars: the book club, where we began, was very important because pedagogy assumes that one person knows and another doesn't, and that's never the case. Similarly, we devoted ourselves to discovering what mirrors for princes are, in terms of genre, but in no way are we experts or didacts on the subject in hand. Permissiveness, however, is something that's crucial for us: to transmit that permissiveness to the participant or the viewer is a key ambition.

We're very keen on the idea of the layman; how does the s/he engage with the work in contrast to the art professional? There's a great quote by Calvin Tomkins in a profile of Siah Armajani that accompanied his solo show at the Parasol Unit last year.[2] Tomkins and Armajani insist on distinguishing between accessibility and availability, and that we have to redeem this idea of populism. Populism doesn't mean lowest common denominator, it actually means making the highest achievements available for the greatest number of people. So things are available, but only accessible according to how much effort you put into something. It doesn't just mean you make everything clear. Permissiveness here is important

Anthony Downey   **Beatrix Ruf**   Slavs and Tatars

What you've just described there is the genre of mirrors for princes. The *Kutadgu Bilig* is one example of the genre that uses the Socratic method. It is about learning *with* rather than *against*; it's about a dialogic learning process.

because it engages with notions of generosity – a gift or an exchange. The idea of a book club is that you're discovering with somebody; there's no leader of a book club.

Another reason we are interested in the genre is that the critique is presented as a form of reciprocation, not as a frontal assault. These are books – codices, texts – which were often written as a gift to somebody. So while they're explicitly saying 'this is how your son should rule', implicitly what they're saying is 'this is how you're not ruling'. We are interested in how critique is delivered effectively through circuity – through the gift, through generosity. We often use the analogy of commemorating something while stabbing it in the back. Actually that's what a lot of these texts do; the first ten pages are praises, whether it's to God or the setting. Most people fall asleep before they get through the introduction because it's the antithesis of our need for immediacy and transparency: they resist shortcuts.

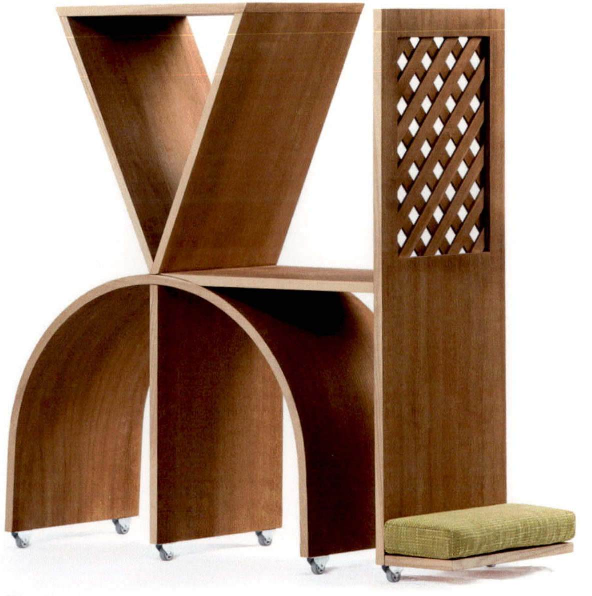

The Noughty Nasals, wood veneer, wheels, fabric, foam, various dimensions, 2014.

قارى، ئۆزى ئۆلگەن ئادەم ئۇنتۇلۇپ، سۆزى يامانغا يوللۇپ قالىدۇ. سۆزۈڭگى ياخشى سۆزلەپ، ئۆزۈڭ ئۆلمەسلىكىنى قالدۇر.

Der Geborene stirbt und verschwindet ohne Spur,
Rede gute Worte, dann ist Dein Wort unsterblich.

Zważ, człowiek się rodzi i umiera, lecz pozostają po nim słowa,
Mów dobre słowa, a pozostaniesz nieśmiertelny.

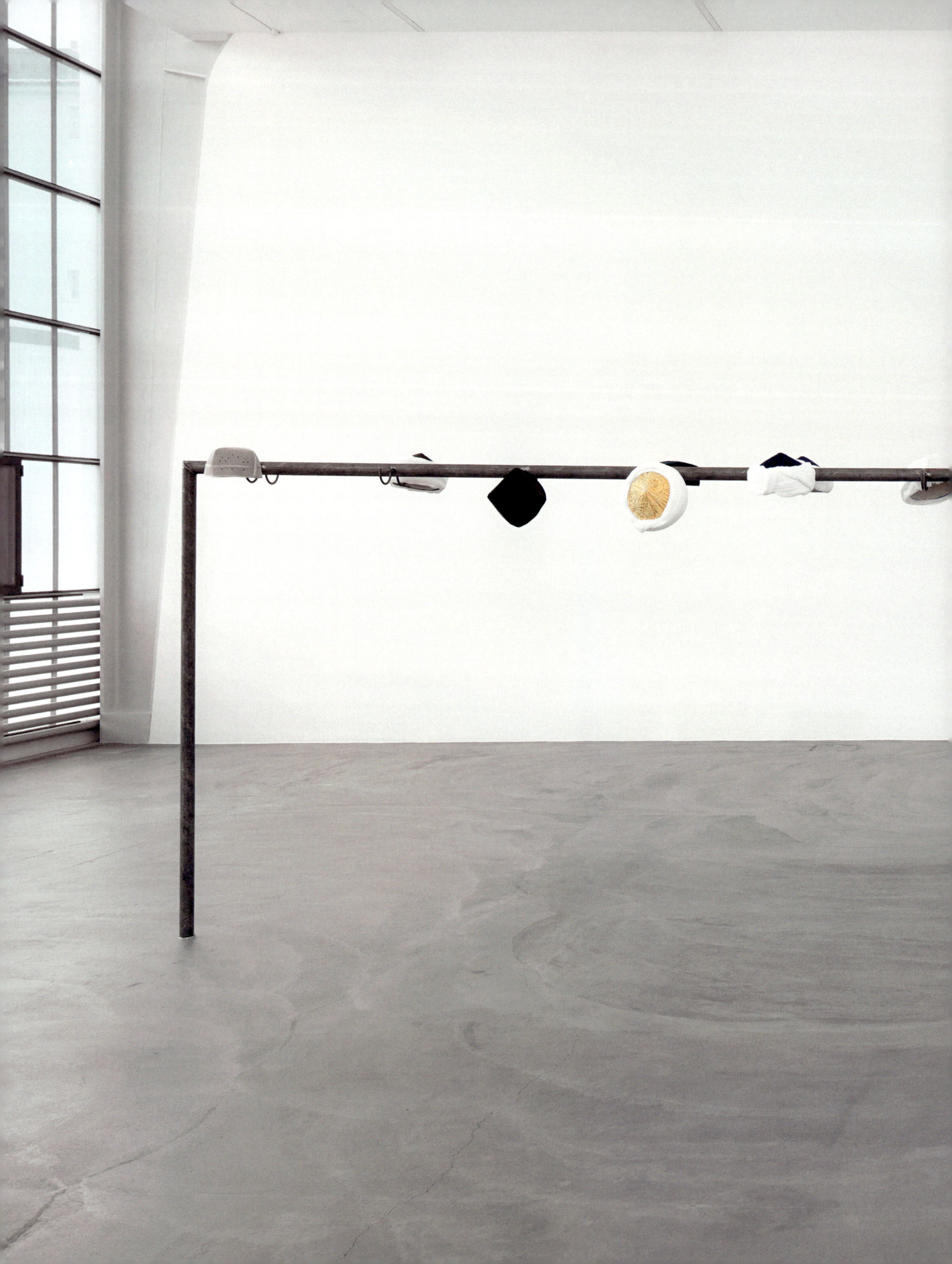

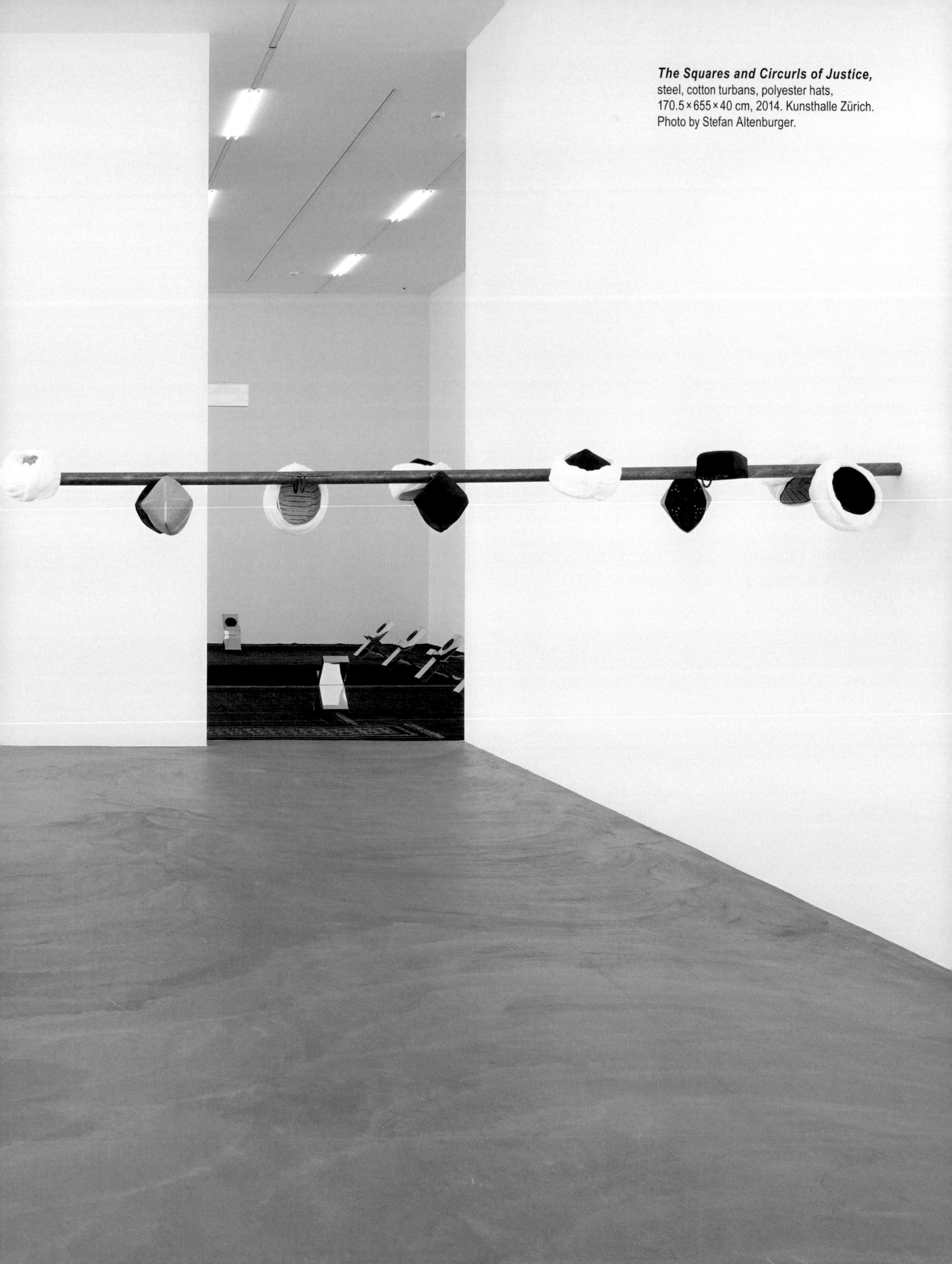

The Squares and Circurls of Justice,
steel, cotton turbans, polyester hats,
170.5 × 655 × 40 cm, 2014. Kunsthalle Zürich.
Photo by Stefan Altenburger.

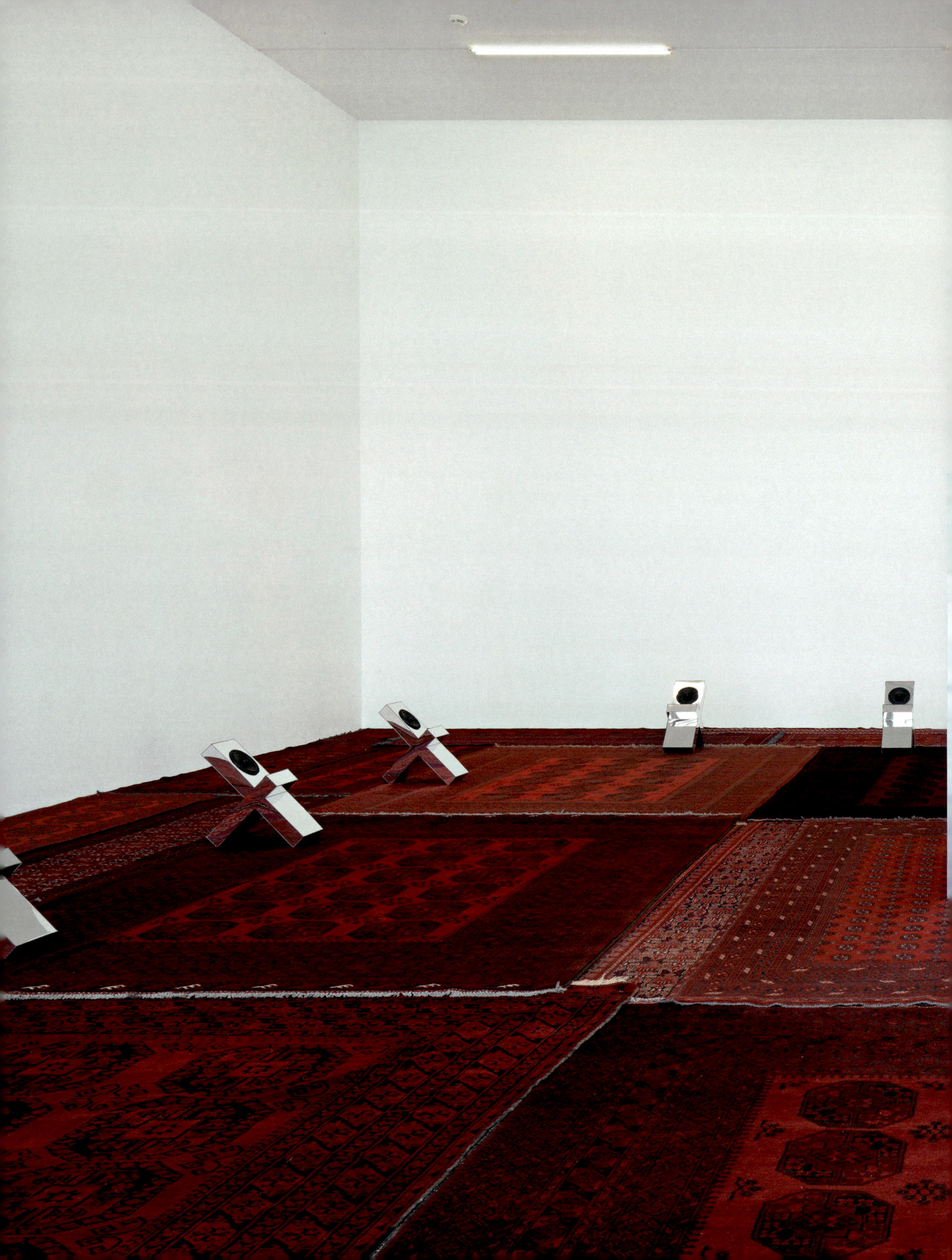

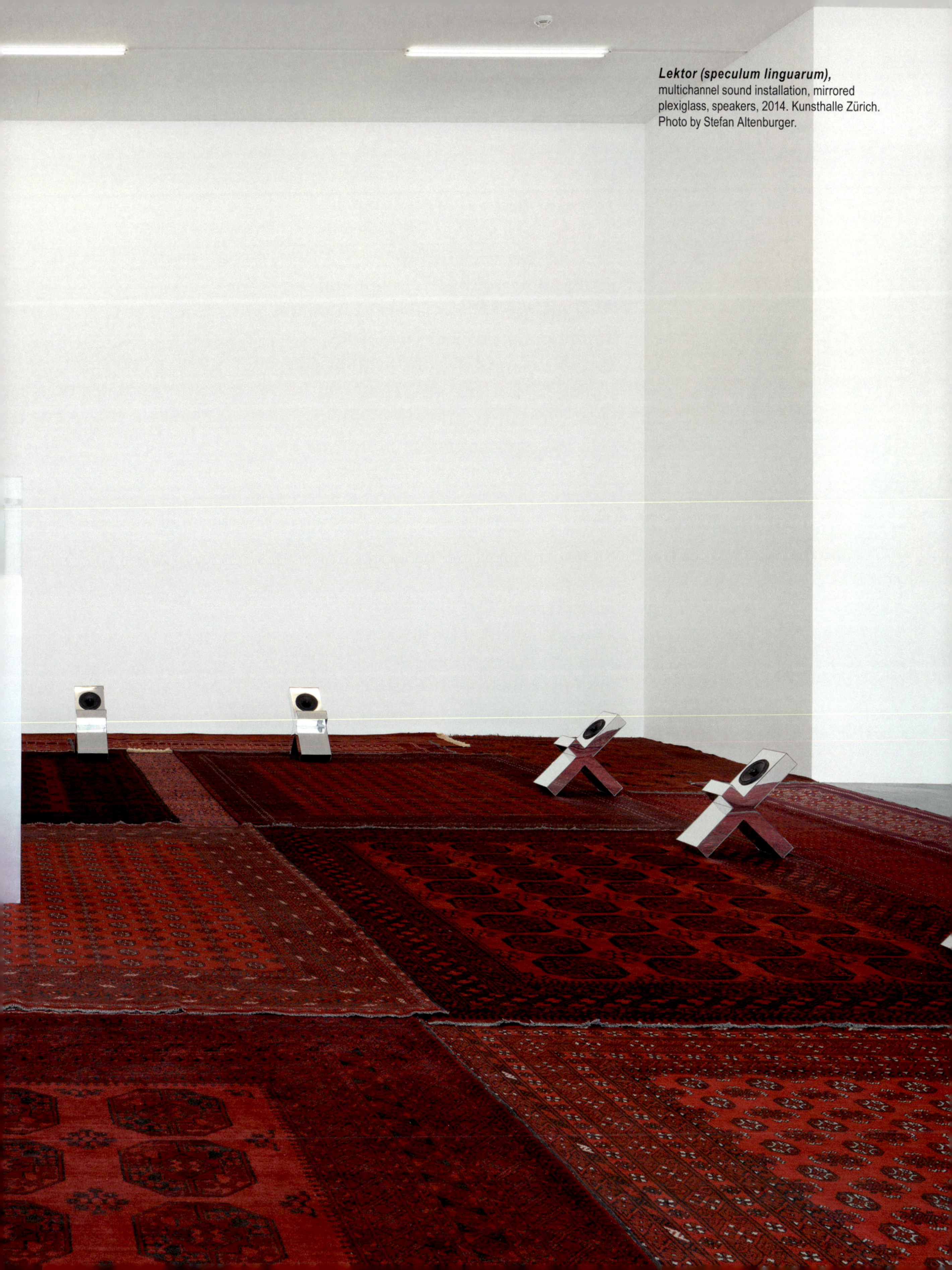

Lektor (speculum linguarum), multichannel sound installation, mirrored plexiglass, speakers, 2014. Kunsthalle Zürich. Photo by Stefan Altenburger.

Anthony Downey   **Beatrix Ruf**   Slavs and Tatars

Bak, doğan ölür; ondan eser olarak söz kalır;
Sözünü iyi söylersen ölümsüz olursun.

كل مولود يموت، ويبقى منه الكلام؛ فإن أحسنت الكلام تغدو مخلدا.

You said that you were interested in how the *Kutadgu Bilig* softens the lines between different disciplines: politics, religion and even science. These terms also play an important role in your work. But this is not scientific or political writing, it's literature. That's an important distinction to make in relation to the question of how to make books that are pragmatic.

And what it does to the narrative form in the process?

Exactly, and this approach is also an ethic. I'd be interested to hear from you on whether you place an importance on the differentiation between morality versus ethics, or image and literality versus metaphor, as an element that also defines the work.

What is born dies, but words remain a sign,
so speak good words and you will be immortal.

We both go back and forth between whether the work wilfully or accidentally employs literality, as opposed to metaphor. When there's a strength to literality, it's in the sense that it's also a smokescreen, like a Hollywood set or a Potemkin village – but hopefully there are different layers behind that village. Whereas with metaphor it's immediately apparent that there's a transmission or translation through something.

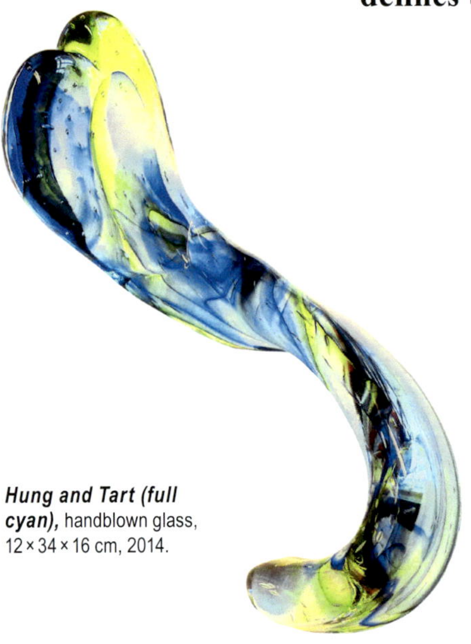

Hung and Tart (full cyan), handblown glass, 12 × 34 × 16 cm, 2014.

Anthony Downey   **Beatrix Ruf**   Slavs and Tatars

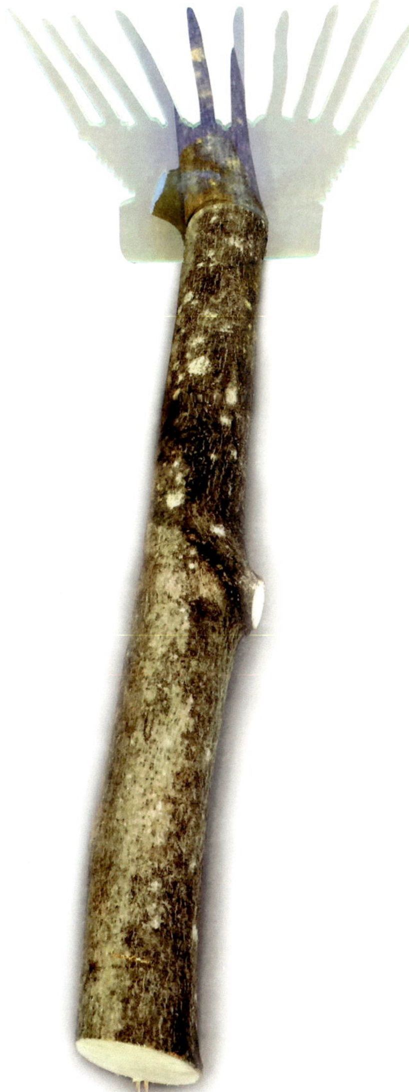

Bazm u Razm (wing 2),
dichroic glass (various
dimensions), wood, 2014.

We pride ourselves on the fact that we do research in four languages, and this was the most significant work we've done in languages that we don't speak – part of a process of willful abstraction. It's a completely new way for us to approach the text.

What's interesting in terms of morality and ethics in Islamic and Muslim medieval literature is that the term *adab*, which means morality, behaviour and virtue, is the same word as that used for literature; *adabiyaat* and *adab* have the same root. The Persians had another term, *akhlāq*, or virtue, so they see these two concepts as different. In Muslim lands a lot of mirrors for princes were incorporating a previous body (or the mistranslation of this process) of Zoroastrian knowledge. So they were adapting the Zoroastrian idea of kinship and religion into a completely different, Islamic context.

We would probably come down on the side of literality more than metaphor, but literality coupled with a kind of misfiring. Our past two or three years of work comes under the umbrella of what we call the Faculty of Substitution, where if you to go from A to B you have to resort to circuity, you can't go straight, you must go to C and D first. So we would argue that *Mirrors for Princes* doesn't have anything to do with politics, as

نىككى نەرسە بىلەن ئادەم قېرىمايدۇ : بىرى ياخشى ھەرىكەت، بىرى ياخشى سۆز.

Mit zwei Dingen ist der Mensch unsterblich,
Das eine sind gute Taten, das andere gute Reden.

Jeśli człowiek odznacza się dwoma przymiotami, nie zestarzeje się,
Jeden przymiot to dobre czyny, a drugi to dobre słowa.

Anthony Downey   **Beatrix Ruf**   Slavs and Tatars

It seems to me that the performativity of language itself is key to understanding what I would describe as the work's dialogic context. The expectation on the audience to engage is not one of an engagement towards a common end, but instead a very physical and material, agonistic thing in and of itself. You have to twist yourself around these works, sometimes literally, but always conceptually. Could you talk about this element of performativity in the work, that sense that something is unfolding?

we understand it in the literal sense; it has more to do with inner politics, or pragmatic questions of self-governance, as opposed to questions of self-help, let's say.

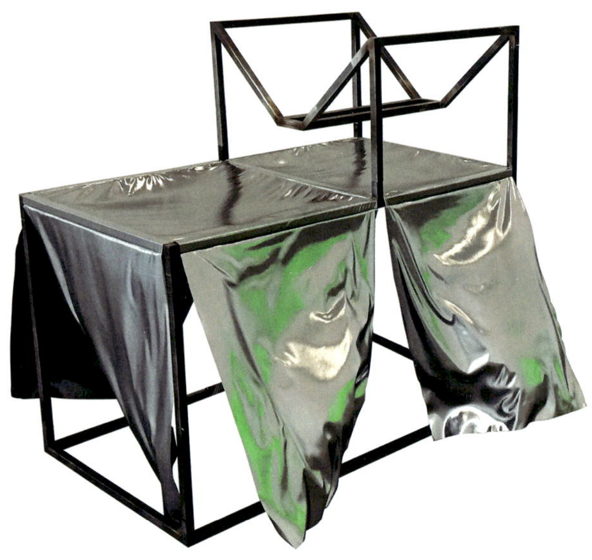

Sheikha, steel, textile, fans, 125 × 80 × 130 cm, 2014.

The question of performativity could be answered through the metaphor of taking the term and flaying it like a piece of meat – breaking it, reifying it, decomposing it and putting it back together. This word is used in our practice often, for example, in our lectures, but we still haven't understood what about our work is performative, other than the way we treat the research.

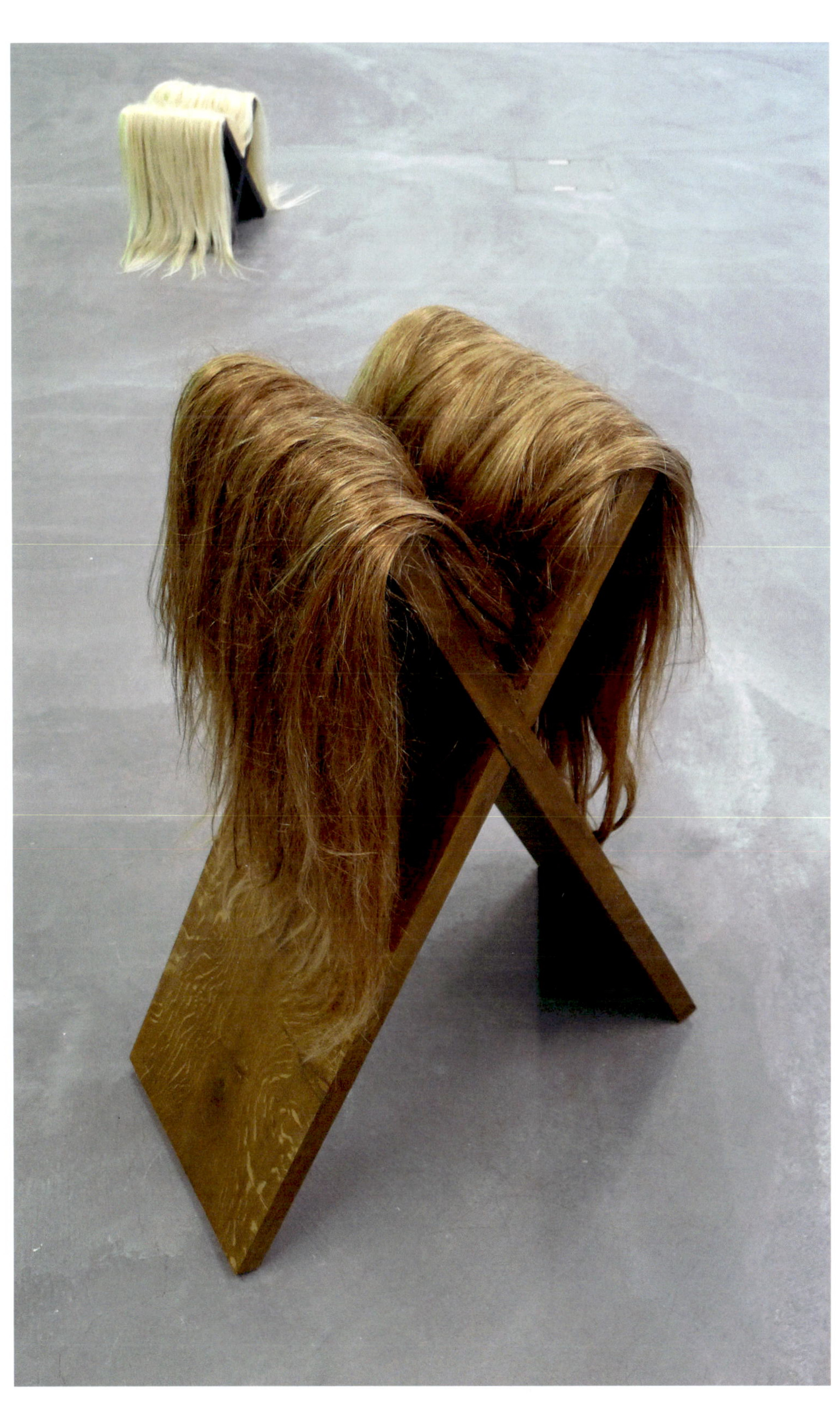

Zulf (brunette) and Zulf (blond), oak wood, hair, various dimensions, 2014. Kunsthalle Zürich.

يفقنىكى ئادەم تۇغۇلىدۇ ، ئۆلىدۇ ، لېكىن نۇتۇق قالىدۇ . ئۆزى كەتسىمۇ ناسى قالىدۇ .

Die Menschen sind geboren und gestorben,
Ihre Worte aber sind geblieben.
Nur durch ihre Worte ist ihr Name geblieben.

Pamiętaj, człowiek rodzi się i umiera, a słowa jego pozostają,
Choć dusza odchodzi, pozostaje jego imię.

Anthony Downey   **Beatrix Ruf**   Slavs and Tatars

**A sort of conceptual gymnastics –
does that work better?**

Perhaps, but again there is a missing element. In our discourse, performativity has a very corporeal kind of vision, and we can't pretend to understand what that corporeal, phenomenological understanding is, because in the lectures we don't see it; perhaps in the work it's there, but not in the lectures.

Another interesting aspect I think we should talk about is the tradition of research-based art – you intentionally position your work in the art world. You could say we're going to go through the university or the academy, but you place it in the art world. Often research-based art is only a success when it translates the document into a different form. You choose to produce objects, all kinds of objects that perform – if you want to use that term.

*Molla Nasreddin:
The Antimodern,*
fibreglass, laquer paint, steel, 165 × 157 × 88 cm, 2012. Nasreddin's pole position – backwards on his donkey – demonstrates the Sufi wise-man-cum-fool's particular take on progress and history, not to mention making for an often awkward exchange between children and their parents. Obliged to hold the old man's belly instead of his back, younger passengers inevitably pester their parents with thorny questions on perspective and time.

To answer the first question of why research in art: when we started out, we had no intention of being artists; what we thought we were going to do was publish one or two books per year and continue our previous careers. The kind of research we were doing wouldn't have sat well, or have been

Anthony Downey   **Beatrix Ruf**

Slavs and Tatars

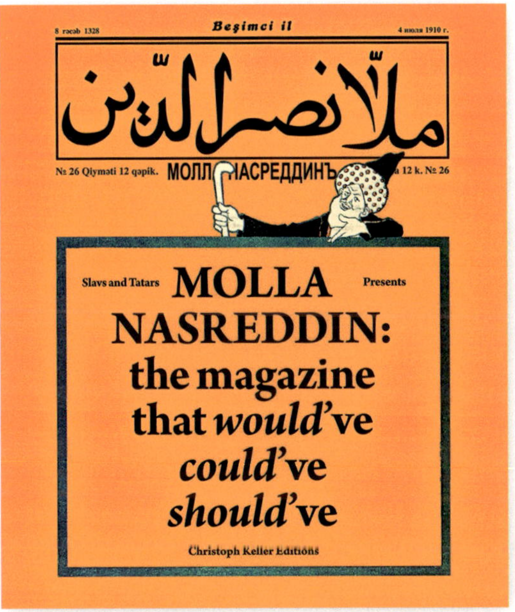

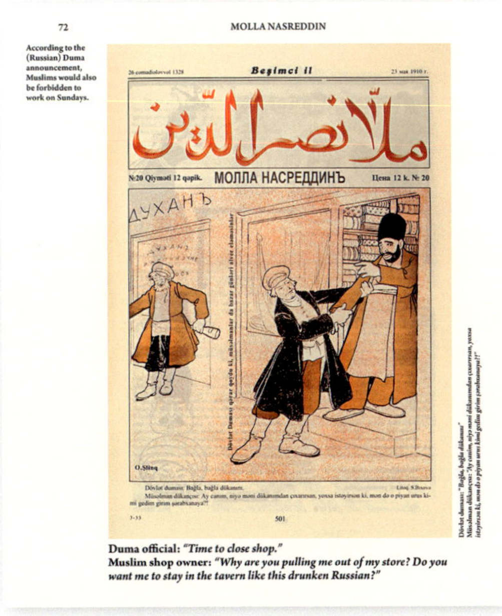

Molla Nasreddin, offset print, 28 × 24 cm, 208 pages, published by JRP|Ringier, 2011.

accepted or supported by any other medium. It is a testament to the elasticity of art as the only medium or discipline – at least to our knowledge – that is constantly questioning its own definition, so that what was outside of art became invited within.

The *Molla Nasreddin* (2011) publication is the best example; this is the kind of historical document that universities and policymakers should have published – it could have fitted into a whole array of different milieus and yet only an art publisher accepted it. From the beginning we were very keen never to show the research as such. In this sense, there is a kind of literality that we abhor. There should be a cardinal rule to prevent exhibiting documents as such, without any intervention – because you don't want to read things on a wall. You want to read things in your bedroom, in your bathtub.

People tend to hide behind the document; it becomes a buttress. It's very important never to allow anything to become an end point, so the document must be revisited as an incitement to do something. After the research we constantly ask ourselves, what are we bringing to the table as artists that historians, linguists, novelists and activists are not? What the hell do we have to say about language politics, about mirrors

سەن ئۆلمەيدىغان بىر ھاياتنى تىلىسەڭ، خۇلقى-مىجەزلىك بىلەن سۆزرۇڭگى ياخشى قىل، تەبى دانا.

Wünschst Du Dir ewiges Leben, Unsterblichkeit,
So lasse Du, Weiser, gute Tat und gute Worte zurück.

O mędrcze, jeśli pragniesz, by dusza twa była nieśmiertelna,
Dbaj dobrze o czyny swe i słowa.

Anthony Downey   **Beatrix Ruf**   Slavs and Tatars

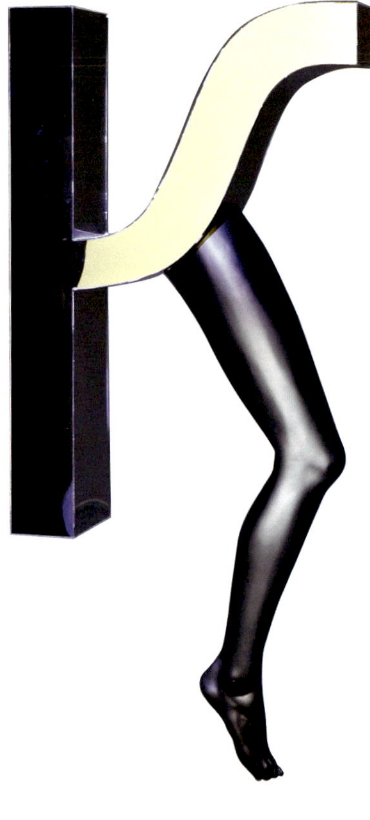

Qit Qat Qa, mirrored plexiglass, fibreglass, steel, 146 × 70 × 50 cm, 2013.

3
Friendship of Nations: Polish Shi'ite Showbiz, 2011, Sharjah Biennial 10.

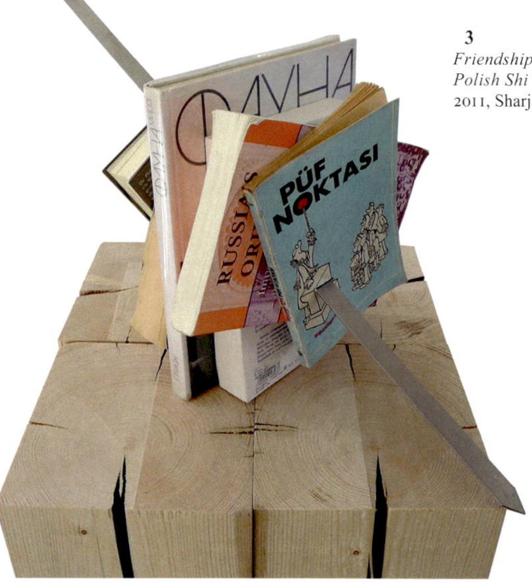

Kitab Kebab, books, metal kebab skewer, 135 × 50 × 50 cm, 2013.

for princes? Otherwise, yes, you should just read the scholarship.

When we started working together, we realised anything we tried to do on walls didn't work. Of course we don't think of our practice strictly as art. Sure, we see that what we do works within art institutions and contexts, but we didn't put anything on a wall for six years, until relatively recently. We never thought we wanted to do sculpture, but were always drawn towards the middle of the space. So it was really about the centre, becoming part of the experience, always going inwards. It began in Sharjah, where everything we created was flat, simple, singular pieces that you could ostensibly hang on the wall; yet we didn't manage to do so: we created a space where you can spend time.[3] There is also the question of craft. The idea of creating a document as an object draws us, whether it's in the context of ethnographic or folklore research – documents as dioramas, illustrating an environment around objects with painted backgrounds, people and wax, in a way that is anathema to the contemporary context. It's a challenge, a question of recreating the estrangement that happens when you create a galactic document that wings between periods of thousands of years. Some of the grooming objects in the Zürich show,

Anthony Downey   **Beatrix Ruf**   Slavs and Tatars

Sometimes these objects also look quite literal; that is, they look like they have a clear linguistic function (the tongue as shape, the mouth as shape), but humour always seems to undermine any easy access to functionality. Humour, slippage and transliteration are also key to the development and not just the ideas of these objects, for example, *Kitab Kebab* (2012, ongoing) and *Qit Qat Qa* (2013).

or even the turban *Wheat Molla* (2011), work within this kind of extended time frame.

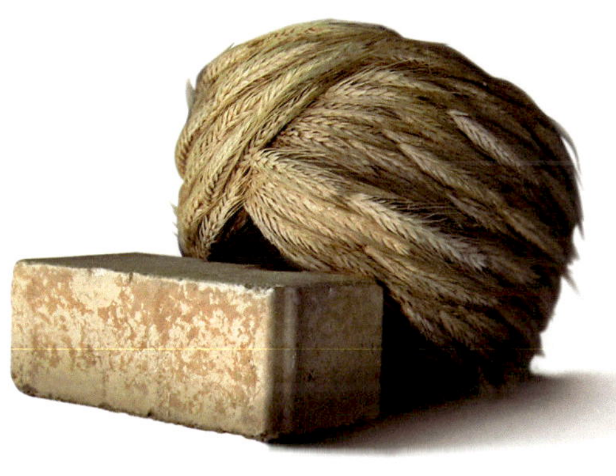

Wheat Molla, wheat, cotton, brick, 30 × 35 × 25 cm, 2011.

Humour also brings an element of generosity, something very warm that otherwise the elaboration of the object could repel. Humour attracts, or diffuses the situation; it also gives you more room to manoeuvre. You can actually be very violent if you're humorous, more pointed without that aggression – a generous way to tease meaning out of its comfort zone.

I want to go back and touch on a number of words that came to me as I looked over the material involved in both the book and installation, *Mirrors for Princes*, and see if they have any further purchase in this context. I was thinking about haunting; there's

Die Zunge habe ich gelobt und getadelt,
Mein Wunsch war das Wort, so habe ich gesagt.

Tak bardzo wychwalałem język, lecz nieraz go przeklinałem,
Wszak chciałem ci wyjaśnić znaczenie słów.

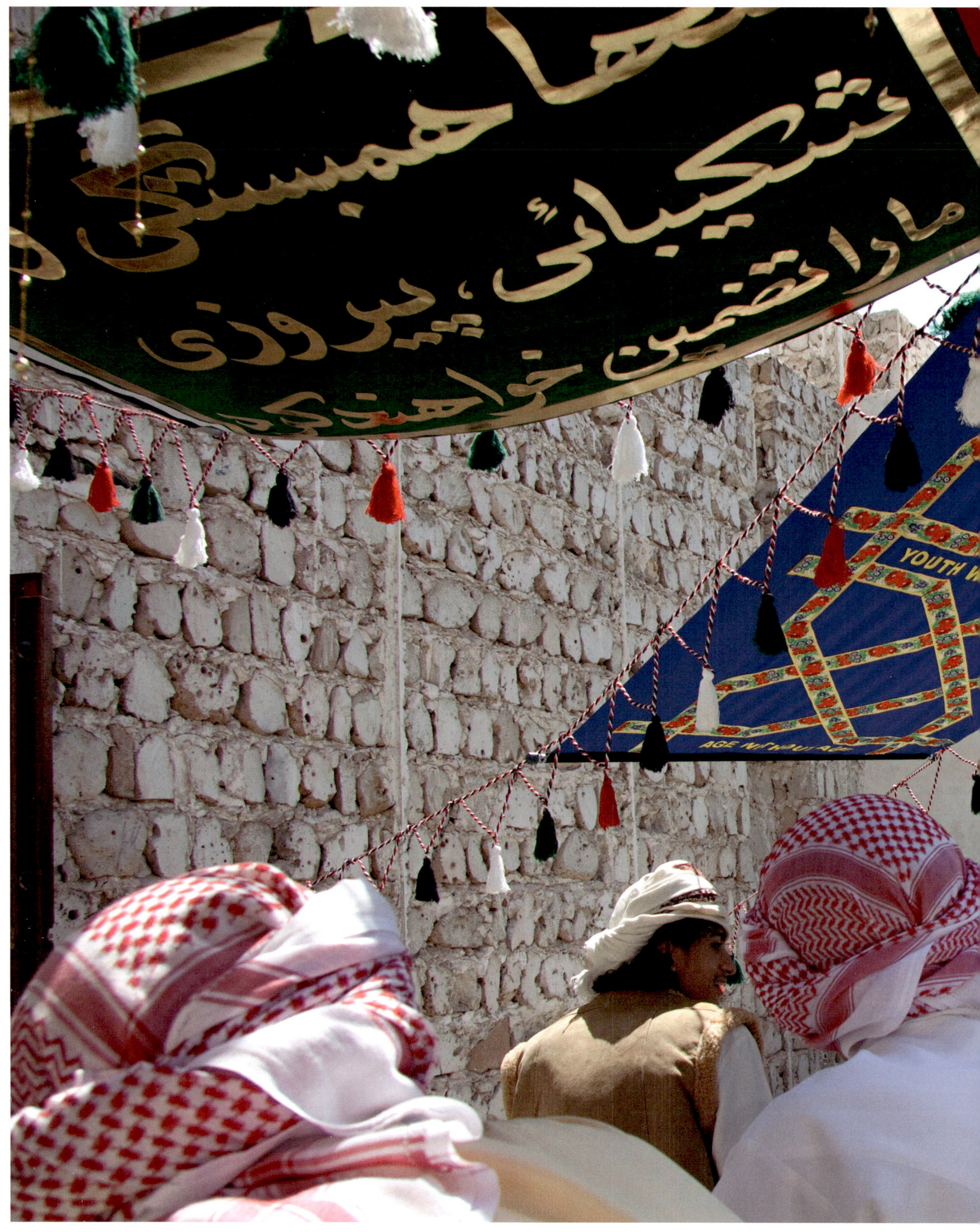

Dili bu kadar övmek ve arada bir sövmekten amacım,
Sana sözün ne olduğunu anlatmaktı.

هذا المديح منّي للسان (الإنسان) والشتمة والذمّ،
بيان لحقيقة القول لك منّي.

The tongue I have praised and chastised,
my wish was the word, thus have I said.

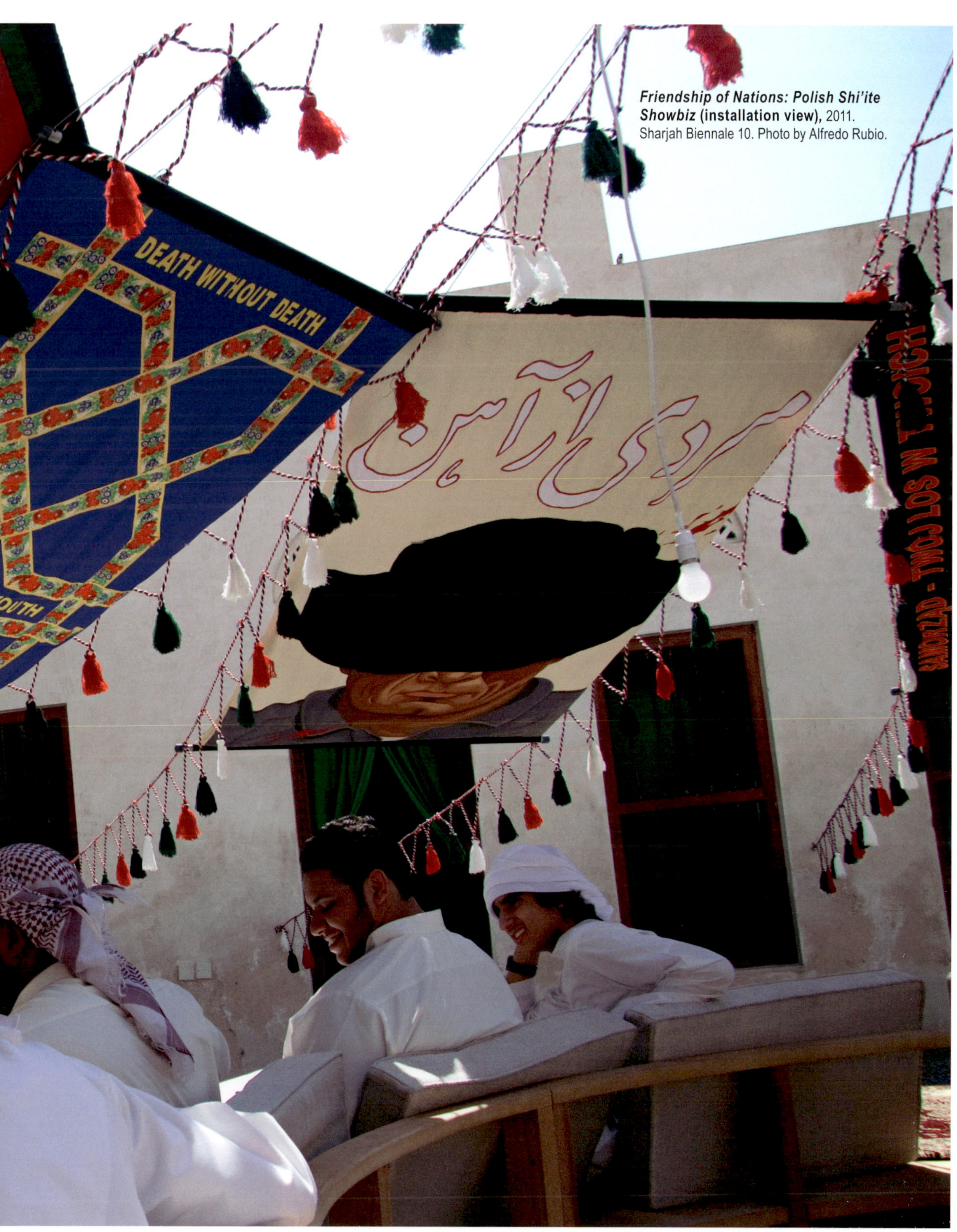

Friendship of Nations: Polish Shi'ite Showbiz (installation view), 2011. Sharjah Biennale 10. Photo by Alfredo Rubio.

همەمىلا سۆزۈڭنى يېڭىسا نۇقۇل ماقۇل كۆرمەيدۇ،
كىشى ھاجەتلىك سۆزۈڭنى سۆزلەيدۇ، يۇسۇز مايدۇ.

Nicht jedes Wort, das gefällt, ehrt den Verstand,
Sprich nur nötige Worte, sie halte nicht zurück.

Każdego słowa i jego znaczenia nie należy skrywać,
Mówić winno się prawdziwe słowa, niczego nie ukrywać.

Anthony Downey   **Beatrix Ruf**   Slavs and Tatars

almost a repression or an exploration of historical oppression – colonisation, imperialism, geopolitics, globalisation, call it what you will. The work as you present it seems to be almost like a 'ghost at the banquet', in a way that is exploring what haunts present-day representations of Islam, Muslims, Slavs and, indeed, Tatars. The submerged genre of mirrors for princes, in particular, seems to haunt political discourse today because that level of discourse is absent, or deferred, and it is precisely that absence that draws attention to the fact of its presence and the need for it. So I'm thinking about *Mirrors for Princes* as a kind of haunting of present-day political discourse, if that works?

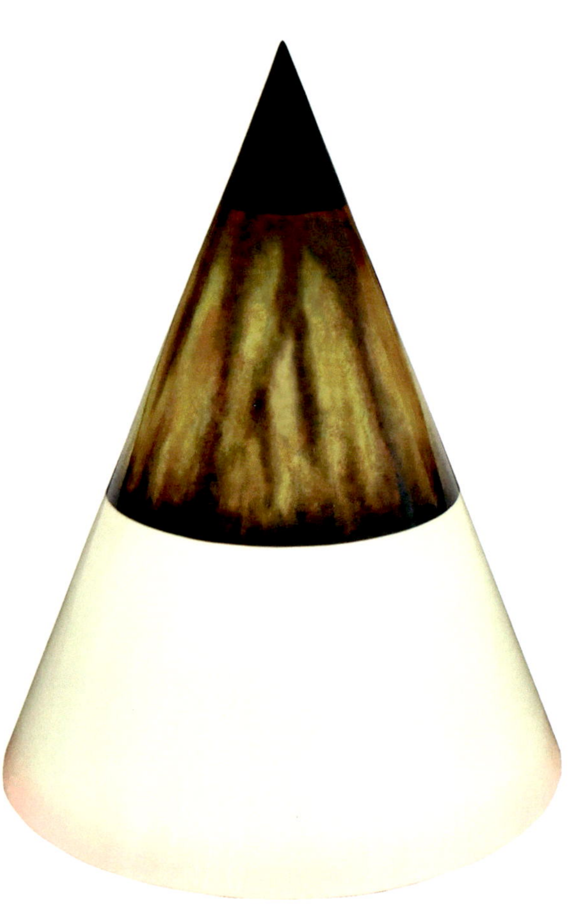

Sharp Eye (Hazel),
fibreglass, acrylic paint,
polyester resin,
125 × 100 × 100 cm, 2014.

Perhaps haunting in terms of excavating the forgotten and overlooked – but not in a frightening sense. Perhaps we could also consider haunting as a form of reoccurence – it's something that is unresolved. Rather than finding or discovering an archive, we work with it as a reoccurring subject.

That which refuses to go away, which refuses to die.

Anthony Downey   **Beatrix Ruf**   Slavs and Tatars

Exactly, it's almost like it repeats itself: it's constantly the same; it comes back under different names in different times.

Because mirrors for princes, as a genre, is now rewritten in a vulgarised form as self-help books, the genre seems to be employing different idioms. But what you have done is excavate the shared element of developing a spiritual context within the political. Nobody talks about faith in the context of politics today. In fact, the notion of faith seems to be excised–

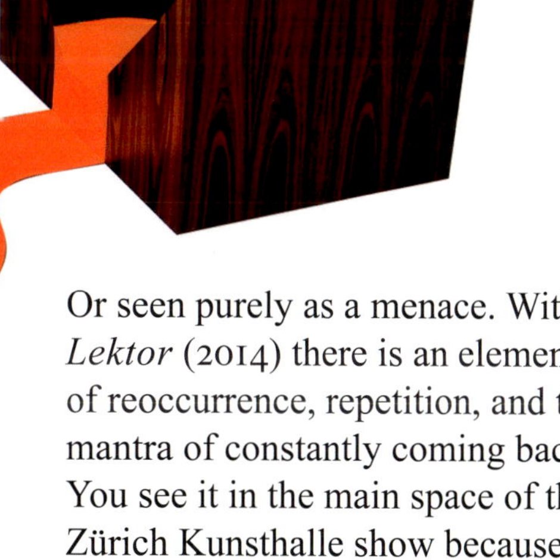

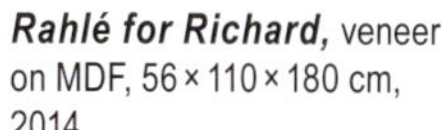

Rahlé for Richard, veneer on MDF, 56 × 110 × 180 cm, 2014.

Or seen purely as a menace. Within *Lektor* (2014) there is an element of reoccurrence, repetition, and this mantra of constantly coming back. You see it in the main space of the Zürich Kunsthalle show because of the presence of four languages in four channels; by the time one sequence ends, the original language has just finished when the destination language is beginning, so there's a kind of linking up to, or trying to catch up to, itself.

It's interesting to talk about ghosting because a ghost's form is changing; there is no given form. That's something that reoccurs in your work; looking at cultural

Anthony Downey **Beatrix Ruf** Slavs and Tatars

Ey yiğit, ben bu sözü oğlum için söyledim;
Oğul benden aşağıdır, bana nasıl denk olur.

هذا القول قلته لابني أيها المغدام؛
إني أسفل منى فكيف يوازيني!

My word have I, my son, spoken to you, oh, son, accept it well!

phenomena in that more concrete, harder, but changed form, which is therefore still there, haunting or reoccurring. These self-help books are probably the least appropriate or the worst ghost that could come out of mirrors for princes.

I'm also thinking about Gavrilov's translation and technique, that mimetic quality of two languages coming together, fighting and contesting one another.[4] It seems Gavrilov translation, as a form, is very much about how the voice is a form of contestation, working in an ephemeral, immaterial sense, to simultaneously haunt another voice.

4

Gavrilov translation is a translation practice often used in Poland and Russia. The language of the original film or news segment is kept audible and almost equal to the destination language. The simultaneous playback of two distinct audio tracks makes for a disruptive experience, touching on issues of legibility and authenticity (the method is often used for news segments and documentaries). This method, of course, would often result in deviations from the original to the 'translated' voice. For a fuller discussion of this technique, see David Crowley's essay in this volume.

You're right, it haunts (maybe we can take the ghost metaphor further); it's a voice that overrides yet serves something, so it's this very strange thing where you're trying to explain in another language what somebody is saying, but while you're doing that, you're speaking over them.

I can't get away from Bakhtin's notion of heteroglossia here; the accumulation of many different voices together to create something that is nonsingular, nonindividual, nonauthentic, nonoriginary, but also accumulative. That heteroglossic moment where meaning emerges

Anthony Downey   **Beatrix Ruf**   Slavs and Tatars

and mutates is not only about contest, it's about agonism and antagonistics; it's about the nonresolution of a specific point or historical moment. Have you guys looked at Bakhtin before?

5
David Joselit, 'On Aggregators', *October*, vol. 146 (Fall 2013): 3–18.

Of course, the dialogic is important, as is the carnival and carnivalesque. We were just reading David Joselit's essay about aggregates.[5] He mentions that the difference with aggregates is that each element retains its own autonomy as opposed to becoming a mash-up or a third thing. Aggregates rely as well on asynchrony, whether through time (in the form of an anachronism) or scale. It's kind of like magnets; when magnets repel, there's a discharge, but perhaps one of agency.

It seems to me that the genre of mirrors for princes hasn't just been chosen because it's a form of historical document that brings together occluded narratives that have been partly forgotten. Nor is it just the reference to political instruction. It seems the reason you've chosen it is that it speaks to the ethos of present-day human behaviour, and perhaps what's missing from today's political discourse. I think this notion of political instruction in the context of the ethos of ethical and human

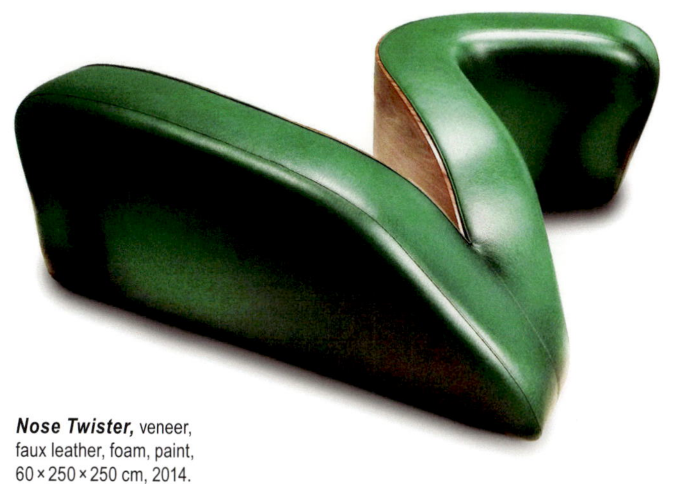

Nose Twister, veneer, faux leather, foam, paint, 60 × 250 × 250 cm, 2014.

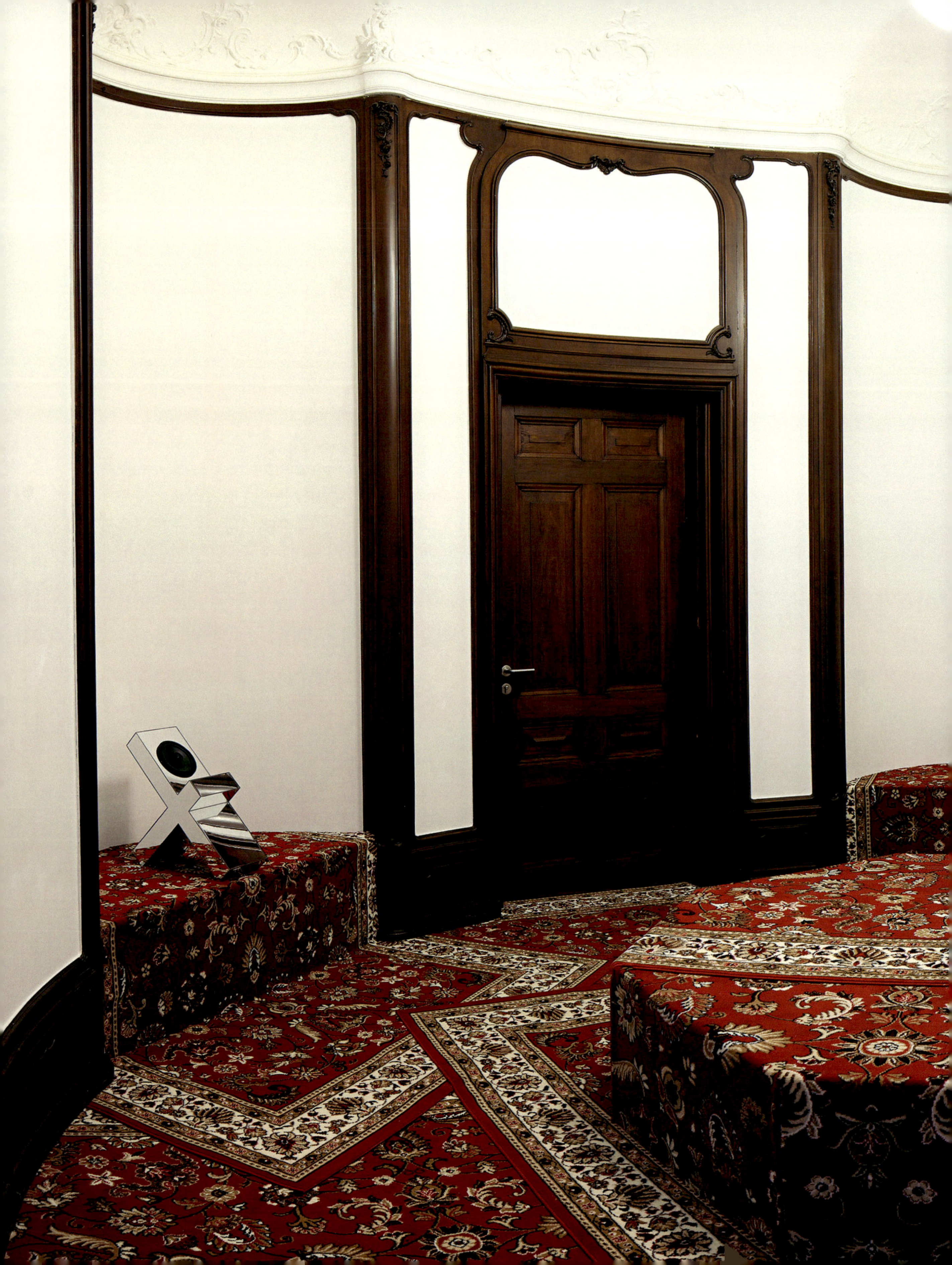

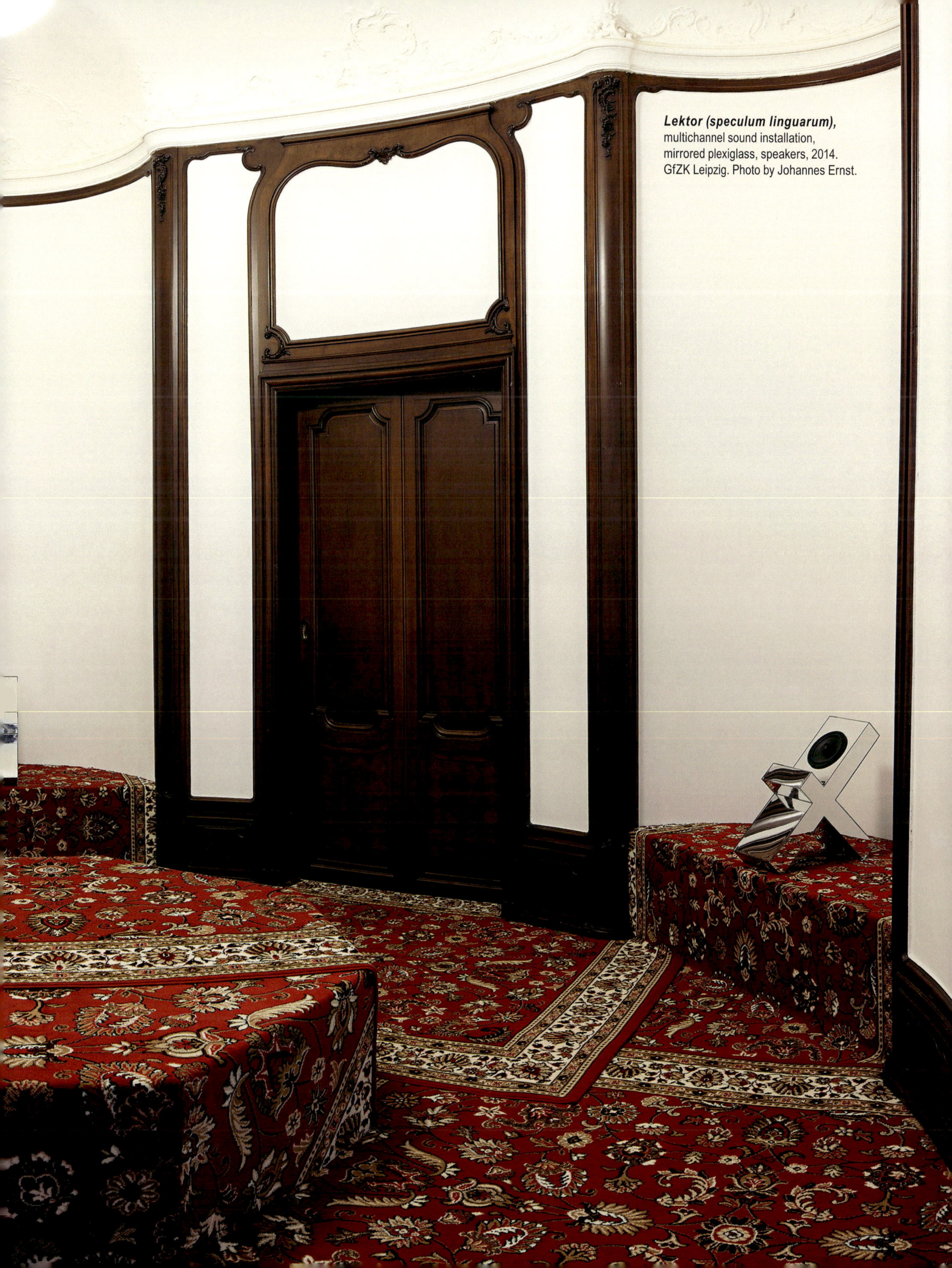

Lektor (speculum linguarum),
multichannel sound installation,
mirrored plexiglass, speakers, 2014.
GfZK Leipzig. Photo by Johannes Ernst.

Anthony Downey   **Beatrix Ruf**   Slavs and Tatars

behaviour seems to be the key debate of our time. Politics seems bereft of imagination, for want of a better term. Does that have something to do with the choice of this specific mirror for princes? What does it have to say to the present moment? How it offers a codependent, historical document or lineage for re-engaging the discussion.

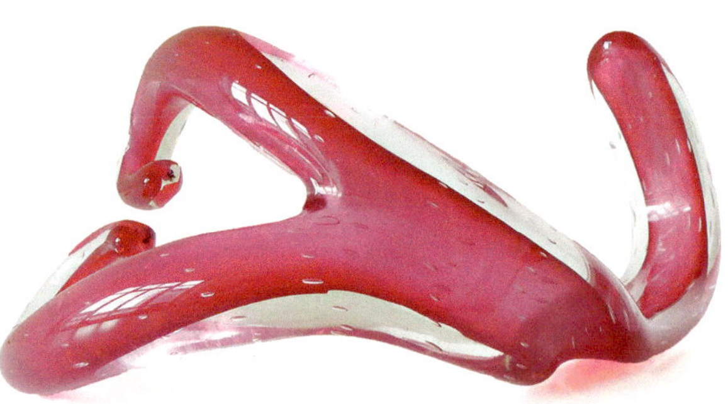

Hung and Tart (split magenta), handblown glass, 15 × 35 × 25 cm, 2014.

We had a great idea for a proposal: if there were a government commission of a public artwork, we could have a mirror for princes text read to visiting dignitaries.

An edited version or extract from?

It's read to you, in its entirety.

So it's formal, instructional?

It's formal and you have to take time to listen, so yes. I think the focus of *Lektor* (2014) on language is important here because everything starts with the enunciation. Whether it's the way heads of state allow themselves to talk about Vladmir Putin or how the language that's used to talk about immigration has evolved in the past ten years. James Scott uses the term *infra-politics*; the private domain of the oral, whether in speech, songs or gestures, as forms of opposition

Anthony Downey   **Beatrix Ruf**   Slavs and Tatars

that escape even the most oppressive regimes. Scott argues that we often look to the most overt and organised manifestations of politics, those most often successfully suppressed, but that we don't ever look at the gestures, the private jokes – those are infra-politics. We are interested in that kind of infra-discourse, the discourse that happens away from sight but, also, within one's self.

And it is this sense of the infra, that which lies beneath or behind, that seems to be made manifest in the objects.

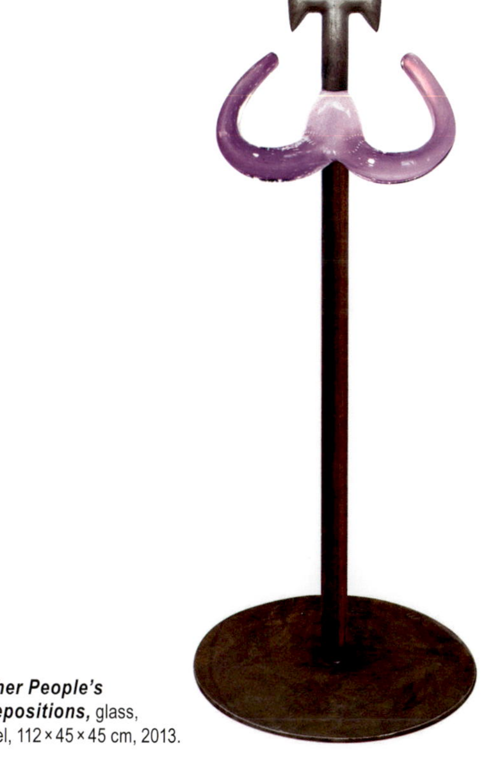

Other People's Prepositions, glass, steel, 112 × 45 × 45 cm, 2013.

To come back to objects, when we started we were very concerned with the spaces that we build – like *PrayWay* (2012), or the riverbeds, as in *Dear 1979, Meet 1989* (2013) – and we always think of a comparison between those seating spaces and a chair. The chair is articulated individually – there's your space and my space. We're always trying to introduce a space where it's not about you and the chair but where one becomes the other. The collective trumps the individual.

You could perhaps see the notion of ethics and advice literature throughout previous works, not just in the current body of *Mirrors for Princes*. Much of our research,

Anthony Downey   **Beatrix Ruf**   Slavs and Tatars

installations and sculptures engage a sense of responsibility towards the other and the world around you.

But not necessarily on equal terms – again, it's an antagonistic, agonistic process.

Even the idea of the oral aspect of reading is interesting. Our challenge is to understand how to reclaim the collective act. How do you reactivate – or activate, even – or redeem the collective act of reading?

Which was the idea of the book club. This is quite a strong, potent, structural element for the rest of your work.

We often see reading as intimate, but perhaps the way to read a book is as though you are reading it aloud to the other person, or, the other extreme, as a text is written solely and exclusively for you.

I see in all your work that you look at things in terms of how the text failed, so to speak, in a historical context and in the chronology of the text being transmitted to different channels and also conditions, in terms of politics or religion. When you think of art and its history, language is bound to fail, as many

Benden sana gümüş ve altın kalırsa,
Sen onları bu söze denk tutma.

فإن ورثت مني فضة وتبر،
فلا تجعله يوازي هذه الوصايا.

If I bequeath to you gold and silver,
do not consider that to be equal to these words.

Anthony Downey   **Beatrix Ruf**   Slavs and Tatars

artists have actively been saying.
In your work, it seems the objects
take on the grammar of language;
they intentionally do not make
language fail, but almost visualise
or materialise language into
objects. So the encounter with this
is actually the absolute opposite of
performativity because it's reading
and not speaking; it's reading and
not the activity of interpretation.
It excludes interpretation almost.

Perhaps *enunciative* rather than
performative might be a better term
– to enunciate, the literal moment
of saying as opposed to the moment
of making meaning, as opposed to
any narrative.

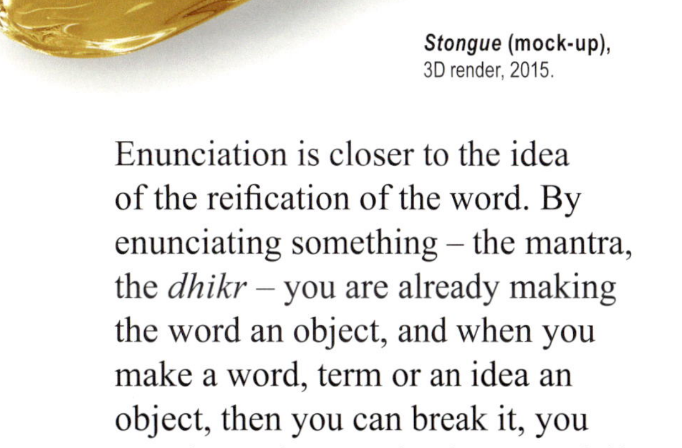

Stongue (mock-up),
3D render, 2015.

Enunciation is closer to the idea
of the reification of the word. By
enunciating something – the mantra,
the *dhikr* – you are already making
the word an object, and when you
make a word, term or an idea an
object, then you can break it, you
can shatter it, you give it a materiality.
How do you give a real, fleshy
corporeality to a term that otherwise
can slip through your fingers?

There seems also to be a moment of
estrangement – the materialisation
or enunciation of that word can
be a moment of estrangement, too.

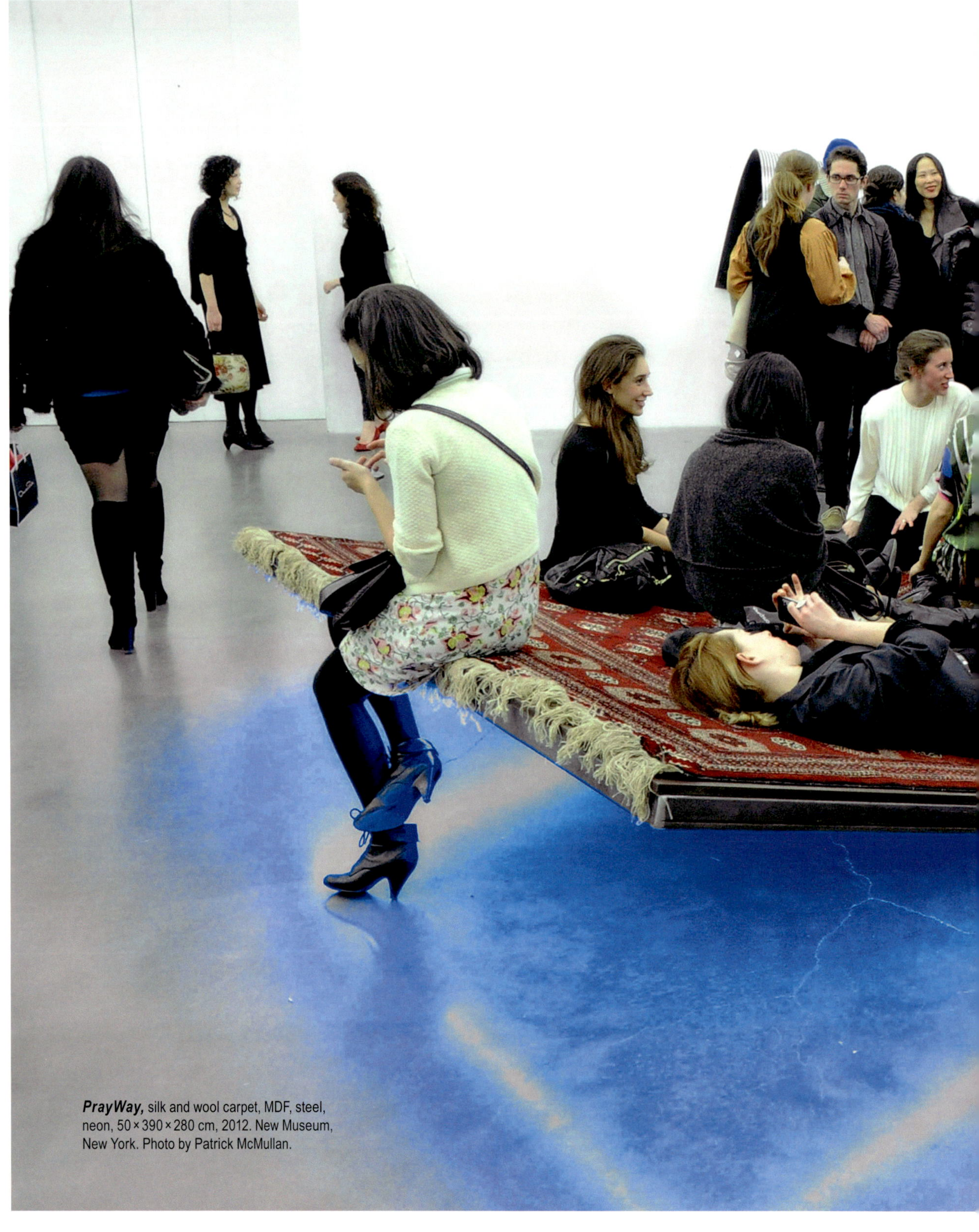

PrayWay, silk and wool carpet, MDF, steel, neon, 50 × 390 × 280 cm, 2012. New Museum, New York. Photo by Patrick McMullan.

Gümüşü bir işe harcarsan tükenir;
Sözümü işe harcarsan gümüş kazanılır.

فما انفقت من تبر بدولي يفنى؛
وبالدرام قولي تكسب التبر

Apply silver to affairs and it will be used up,
but apply my words and you will gain silver.

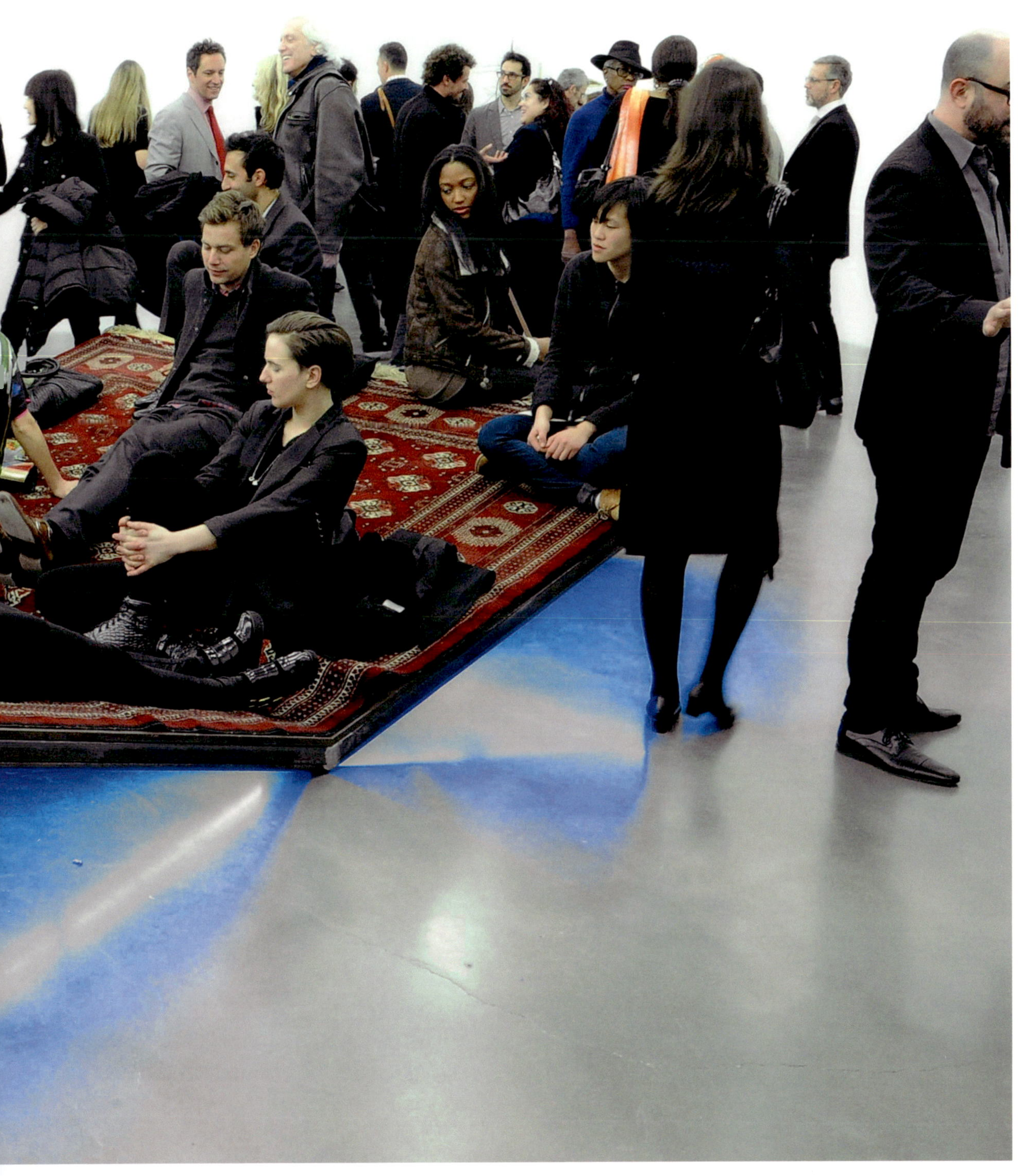

Von Mensch zu Mensch wird das Wort vererbt,
Der Nutzen, das geerbte Wort zu behalten, is gross.

Słowa dziedziczy człowiek od człowieka,
Wielka jest korzyść z odziedziczonych słów.

Anthony Downey   **Beatrix Ruf**   Slavs and Tatars

You've got to work hard at this – every time I see your work I get a totally different experience, and you have to be ready to absorb and engage this difference. Maybe this goes back to your notion about accessibility and availability.

Vulgarisation is also something we could talk about as a question of profanity and the sacral. We keep talking about the talisman or the totem, creating works that have or suggest a ritualistic quality, but at the same time there is a very clear process of vulgarisation.

It has a rich meaning, the term *vulgar* – it's not just a simile for scatological. You know *vulgate* is actually the common speech of the people, the vernacular. The vulgate Bible was prepared by St. Jerome in the fourth century BC, and handed down to the people and accepted as the recognised version, thereafter making the Word of God more widely accessible to the individual, and this is the origin of the notion vulgarisation. A vulgarisation can be the secularisation of the sacred.

This is a tension that we have within our own practice, and within our dynamic. It's again this idea of the repelling magnets – on one end we're

Kişiden kişiye, miras olarak söz kalır;
Vasiyet edilen sözü tutmanın faydası çoktur.

يبقى البيان من الإنسان للإنسان ميراثً،
وقوائد الكلام الموصى به كثيرةً.

Words are one man's legacy to another.
So hold on to the legacy of my words, and the profit therefrom will be a hundredfold.

Anthony Downey   **Beatrix Ruf**   Slavs and Tatars

invested in the printed word, and yet the printed word profanes the sacrality of texts, the very thing that we seek to preserve.

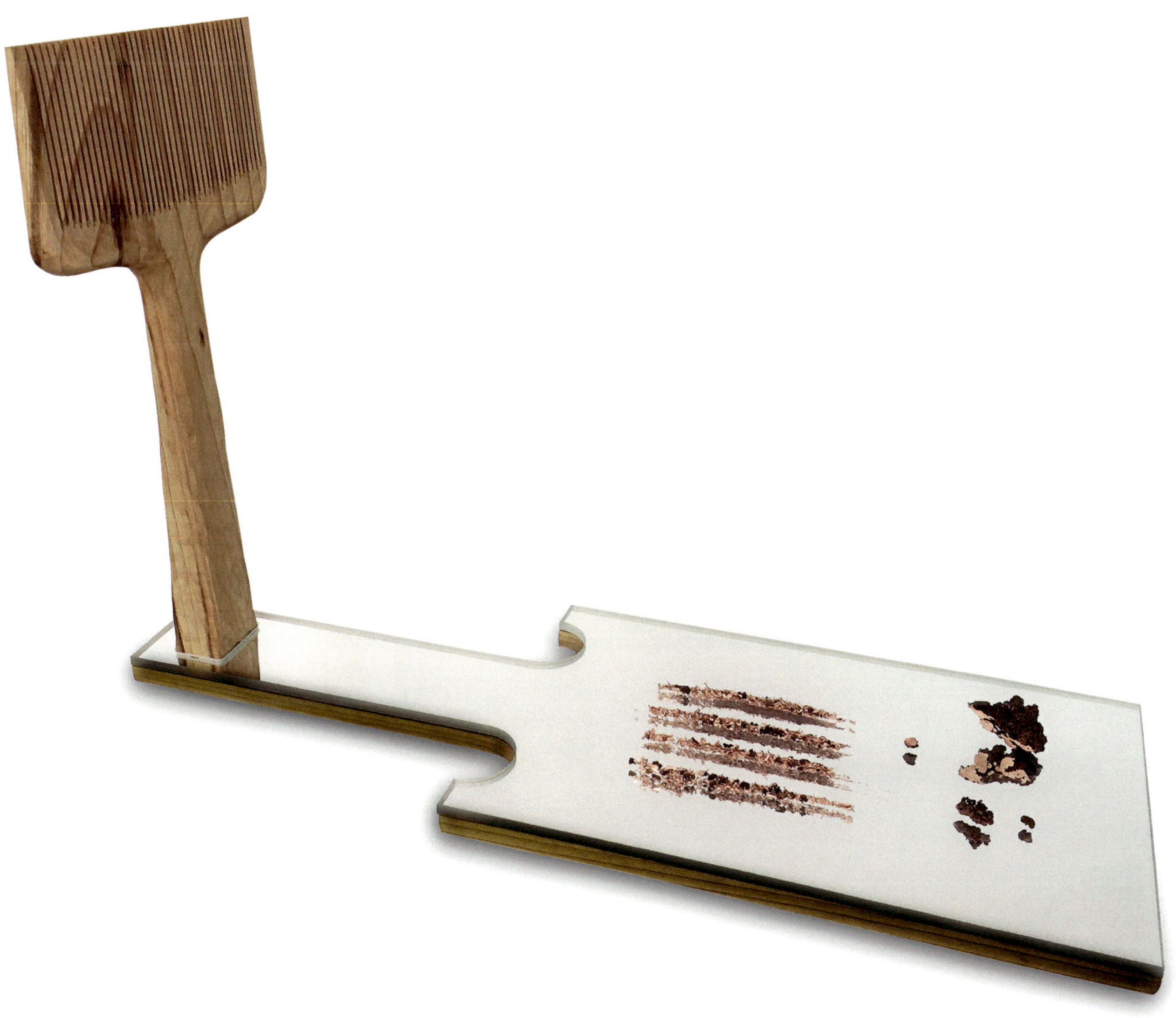

5 o'clock shadow, linden wood, mirror, shaved copper ore, 18 × 48 × 31 cm, 2014.

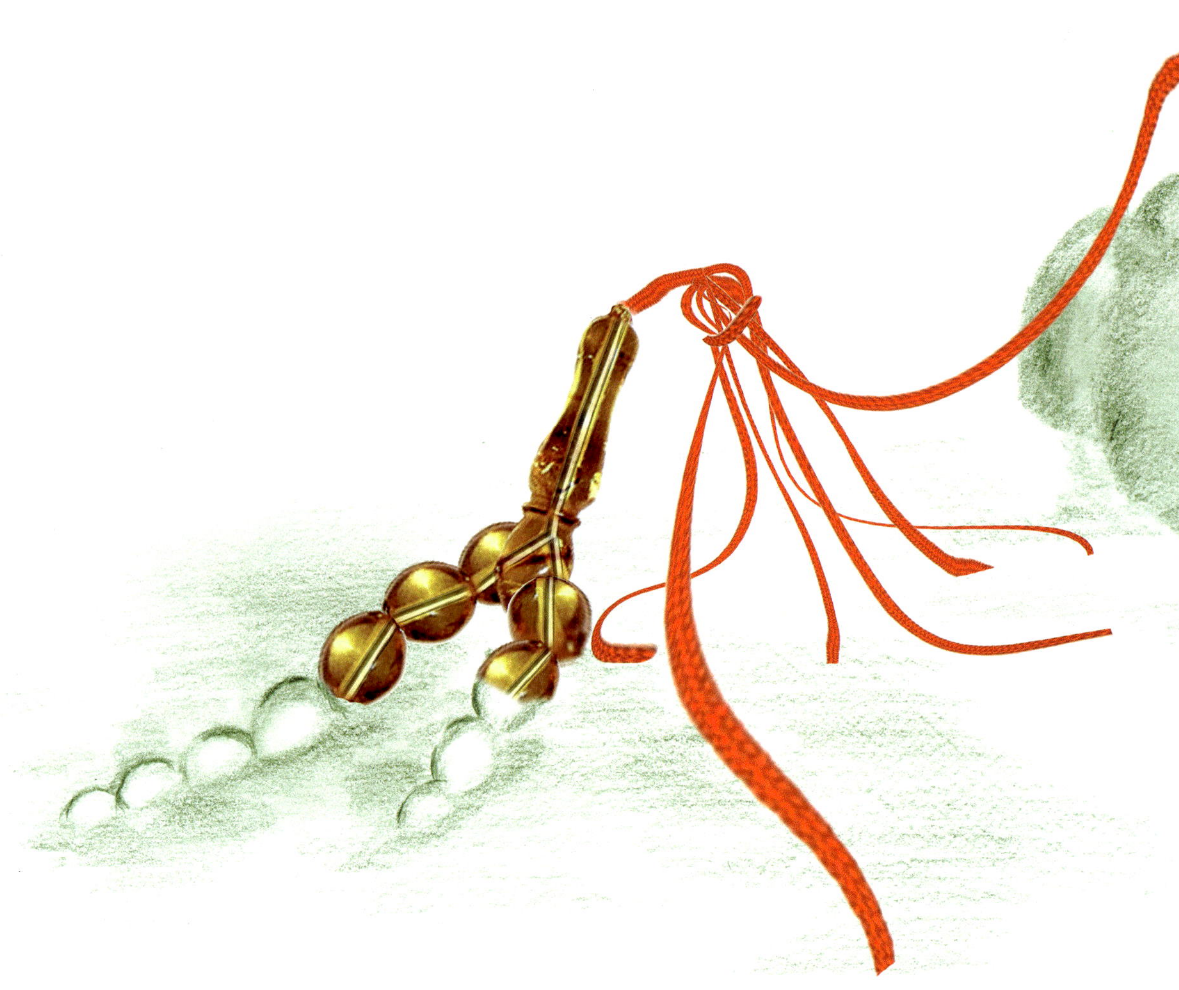

Söz yağız yere mavi gökten indi;
Kişi kendine sözüyle değer verdirdi.

بيخط الكلام من السماء الزرقاء إلى الأرض السمراء
و المر ء بالقول يمنح لنفسه قيمتي.

Speech descended from blue heaven to brown earth,
and it is by means of speech that man ennobles his soul.

AÂ AÂ AÂ UR, sketch
for public sculpture, 2014.
Skulpturenpark Köln.

Fate, Fortune and Governance in the Medieval World

Neguin Yavari

The juxtaposition of fate and governance is a salient fixture of premodern historical writing from around the globe. This pairing of seeming contraries has been conventionally interpreted as follows. Fate and/or fortune were dear to the medieval heart, bound as they were by piety and religiosity. The hegemony of fate and fortune over human affairs accommodated in the political realm the hegemony of tyranny. That corrosive nexus ended with the onslaught of secularism and the separation of religion from politics, otherwise known as the birth of the modern world. But does piety, or faith, render inevitable the subordination of politics to religion? Is secularism a historical process, born sometime in the sixteenth century (or the one after, or the one after that, depending on who you ask), or is it comprised in an ideational constellation that dates at least as far back as the Old Testament? This essay explores the interplay of fate, fortune and governance in two Islamic mirrors for princes from the eleventh century, to argue that a reconsideration of languages of authority in medieval Islam could lead to important questions bearing directly on the study of political thought in the modern period.

Scriptural influence – in the form of structure, content, metonymy and synecdoche – on political thought is pervasive. In Exodus and in subsequent Abrahamic scriptures, God demands justice and good governance for his peoples, warning the pharaoh to put an end to tyranny and iniquity. The pharaoh, as is well known, fails to heed good advice, and his downfall is thereby availed. The alternate paradigm,

Ein Meer ohne Grund ist das Herz des Menschen;
Eine Perle auf seinem Grund ist das Wissen.

Serce ludzkie jest jak morze bez dna;
A wiedza niczym perła co na dnie leży.

good rulership, is henceforth contingent upon receptivity to advice. The exhortation to good rule is the primary subject matter in mirrors for princes, manuals of governance that proliferated in the Christian and Islamic worlds in the medieval period, although that literature enjoys a much longer history. In 1889, a manual on the vizierate was discovered in the tomb of an Egyptian vizier, which subsequent research has dated to the second half of the reign of Ahmose, founder of the eighteenth-

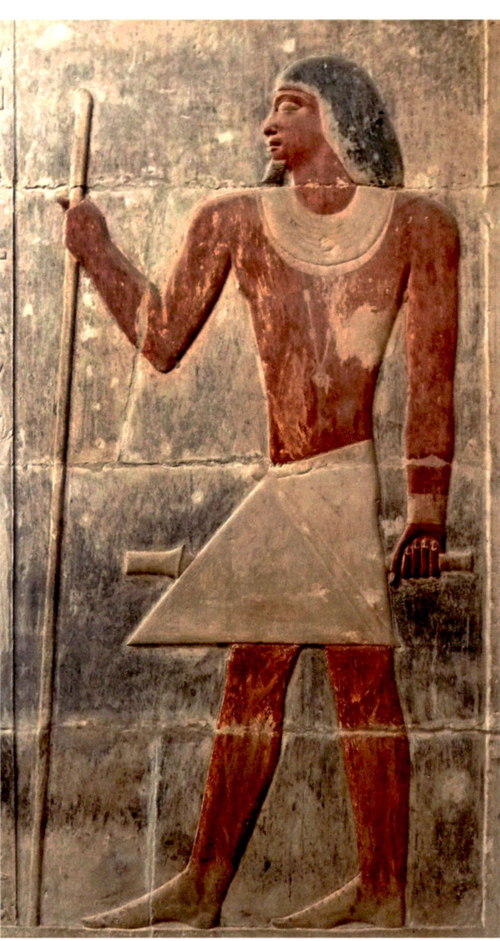

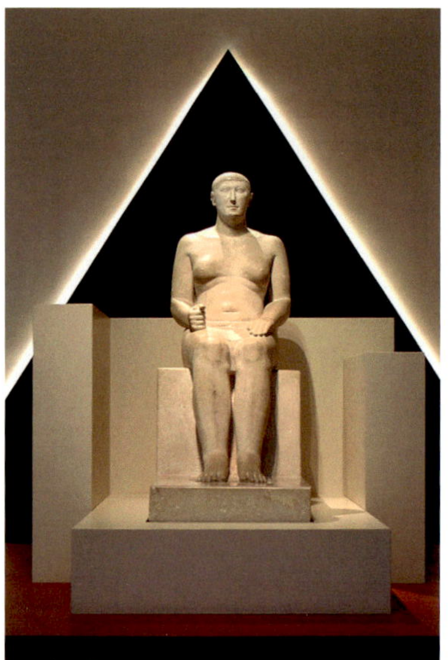

Statue of **Hemiunu** (3rd millennium BCE), vizier and thought to be the architect of the Great Pyramid of Giza. Source: *Roemer- und Pelizaeus-Museum*, Hildesheim, Germany. *(top)*

Kagemni, vizier to King Teti (2354-33 BCE), Sixth Dynasty of Ancient Egypt. Source: *perankhgroup.com (left)*

century dynasty.[1] Mirrors rely on past exemplars, semiotic codes and moral teachings to edify rulers and to educate them in the taming of their innate inclination to injustice, tyranny and abuse of power.[2] Reason, prudence, liberality, decisiveness and vigilance were often evoked as the requisites for stable rule, along with receptivity to advice and a willingness to take on board lessons that past rulers had learned

[1]
The Duties of the Vizier: Civil Administration in the Early New Kingdom, ed. and trans. G. P. F. van den Boorn (London: Kegan Paul International, 1988), 344.

[2]
For a genealogy of mirrors for princes, see: Neguin Yavari, *Advice for the Sultan: Prophetic Voices and Secular Politics* (New York: Oxford University Press, 2014), 7–44.

the hard way. Associated with tyrannical rule, as Robert Dankoff has asserted,[3] the battle of counsellor and king came to an end in Europe, according to Judith Ferster, when parliaments replaced counsellors as the primary vehicle for delimiting princely power.[4] In the Islamic world, mirrors for princes persist until the early twentieth century, albeit with a considerably shrunken readership.

Their quaint instructions on the etiquette of serving dinner to esteemed guests or the proper decorum for dining with the king notwithstanding, mirrors offer powerful political visions, and are substantially more critical of power, and of religious dogmatism, than their superficial praise and prayer for the prince might suggest. Alongside lessons from the past, the exhortation to good rule was almost infallibly clad in the observance of God's rules. But the mirrors convey an infinitely more complicated and nuanced juxtaposition of history with religion, or its avatar, that is, fate. While the latter pertains to the future, and is unstable, the past – the stuff of history – is impervious to change. Why teach about the past, if the purpose of instruction is to procure the future? Fate, in this regard, is the nemesis of history: it is invoked to explain reversals and sudden changes, whereas a solid historical account attempts to explain events and developments in terms of long-term currents and distant causes. In a way, history works to undermine fate: it classifies and theorises cause and effect to explain what may appear as unexplained. In medieval parlance, history is weaponised in mirrors for princes to protect against instability, and to overcome fate, as we shall explore below. We will also learn that orthodoxy and adherence to the good religion is frequently invoked to augment the power of secular authority and as a buffer against revolutionary ideology.

Lore has it that in 1086, when the power of the Turkic Sultan Malikshāh (d. 1092) of the Saljūq Dynasty (r. 1040–1194) was at its zenith, he asked his Persian tutor and vizier, Nizām al-Mulk (d. 1092), to prepare a manual for governance. The vizier complied and, drawing on his own learning and experience, the teachings of past masters, and accounts of the deeds and words of Muhammad, produced the *Siyar al-mulūk* (*The Way of Kings*), in fifty chapters:

3
Yūsuf Khāss Ḥājib, *Wisdom of Royal Glory (Kutadgu Bilig): A Turko-Islamic Mirror for Princes*, trans. and ann. Robert Dankoff (Chicago: The University of Chicago Press, 1983), 4.

4
Judith Ferster, *Fictions of Advice: The Literature and Politics of Counsel in Late Medieval England* (Philadelphia: University of Pennsylvania Press, 1996), 174–87.

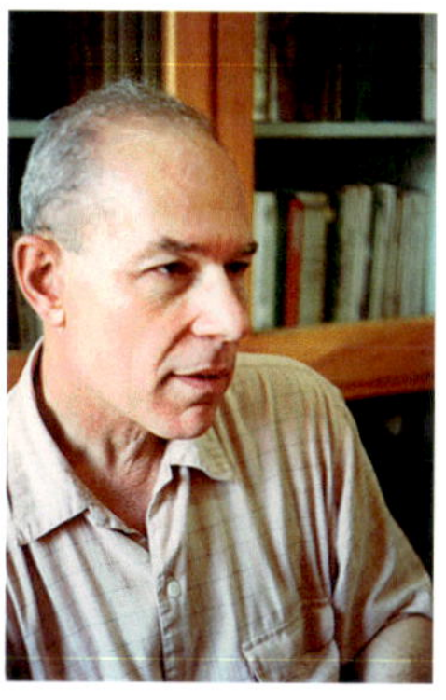

Robert Dankoff
has the honour of having translated the two mastodons of Turkic literature: Along with *Kutadgu Bilig*, the 11th-century epic poem of advice literature by Yūsuf Khāss Ḥājib, *Divan e Lughat al-Turk* (*Compendium of the Languages of the Turk*) is considered to be one of the foundational texts of Turkic literature, the equivalent of *The Iliad*, the *Nibelungenlied* or *The Shah-Nameh*. The Turkish government has sponsored translations of the Divan into more than 20 languages, including modern Turkish, proudly celebrating the millennial anniversary of its author in 2008. Courtesy Robert Dankoff.

Solange der Mensch diese Perle nicht aus dem Meer holt, Solange ist es gleich, ob Perle oder Kieselstein.

Dopóki człowiek nie wydobędzie perły z morza, Wszystko mu jedno, czy to kamyk czy perła.

Kişi inciyi denizden çıkarmadıkça,
O, ister inci olsun ister çakıl taşı, fark etmez.

والدرء ما لم يستخرج الدر من مكنه
فلا فرق ان كان درا و حجرا،

If he fails to bring the pearl up out of the sea it could just as well be a pebble as a pearl.

No king or emperor can afford not to possess and know this book, especially in these days, for the more he reads it, the more he will be enlightened upon spiritual and temporal matters, the better he will appreciate the qualities of friends and foes; the way of right conduct and the path of good government will be open to him; the rules for the management of the court, the audience-hall, the divan, the royal palace and the parade ground, and the methods of administering the taxes, transacting business and settling the affairs of the people and the army will be clear to him; and nothing in the whole realm whether great or small, far or near, will remain concealed (if Allah wills – be He exalted).[5]

5

Nizām al-Mulk, *The Book of Government or Rules for Kings*, 2nd ed., ed. and trans. Hubert Darke (New York: Routledge and Kegan Paul, 1978), 1–2.

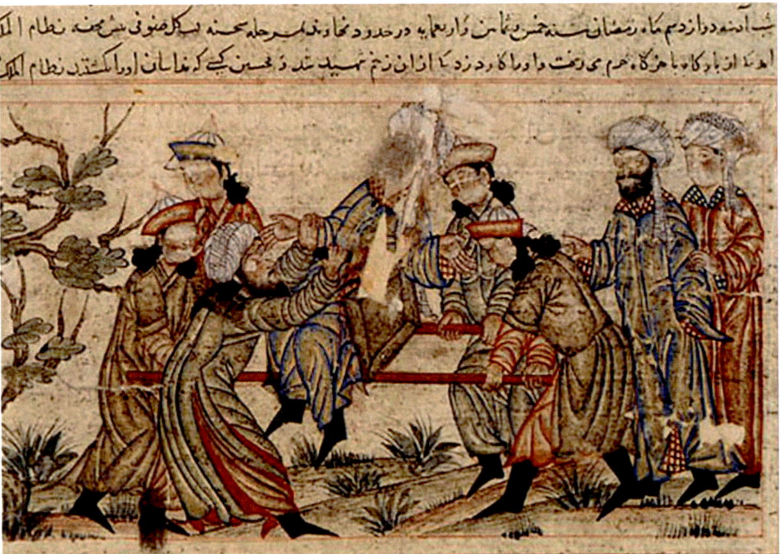

A 14th-century painting shows **Nizām al-Mulk** being fatally stabbed by an agent of the Order of the Assassins, a secret Nizari Ismaili sect. Source: *Topkapi Palace Museum*.

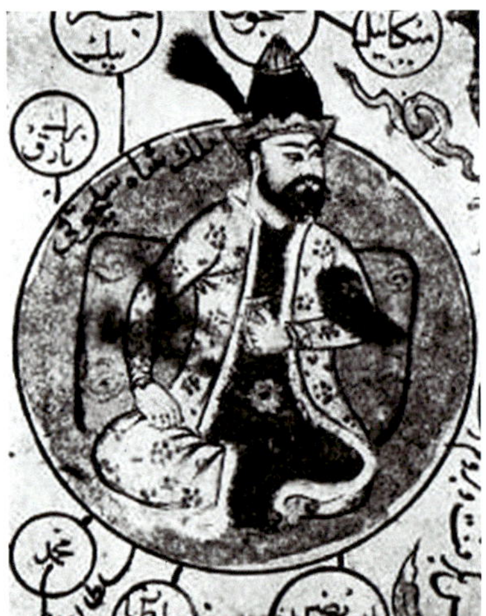

Jalal al-Din Malikshāh, Saljūq Sultan and nominal head of state, lent his name to the Jalali calendar, adopted in 1079. Considered to be one of the most accurate in the world, the Jalali is a sidereal calendar, drafted in part by Omar Khayyam, and need not recourse to a leap-year. A version of it is still in use today in Iran and Afghanistan. Source: *simerg.com*

The turning of the wheels of fortune and kingship enjoy a direct and unmediated relationship in Nizām al-Mulk's work. God chooses in every age and in every time,

[O]ne member of the human race, and having endowed him with the interests of the world and the well-being of His servants; He charges that person to close the doors of corruption, confusion and discord, and He imparts to him such majesty and dignity in the eyes and hearts of men, that under his just rule they may live their lives in constant security and every wish for his reign to continue.[6]

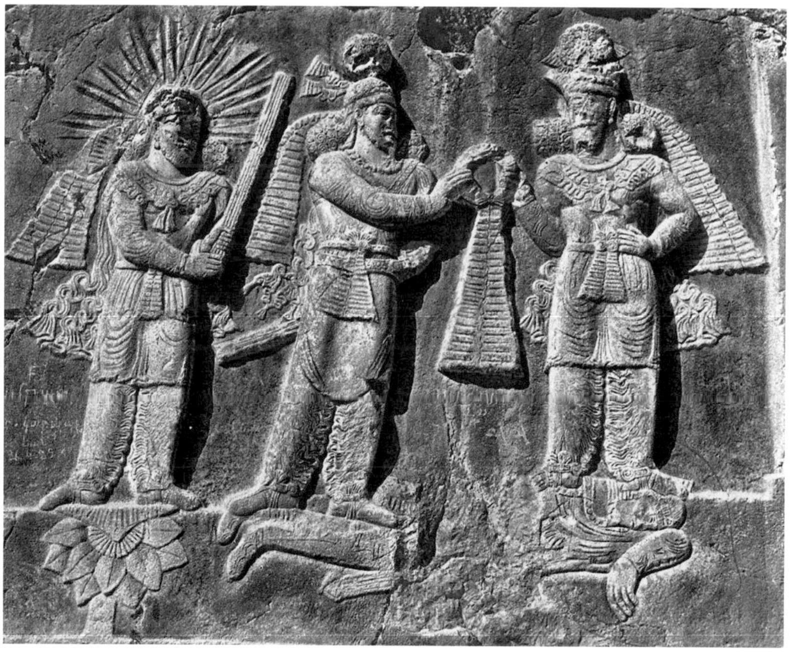

'Investiture of Ardashir II (r. 379–383) (center) by the supreme God Ahura Mazda *(right)* with Mithra *(left)* standing upon a lotus. Trampled beneath the feet of Ahura Mazda and Ardashir II is an unidentified defeated enemy. Of interest are the emanating sun rays from the head of Mithras. Note the object being held by Mithras. This may be some sort of diadem or even a ceremonial broadsword, as Mithras appears to be engaged in some sort of 'knighting' of Ardahsir II as he receives the ***Farr*** (Divine Glory) diadem from Ahura Mazda.' Source: *rafigh1367.blogfa.com*. Photo by Abou Soudavar.

In the original Persian, it is *farr*,[7] or royal glory, that marks the chosen one. He who possesses *farr* is blessed with the requisites of just rule; he is of moral excellence and mental acuity. God's punishment for disobedience to the king or disregard for divine law is the disappearance of kingship altogether, and the inauguration of civil strife and destruction, 'and through the wickedness of such sinners many innocent persons too perish in the tumult'.[8] *Farr* finds a new home, and a new king comes about.

While the selection of the king may be a divine prerogative, it is the wisdom of the king that employs good counsel and protects and preserves rule. The wisdom of Malikshāh, Nizām al-Mulk wrote,

> [I]s like a taper from which many lamps have been lighted; by its light men find their way and emerge from

> darkness. He has no need for any counsellor or guide; nevertheless he is not without cares, and perhaps he wishes to test his servants, and assess their intelligence. So when he commanded his humble servant to write down some of the good qualities that are indispensable to kings [...].[9]

9 Ibid.

Although morally excellent, and wise, the king is in need of advice. Among the first lessons learned is that although good kings are pious, uphold religious law and embody God's will, their success in this world is measured not by their piety but by their ability to rule with wisdom and discernment, qualities which are acquired and not innate, and which are purveyed by others, that is, their counsellors. Self-restraint, or receptivity to advice, is the cornerstone of just rule, for if the king learns to rule himself he will be able to rule others. To avert God's wrath, he needs to be fair and equitable in dealing with his subjects. Apart from justice, the ruler must learn to bridle his passion, avoid the mistakes of others, and keep women, flatterers and people of bad religion at a distance.

This last injunction of keeping heresy at bay is the key to the ruler's mastery over religion. If and when deployed as the arbiter of good faith, it is the king who is authoritative. The ruler, Niẓām al-Mulk insists, must take an active part in ideological currents in the empire, and engage in frequent debate and exchange with the learned and with religious rulers. To that end, he must maintain familiarity with ideological currents. In *Siyar al-mulūk*, he writes:

> It is incumbent upon the king to enquire into religious matters, to be acquainted with the divine precepts and prohibitions and put them into practice, and to obey the commands of God (be He exalted); it is his duty to respect doctors of religion and pay their salaries out of the treasury, and he should honour pious and abstemious men. Furthermore, it is fitting that once or twice a week he should invite religious elders to his presence and hear from them the commands of The Truth; he should listen to interpretations of the Qur'an and traditions of the Prophet (may Allah pray for him and give him peace);

Le fric,
c'est pas
si chic,
dit le
Tajik.

and he should hear stories about just kings and tales of
the prophets. During that time he should free his mind
from worldly cares and give his ears and attention
[wholly] to them.[10]

Debate with the *ulamā* (the learned, the clergy) will become
a habit, the vizier explains, and once the prince learns the precepts
of the *sharī'a* (divine law):

> [T]he way of prudence and rectitude in both spiritual
> and temporal affairs will be open to him; no heretic
> or innovator will be able to turn him from that path.
> His judgement will be strengthened and he will
> increase in justice and equity; vanity and heresy will
> vanish from his kingdom and great works will spring
> from his hands. The roots of wickedness, corruption
> and discord will be cut out in the time of his empire.[11]

Debate and exchange with various strands of learning and wisdom
is the overarching frame of the second mirror under consideration
in this essay as well. A few years before Nizām al-Mulk and
living further east in the city of Kāshghar, in present-day Chinese
Turkestan, another vizier, Yūsuf Khāss Hājib (d. 1085), this one
serving the eastern Ilig Khānid (or Qarakhānid as the dynasty
is known in the 'West') ruler (r. 1032–1211), Hasan b. Sulayman,
known as Tabghach Bughrā Qara Khān (d. 1075), authored a mirror
for princes entitled *Kutadgu Bilig* (*Wisdom of Royal Glory*). Yūsuf
Khāss Hājib's opus is a *masnavī* in 4468 couplets on the interface
of fate with fortune, religion with reason, and kingship with divine
rule. Remarkable in Yūsuf Khāss Hājib's rhymed mirror is the
explicit and much celebrated twinning of wisdom with good
fortune – to enjoy a stable and peaceful reign, that is. Like Nizām
al-Mulk's king who possesses *farra*, or Machiavelli's prince blessed
with *fortuna*,[12] Yūsuf Khāss Hājib's king is privileged with *kut*
(*qūt* in Chagathay) – that je ne sais quoi which marks a just prince
and elevates him into an exemplar of justice and virtue. *Fortuna*,
farr or *kut* is the very antonym of politics and of stable rule,
the fickleness of which only wisdom and virtue can overcome.

10
Ibid., 59–60.

11
Ibid.

12
Niccolò Machiavelli, *The Prince*,
see: http://www.gutenberg.
org/files/1232/1232-h/1232-h.
htm#link2HCH0025/ (accessed
23 October 2014); see also
Alison Brown, 'Philosophy
and Religion in Machiavelli',
in *The Cambridge Companion
to Machiavelli*, ed. John M.
Najemy (Cambridge: Cambridge
University Press, 2010), 157–72.

Kut, or good fortune, is paired with *bilig* (or wisdom) in mirrors for
princes as a recipe for staving off good fortune's unruly twin, namely,
fate. The rule of fortune, the king is told, is only procured through the
observance of reason. As in Nizām al-Mulk's text, religion is indirectly
but explicitly subordinated to political rule. The crossover between
fortune and governance, as well as between fate and politics, in the
Kutadgu Bilig is also embodied in the cast of characters:

> First I speak of the king, Rising Sun – I shall explain
> this name, gentle reader! Then I speak of Full Moon –
> the sun of blessed Fortune receives its light from
> him! 'Rising Sun' stands for Justice and 'Full Moon'
> for Fortune. Then I speak of Highly Praised – he is
> the personification of Intellect, which raises a man's
> estate. Finally, I speak of Wide Awake – he represents
> the Last End. Upon these four things I have based
> my discourse.[13]

Apart from the allegorical valences of its characters, Yūsuf's mirror
for princes is remarkable for its narrative form as well as its unusual
content. Instead of anecdotes, and alongside tales of kings and prophets
past, and instructions on morals and manners, Yūsuf's mirror has a
frame story that is pursued from beginning to end. Various topics are
explored in the guise of dialogues between the various characters, each
signifying several allegorical valences. Royal aura is juxtaposed with
reason in the dialogues between the king and his vizier, and as the cast
expands with the unfolding of the narrative, the active life spars with
renunciation and isolationism, and religion with statecraft.

In contradistinction to the rash princes and sultans addressed in most
mirrors, Yūsuf Khāss Hājib's mirror tells the tale of an enlightened,
just and virtuous king. He was given the name Rising Sun by a sage,
he tells his vizier, 'in likeness to my character. The sun you see, never
wanes but is always full, its brightness is constant and excellent. That is
I am too: full of justice, and with no deficiency'.[14] The sun is stable, and
'its foundation firm: the constellation of the sun is Leo; its house never
moves and so it never falls to ruin. My nature is uniform: I never change
to something other than light'.[15]

13
Yūsuf Khāss Hājib, *Wisdom
of Royal Glory*, 1–35.

14
Ibid., 66.

15
Ibid.

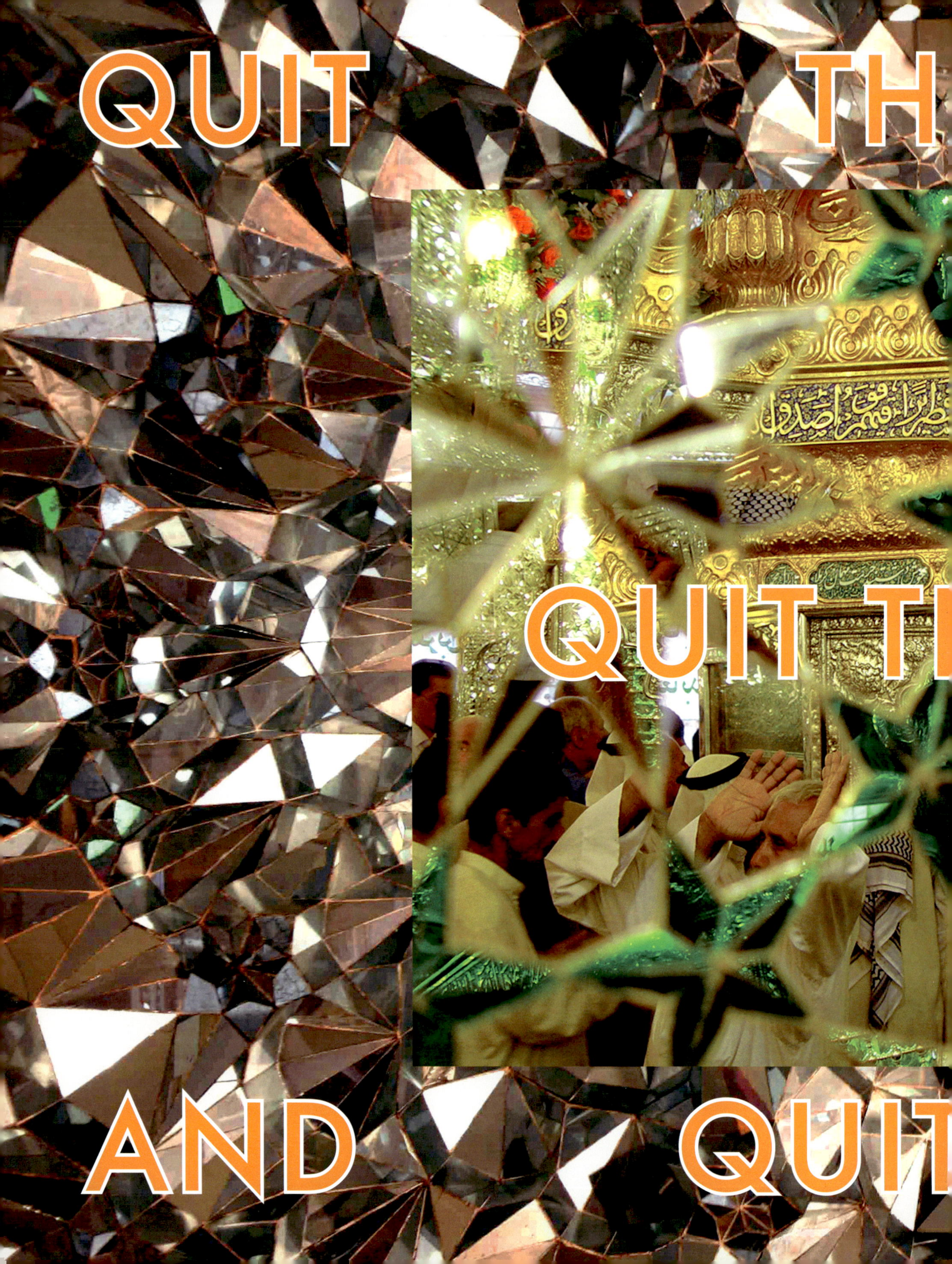
QUIT
TH
QUIT TI
AND
QUIT

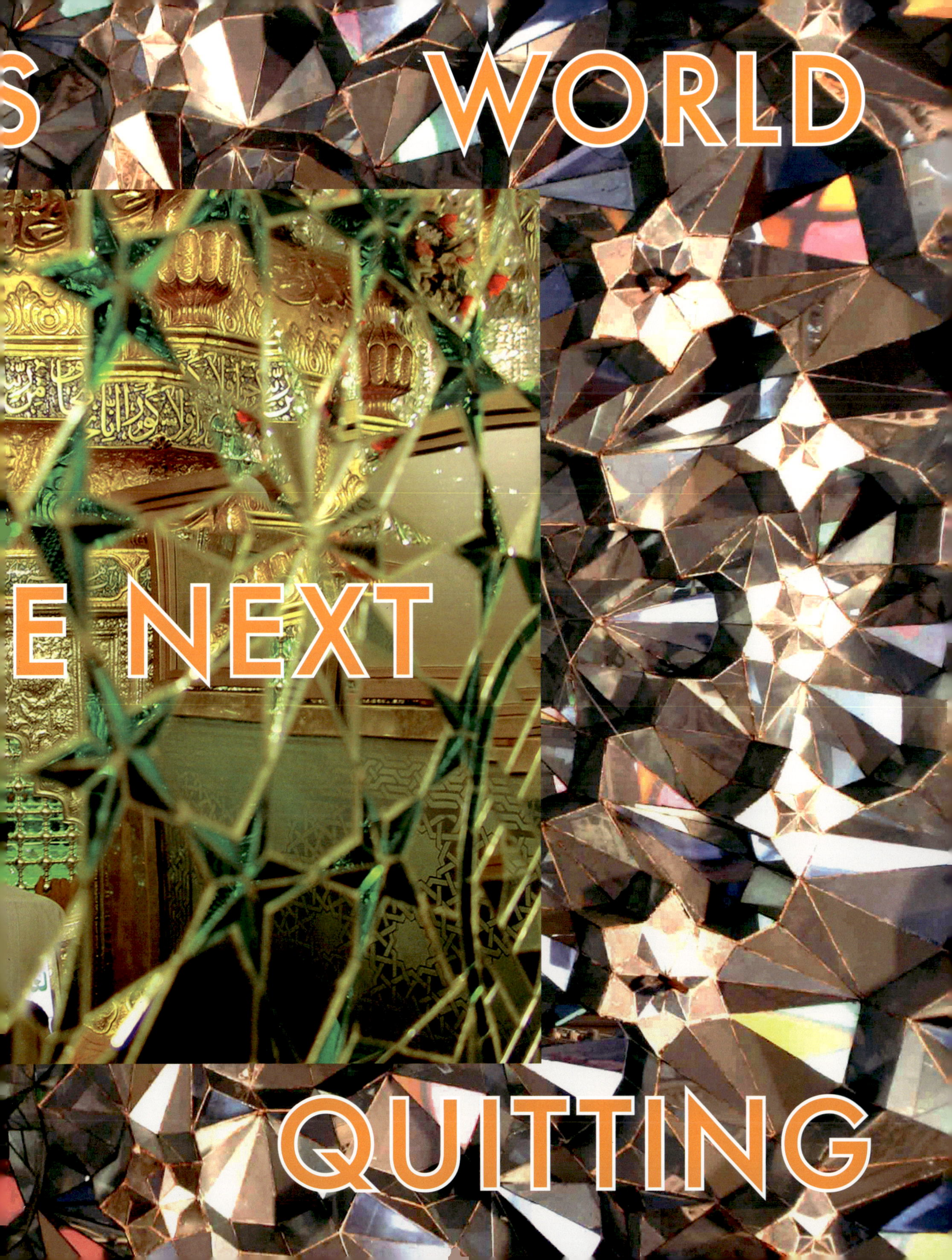
S
WORLD
E NEXT
QUITTING

Rising Sun longs for a good vizier, and his chamberlain presents him with Full Moon, who has travelled from far away, lured by the king's stellar reputation. After a gruelling interview, Full Moon is offered the position. The king's justice, probity and wisdom enthused

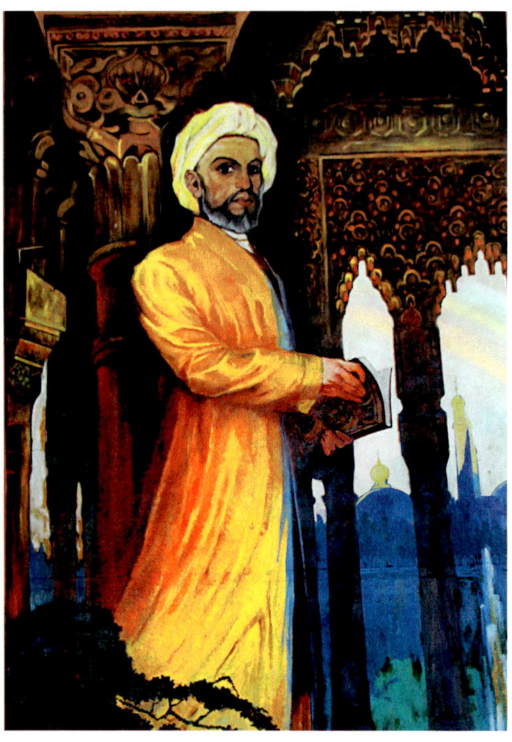

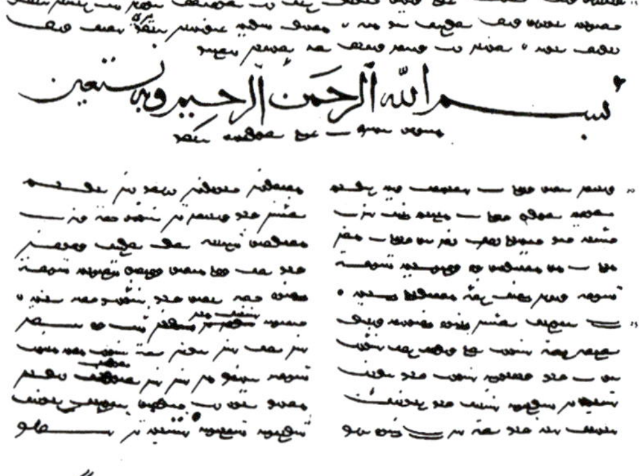

An excerpt from **Kutadgu Bilig**, in Uighur script, from the Vienna (Herat) manuscript of 1439. *(top)*

Yūsuf Khāss Hājib, the 11th-century poet from the city of Balasaghun, the capital of the Karakhanid Empire, in modern-day Kyrgyzstan. Photo from painting inside Hājib's tomb. *(left)*

the good vizier, who announced: 'You are worthy to be served, and Fortune opens her gate when the worthy one is served'.[16] Full Moon's handling of the kingdom's affairs was exemplary: 'Lamb and wolf walked together. And as the realm continued to thrive and justice to be administered, the king's Fortune daily rose. Thus for a while did he bask in the royal glory'.[17] But the vizier's tenure in office was cut short by the waning of fortune, instigated by his unrivalled success: 'Full Moon had realised all his wishes. Now his life was used up and his good would remain behind. His moon that was full now began to wane, his summer that was bright now turned to grim winter'.[18] On his deathbed, Full Moon entrusted the king with care of his son, Highly Praised. True to his father's legacy, Highly Praised administered the empire with utmost care, wisdom, virtue and intelligence, and 'thus his Fortune grew perfect'.[19]

16
Ibid., 70.

17
Ibid., 73.

18
Ibid., 74.

19
Ibid., 97.

One day, Rising Sun asks Highly Praised how it was that he learned his virtues: 'Listen now, Highly Praised. When your father died you were still too young to have profited from his care [...]. How is it then that so much Wisdom is gathered in your person?' Through seeking God's favor, Highly Praised responded:

> Through grace of God his way is straight,
> Wisdom to him now opens her gate;
> Fortune's sun shines daily brighter,
> And he though once small now is great.[20]

The king rejoices in the wisdom of his vizier. Shortly thereafter, and wary of losing his trusted vizier, he asks Highly Praised to recommend a spare. Highly Praised suggests his brother, a sage who is 'very wise and virtuous, pious and wakeful [...]. His name is Wide Awake'.[21] But Wide Awake, who has renounced the world, refuses to heed the king's call to duty. 'Ought I to give up service to the Lord Creator, and take up service to a creature?'[22] The transient world is unstable, Wide Awake claims: 'Inconstant Fortune comes to every man in turn and quickly grows old. I have no need of this world, nor of Fortune's feverish spell'.[23] Fortune is the enemy of piety, and not a good thing as it estranges one from God and is the ruin of religion.[24]

In defense of this world, however, Highly Praised too summons godliness:

> God created two abodes for us His creatures, paradise
> and hell. Now if every man is ought right this world
> alone, day and night, neglecting the service of God
> completely, then indeed paradise would remain empty.
> But God gave man two each of eyes and ears, one for
> attending to this world, one for the next; and two hands,
> one to grasp this world and one the next; also two feet,
> one to walk this way and one to walk that.[25]

Is Highly Praised's comment a secular opening? It is and it isn't, for the triumph of fortune over fate is always incomplete and transient. Highly Praised next tells the king that renunciation is not the way of God, for He wishes His servants to engage with the world, eradicate evil,

20
Ibid., 98–99.

21
Ibid., 143.

22
Ibid., 195.

23
Ibid.

24
Ibid., 155.

25
Ibid., 160.

Anlayış ve bilgi çok şeydir;
Eğer bulursan onları kullan ve uçup göğe çık.

فالفهم والعلم أمران قيّمان؛
فاستخدمهما حيث وجدتهما، ثم حلّق في جو السماء.

Fine things indeed are wisdom and intellect:
put them to work, if you possess them, and you will soar to heaven!

crush infidel armies, and open the way for Islam and for the *shari 'a*.[26] Moreover, Highly Praised, at the pinnacle of his career and fully trusted by the king, has a change of heart. 'He examined his own character and conduct, and concluded that he had wasted his life and youth. Gradually the eye of his heart opened to the light. He conceived the desire to radically purify his heart'.[27] But true to his own advice, he hesitated to seek out the opinion of trusted confidants and virtuous men. Wide Awake convinces him to return to the king's service, advice that Highly Praised duly follows. A short while hence, Wide Awake falls ill and dies, leaving a disciple, Testament, to comfort his brother. Testament advises the vizier to return to his duties and to serve the king loyally and administer his realm with justice.

In his words and in his actions, as well as in his own person, Highly Praised serves as a mirror for the king. He is a good vizier begat by another good vizier, and personifies wisdom. He is diligent and dutiful, and provides exemplary service for the king. He spreads justice and clemency, and does not hesitate to rely on the sword when necessary. And in his heart, he pines for ascetic virtues. His wisdom, which knows no bounds, prevents him from following his heart, even if the drive and the passion are not for vice, but for complete and full renunciation to the will of God. The secret to good rule, as well as the key to the good life, as reflected in the words and actions of Highly Praised, is that true godliness lies not in shunning this world, but in accepting its defects and accommodating its imperfections, without straying from the path of righteousness. Towards the end of his opus, Yūsuf Khāss Hājib gives counsel to himself:

> Here is the path of Religion and the path of the World.
> Stray not from this path or you will howl in hell. If it is
> this world you desire, here is the way; and if you desire
> the next world, this is the path you must follow. Perform
> your duty as God's servant […]. You will find the place of
> honour in both the worlds.[28]

If wisdom is the key to acquiring virtue and embodying justice, which is the way of God, then how can wisdom stand in the way of renunciation, constant prayer and wholesale dedication to divine demands? It is this very paradox that lies at the heart of mirrors for princes, and reflects the

26
Ibid., 217–23.

27
Ibid., 223.

28
Ibid., 253–55.

political and ethical norms and values of the societies in which
they were read and reread most enthusiastically.

In telling the king to rule with justice but to simultaneously serve
God, to heed fortune but beware of fate, Highly Praised is echoing
the teachings of Nizām al-Mulk and other counsellors before him.
Justice is the protection against fortune; it is also the path to salvation:
'Since God granted you Fortune, keep a virtuous heart'.[29] Viziers
regularly warn against vice, violence and rash decision-making, but at
the same time, they remain fully cognisant of the exigencies of power.
A fourteenth-century Egyptian historian, Taqī al-Dīn al-Subkī (d. 1355),
has left an account of an audience between the Nizām al-Mulk and
Imām al-Qushayrī (d. 1074), among the eleventh century's most
venerable and learned of clerics, and a Sufi leader as well:

> The Imam al-Qushayrī has said that one day he went
> to visit Nizam al-Mulk, and the Vizier was being
> attended by his dressers. Eighty of them had lined up
> on his left and eighty on his right, each fussing over
> one aspect of his garment. Al-Qushayrī cast a glance
> of disdain, which was quickly apprehended by Nizam
> al-Mulk. He said, 'O Master, these eighty dressers are
> only a token of the more than 80,000 servants that I have.
> But I assure you, I have never exposed myself in their
> presence. It is only because the prestige of the office is
> dependent upon observance of such protocol. And the
> government is strengthened by it'.[30]

Similar to Highly Praised, Nizām al-Mulk's fictional counterpart,
the vizier harboured strong affinities with Sufi shaykhs of his time,
even before his appointment at the Saljūq Court. An anecdote to
this effect is recorded in the history of Ibn al-Jawzī (d. 1201). When
asked about the reason for his attraction to Sufi shaykhs, the vizier
remembered a piece of advice dealt to him when he was serving as a
lowly bureaucrat. A Sufi had told him, 'Serve the person whose service
will one day serve you. Do not occupy yourself with the duties of a man
whom dogs will eat tomorrow'. Nizām al-Mulk could not make much
sense of those words. But the prince he served had a pack of ferocious
dogs, trained to devour strangers at night. The following evening,

29
Ibid., 231.

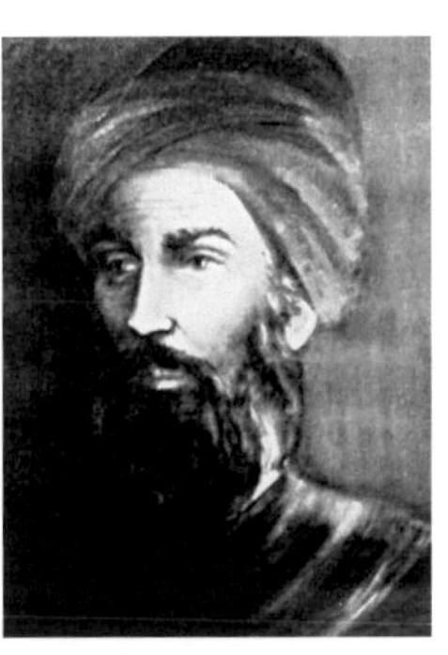

Imām al-Qushayrī
Source: *muslimheritage.com*

30
Taqī al-Dīn al-Subkī, *Tabaqāt al-Shāfiʿiyya al-kubrā*, vol. V, eds. M. M. Tanahi and A. M. al-Hulw (Cairo: ʿIsa al-Babi al-Halabi, 1967), 316.

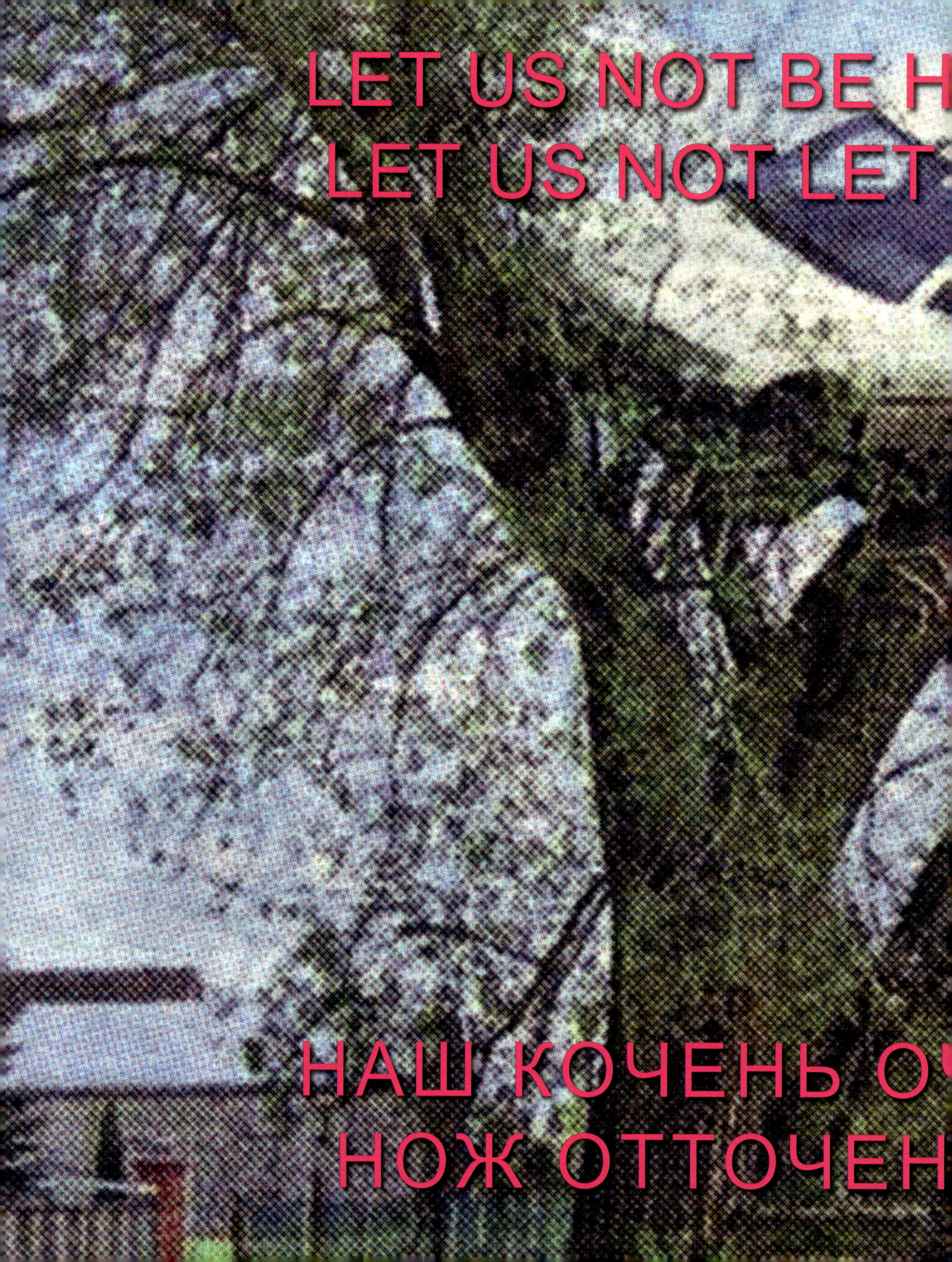

LET US NOT BE H
LET US NOT LET

НАШ КОЧЕНЬ О
НОЖ ОТТОЧЕН

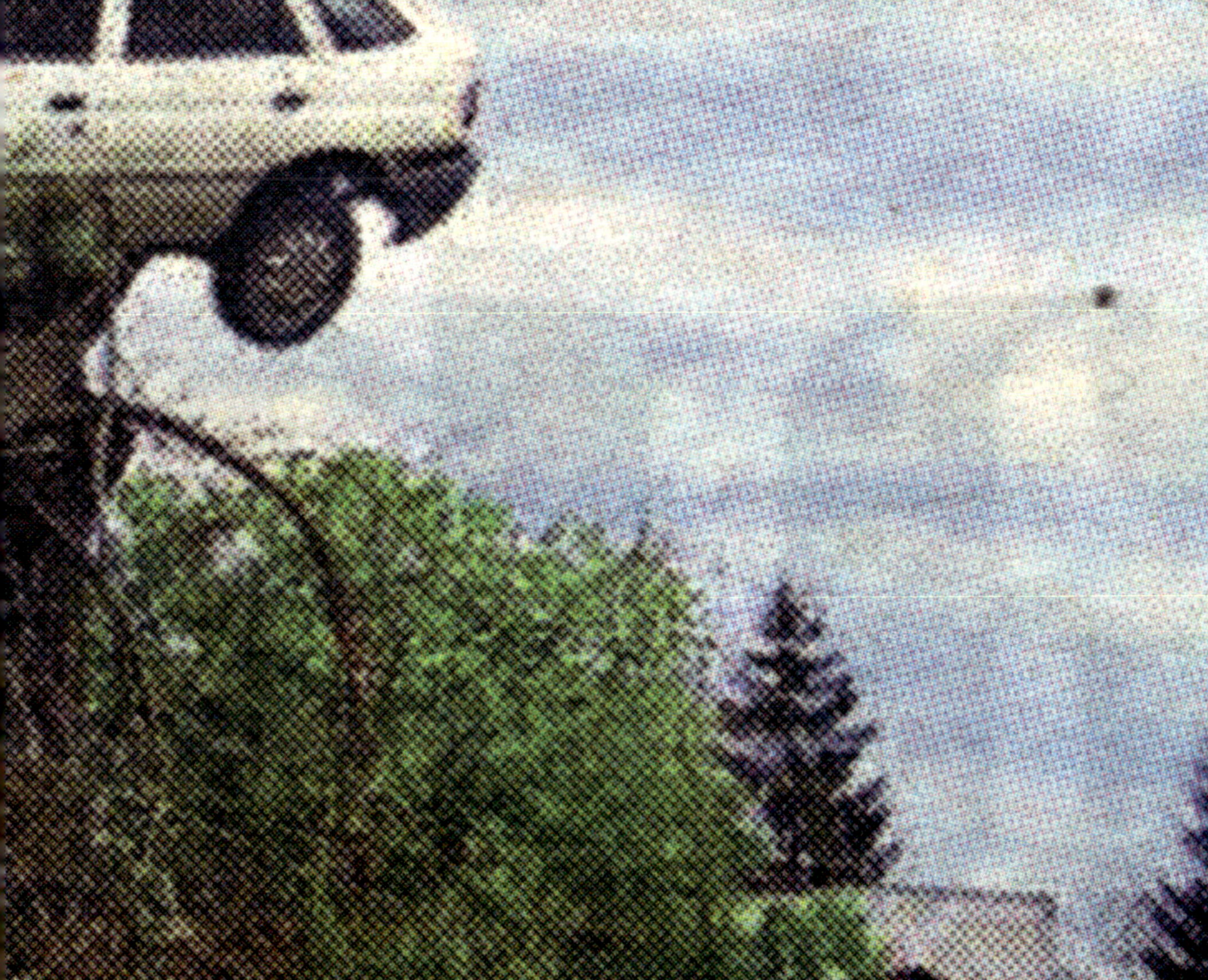
ADS OF LETTUCE
NIVES UPSET US
ЕНЬ ОЗАБОЧЕН:
ТОЧЕН ОЧЕНЬ!

in a state of intoxication, the prince ventured onto the palace grounds, and the dogs tore him to pieces. Nizām al-Mulk is believed to have said: 'It was then that I realised the significance of the oracle the Sufi had told me. I admire people with foresight and prudence'.[31]

31
Abū al-Faraj 'Abd al-Rahmān b. 'Alī b. al-Jawzī, *al-Muntazam fī tā'rikh al-mulūk wa al-'umam*, vol. IX, (Hyderabad: Osmania, 1940), 64–69. My translation.

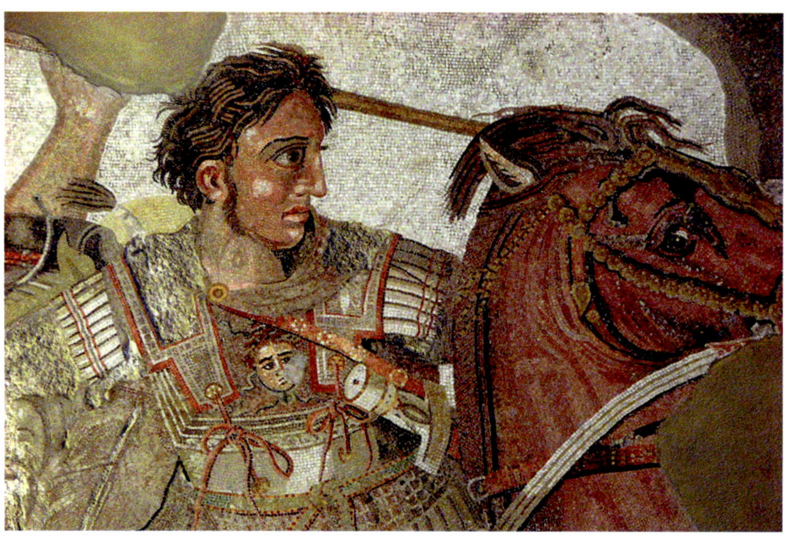

Alexander the Macedonian, 356–323 BC. Source: *cais-soas.com*

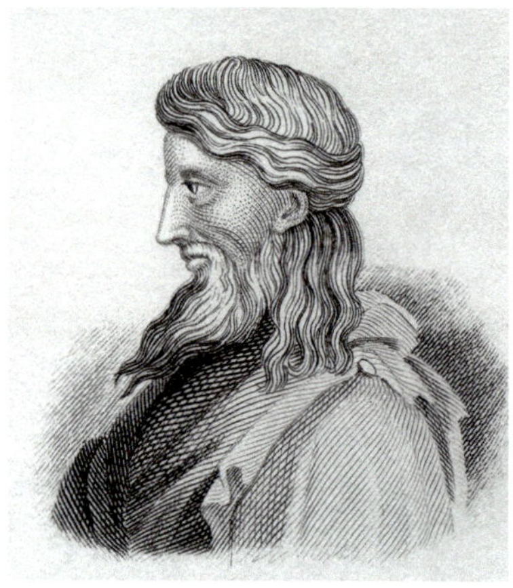

Callisthenes was critical of Alexander's adoption of Persian customs, in particular, proskynesis, a traditional Persian act of bowing before a person of higher rank. Private collection Ken Welsh/Bridgeman Images.

Death, as the paradigmatic sign of the Divine, is a multifarious presence in mirrors for princes. Instructions on a medley of virtues, from equestrian skills to moral rectitude, physical prowess and piety in practice, offer, at the end, little in the way of protection against instability, the waning of fortune and the triumph of fate. Literally, too, most viziers are destined for an early death, often murdered by the sultan they so loyally serve. Alexander the Macedonian (d. 323 BCE) was complicit in the murder of Callisthenes (d. 328 BCE),[32] his tutor who refused to prostrate himself before the king; the 'Abbāsid caliph Hārūn al-Rashīd (d. 809) ordered the execution of Ja'far the Barmakid (d. 803), the fabled vizier and protagonist of the *One Thousand and One Nights*;[33] Nizām al-Mulk was stabbed to death on Malikshah's orders,[34] and countless others, including Amīr Kabīr, whom the Qajar dynast murdered in 1852,[35] and finally, Amīr 'Abbās Hoveydā, Muhammad Rezā Shāh Pahlavī's long-suffering loyal prime minister, imprisoned on trumped-up charges in the final weeks of the Pahlavī regime,[36] and left for dead by the king when he fled Iran in February 1979.

32
Marie Louise Chaumont, 'Callisthenes', *Encyclopaedia Iranica Online* (December 1990). See: http://www.iranicaonline. org/articles/callisthenes-the-name-of-a-greek-historian-of-the-period-of-alexander-the-great-q/ (accessed 23 October 2014).

33
On Ja'far's life see: Tayeb El-Hibri, *Reinterpreting Islamic Historiography: Hārūn al-Rashīd and the Narrative of the 'Abbāsid Caliphate* (Cambridge: Cambridge University Press, 1999), 17–58.

34
Yavari, *Advice for the Sultan*, 109–42.

35
Abbas Amanat, 'The Downfall of Mirza Taqi Khan Amir Kabir and the Problem of Ministerial Authority in Qajar Iran', *International Journal of Middle East Studies*, vol. 23, № 4 (November 1991): 577–99.

36
Abbas Milani, 'Amir-Abbas Hoveyda', *Encyclopaedia Iranica Online* (March 2012) http://www.iranicaonline.org/ articles/hoveyda-amir-abbas/ (accessed 23 October 2014).

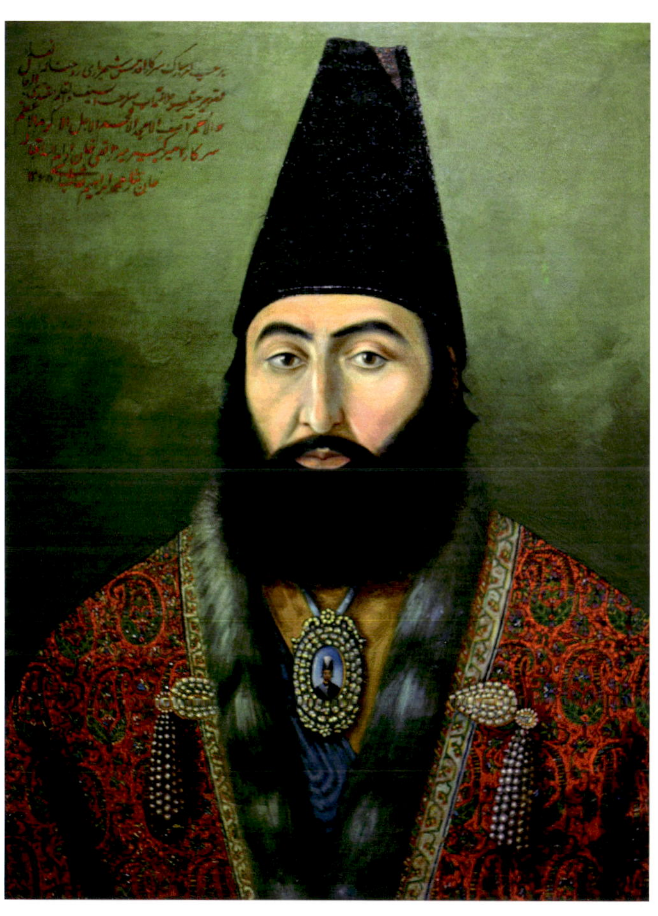

Mirza Taghi Khan Farahani, aka Atabak aka Amir-e Nezam aka **Amīr Kabīr**, served as prime minister of Persia under Naser al-Din Shah. Portrait by Muhammad Ibrahim Naghashbashi (d. 1851). Source: *irangazette.com*

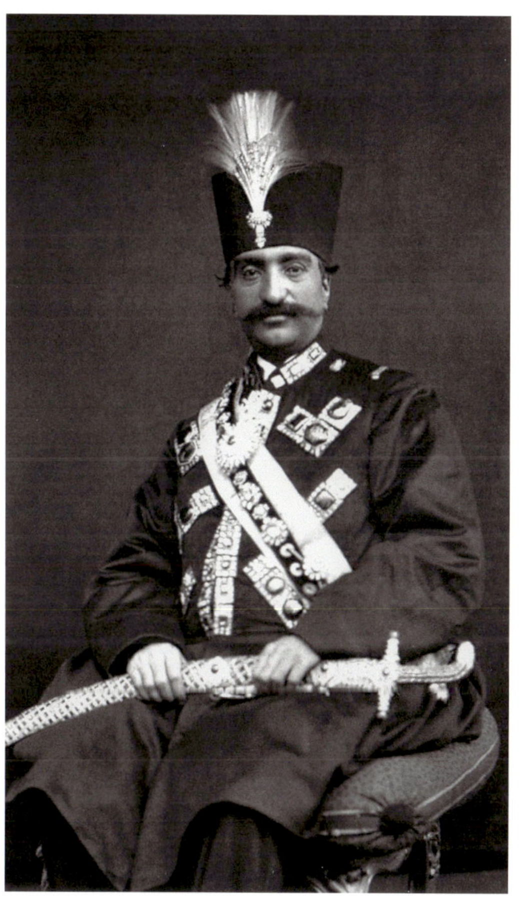

Nāser al-Dīn Shah Qajar, photographed by Nadar, ruled Persia from 17 September 1848 to 1 May 1896, when he was assassinated. Source: *iranvisitor.com*

Buna benzer Türkçe bir atasözü vardır; işte onu söylüyorum, şöyle der:

هناك مثل تركي يشبه هذا الكلام
ها أنذا أقوله.

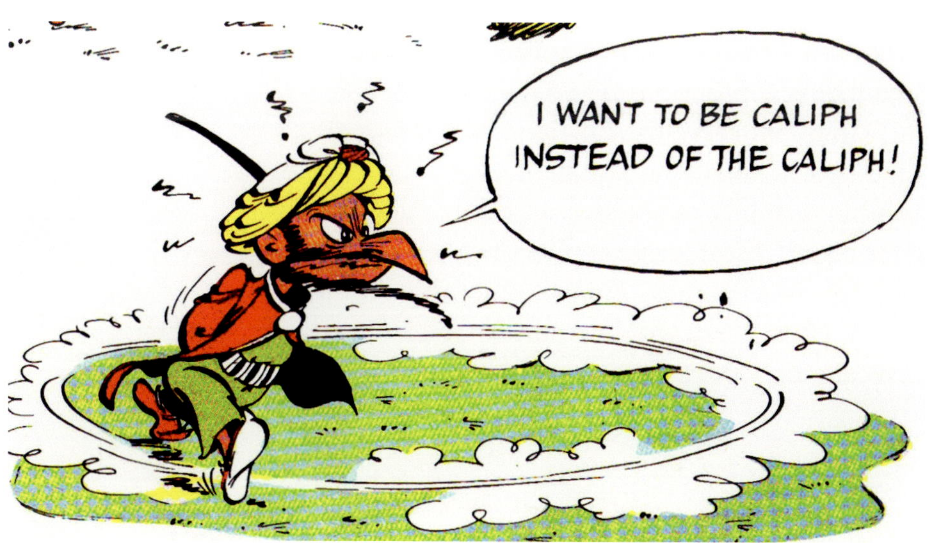

Son of the vizier to the Abbasid Caliph Harun Al-Rashid, Ja'far ibn Yahya Barmaki aka **Jafar the Barmakid** was allegedly beheaded for having an affair with the sister of the Caliph, Abbasa. Jaffar's depiction in recent popular culture has been somewhat less kind: often taking up the role of scheming villain, sorcerer or magician in video games (*Prince of Persia*), films (Disney's *Aladdin*), even French bande dessinée (as *Iznogoud* in the eponymous French comic strip). Comic by Goscinny and Tabary, 1978.

The following Turkish proverb has come down illustrating this point:

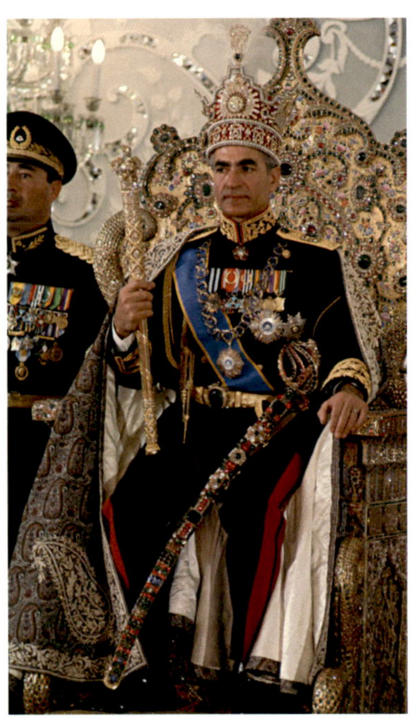

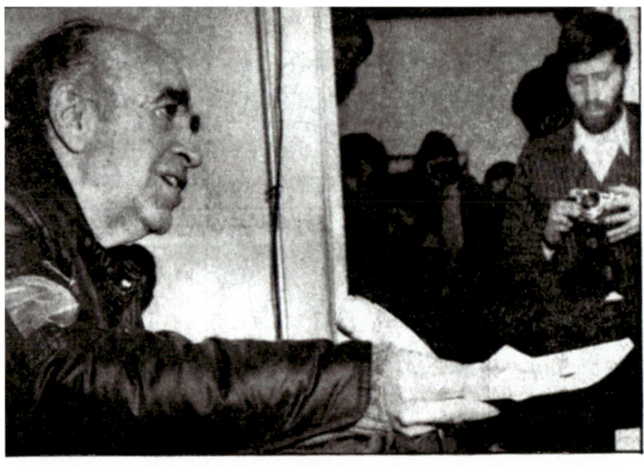

Muhammad Reżā Shāh Pahlavī at his coronation in 1967. Courtesy James L. Stanfield

Amīr ʿAbbās Hoveydā during his trial in a Tehran court in 1979. Source: *parstimes.com*

The fatal dance between purveyors and recipients of advice, or the grammar of premodern politics, rests on rhetoric, allegory, irony, code, myth and paradox to disambiguate a positivist, linear relationship between past and future, religion and politics, fortune and rule. In twinning history with fate, fortune with governance, and religion with politics, mirrors for princes authorise political rule and circumscribe, simultaneously, the exercise of power. They teach the secret to long rule, and reflect the inevitability of demise. They bolster and undermine rulership in the same breath. It is appropriate to end with an anecdote from the late-twelfth/early thirteenth century *Jawāmiʿ al-hikāyāt* of Muhammad ʿAwfī. Mahmūd the Ghaznavid Sultan (d. 1030) is said to have asked one of his confidants if he had read anywhere that viziers were enemies of kings. He hadn't, the courtier replied, but he had read often that only fools seek the vizierate. 'Kings cannot share their kingdoms', the courtier continued, 'they will first honour and respect their viziers, and after a week, the seeds of animosity and resentment are sown'.[37]

37
Muhammad ʿAwfi, *Jawāmiʿ al-hikāyāt*, ed. Muhammad Ramezani (Tehran: Kulalih Khavar, 1956), 48–49.

'On Difference' in Mirror for Princes
A VIEW FROM MEDIEVAL INDIA

Manan Ahmed Asif

When the historical teledrama *Chanakya* debuted in 1991 in India, it immediately became wildly popular. The director, writer and actor Chandraprakash Dwivedi dramatised the life story of philosopher Cānakya – also remembered as Kauṭilya and Vishnugupta – who plucked a boy, Chandragupta (340–293 BCE), from obscurity, trained and raised him, and then helped him become the founder of the

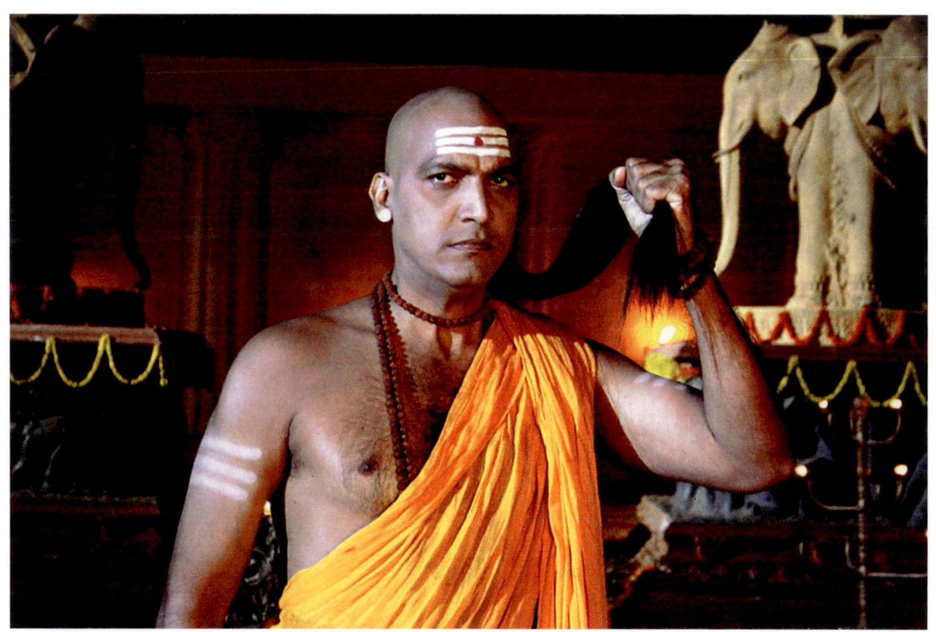

Akshay (played by Deepraj Rana) in **Chanakya,** a 47-part epic Indian television historical drama.
Source: *great-treasure.blogspot.de*

Aklın süsü dil, dilin süsü sözdür;
Kişinin süsü yüz, yüzün süsü gözdür.

زينة العقل اللسان وزينة
اللسان وزينة المرء وجهه وزينة الوجه العين

The adornment of the intellect is the tongue,
and the adornment of the tongue is speech;
the adornment of a man is his face,
and the adornment of the face is the eyes.

great continental Mauryan Empire. Over forty-seven episodes, the serial followed the journey of Cānakya as he helped destroy the illegitimate king in Nanda and installed Chandragupta Maurya on the throne of Magadha in 321 BCE. Dwivedi, using a heavily Sanskritised language and Brahmanical rituals, highlighted the aphorisms and advice that Cānakya provided to Chandragupta who had historically become known as a universal king – a *chakrāvārtin*. Dwivedi's Chanakya acted out a dominant theme of twentienth-century India – the 'discovery' and political usage of 'ancient' Indian texts to argue anticolonial and proto-nationalist claims. To recreate this history of India, Dwivedi relied on a text ascribed to Cānakya and widely known as the *Arthaśāstra* (*The Science of Wealth and Governance*). The *Arthaśāstra* was lauded throughout the twentieth century as a premier example of an Indic mirror for princes, akin to Machiavelli's *The Prince*. This genre of literature, often termed *specula principum* or *Fürstenspiegel*, focused on giving advice to the king on matters of governance and strategy and was a perennial favorite among scholars of statecraft and literary theorists. In *Chanakya*, Dwivedi used *Arthaśāstra* to present a fully realised and unified India as 'akhand Bharat' – the first national state in India – a depiction of mediated advice for the political crises of the early 1990s.

Chanakya had followed the unprecedented successes of televised dramatisations on the Indian national broadcast channel, Doordarshan. In the late 1980s, across the subcontinent, truly massive audiences had watched the gilded reenactment of Indian epics *Mahabharata* and *Ramayana*.[1] These serials presented an ancient, 'unified' kingdom of Bharat that stretched from immemorial times and ritual into the universal time of contemporary India. The language and rituals depicted in the serials marked a 'saffron' history – religiously and politically conservative – that erased diverse traditions of being from Indian pasts to highlight only the right-wing Hindu understanding of the past.

By the beginning of the '90s, postcolonial India had experienced two decades of separatist movements in Kashmir, in Assam and in Punjab. When, in 1992, Hindu nationalists destroyed the medieval mosque bearing the name of the Mughal Emperor Babur in Ayodhya, riots broke out across the country, with massive pogroms against the Muslim

1

Mahabharat (prod. B. R. Chopra, dir. Ravi Chopra) ran for 94 episodes from 1988 to 1990 and *Ramayan* (prod. Sagar Enterprises, dir. Ramanand Sagar) for 78 episodes, from 1986 to 1988. Both teledramas were aired on DD National, a channel of Doordashan, the Indian public service broadcasting corporation.

populations. The claim of Hindu nationalists was that the mosque itself represented a destruction of the birthplace of Ram, and they were now going to restore this sacral site to its proper glory. The teleserials of *Ramayana* and *Mahabharata*, as 'historical reenactments', created a historical memory where only a sacral commitment had existed.

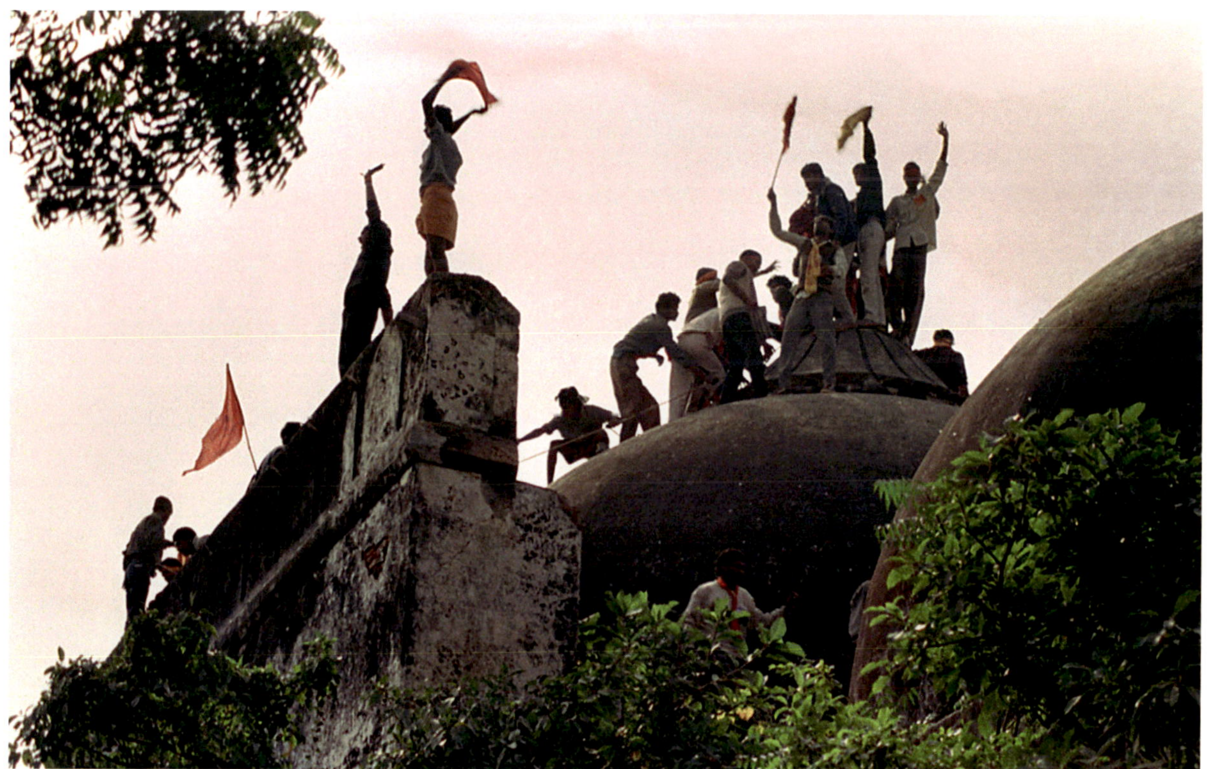

Ayodhya riots at the Babur mosque in Uttar Pradesh, India. Copyright Douglas E. Curran/AFP.

The philosopher and conquering king relationship reenacted in *Chanakya* had similarly aligned absolute power alongside absolute certainty in dogma and birthright. The warrior king and his wise adviser now came to advise the broad right-wing Hindu politicians on how to answer the question of difference in India – religious, ethnic, sectarian, political – by majoritarian power and violence.

If this was the near present of pedagogic and didactic literature collectively known as mirrors for princes in India, then what are its pasts? What genealogies of thought, and practice, can we trace in the broad contours of the landscape across West and South Asia?

Bilgilinin sözünü dinle, itiraz etme;
Sana sorulmadan da sözünü söyleme.

A wise man has said:
Be not insolent, nor speak before you are bid to.

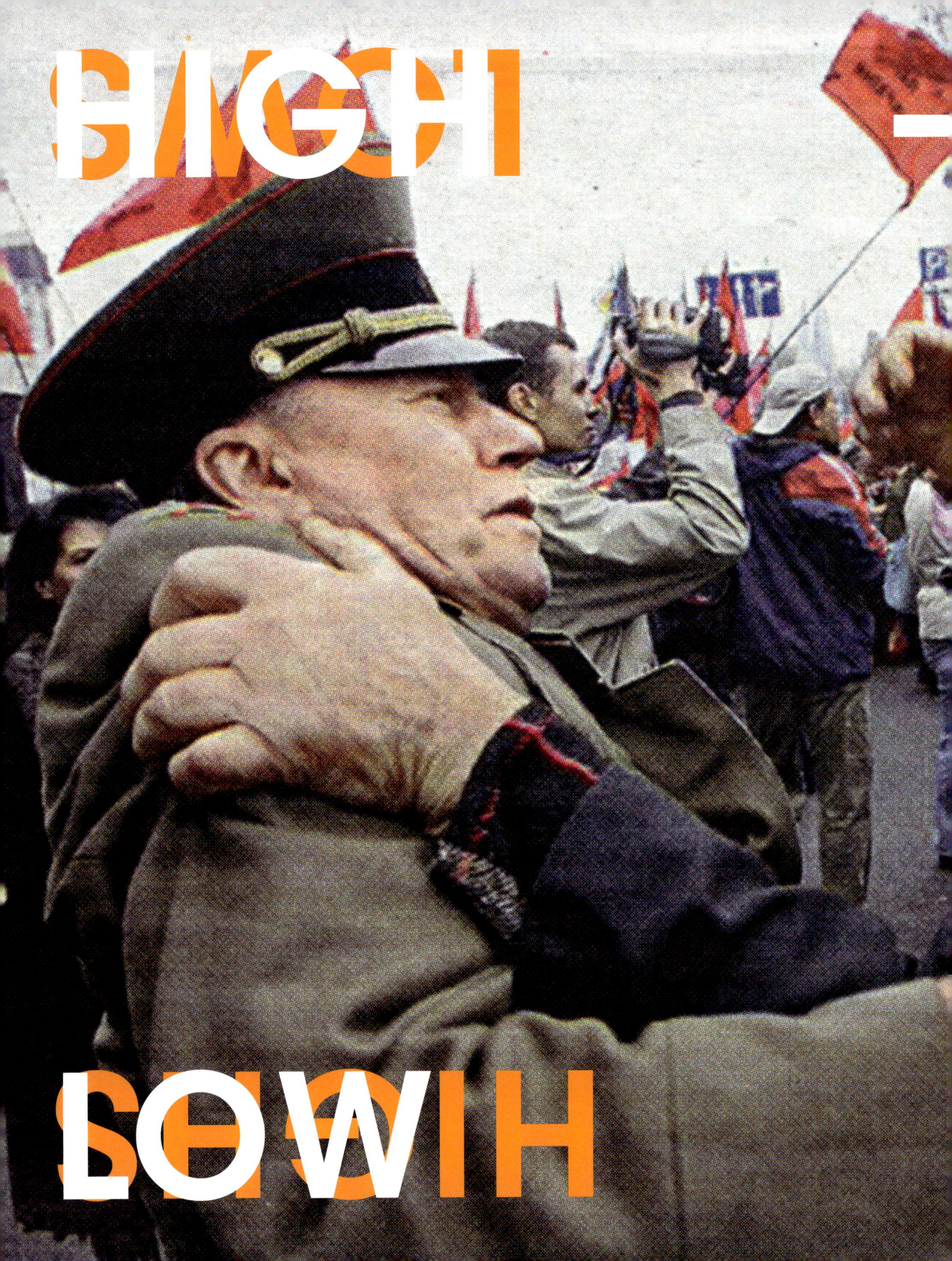
HIGH
LOW

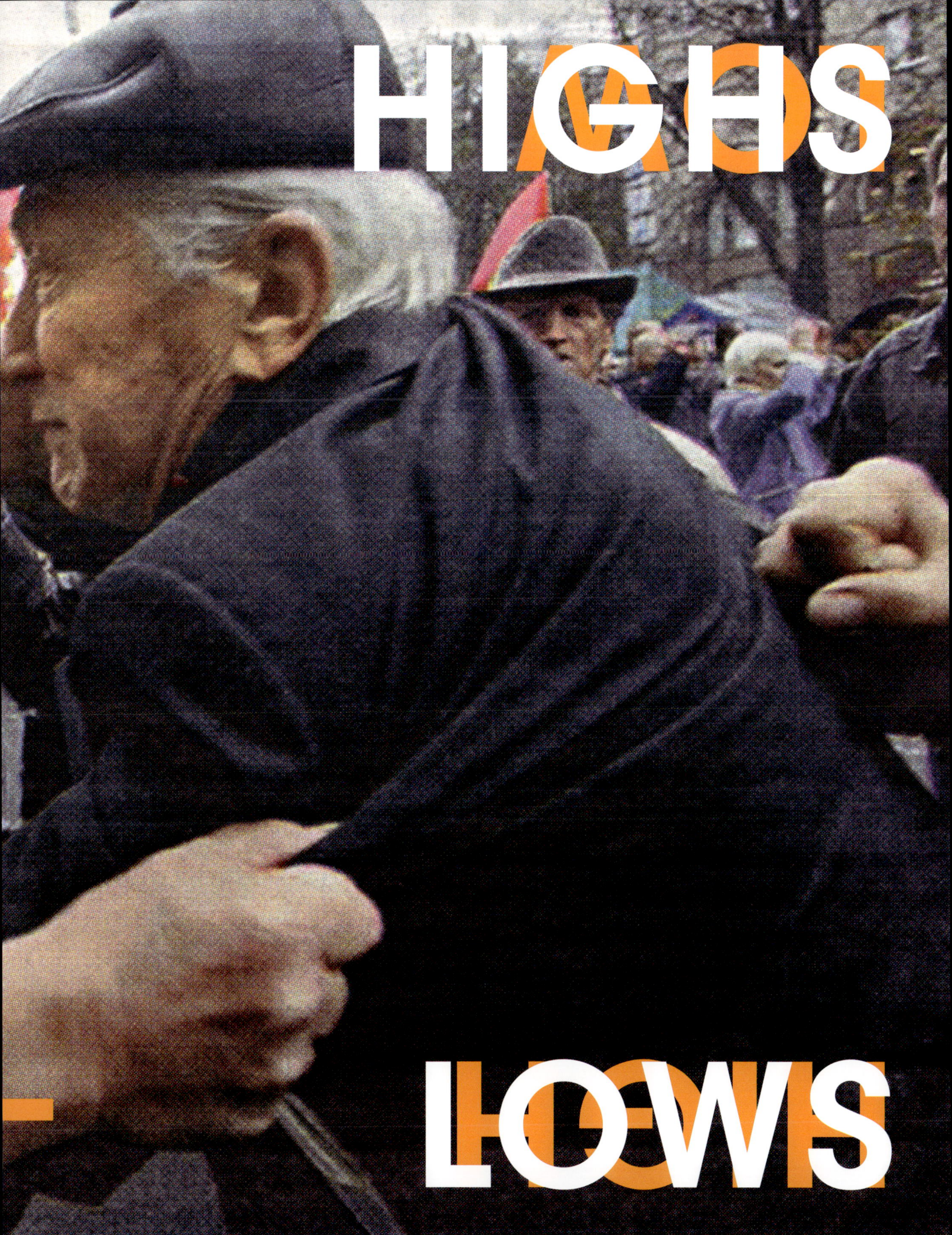
HIGHS
LOWS

This essay will present three temporally specific but overlapping genealogies of advice literature in India. They overlap in languages, in forms, in their relationship to power and in the impact of their thoughts. They inform us of a conceptually, textually and politically enmeshed milieu that extended from the Nile to the Ganges. In this milieu, conceptual figures such as 'king', 'minister' and 'philosopher' travelled in these texts in languages as diverse as Sanskrit, Arabic and Persian, and were used to enact and entrench political regimes which often faced military opposition, even when they shared this political universe. A question that will linger silently under this essay is, how did we, the moderns, end up with such a different way of being different?

The first genealogy we trace is that of the *Arthaśāstra*, which is the earliest, but also the latest and most recognisable in our political present. The second genealogy is that of the *Pañcatantra*, which begins in 300 CE and fades after the thirteenth century. The third is the genealogy of neo-Aristotelian ethics that emerges in conjunction with the Mughal Empire in the sixteenth century and disappears under colonisation's sweep of the past. In these overlapping genealogies, we can trace three distinct notions of subjective difference: the subjectivity of the righteous birthright ruler who creates and manages difference; the subjectivity of natural and naturalised difference that itself creates an autonomy of understanding through dialogue; and the subjectivity that is arrived at by adopting an ethics that is distinct from religious difference.

Part I.

A unitary text called *Arthaśāstra* was not discovered until the twentieth century. However, references to and excerpts from it circulated widely in many Sanskrit commentaries and critiques across medieval India. In 1904, in Mysore, a Dr. R. Shamasastry was given the full text of *Arthaśāstra*, written on palm leaves in the *grantha* script, by a pandit. He published the text in 1909 and an English translation in 1915. It is then that the text entered philological enquiry, as did the process of enacting the thought of Cānakya as an 'Indian' political philosopher speaking directly towards a Brahmanical Indian king.

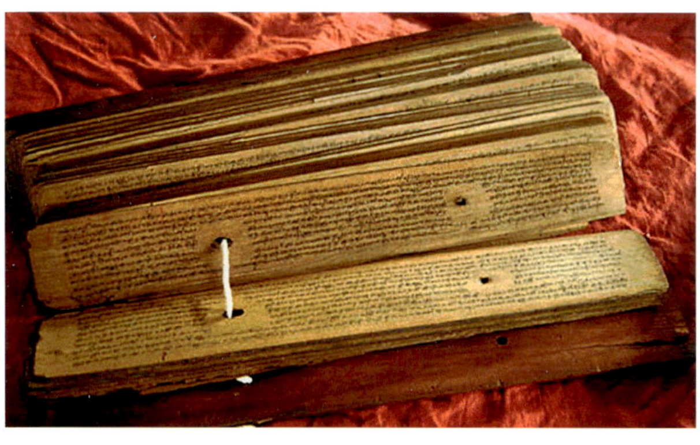

Arthaśāstra Manuscript Source: ourkarnataka.com

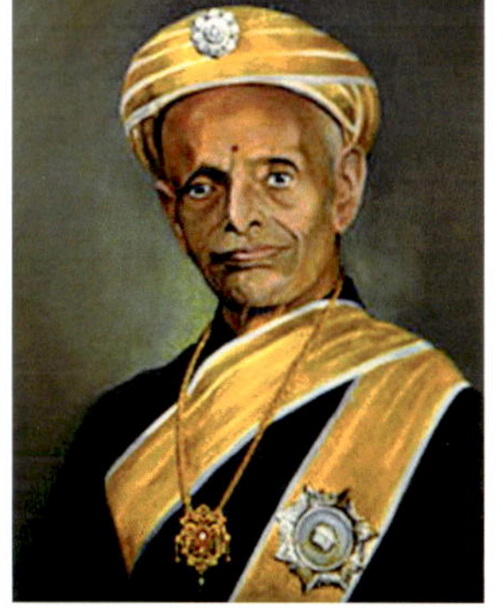

Dr. Rudrapatnam Shamashastry discovered the *Arthaśāstra* in Sanskrit. Though written 2,400 years earlier, the classic work was discovered as late as the 20th century. Source: *outlookindia.com*

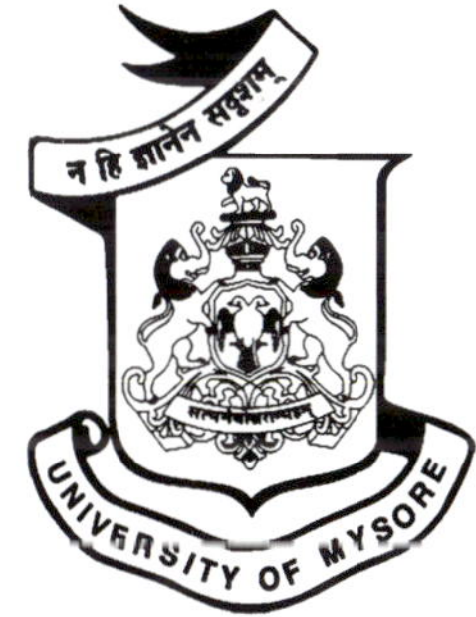

Oriental Research Institute (ORI) at Mysore is a research institute which collects, exhibits, edits and publishes rare manuscripts in Sanskrit and Kannada, with a few works in English, Tamil and Telugu. Formerly it was known as the Oriental Library. Logo of University of Mysore, India.

The *Arthaśāstra* contains 15 books – 150 chapters with roughly 6,000 verses in total. The first five books deal with the training of the king and his daily routines: the administrators, laws, crime, taxation, salaries, etc. – in other words, all of the domestic affairs that concern the bureaucracy. From books seven through thirteen, it focuses on foreign policy, diplomacy, war and conquest, and governance over the conquered. The last books deal with occult and philosophic practices. At the heart of the text, in book six, is the theoretical foundation of the text itself. It is there that *Arthaśāstra* defines the characteristics of the king and his adviser. The king, it states, is from noble birth, has intellect, is willing to learn, is brave and resourceful, eloquent and bold, well trained in arts and governance, sweet in speech, and without passion, anger, greed and fickleness. Most importantly, the king should follow the advice of his counsellor. The adviser should be of the highest rank, a native of the land, trained in all arts and logics, and be able to provide guidance to the king in governance; 'Only a king who is wise, disciplined, devoted to a just governing of the subjects and ever conscious of the welfare of all beings will enjoy the earth unopposed'.[2] Crucially underlining that imperative, *Arthaśāstra* notes that, 'A king can reign only with the help of others; one wheel alone does not move a chariot. Therefore, a king should appoint advisers and listen to their advice'.[3] This sets up the basic foundation of political philosophy in *Arthaśāstra* with an ever-learning, and ever-conquering king in dialogue with an ever-wise and advising philosopher.

The *Arthaśāstra* manages political difference via the means and tools of subversion, violence and surveillance. The king is advised to set up a network of spies in the land, to use conspiracies and rumours to

2
Arthaśāstra, 1.5.17, quoted in Nabi Bakhsh Khan Baloch, *Fathnama-i Sind 'urf Chachnama* (Jamshoro, 1963), 143. All translations mine.

3.
Ibid., 1.7.9.

manage political dissent. The effort of the *Arthaśāstra* is to argue for political power to overcome difference. It is not too difficult to imagine why this particular 'advice manual' would catch the attention of rightist Hindu nationalists in the twentieth century – it poses difference as awaiting surrender or conquest under a *just* king who is necessarily of good birth and conduct.

Part II.

The *Pañcatantra* (Five Fables) tales, composed in approximately 300 CE, articulated a different type of advice on how to handle political life. The power of birthright, might and righteous claims existed alongside a dialogic model with difference highlighted as the very basis of conversation. These tales featured nonhumans – animals and birds – whose conduct was rooted in natural difference, yet who gathered in conversation to govern, adjudicate and seek redress. They were clearly meant to give advice to humans, and to be used as didactic and pedagogic materials.

The sources for some of these tales are in the Buddhist *Jātaka* tales; some are found in other *dharmaśastra* texts such as *Mahābhārata* and *Vikramacarita*, and sometimes they use aphorisms from the *Arthaśāstra*, though they subvert or make them incompatible with the story. Unlike the *Arthaśāstra*, where the tone is factual, direct, ruthless and pragmatic, these tales are broadly conversational in nature, with little direct explication of meaning, allowing for multiple interpretations in their readings. These short tales spread across Asia in more guises and forms than any of us can possibly imagine, with recensions available to us in Tibetan to Bhasa and in over fifty other languages.

The brief framing story discusses the plight of King Amaraśakti who has three 'foolish' sons who need training and educating. He asks a wise *brāhmaṇa*, Viṣṇuśarman, to make them suitable for kingship. Viṣṇuśarman composes five books illustrating proper conduct, *nīti*, or kingly conduct, *rājanīti*. Yet unlike *Arthaśāstra*, the tales in *Pañcatantra* are multivocal and highly aware of difference as a categorical classification system. An early very popular tale, *Indigo Jackal*, recognises that the capacity to harm is inimical to power:[4]

4

Viṣṇuśarman, 'Indigo Jackal', in *Pañcatantra*, ca. 300 CE, I-II, quoted in A. Venkatasubbiah, 'Pancatantra Studies', *Annals of the Bhandarkar Oriental Research Institute*, vol. 15, № 1 (1933–34): 39–66.

There was a certain jackal, Caṇḍarava by name, who
lived in a jungle. Once, overcome by hunger, he entered
a town and was attacked by dogs. He took shelter in a
vat of indigo solution. When at last he managed to steal
back to the jungle, he found that his body was coloured a
deep blue. Because of this blue colour, the lion, tiger, wolf
and other denizens of the jungle did not recognise him
as a jackal. They thought that he was a strange animal,
and, being afraid, wanted to run away. For it is said,
'The wise person who desires his own welfare does not
trust someone whose behaviour, family and prowess are
unknown'. But Caṇḍarava realised they were afraid of
him and said: 'O wild animals! Why do you flee in terror?
I have been created by Indra to rule over the animals of

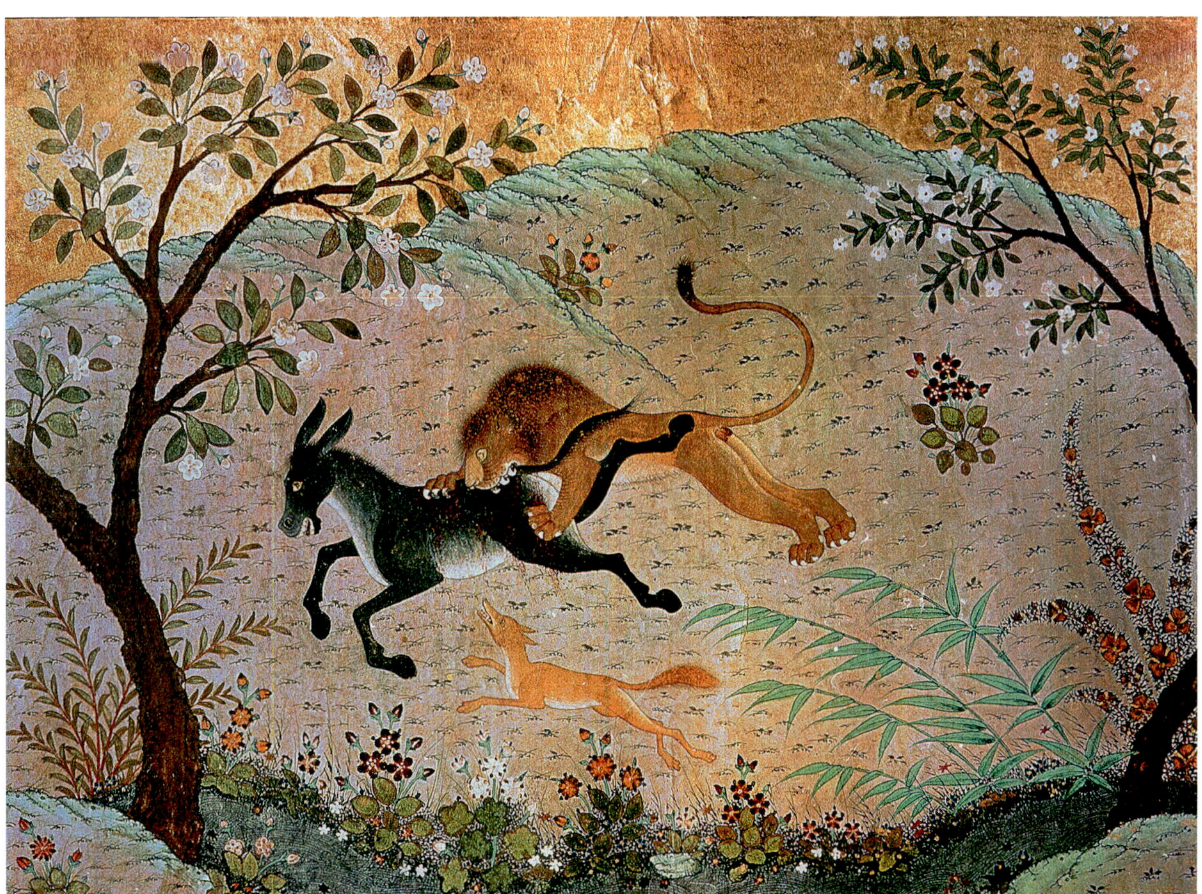

Panchatantra, an ancient Indian collection of animal fables. Copyright *Werner Forman Archives*.

91

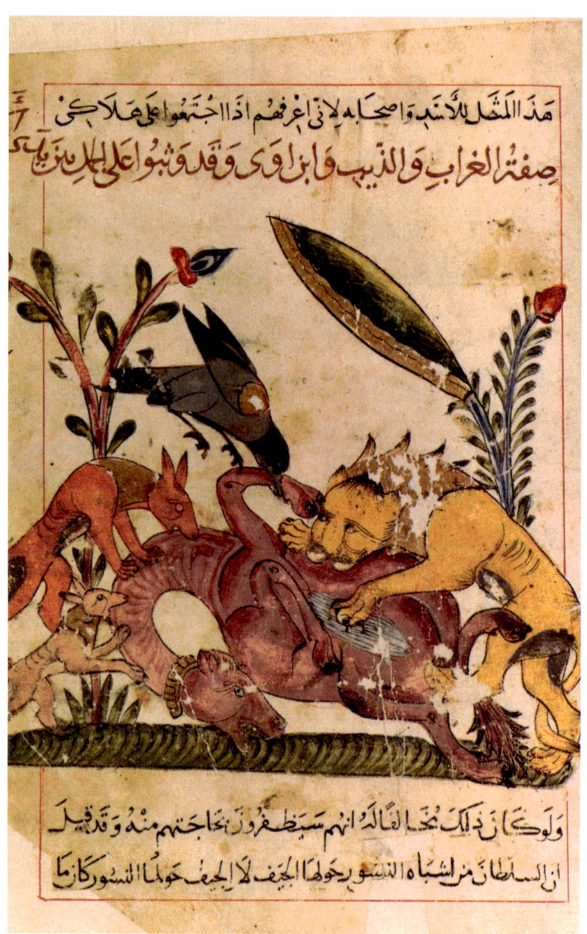

The evil jackal **Damanaka,** the Lion, the Crow and the Wolf attacking the Camel. Source: *Kalīlah wa Dimnah* by Esin Artil.

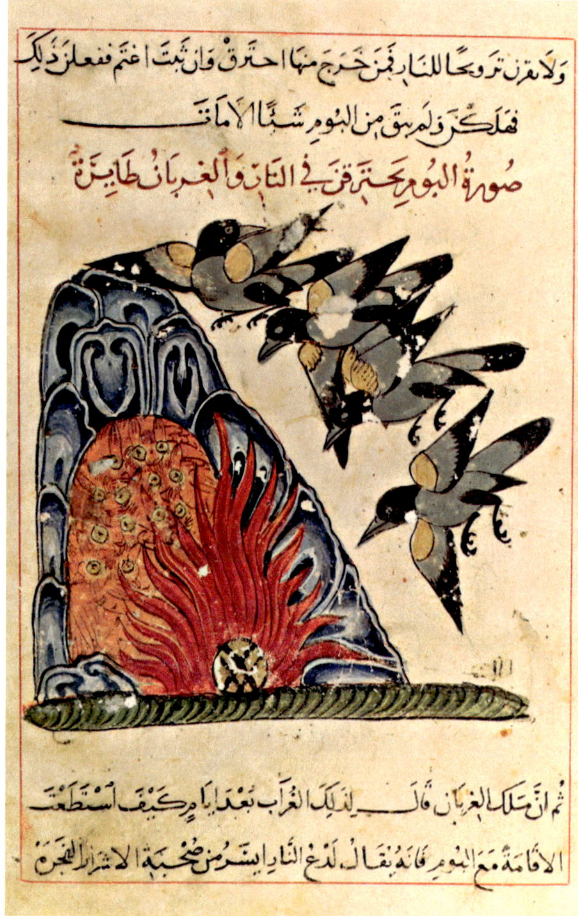

The Indian original, **Kākolūkīyam** – of crows and owls. A Syrian painting of a parliament of owls, trapped in a cave and set on fire by their traditional rivals, the crows. The crows flap their wings to further fan the flames. Source: *Kalīlah wa Dimnah* by Esin Artil.

the jungle, who have no ruler. Caṇḍarava is my name and you can all live in happiness under my rule'. Having heard his words, the hosts of wild animals – lions, tigers, leopards, monkeys, hares, deer, jackals and the rest – bowed down to him and he made the lion his minister, the tiger his chamberlain, the leopard the keeper of his betel-box, the elephant his doorkeeper and the monkey his umbrella-bearer. But those jackals who were his own kind were all expelled from the kingdom. And while he was thus enjoying the splendour of the kingdom, the lions and the rest, having killed wild animals, laid them down before him. And he, in accordance to *dharma*, distributed the flesh to them.

While time passed in this way, one day, in the assembly
hall, having heard the chorus of voices of jackals
howling in the vicinity, the hairs on his body stood,
and he leapt up and howled with them. The lions and
the rest, having heard this, realised that he was a jackal,
bowed their heads in shame: 'We have been deceived by
a jackal, therefore let it be killed'. Hearing that, he tried
to flee, but was torn to pieces by the tiger and died.

Here, the duplicity of the king creates a fissure, which is not overcome
even with his just conduct. This skeptical outlook on royal power,
and the capacity of the courtiers to strike back, permeates the fables.
Twinned with that reading is the argument for the specific nature of
the jackal who is not suited for kingship – this argument is developed
in a series of other tales. For example, in the framing story of the third
book, an assembly of birds – geese, cranes, cuckoos, peacocks, owls,
pigeons, partridges, skylarks, etc. – comes together to elect a king
because Garuḍa the bird-king is preoccupied and negligent in his duty
to care for his subjects.[5] The society of birds debates and decides to
elect the owl after the owl convinces them of his wisdom. However,
just as they are about to crown him king, a crow suddenly appears and
interrupts the procession. The crow points out that the owl's nature is
fierce, cruel and terrifying and evil-minded, and that he will be unable
to protect his subjects. Similar to the *Indigo Jackal*, the tale of the
owl points towards a base-character for rulers, yet it also foregrounds
the capacity of the ruled to counsel and to confederate to protect the
greater good.

These tales, with their divergent meanings and gentle assertions
of difference, entered first the Pahlavi Sassanian Court of Khusru
Anushirwan (d. 579) and then were translated into Arabic by Abdullah
ibn al-Muqaffa in 750 CE as *Kalīlah wa Dimnah* (*The Fables of
Kalilah and Dimnah*). Ibn al-Muqaffa (d. ca. 756), a Persian convert,
converted the framing story of the King Amaraśakti into that of King
Khusru and his philosopher physician Burzōy, who travels to India to
acquire scientific knowledge and wisdom about governance. The tales
concern the jackal Dimnah who is striving to acquire power by any
means necessary, and his brother Kalīlah, who tries to dissuade him
and divert his intentions by moral teaching. The two are advisers to

5
Ibid., 3-01.

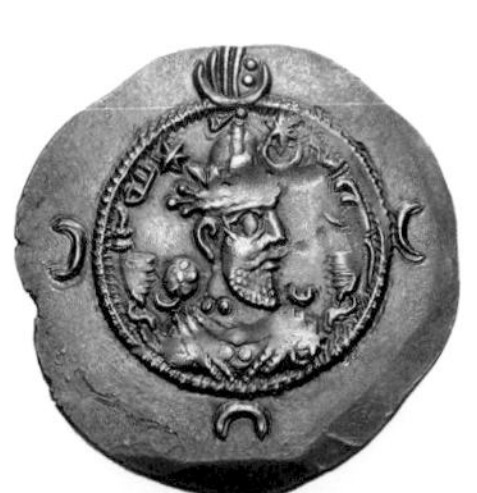

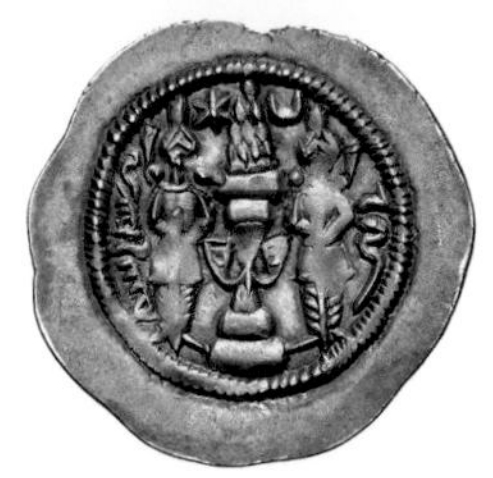

Coins of *Khusru (I)
Anushirwan,* the 22nd
Sassanian Emperor of Persia,
epitome of the philosopher
king. Copyright *Classical
Numismatic Group, Inc.*

the King of the Beasts – the Lion – and they are eventually executed via trial after Kalīlah's scheme to become king fails.

In *Kalīlah wa Dimnah*, Ibn Muqaffa, who wrote a series of other works on wisdom in Arabic, including *Adab al-kabīr* (*The Comprehensive Book of the Rules of Conduct*) and *Ā'in nāmeh* (*The Book of Proper Conduct*), created one of the most powerful and influential genres of advice literature for the Arabic and Persian literary and political cultures. It spread throughout the various courts in the vast Islamic realms and was commented upon, reinscribed and rewritten numerous times. A prominent example of the development of its stature as advice literature is in the *Rasa'il Ikhwan al-Safa'* (*Brethren of Purity*) – compiled in the late tenth century – where, alongside animals and humans, *jinns* enter into a ferocious debate about morality, ethics, faith and governance.

More directly, *Kalīlah wa Dimnah* reentered India through numerous forms – Firdausi's *Shahnamah* (*Book of Kings*), completed in 1010, al-Biruni's *Kitab al-Hind* (*Book of India*) completed in 1030, Abu'l M'aati Nasru'llah's *Anvār-i Suhailī* (*The Lights of Canopus*), composed in 1121, and Farīd al-Dīn Aṭṭar's *Manṭiq al-ṭair* (*Speech of the Birds*), completed in 1178. With these companions in advice, these texts emerged as foundational exegetical texts on governance and royal conduct for the Indo-Persianate rulers of northern India from the twelfth century to the eighteenth. In these texts, difference was overwhelmingly understood through dialogue and refracted through pragmatic politics.

A key example of the pedagogic and utopic mirror for princes genre, the *Chachnama*, was composed in Uch Sharif in 1216. The *Chachnama*, among other things, acts as a manual for advice to the local Muslim rulers. The world of the early thirteenth century within which *Chachnama* took place was politically heterodox and increasingly unstable. There were multiple claimants for the city of Uch Sharif and the ruler, Qabacha, needed to make alliances with the neighbouring principalities in Gujarat to fend off the challenge from Lahore. The political imagination deployed in the *Chachnama* sought to reimagine Islam's moment of origin in the Sind province to argue for a future utopia where natural difference can coexist.

Chachnama was written as an explicit history of Islam's arrival to Sind and was dedicated to Sultan Qabacha's chief minister 'Ain al-Mulk-Abu Bakr al-Ash'ari. Although it became known to the world as *Chachnama*, the book was originally titled *Kitāb-i Hikayāt-i Rai Dāhir bin Chach bin Sila'īj wa halāk shudan ou badāst-i Muhammad-i Qasim* (*The Book of Stories of the King Dahir bin Chach bin Sila'ij and His Death at the Hands of Muhammad bin Qasim*'). The text precisely labels itself a *hikayāt* (stories, often told and heard orally), a *ta'rīkh* (history) and a *dastān* (epic) –

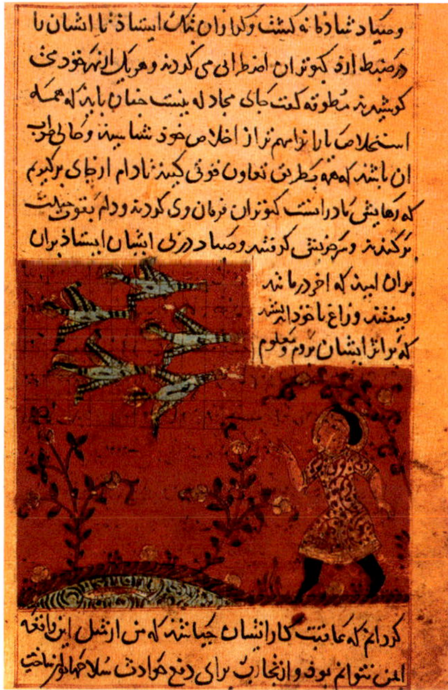

The Birdcatcher and the Doves

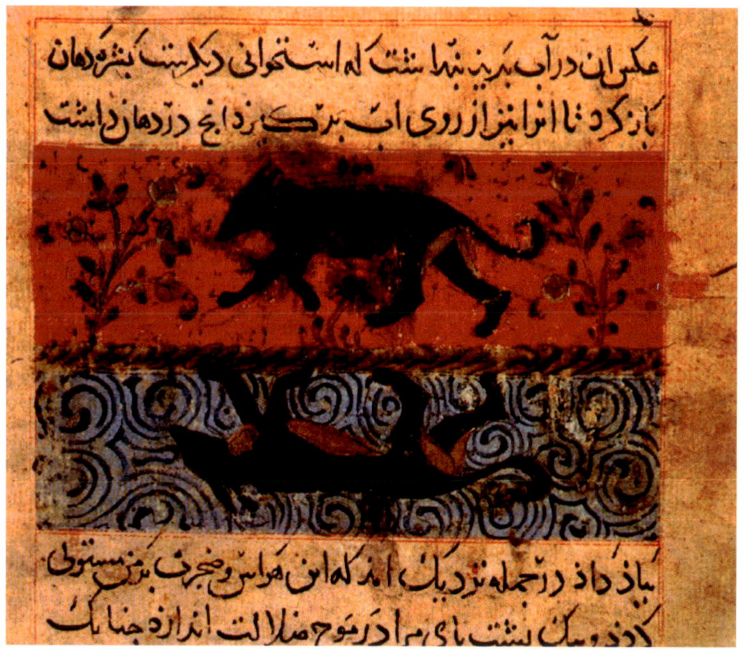

The Dog and Its Reflection in Kalīlah wa Dimnah. Source: kilyos.ee.bilkent.edu.tr (both)

and participates in those narrative voices accordingly. In its format, the narration of particular 'historical' episodes is sprinkled with discursive details of good governance and guidelines for conduct. *Chachnama* specifies a hierarchical distinction between the ruler and the ruled that evokes the arguments of *Pañcatantra*. Hence, the *Chachnama* provides a dialogic framework for royal conduct, which posits difference as mutually understandable – even if it is incommensurate, as the jackal is to the lions or the owl is to the other birds.

95

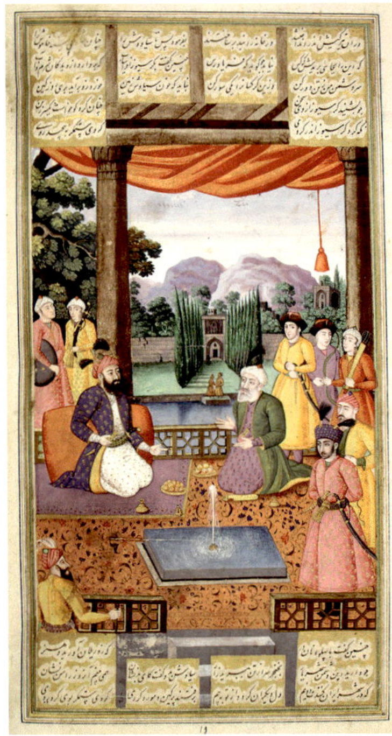

Scenes from the **Shahnamah** (*Book of Kings*), depicted as Iranian *qahveh khaneh* (coffee-house) painting, a vernacular style distinguished by its distance from the court arts. Source: *The Metropolitan Museum of Art*, New York, *metmuseum.org (top)*

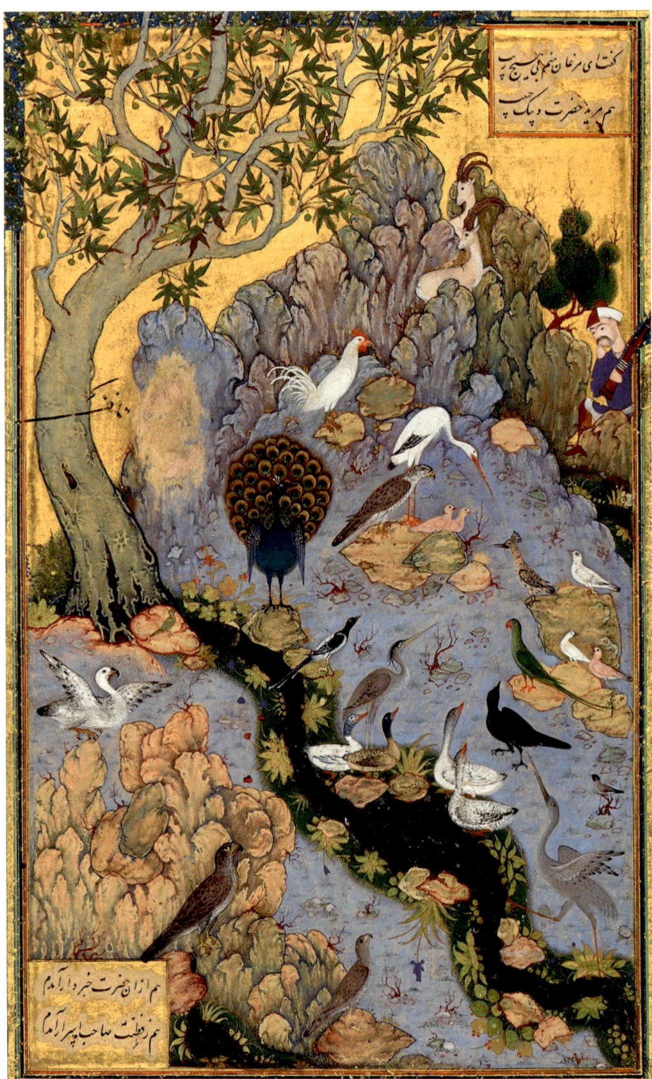

16th-century illuminated page of **Manṭiq al-ṭair** (*Speech of the Birds*), the 12th-century epic poem. Eight centuries later, theatre director Peter Brook had the poem adapted by Ted Hughes and enlisted a troupe of actors, including Helen Mirren, to travel to the Sahara to stage the piece in front of an audience with whom they shared neither common language nor culture. Painting by Habiballah of Sava. Source: *The Metropolitan Museum of Art*, New York, *metmuseum.org (above)*

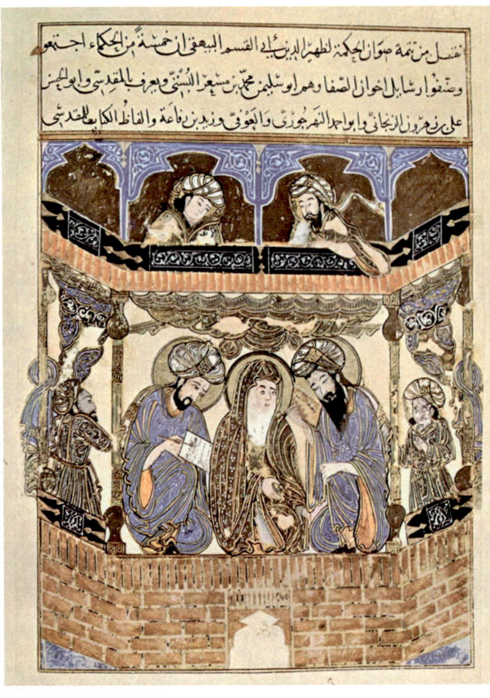

Rasa'il Ikhwan al-Safa' (*Brethren of Purity*) Arabic manuscript illumination from the 12th century CE. Source: *muslimheritage.com (left)*

96

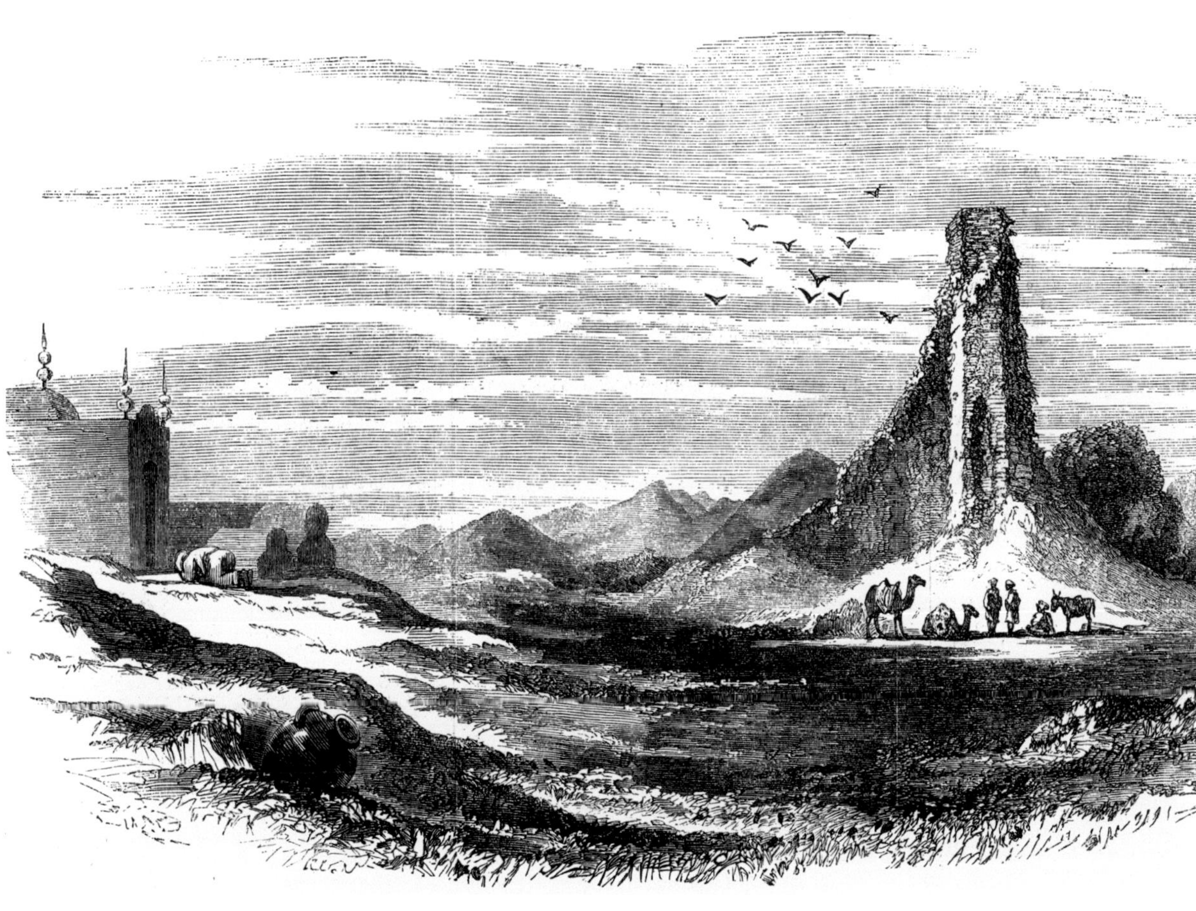

Brahmanabad, the historic capital of the Arab empire in Sindh. Courtesy Dr. Frances W. Pritchett. Source: *Illustrated London News*, February 28, 1857, 187.

The first attempt to delineate a political theology of difference and power is narrated in the text, in the section pertaining to Sind before the arrival of Islam – during the reign of Chach. The Brahmin Chach is attempting to conquer the various principalities in Sind and unite them under his rule. He faces resistance at the fort city of Brahmanabad and lays siege to it. Eventually the siege is broken and Brahmanabad is taken, but Chach faces an antagonistic population which is largely Buddhist and which pays tribute to the central Buddhist temple. Chach suspects that this Buddhist priest was behind the resistance of the people, and vows to 'peel off the skin' of the priest and 'give it to the Royal drummers so that they can stretch it across their drums and beat it to shreds' (*o ditan-ra budham ta dar tabalha kushand o mi zanand ta para para shavad*).[6] After settling the affairs of the new state, Chach turns his attention to the priest who had defied him:

6

Baloch, *Fathnama-i Sind ‘urf Chachnama,* 30.

Then asked: Where is that magician Buddhist (*samani*)
so that I can see him. They said: He is an ascetic (*nāsik*)
and will be with the ascetics. He is one of the wise ones
of al-Hind and a servant of the temple (*Kanohār*) –
they praise his miracles and his spiritual gain. He is so
powerful that he has ensnared the whole world in his
spell and those that he supports, succeed.[7]

Chach takes a large retinue and sets off to find and kill the Buddhist
priest. He orders the troops to stop at a distance from the temple,
and tells them that he will proceed alone. He explains that when he is
done conversing with the priest, he will give them a signal and, at that
moment, they are to descend upon the temple and kill the priest.

Chach approaches the priest, and finds him sitting alone on the ground,
making little clay images (*asnām*) with his hands, and then marking
them with a seal. He addresses Chach, 'So the son of Sila'ij the priest
has arrived?' Chach replies, 'Yes, O ascetic Buddhist'. 'Why have you
come?' 'I am your disciple and I have come to pay my respects'. Chach
offers the priest a return to Brahmanabad to take over the important
religious duties. The priest replies that he has no need to take part in
political matters and he is content to stay in his temple. Then Chach
asks:

> So why did you resist me in taking Brahmanabad?
> The priest replied: When the ruler Agham had passed
> away and the young prince became the Raja, I reluctantly
> took the task of giving him advice. Though in my view
> all matters of this world are matters to be shunned. Now
> that you are the ruler of the world, I am willing to obey
> you, but I fear that you will take your revenge on the
> temple and destroy it. Chach replied: It is always better
> to worship the Buddha and to attain perfection in his
> path. If you need any thing from me, you simply ask.[8]

Unlike the *Arthaśāstra*, the advice-giver in *Chachnama* is reluctant
to give advice. Chach continues to offer the priest riches and he declines
each time. In the end, he makes one request: 'the Buddhist temple
of Kanohār is ancient and decrepit. If you repair it, you will earn the

7
Ibid. 31.

8
Baloch, *Fathnama-i Sind
'urf Chachnama.* 32.

Die rote Zunge ist der Feind des schwarzen Hauptes,
Wieviele Häupter sie auch verzehrt hat,
Noch immer verzehrt sie sie.

Czerwony język jest nieprzyjacielem czarnej głowy,
Ileż głów już zjadł i nadal jest nienasycony.

gratitude of the believers'. Chach quickly agrees and leaves the priest.
He returns to his troops and orders them back to Brahmanabad.

'Why did you not let us kill the priest?' Chach's minister enquires
of him. He replies:

> I saw something that was not trickery nor magic (*hargiz
> dar vai sahār o sh'baida nist*). I examined it carefully
> with my eyes. When I sat down next to him, I saw a
> demon, ugly and fearful (*makruh o sahamnak*), who
> stood next to him. His eyes glowed like embers glowing
> or rubies; his lips fat and drooping; his teeth sharp
> like spears. And he looked to strike someone. I was
> frightened when I saw him and I dared not speak to
> the priest as I had indicated to you, because I knew
> he would kill me. So I made peace with him and left.

In setting up this conflict among two religions – Brahmin and Buddhist
– *Chachnama* specifies a hierarchical distinction between the ruler
and the ruled. It asserts that ways of sacrality, though overlapping,
have contentious claims to political power. The stand-off between
the political power of the ruler, as represented by Chach, and the sacral
power of the Buddhist, as represented by the demon with ruby eyes,
rests on a specific idea of religious difference. Chach affirms this in his
discussion with the priest when he proclaims that his intention is to seek
the higher truth in life through service. Thus, for Chach, the reason for
compromise was both an understanding of religious efficacy in political
life, as well as a grasp of the vortices of power. In recognising, and
fearing, the Buddhist demon, the Brahmin Chach agrees to a political
detente. In recognising the political power of Chach, and asking him
for material aid, the Buddhist priest also agrees to a political detente.

Chachnama's advice, like that of the *Pañcatantra*, is to recognise
difference and assert that this recognition is mutual and a necessary
condition of enacting power and coexisting.

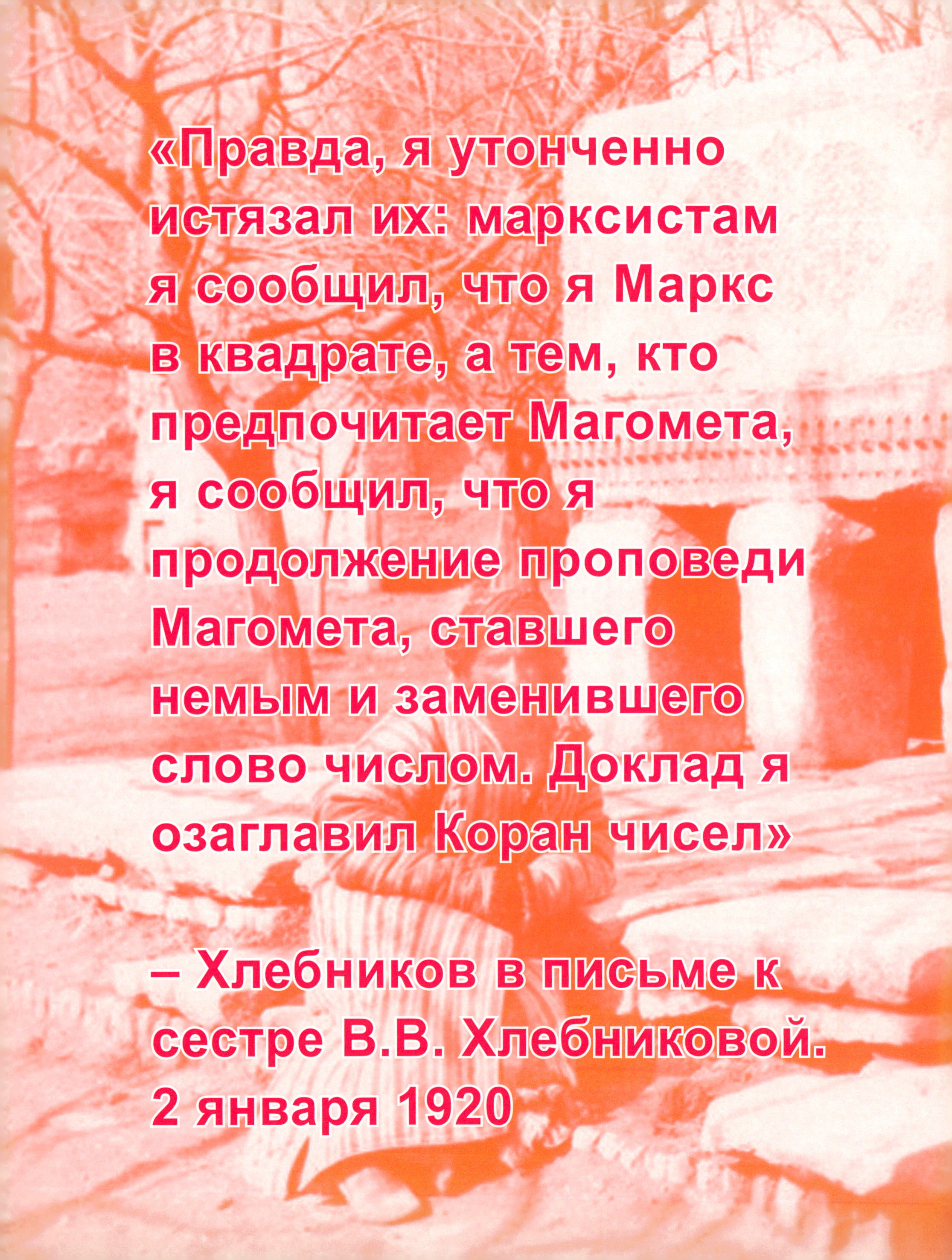

«Правда, я утонченно истязал их: марксистам я сообщил, что я Маркс в квадрате, а тем, кто предпочитает Магомета, я сообщил, что я продолжение проповеди Магомета, ставшего немым и заменившего слово числом. Доклад я озаглавил Коран чисел»

— Хлебников в письме к сестре В.В. Хлебниковой. 2 января 1920

«I announced to the Marxists
that I represented Marx
squared, and to those who
preferred Mohammed
I announced that I was the
continuation of the teachings
of Mohammed, who was
henceforth silenced since the
Number had now replaced
the Word. I called my report
the Koran of Numbers»

– Khlebnikov in a letter to
his sister Vera 1920

Part III.

As the Mongol armies overturned the centuries-old Baghdad-based Caliphate in 1258, a massive migration of refugees towards Cairo and Delhi reset global and local politics in the thirteenth century. In this newly made world, political and religious difference lost its dialogic capacity and became intransitive. The philosopher–king relationship as a key formulation of advice literature is reinvigorated in the Persian advice literature in the fourteenth century as the Turko-Mongolian Muslim elite attempt to ground and grow their new imperial dynasties in Delhi. Unlike in the *Arthaśāstra*, the king does not have a birthright to the throne and is a fallable human who is unsure of his own capacity to be a just king. The role of the philosopher and teacher, then, is to articulate a political theology for the king but also illustrate the concerns of the citizenry. Tracing the genealogy of thought from the pseudo-Aristotelian *Secretum secretorum* and the Arabic *Kitāb sirr al-Asrar* (ca. 940s), these advice manuals focused on Alexander's conquest of India and the role played by Aristotle as his philosopher-adviser. This tradition of ethical advice emerged from the same translation projects that made Ibn al-Muqaffa's *Kalīlah wa Dimnah* possible in the eighth century. In the 'Abbasid courts of the tenth century, a comprehensive translation project brought Greek and Syriac texts – especially philosophical and scientific – into Arabic, as well as texts from Sanskrit and Pahlawi. The emergence of Aristotelian thought and ethics in the tenth century was itself a response of the 'Abbasid Empire to think about difference in the socially and politically diverse areas formerly of the Byzantine and Sassanid empires. The key advice texts in this intellectual tradition were the *Siyāsatnama* (*Book of Politics*) by Nizam al-Mulk (1018–92) and *Qabusnama* (*Book of Qabus*) by Qabus ibn Vushmgir (d. 1012).

From the movement of refugees congealed new forms of political power centred in Delhi – that which we call the Delhi Sultanate. These intertwined Turkic warlords and their descendants saw a world very different than that of the *Chachnama*. The measure of land became the conquest of land – with material and textual proclamations of universal kingship. How is one to be a just king in this new world order? An order that is expansionist and internally riveted? A key early political advice manual that answered this question was Ziyā al-Dīn

Two charts for determining whether a person will live or die based on the numerical value of the patient's name from an 1264/1848 copy of ***Kitāb sirr al-Asrar,*** a medieval treatise also known as *Secretum Secretorum* aka *The Book of the Secret of Secrets*, aka *The Book of the science of government: on the good ordering of statecraft.* Source: *nlm.nih.gov*

والشفا وان كان القمر في الجوزا والسنبله والحوت
دل على توسط العمر وان كان القمر في القوس والاسد
والدلو والعقرب فيدل على طول العله والابطا في البرؤ
والله اعلم حساب للمريض وهو انك تحسب اسم المريض
واسم اليوم الذي انت فيه وتضيف اليه ما قد مضى من الشهر
العربي الذي انت فيه وتزيد عليه عشرين من القوس ثم
تسقط الجميع ٣٠،٣٠ والذي يفضل معك هذا الاسقاط
تدخل فيه الجدول وليكن احدهما لوح الحياه والثاني لوح الموت
وتطلب ما قد بقي معك من العدد واي لوح اتفق فان كان
لوح الحياه فالحياه وان كان لوح الموت فللموت والله اعلم

لوح الحياه   لوح الموت

٣	٢	١
١٣	١١	٧
١٧	١٦	١٤
٢٨	٢٠	١٩
٢٨	٢٦	٢٣

٦	٥	٤
١٠	٩	٨
١٨	٢٥	٢٢
١٥	٢٤	٣١
٣٠	٢٩	٢٧

غيره حساب
الغالب والمغلوب
احسب اسم الطالب
والمطلوب حل اسم
وحده اسقطهم ٩٩
وانظر ما بقي معك فان النود
يغلب ما فوقه من الافراد
وما ختمه من الازواج والزوج

[illegible]

فائدة اذا اردت ان تعلم الحاكم كم يقيم حكمه في ذلك الولاية
الذي يتولاها فاحسب اسمه واسم اليوم الذي دخل فيه بالجمل
الكبير واسقط الجميع خمسة خمسة وانظر ايش يبقى معك
بعد الاسقاط فان بقي واحد او اثنين بعد لا سريعا ولا يقيم الا القليل
وان بقي اربعه او ثلاثة يقيم مدة طويلة وان بقي خمسه فانه يكون في

فارقب لسانك إن رمت حفظ رأسك
فإنه في كل يوم يتهددك

Başını kurtarmayı istersen, dilini gözet;
Dilin her gün senin başını tehdit eder.

Hold your tongue if you would keep your head;
Before the tongue the head's a coward.

Baranī's (ca. 1285–1356) *Fatāwā-i Jahāndārī* (*Precepts of World Rulership*). Attached to the Delhi Tughluq courts (ca. 1300–50), Baranī's advice drew upon the relationship between an able king, who is susceptible to corruption and ill temperament, and his adviser who steers him through deliberation towards ethics and good governance. After Baranī, manuals of advice continue to evolve into a specifically Turko-Indian formulation.

This is the third geneology that we see in the history of understanding difference in medieval India. It begins with the transcreation by Nasīr al-Dīn Tusi (1201–74) of Aristotle's *Nicomanican Ethics* in his *Akhlāq-i Nasīrī* (*The Nasirian Ethics*). Tusi's ethics separates itself from the mirrors for princes genre into a separate genre of *Ikhlaq* literature – a genre where ethics and conduct is explicated. The works which follow, Amir Khusrau's *Tughluqnama* (*Book of Tughluq*), written in 1320, Qazi Hasan's *Akhlāq-i Humayuni*, written in 1469, or Abu'l Fazl's *'Ain-i Akbarī* (*Constitution of Akbar*), composed in the 1580s, present this particular didactic, neo-Aristotelian ethics of governance and conduct.

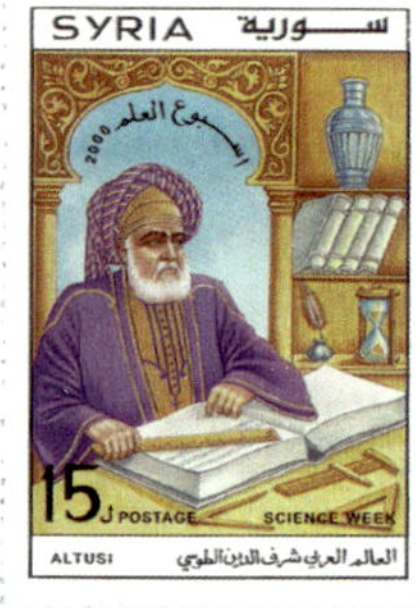

Nasīr al-Dīn Tusi
commemorated by a
Syrian stamp in 2000.
Source: *jeff560.tripod.com*

The Mughal Empire in the sixteenth century, under Jalaluddin Akbar, adopts *The Nasirian Ethics* as the dominant paradigm for the early modern world in South and Central Asia. Here, the model of *tolerance* is the model for recognising and reconciling difference. Akbar's *suhl-e kul* (universal peace) was the official political strategy that emerges from this ethics. It regarded the ideas of balance, of harmony, of the duty of the governor to the governed, and the reliance on the intellect, as key aspects of governorship. The adviser is missing or is relegated to a smaller stature as a confidant. The public and the king are in direct communication. The holistic conversations between various Jesuits, Franciscans, Brahmins and Sheikhs in the courts of Akbar (and his descendants) were conducted under this broad ecumene. These conversations were captured in accounts of Portuguese, Italian and French travellers and observers, and themselves became didactic and explicatory texts for seventeenth-century Europe. The Radical Enlightenment's debt to Mughal thought has rarely been acknowledged but it is historically undeniable.

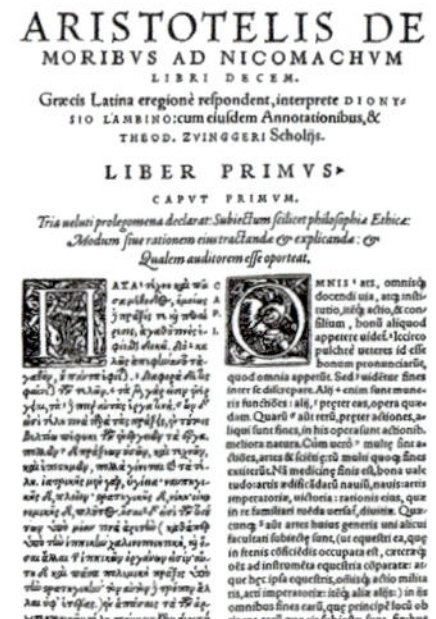

Aristotle's **Nicomachean
Ethics** (*Aristotelis De
Moribus ad Nicomachum*)
in Greek and Latin. Drawn
from his lectures at the Lyceum,
Aristotle's most well known
book on ethics was either
edited by or dedicated to his
son, Nicomachus. Source:
Universitätsbibliothek Basel.

The Mughal dispensation ended with the British colonial regime, which began its own project of translation in the mid-eighteenth century. The advice literature for East India Company officials did not include Persian or Arabic texts – rather, these were the Greek and Roman histories, along with near contemporaries such as Thomas More's *Utopia* or Montesquieu's *Persian Letters*, among others. Yet, the Orientalists did begin the act of translating these Indic texts as exemplars of the advice manual.

Persian Letters by Montesquieu, an epistolary novel as social commentary: namely the account of a trip to France by two Persian noblemen, Usbek and Rica. Source: *educ.fc.ul.pt*

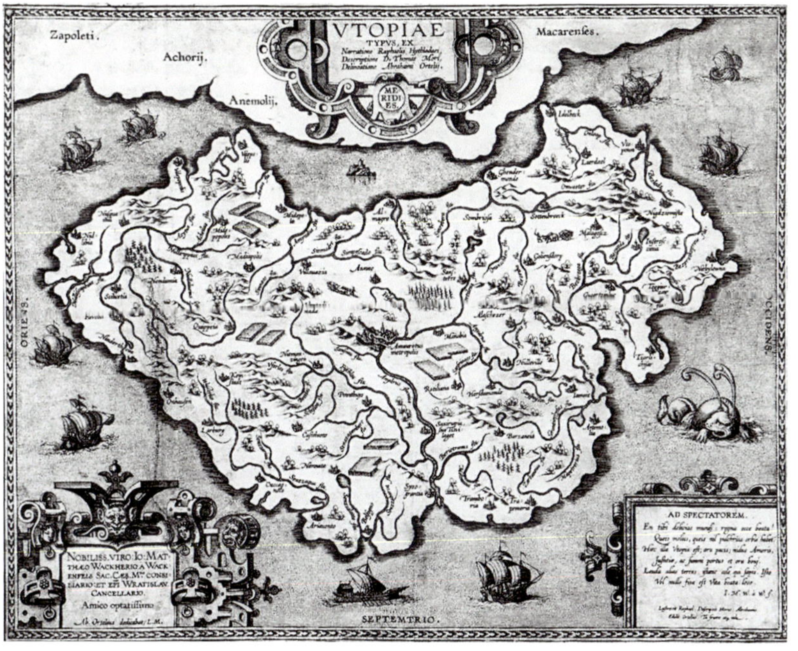

Abraham Ortelius's map of **Utopia** circa 1595. Source: *artsandsciences.colorado.edu*

As we make a temporal return to the postcolonial era, and the emergence of the *Arthaśāstra*, we see in these three genealogies the evolution and dispersion of advice manuals. We see a landscape that is polyglot and heterogeneous in language, ritual and social practices and, as a result, we see differing political understandings. The *Arthaśāstra* demanded that difference be erased with purpose from one privileged vantage point. The *Pañcatantra/Chachnama* offered a dialogic understanding that does not negate difference but instead allows difference to operate in a logic of coexistence. The neo-Aristotelian *Nasiri* model asks that a distinct vantage point outside of religious difference is needed to produce an ethics of coexistence.

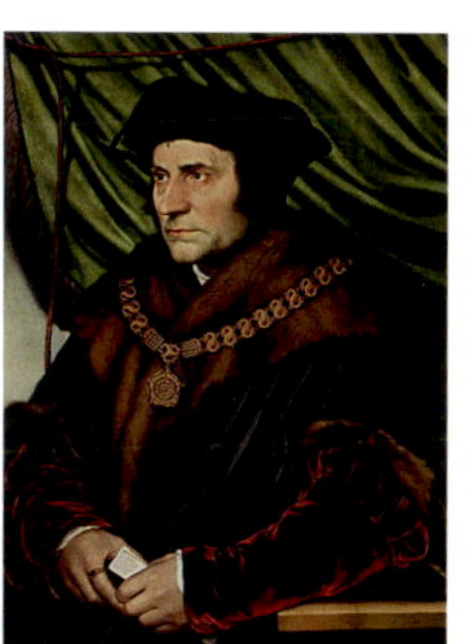

'We asked him many questions concerning all these things, to which he answered very willingly; we made no inquiries after monsters, than which nothing is more common; for everywhere one may hear of ravenous dogs and wolves, and cruel men-eaters, but it is not so easy to find states that are well and wisely governed'. **Utopia** (1516) by Thomas More. Source: *artsandsciences.colorado. edu*

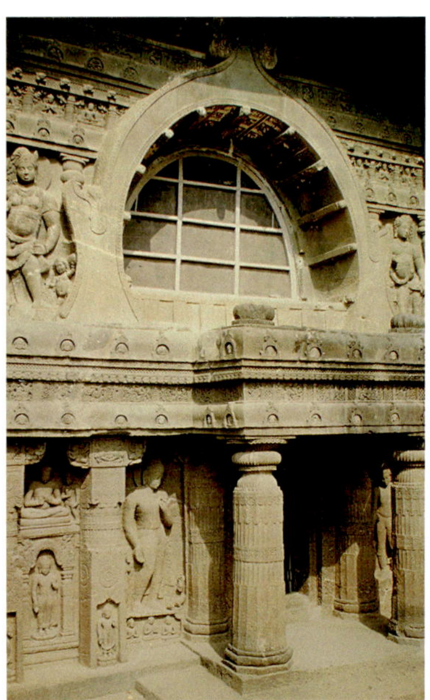 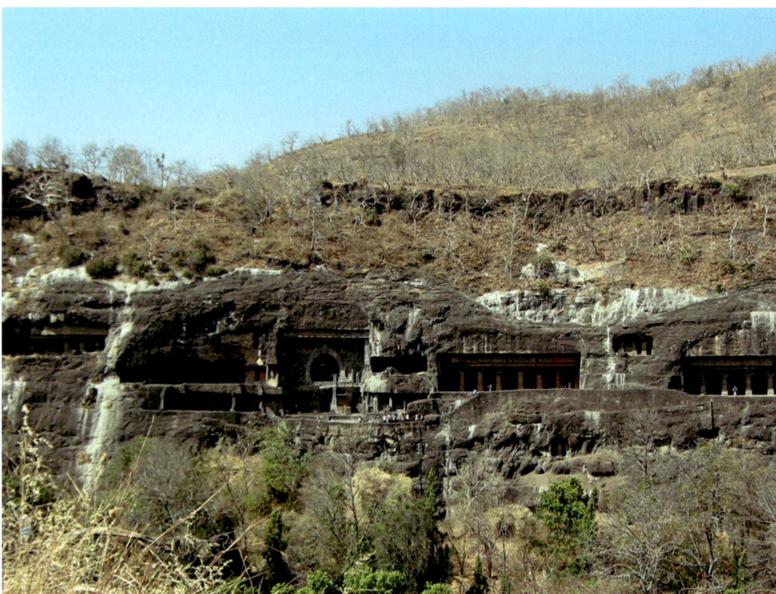

Ajanta Caves, aka the **Pañcatantra Caves.** Source: *Wikimedia Commons.*

What models are left with us? The hardening of difference under colonial regimes as a politics of exclusion and annihilation makes these genealogies seem like wiped-out traces on an old map. Yet the persistence of stories, from the *Pañcatantra,* from the *Chachnama,* in our contemporary world reminds us that political advice catering to the upkeep of empire falls with the empire – but stories designed to make us human live with us.

Mirror for Princesses

Anna Della Subin

The sun eyed the horizon; the earth wrapped herself in saffron silk and ringed her eyes with kohl. The grey moon waited patiently, quietly tolerating their nightly games. At her dressing table, the beautiful and devout Princess Ornament-on-World sat with her maidservant, a wise old woman called Highly Aged, and gazed into the looking glass.

How do I look?

'As a poet once said, "Who can see your face in the moonlight, like milk in milk?"[1] replied Highly Aged.

O swan-haired one, your eyes have grown faint. But your wisdom remains undimmed – I am in need of it.

'Tell me, Princess'.

You know King Rising Sun has asked for my hand in marriage. He wants me to bear his children, and to stand with him at the helm of the state. But motherhood, and guiding the kingdom, will take me away from my contemplation of God. Even thinking of marriage distracts me from Him. Yet should I devote my life fully to God, I would surely abandon the affairs of the realm, and my obligations to it.

'"Thoughts cannot solve the contradictions of the soul", as the philosopher said. "Thoughts mirror themselves in other thoughts, instead of mirroring a destiny".[2] But this conflict you imagine is an illusion'.

[1] Excerpted from an advice poem spoken by an older woman, in which she advises a younger friend not to rush off to her lover too hastily. Collected in the *Gathasaptasati*, an anthology of anonymous poems in Maharastri Prakrit gathered in the first century CE. Translated in *Grow Long, Blessed Night: Love Poems from Classical India*, ed. and trans. Martha Ann Selby (New York: Oxford University Press, 2000), 145.

[2] Emil Cioran, 'The Book of Delusions' (1936), trans. Camelia Elias, *Hyperion*, vol. V, issue 1 (May 2010): 71.

The Curious Case Of Solomoniia Saburova

'Have I ever told you about Solomoniia Saburova?[3] She was the wife of the Grand Prince Vasilii III. Her looks were radiant and charm poured from her tongue. But for twenty years she failed to become pregnant. Desperate to conceive an heir to the throne of Muscovy, she took pilgrimages and potions and consulted with sorceresses, and embroidered a tapestry to Saint Sergius with her plea. I helped her stitch when her eyes grew tired. But all to no avail – against her will, Vasilii divorced her, evicted her from the Kremlin and forced her to enter a monastery. As they tonsured her, she trampled on her veil and even called on God to avenge so great an indignity. She was smacked by the prince's vizier. Rumour has it, a few months after she entered the nunnery, she gave birth to a son, but would let no one see him. Meanwhile, Vasilii remarried and sired an heir, Ivan the Terrible. Centuries later, a tiny crypt was discovered next to Solomoniia's tomb. Inside, they say, was a doll dressed in a baby's white shirt'.

3
Information on Solomoniia Saburova (1490–1542) cited in Isolde Thyrêt, *Between God and Tsar: Religious Symbolism and the Royal Women of Muscovite Russia* (DeKalb, IL: Northern Illinois University Press, 2001), 35.

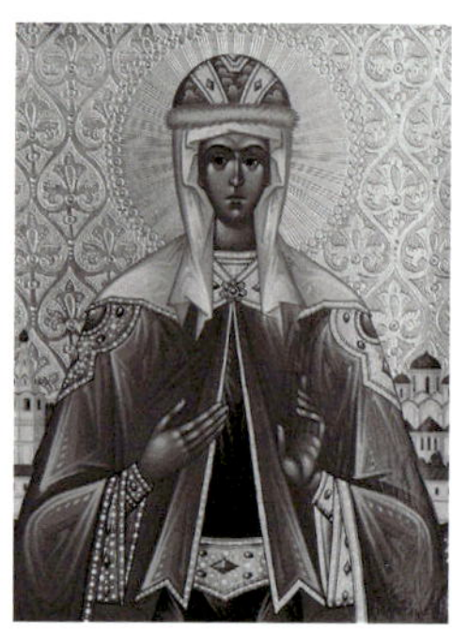

Solomoniia Yuryevna Saburova
Source: *ikona33.ru*

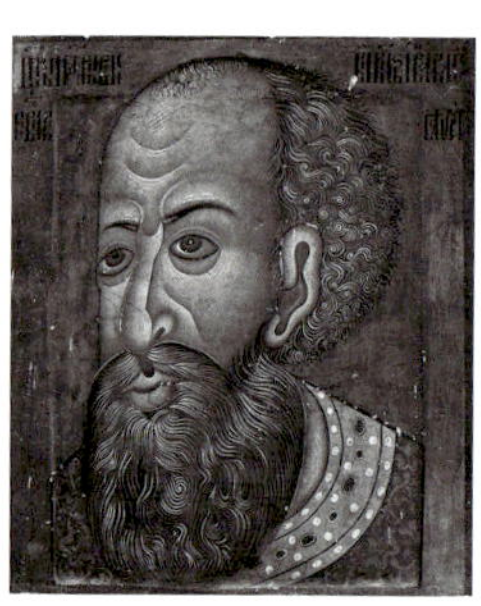

Grand Prince Vasili III Ivanovich
Grand Prince of Moscow, ruler from 1505 to 1533.
Source: *glazo.livejournal.com*

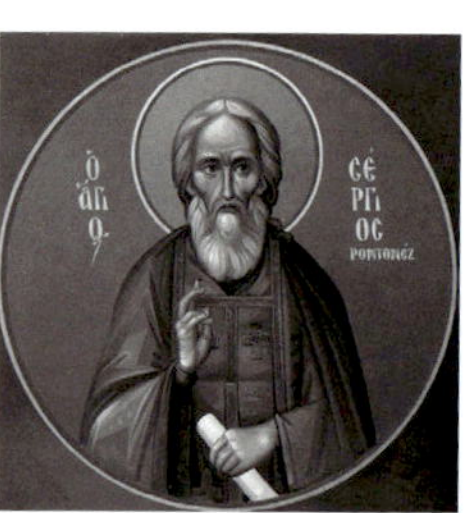

Saint Sergius
Source: *kopsidas.com*

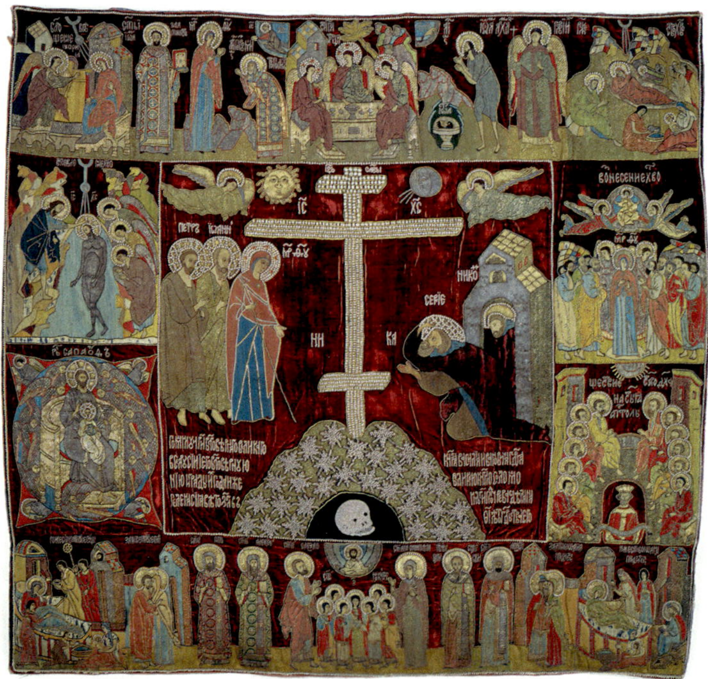

The appearance of the Virgin to St Sergius of Radonezh, red embroided drapery. Source: *pravoslavie.ru*

Der Stumme ist von Natur aus verschlossen,
Seine Zunge redet nicht.
Der Dumme ist so beschaffen,
Dass seine Zunge die Worte nicht verbirgt.

Niemowa język ma uwiązany,
A głupiec słów swych nie jest w stanie ukryć.

'Coerced into otherworldliness, even in her social isolation Solomoniia's obligations to the state, as befitting her royal rank, did not end. Her story was swiftly rewritten: she had renounced her conjugal right for the sake of the perpetuation of the grand prince's line. Or she had begged Vasilii to let her leave the palace, claiming that courtly life had become a distraction from God. As a nun, Solomoniia inhabited a new role in the state: that of intercession with God for the prosperity of the prince and his realm. Her newfound –

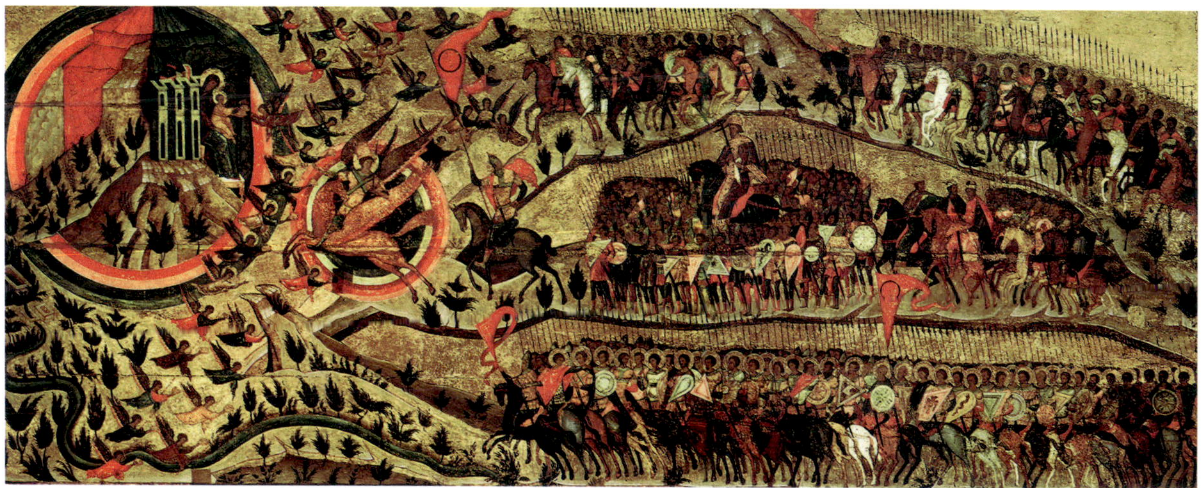

Blessed Be the Host of the Heavenly Tsar (alternatively known as Church Militant). Russian icon, ca. 1550–60, from the Uspensky Cathedral in the Moscow Kremlin, representing the fall of Kazan. Source: *tretyakovgallery.ru*

though unwanted – spiritual fecundity was a political responsibility that lasted long beyond her death. From the afterlife, Solomoniia divinely sanctioned the Muscovite autocracy. She was known for her miracles: once, she appeared to a marauding Lithuanian warlord in a nightmare, where she burned his right hand with a candle. The vision paralysed him, and the region was saved from invasion. After capturing the city of Kazan, a victory against the Tatars, Ivan the Terrible – that heir another woman had borne – visited Solomoniia's relics to offer thanks. She had become a saint in spite of herself'.

'Despite her infertility – and her unseeded faith – Solomoniia incarnated both the divine spirit and the state. You see, my dear Ornament, the womb of a princess always conceives twins'.

Highly Aged, your genius is like rosewater mixed with camphor and musk – its fragrance cannot remain hidden. But what a sad story you tell! What a sorry lot befell this princess. Unable to have children, used by the state that abandoned her and by the orthodoxy she did not want to take up…

'Her life was tragic, it is true. But perhaps Solomoniia is having the last laugh. Isn't the ultimate aim of stately life to create an immortal name for yourself? As the old sage Yūsuf Khāss Hājib said, the man with renown does not die when he dies, no matter how long he rots in the black earth's folds. "Seek not life, seek a good name, for as long as you have that you are alive and smiling".[4] The improbably good name of Solomoniia Saburova lives on'.

Lost in thought, the Princess glanced upwards, her eyelashes as curled as a question mark. In a letter to me, King Rising Sun confided that he's grown weary of handling the affairs of the realm by himself and that he desires a son. But what about me? Can motherhood itself be a form of statecraft?

'O Princess, my cheeks that haven't blushed in centuries are reddened in your service', Highly Aged replied. 'Gods may hatch from lotuses and sea foam and the footprints of greater gods, but kingdoms are born and managed by mothers. In Egypt, within only a few decades, mothers gave rise to *two* kinds of governments – a colonial regime and then a nascent nation…'.

A Mammary Politic

'When the British conquered the country, they pointed to the lives of its princesses as one of the reasons why Egypt was entirely unfit to govern itself.[5] The reports of European travellers who had penetrated the Khedive's palace, muddled with tales from the *Thousand and One Nights*, told of captive, cloistered harem girls, playthings of despots, who lived pampered and perverse existences in clouds of twisted smoke. Besotted and outraged, the British surmised that the harem

4
Cited by Yūsuf Khāss Hājib in *Kutadgu Bilig*, ca. eleventh century. *Wisdom of Royal Glory (Kutadgu Bilig): A Turko-Islamic Mirror for Princes*, trans. Robert Dankoff (Chicago: University of Chicago Press, 1983), 232.

5
Lisa Pollard, *Nurturing the Nation: The Family Politics of Modernizing, Colonizing, and Liberating Egypt, 1805–1923* (Berkeley: University of California Press, 2005).

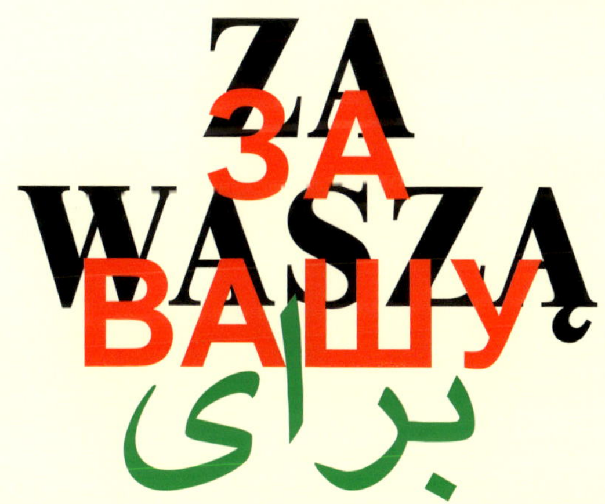

W JMIE
BO IMЯ
بہ نام
حدا
BOGA
БОГА
ZA
ЗА
WASZĄ
ВАШУ
برای
I
NASZĄ
НАШУ
آزادی
WOLNOŚĆ
ВОЛЬНОСТЬ
و ما
شما

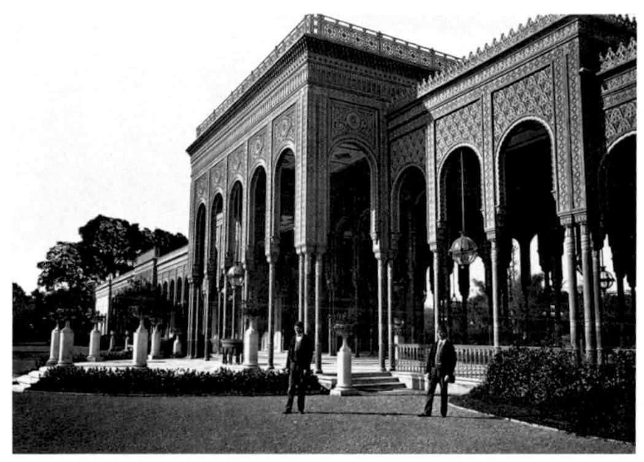

Designed in the 1868, the Gezirah Palace, also known as the **Khedive's Palace**, was one of the Egyptian royal palaces of the Muhammad Ali Dynasty. Today it goes by the no less ornate moniker: Cairo Marriott Hotel & Omar Khayyam Casino. Courtesy *The Metropolitan Museum of Art*, OASC licence.

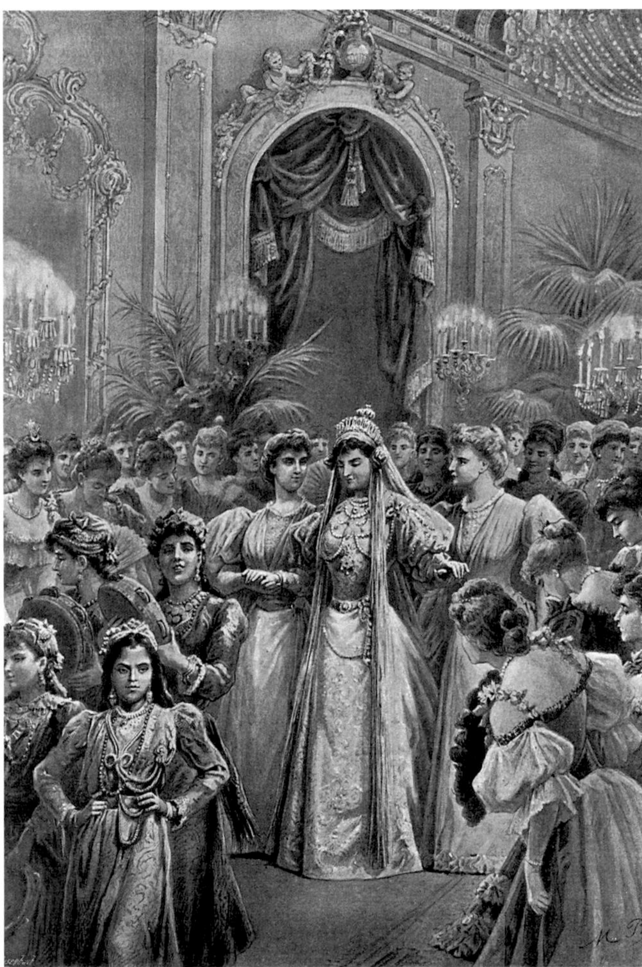

The marriage of the Khedive's sister, the bride's procession forming in the interior of the Harem. *The Graphic* (London), Saturday, March 2, 1895; Issue 1318.

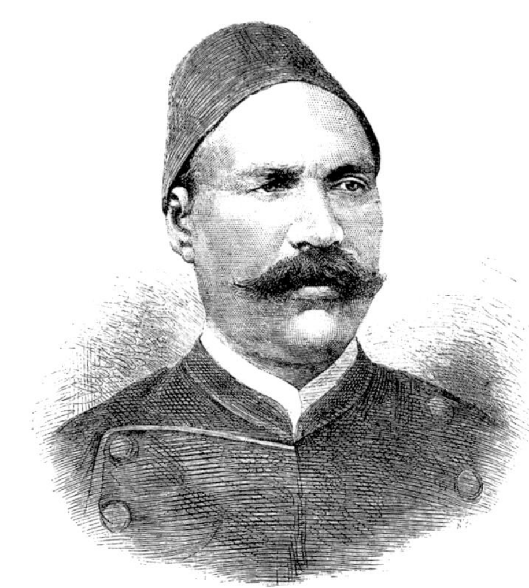

Colonel Ahmed 'Urabi or Orabi, also known as Ahmad Arabi, Arabi Pasha and 'El Wahid' (the Only One), led the uprising against the Khedive Tewfik Pasha. Source: *archiv.ucl.cas.cz*

was having a pernicious effect at the highest levels of government. In this mysterious hothouse, mothers were raising generations of indolent sons who were ill-suited to rule. The British used it to justify their open-ended stay in Egypt, as a way of saving the Egyptians from themselves. And so Egypt's quest for self-rule began with the transformation of household affairs'.

'Nationalism took on a mommying tone: mothers, it was argued, were the best conveyers of the values of the revolution, as they, above all, forge the morals of their children. This began at the breast. As a Turkish proverb goes, "If good character enters a man with his mother's milk, it does not depart until death takes hold".[6] Or Rousseau: "Let mothers

6
Cited in the *Kutadgu Bilig*, 68.

deign to nurse their children, morals will reform themselves".[7]
Advertisements for Lactagol baby formula, antitoxin to the sins of
the ancient regime, urged mothers that their most sacred duty was to
raise healthy sons for the nation. I saw a cartoon in the paper depicting
Mother Egypt, a chic, veiled woman in high heels, sitting on the back
of the Sphinx and breastfeeding an infant Bank Misr, the newly founded
national bank. Jealous siblings – foreign banks – with nefarious
intentions stalk the baby, but, nursed on his mother's milk, he will live.
And if the home were well organised and clean, the baby would thrive.
The idea spread of *mamlaka fil bayt*, or "home as kingdom": order
in the pantry, like a little Platonic republic, assured order, health and
flourishing at every level of the nation'.

My dear Highly Aged, the Princess chimed in, I don't
imagine the King will expect me to maintain harmony
in the realm by reorganising the palace kitchens.

7
Jean-Jacques Rousseau, *Emile,
or On Education*, trans. Allan
Bloom (New York: Basic Books,
1979), 46.

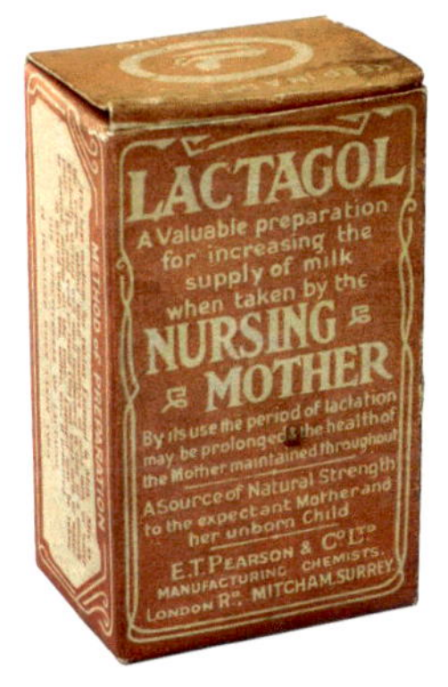

Carton of *'Lactagol',* by
E.T. Pearson & Co., Ltd.,
English, 1920-1955. London
Road, Mitcham. Source:
Science Museum, London,
United Kingdom.

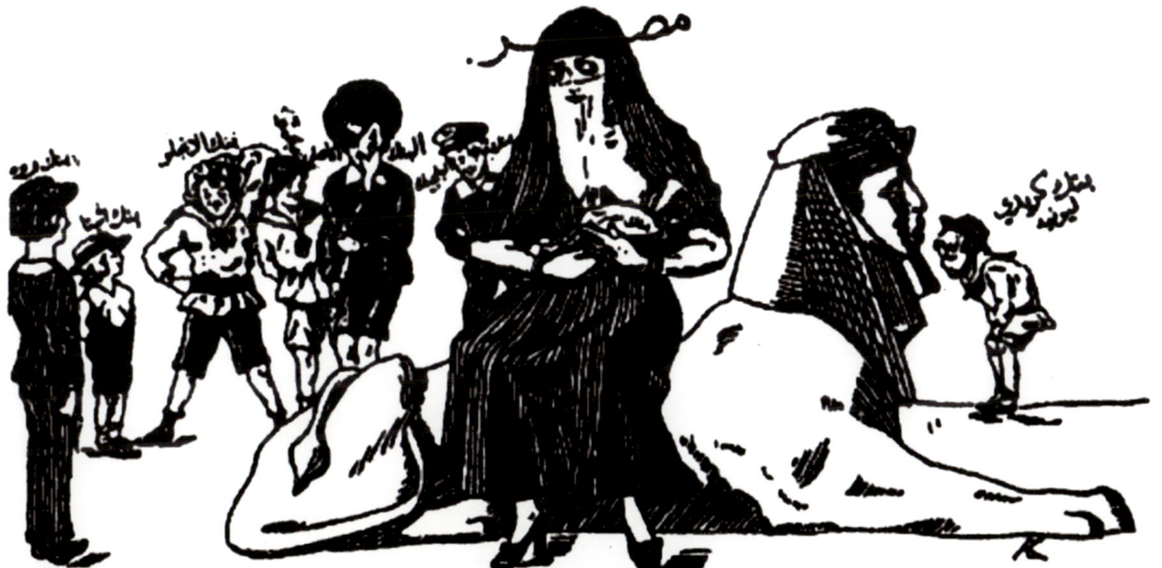

'The baby will live if he continues to nurse from the breast of his mother'.
Illustration by Al-Lata'if al-Musawwara from the book *Nurturing the Nation: The Family Politics
of Modernizing, Colonizing, and Liberating Egypt, 1805–1923*, by Lisa Pollard.

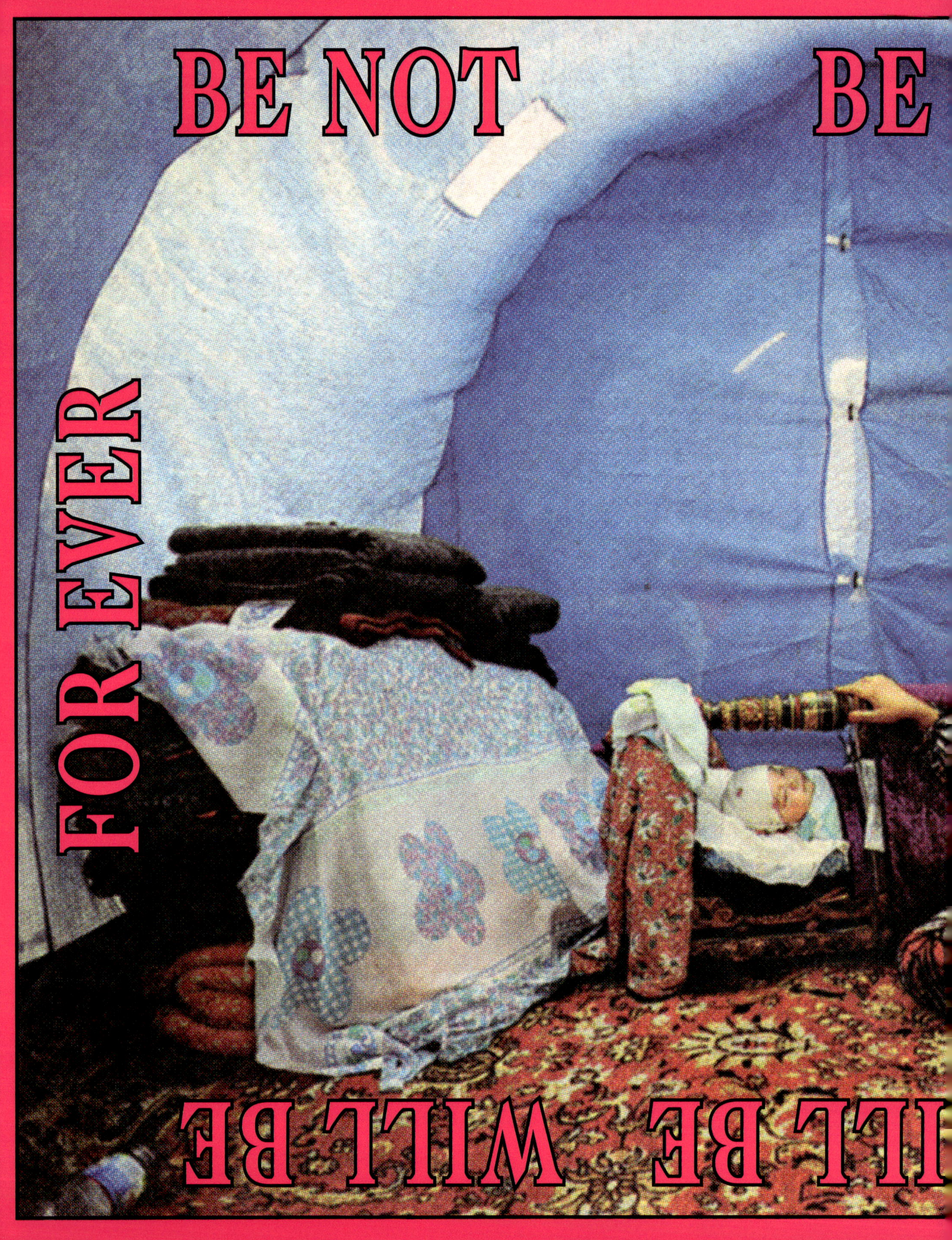

BE NOT
BE
FOR EVER
ILL BE WILL BE

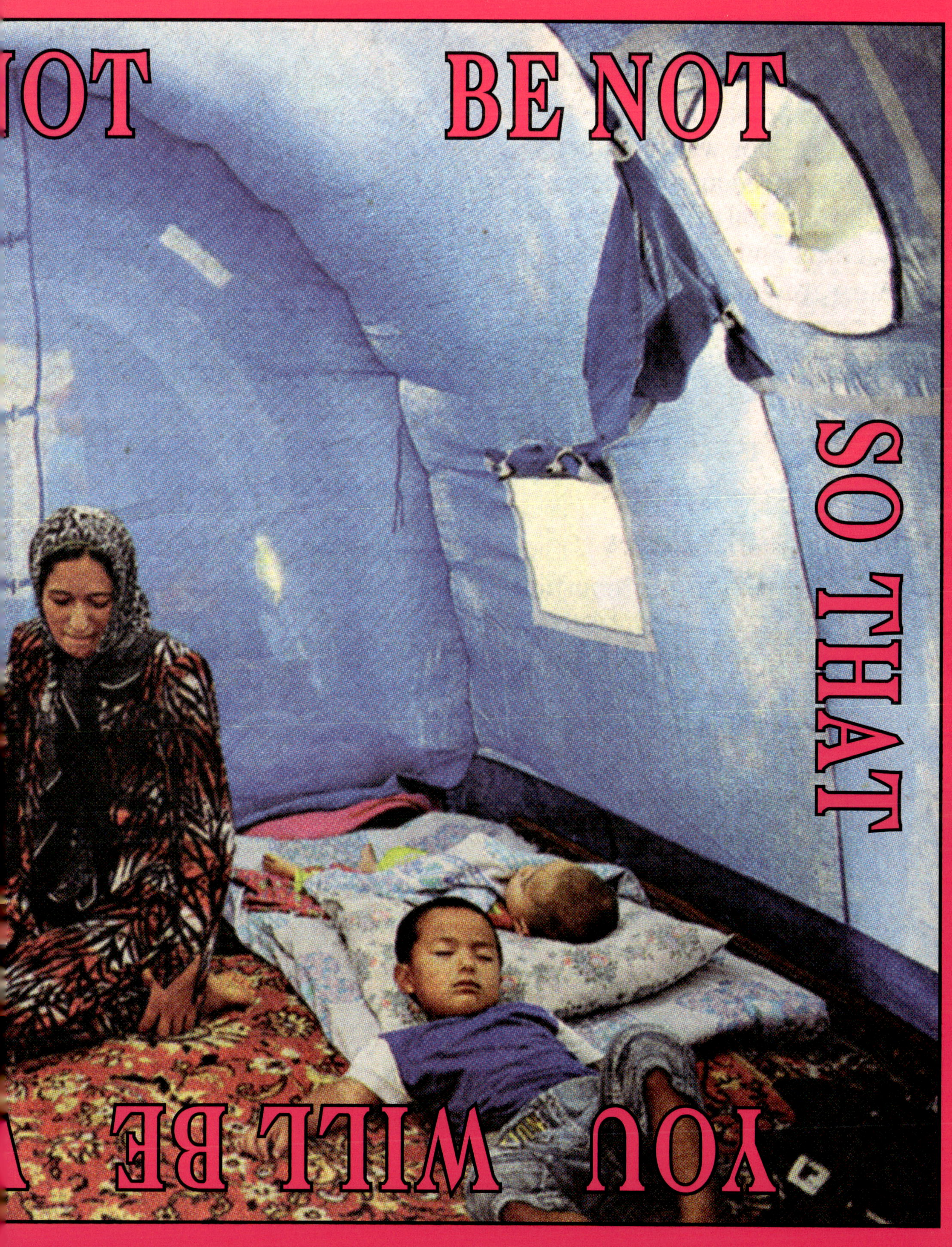
BE NOT
SO THAT
YOU WILL BE

'Fiction is the essence of statecraft, O sparkling Ornament. Like conjuring the most fantastical fairy tale, politics is an act of creation that brings a subject into existence. And so fiction becomes fact. All this maternal talk generated a feeling that Egypt was a family, a natural, self-determining unit, and eventually, it became just that. Moreover, the *love* of country it gave rise to was real – and crucial. What else could ever compel a people to follow the laws of the land, to fight and to die for it, all for a fable? You see, my cherished gem, why mothers are so vital to statesmanship, as they, above all, deal in love. But one must tread with care. As the love-struck poet sang,

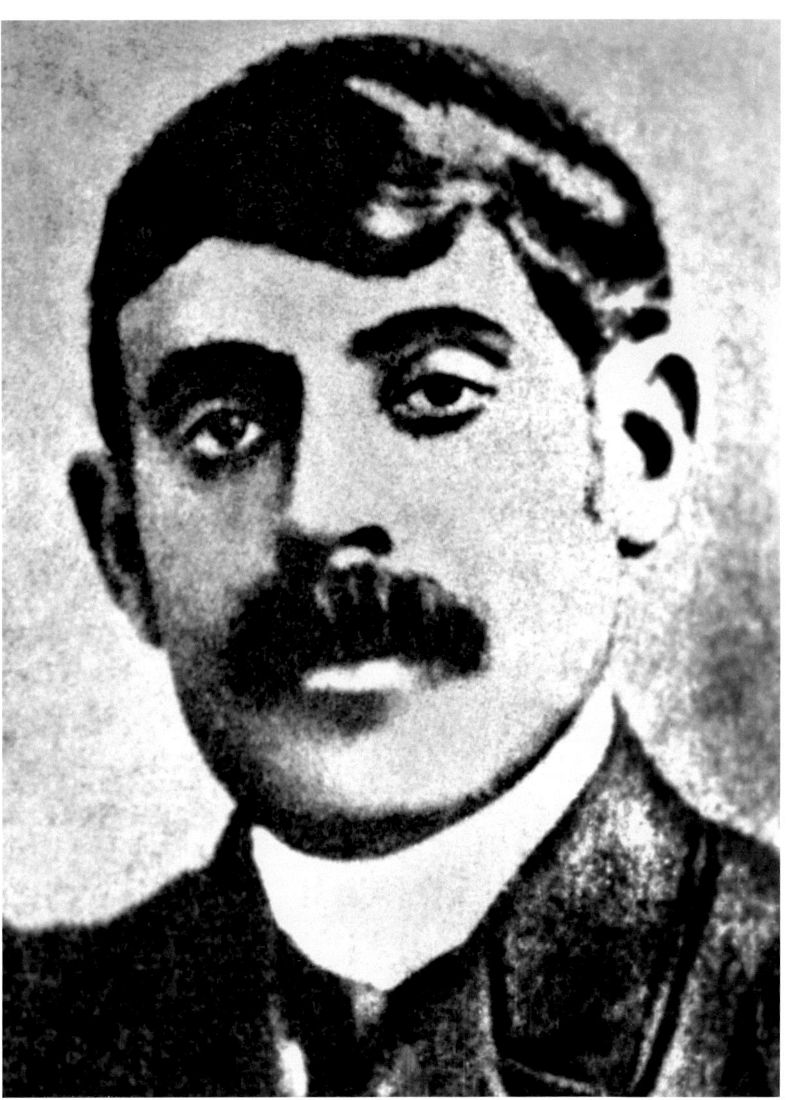

Egyptian jurist **Qasim Amin** (1863–1908) doing his best Marcel Proust. One of the founders of the Egyptian national movement and Cairo University, Amin returned to Cairo after a stint studying in France, determined to change the condition of women in his native country. Courtesy AFP.

She creates and she destroys:
Her navel is a lotus swaying
inside a lake, where water lilies
bloom into breasts. Her thick hair
streams down Her body, a garland of heads
hanging around Her neck. Even those earrings
    children's corpses
look stunning against the Mother's ears'.[8]

What a ghoulish sight! I don't understand,
O wizened one. How could a hug strangle an army?

'Mothers birth the nation, but they may also breed dissent. "A good
mother is more beneficial to the species than a good man, and a corrupt
woman is more damaging than a corrupt man",[9] as an Egyptian feminist
once declared. A father might discipline with physical punishment. But
mothers can indoctrinate their children into seditious beliefs by giving
or withholding that most potent force of all…'.

O Highly Aged, how could one not just burst with love,
like a ganglion of lightning? exclaimed the princess,
allowing a daydream of motherhood to flicker past her
emerald eyes.

Indoctrinate with Love

'Sublime Ornament', her seasoned maid replied, 'this very same
thing once terrified a great nation. It was called Momism – a fear
of the soft power of Mom that gripped America. During the Second
World War, when millions of women entered the workplace for the first
time and occupied jobs once filled by men, there was the sense that
masculinity itself was under threat. A crank called Philip Wylie wrote
a bestselling book that, ridiculous as it was, became taken seriously
in high circles.[10] According to his theory of evolution, every female
is a princess until she mates. Then, she smotheringly presides over a
collectivist society, like a queen ant. Liberated from the household tasks
of preindustrial women, Wylie surmised that Mom had way too much
time on her hands, which she spent in getting her sons and husbands

---

8
A hymn to Kali by the Bengali poet Kamalakanta Bhattacarya (1769–1821) in *Singing to the Goddess: Poems to Kali and Uma from Bengal*, trans. and ed. Rachel Fell McDermott (Oxford: Oxford University Press, 2001), 36.

9
Qasim Amin (1863–1908), a man often referred to as 'the Arab world's first feminist'. See Qasim Amin, 'The New Woman', trans. Raghda el-'Essaqi and Lisa Pollard, (unpublished ms. Cairo, 1995), 9. Qasim Amin, cited in Pollard, *Nurturing the Nation*, 159.

10
Philip Wylie, *Generation of Vipers* (New York: Pocket Books, 1942). The American Library Association selected *Generation of Vipers* as one of the best nonfiction works of the first half of the twentieth century.

Des Wissenden Worte nehmen nicht ab,
Des fliessenden Flusses Wasser nimmt nicht ab.

Słów człowieka mądrego nigdy nie jest dosyć,
Ani czystej wody źródlanej nie może zabraknąć.

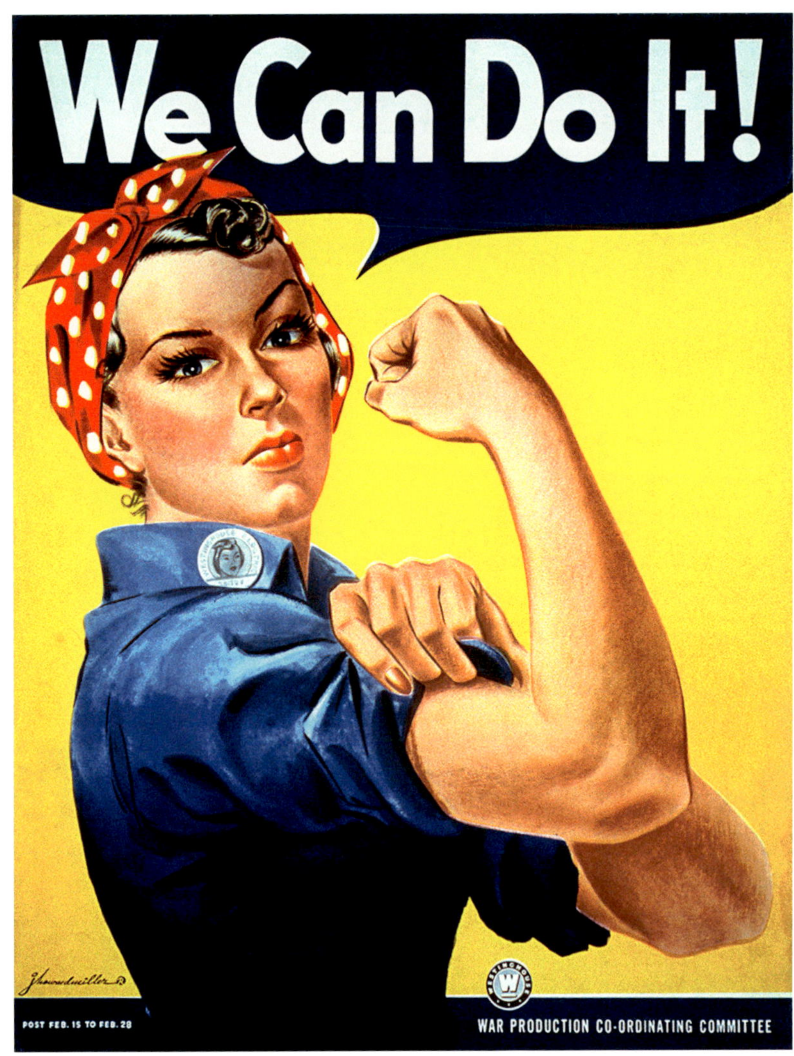

We Can Do It! 'The wrinkles of a nation are as visible as those of an individual', wrote Emil Cioran, image by J.H. Miller. Source: *National Museum of American History*.

to adore her. Her instruments of indoctrination included hugs, pies of various fruits, and guilt, but above all, "that lion crouching on the threshold", the tongue. Mom was "all tongue and teat and razzmatazz". But she, terrifyingly, was the one teaching her children language'.

'"Men should either be caressed or crushed", as Machiavelli said.[11] Mom was doing both. Edward Strecker, the president of the American Psychiatric Association, declared that the millions of men who had been rejected or discharged from the army during WWII were the creations of overbearing mothers. Mom posed a threat to national security.

11
Niccolò Machiavelli, *The Prince*, trans. Quentin Skinner and Russell Price (Cambridge: Cambridge University Press, 2003), 9.

As Cold War hysteria hit, American mothers were held responsible for keeping the communist plot out of the home. But who could tell whether they weren't the ones stirring it? Wylie was an adviser to the Atomic Energy Commission and advocated for the H-bomb, arguing that nuclear armament was the best way to eradicate Momism. But even Enola Gay had been someone's mother. As the poet said,

Love's ways are like this:
as curled as the tendrils
of a new cucumber.[12]

'Wylie proclaimed Mom the third point in an American trinity, with Bible and Flag', Highly Aged continued. 'It's funny how, attempting to demonise mothers, he truly apotheosised them'.

I fear I've done the same with my own mother, Drone-on-World, the princess replied. You know how we've never got along. But now as I'm about to marry the king, I feel I need her blessings, not only for my own sake but that of the realm… Do you think it is strange?

'It may be, O Princess, that politics is just not practicable without the divine spirit. The state is simply a mixture of everyone's particular self-interests. What can bind it together and elevate the people to strive for some sort of greater public good? In Solomoniia's case, the authority of the monarchy was sacralised by the Orthodox Church. Communist regimes give rise to cults of charismatic leaders. Or in a democracy, civil religion seeps in. As Eisenhower said to me, "Our form of government has no sense unless it is founded in a deeply felt religious faith – and I don't care what it is".[13] Every realm needs something, anything, to sanctify it. It might even be your mother'.

O Highly Aged, you are the lamp in the fading light.
But something troubles me: in the quest for power,
it seems so easy to harness the divine for my own
advancement in this world. But then I will surely ruin
my chances of paradise in the next. How can I have it all?

12
From the *Gathasaptasati*, in *Selby, Grow Long, Blessed Night*.

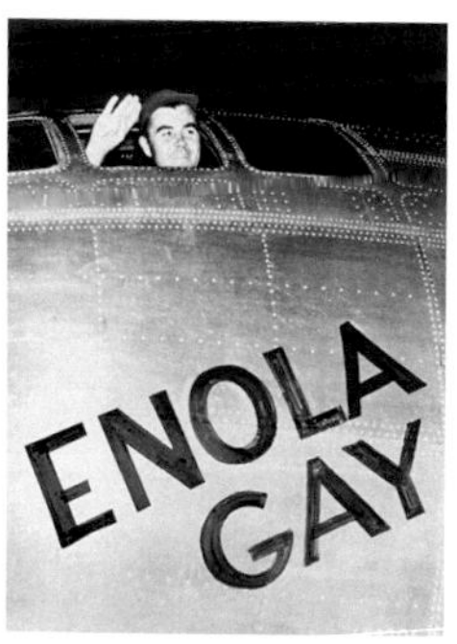

Enola Gay
The namesake of the airplane that dropped the bomb on Hiroshima during WWII, Mrs. Enola Gay Tibbets was a Sagittarius – the sign of the archer, or those who take aim. Source: *Wikimedia Commons*.

13
Dwight D. Eisenhower, 'Address at the Freedoms Foundation' (Waldorf-Astoria, New York, 22 December 1952).

Carnal Selfie

'O pious jewel, have you ever heard of Rabi'a al-Adawiyya?
She used to walk down the streets of Basra in the eighth century,
holding a pitcher of water in one hand and a flaming torch in the other.
When people asked what she was doing, she would say, "I am going to
quench the fires of hell and burn down paradise. For people should not

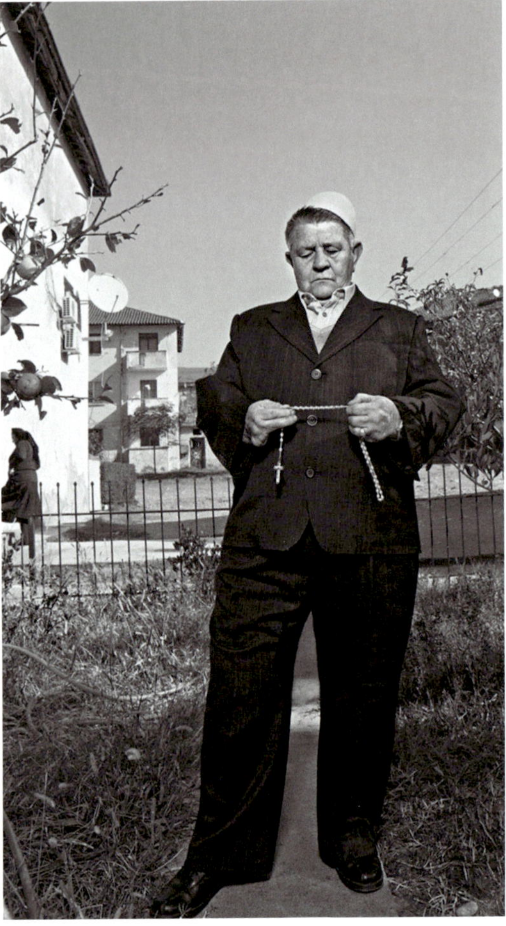

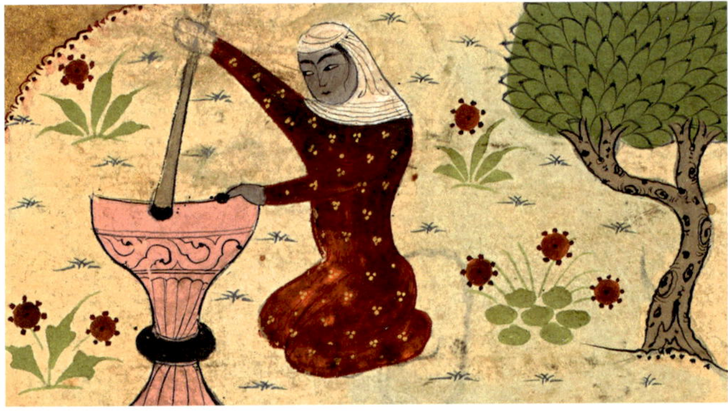

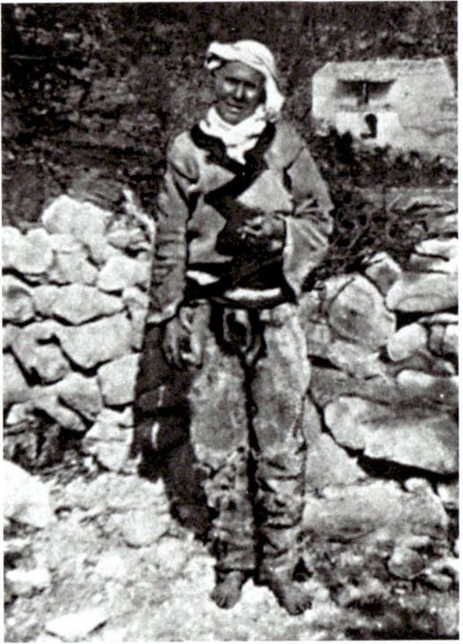

Rabi'a al-Adawiyya The
poet Attar sang her praises:
'If all women were like the one
we have mentioned, / Then
women would be preferred to
men. / For the feminine gender
is no shame for the sun, / Nor
is the masculine gender an
honor for the crescent moon!'
Courtesy Javaz at British
Library.

Another response altogether
to the ills of patriarchal society,
the **Albanian sworn virgins**
take a vow of chastity in order
to enjoy the lifestyle and
benefits of men, which includes
carrying a gun or hanging out
with other men in cafés all day
while women do the brunt of
the work. Sources: Jil Peters
(left). Edith Durham/Royal
Anthropological Institute *(right)*.

worship from fear of punishment or hope of reward, but only for love
of God".[14] When her arm became tired, she would make me hold the
jug. Princess, you must think of paradise as Rabi'a did, as a purely
spiritual state – that of complete union with God. Heaven is like being
milk in milk. To get there, you must obliterate your carnal self, the
wayward, hungry *nafs*. It is one of the three things that are bad when

14
This is my own wording of this
often told / reimagined story of
the Sufi saint Rabi'a. See also
Margaret Smith, *Rabi'a the
Mystic and Her Fellow Saints
in Islam* (Cambridge: Cambridge
University Press, 1928).

Men
are from
Murmansk

Women
are from
Vilnius

they are fat, according to the old sage Yusuf, along with your falcon and your dog. As he put it, "if your carnal self gets a thick neck like a camel stallion, it will drag you wailing to the Fire"'.[15]

'Recite after me: "The country of *I* and *We* forsake; thy home in Annihilation make", as the martyred poetess[16] sang. Rabi'a lived there, sleeping with a brick as a pillow. Her austere hut was like a marsh made from her tears. She depended entirely on God for her subsistence. When, after days of fasting, she was cooking a meal for herself and needed an onion, a bird flew overhead and dropped one into her frying pan, already peeled. Many sought her hand in marriage but she rejected them all. It's said that when Hasan of Basra proposed to her, Rabi'a replied: "The contract of marriage is for those who have a material existence. But I have ceased to exist and have passed out of Self. My existence is in Him, and I am altogether His".[17] How's that for a rejection, O Princess? When she went on hajj, the Ka'ba got up and walked over to meet her along the way. But although Rabi'a lived in celibacy and extreme solitude, many have followed her path while remaining in societal life. At worst, you can consider your marriage to King Rising Sun as a purgative of sorts for the soul, a training in patience, which is one of the steps on the way. But maternity will be for your spiritual benefit. As the Prophet said, "Paradise lies at the feet of mothers"'.

> You are truly the zephyr that wafts from the east and
> opens the way to the hereafter. But I don't see how, in my
> daily life, I could practice this. How could I annihilate
> my self and then put the children to bed?

'The beguine Marguerite Porete imagined it as an act of *decreation* – a metaphysical one – requiring seven steps. "One must crush oneself, hacking and hewing away at oneself to widen the place in which Love will want to be", she advised in *The Mirror of Simple Souls*.[18] "Love dares the self to leave itself behind", as the poet sang.[19] When one has become utterly empty of will, into the void the numinous spirit floods in. In this state of nothingness, Marguerite wrote, "God of his divine majesty sees himself in her, and by him this Soul is so illumined that she cannot see that anyone exists, except only God himself, from whom all things are".[20] The soul becomes the place for the deity's

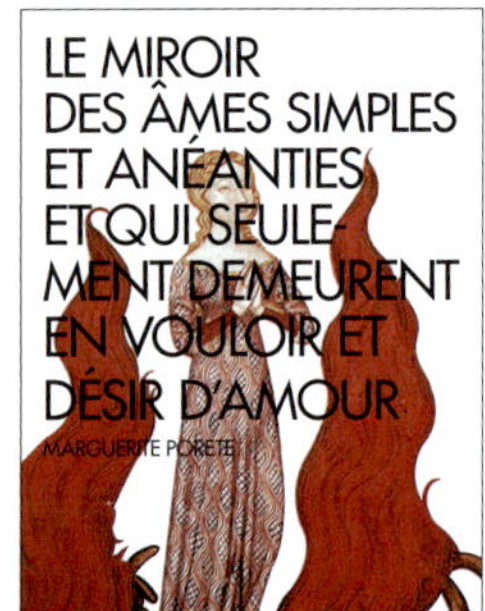

The Mirror of Simple Souls is an early 14th-century work of Christian mysticism by Marguerite Porete. The full title lets slip the love mysticism shared by Christianity and Islam in medieval times. Source: *Éditions Albin Michel*.

15
Cited by Yūsuf Khāss Hājib in *Kutadgu Bilig*.

16
The Iranian poet and theologian Fatimah Baraghani, also called Táhirih. She was executed for her Bábi faith in Tehran in 1852, wearing a bridal dress.

17
A story of Rab'ia told in Attar's *Memoir of the Saints* (*Tadhkirat al-Awliya*), ca. 1200. Cited in Smith, *Rabi'a the Mystic*.

18
Marguerite Porete, *The Mirror of Simple Souls*, trans. Edmund Colledge, Judith Grant, J.C. Marler (Indiana: Notre Dame Press, 1999), 142.

19
Anne Carson, *Decreation* (New York: Knopf, 2005), 162.

20
Porete, *Mirror*, 145–46.

infinite self-reflection: God's mirror. And as the place where God sees God, the soul herself becomes God. So the obliteration of the self is actually a process of deification, a bit like what happened to Solomoniia in her barrenness. Marguerite Porete was burnt at the stake for heresy. But as Al-Kalabadhi said, "He is burnt who feels the fire, but he who is fire, how shall he be burnt?"'[21]

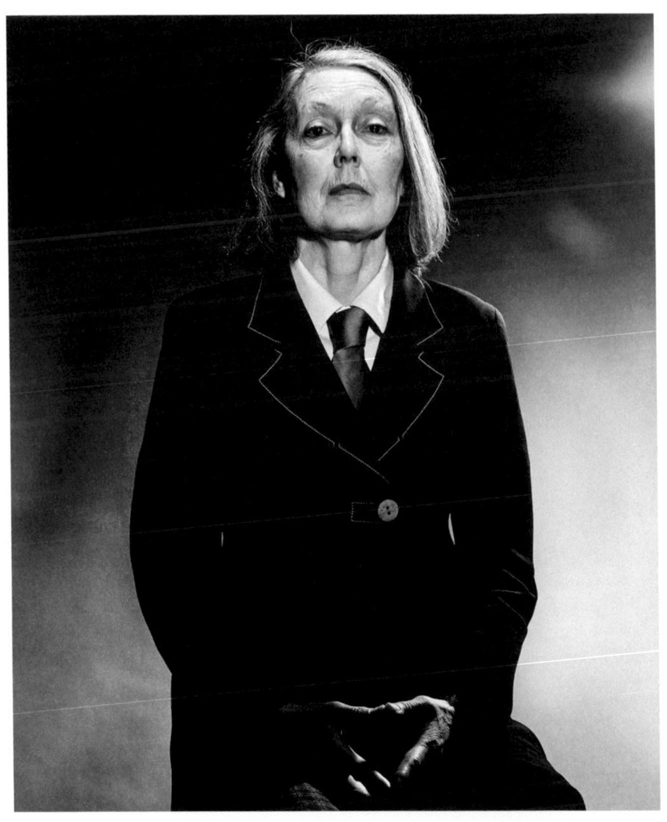

In her work on Sappho, the classicist and poet **Anne Carson** wonders whether it is a coincidence that the Greek poets who first sang of Eros were also the first to leave poems in written form, following the development of the alphabet in the 7th and 6th centuries BCE. "To put the question more pungently, what is erotic about alphabetization?" she asks. Copyright Jeff Brown, published in *The New York Times*.

You are the mirror for this simple soul, the princess marvelled. But I cannot help but wonder, if all people took up such a path, how could the state continue to exist? Would the kingdom dissolve into chaos?

'It's true, princess, all government and even ecclesiastical authority would be totally subverted. I am old and my hair is like the feathers of a seagull. But perhaps there is a way for the realm to still hold together. The way forward, I think, is as a great sage once said: "Man is called to become in the image of an angel"'.[22]

21
Smith, *Rabi'a the Mystic*.

22
Norman O. Brown, *The Challenge of Islam* (Santa Cruz: New Pacific Press, 2009), 98.

Bilgisiz kişinin gönlü kumsal gibidir;
Nehir aksa olmaz, orada ot ve yem bitmez.

نفس الجاهل كالرمال القاحلة؛ لا تنبت فيها الحشائش ولو جرت عليها الأنهار.

But fools' hearts are like a sandy waste: though a river flow into it, it does not fill up and vegetation cannot take root.

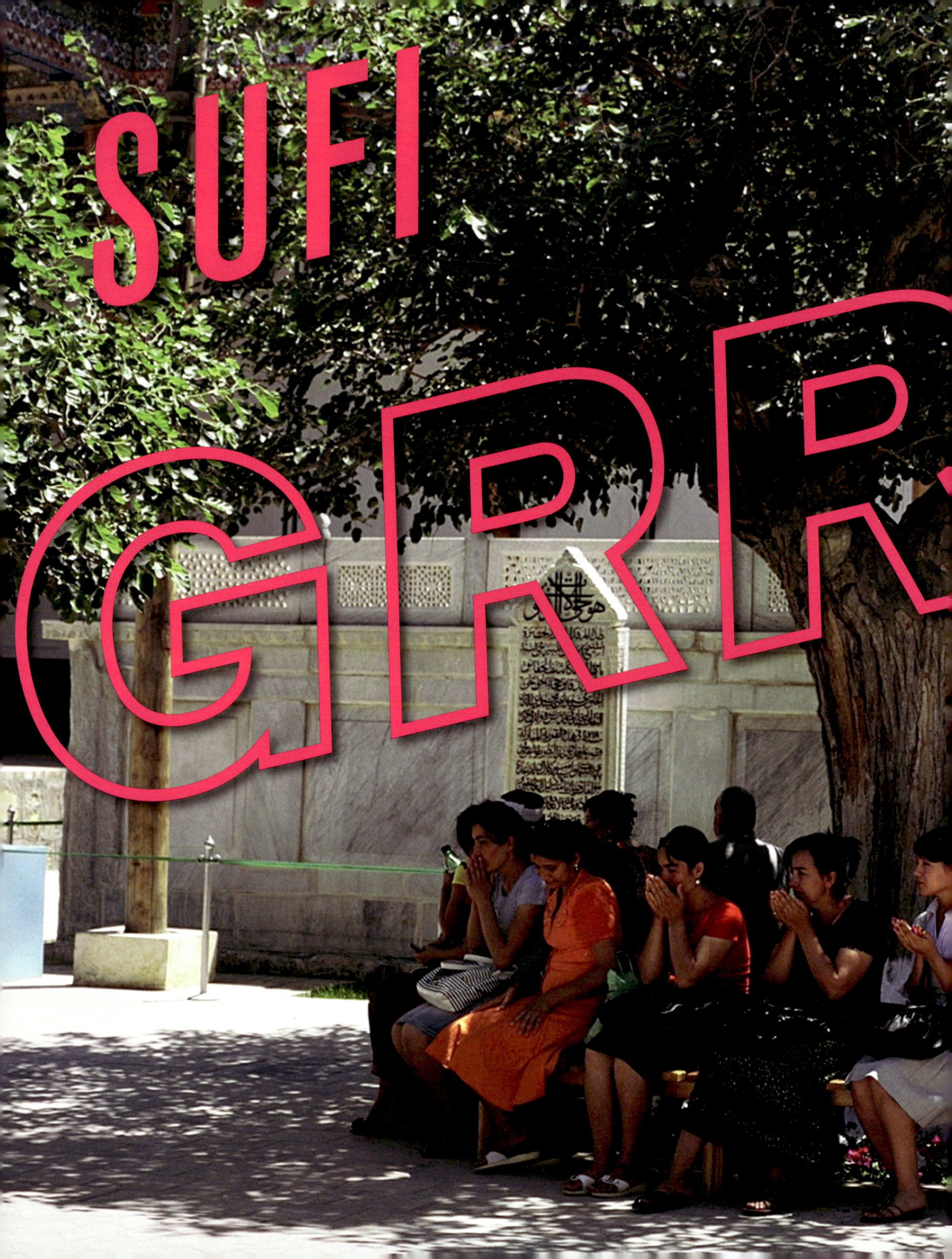

SUFI
GRR

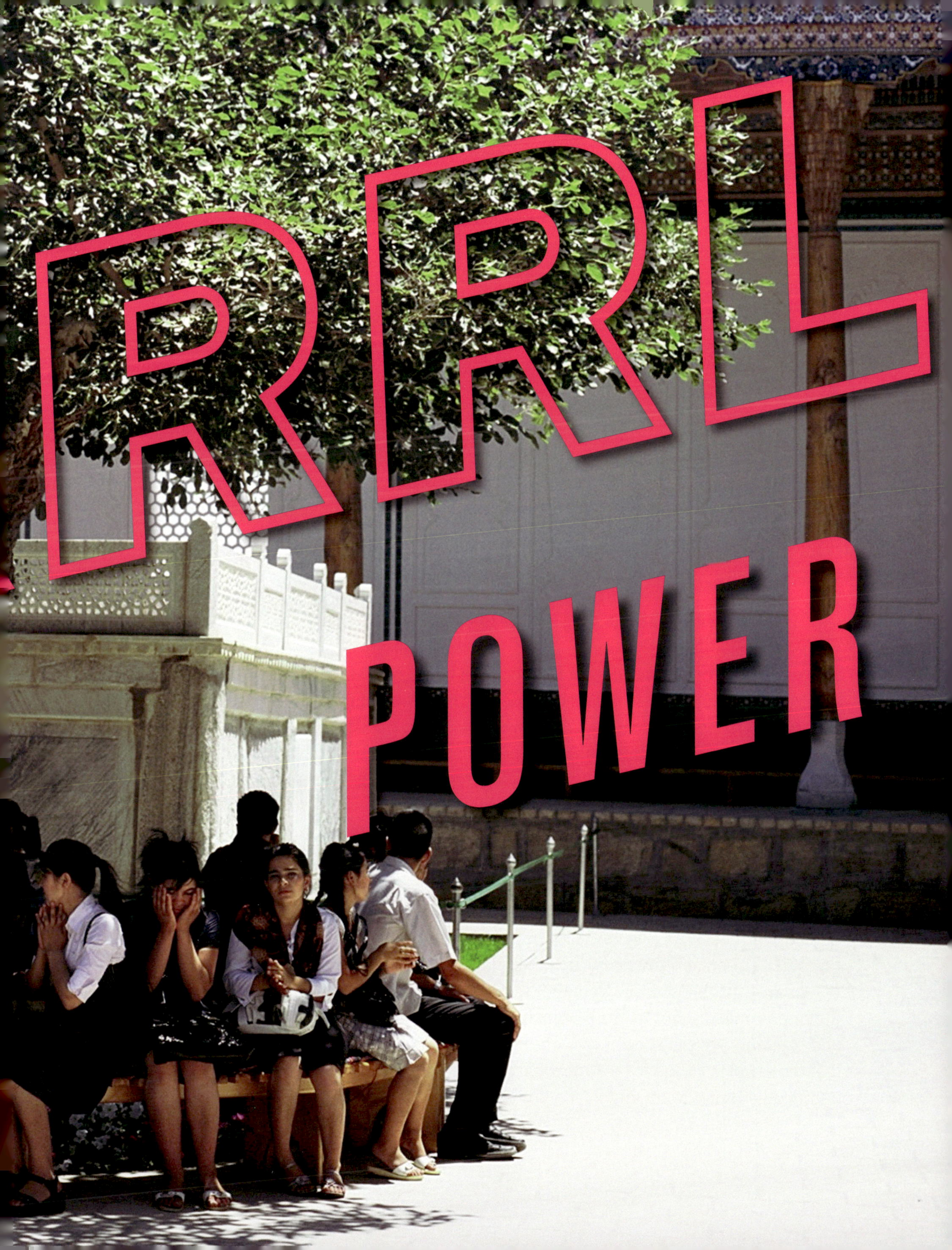
RRL
POWER

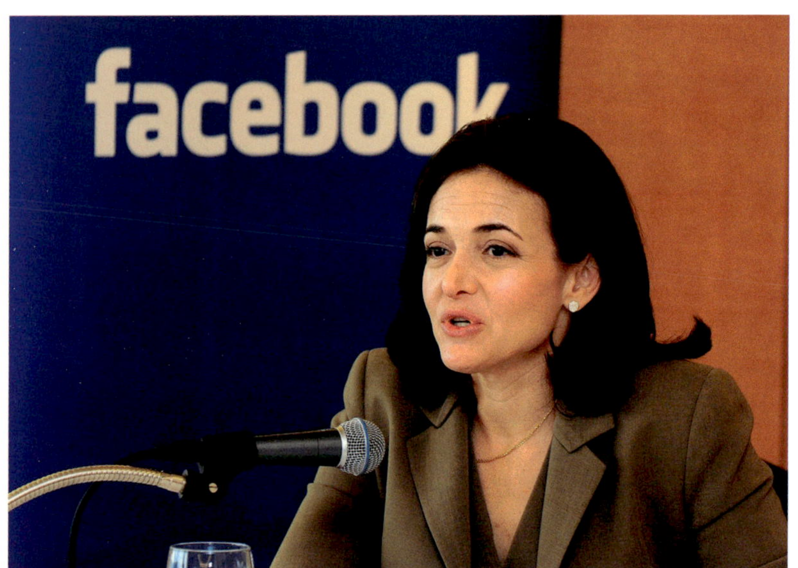

One of the top execs at Facebook, **Sheryl Sandberg** has spoken publicly about her struggles with impostor syndrome. This psychological condition common among women – with its conviction that the world is an illusion and the self a fraud – may actually bring her closer to achieving bodhisattva-hood. Photo by *Yonhap/EPA*, via *Landov*.

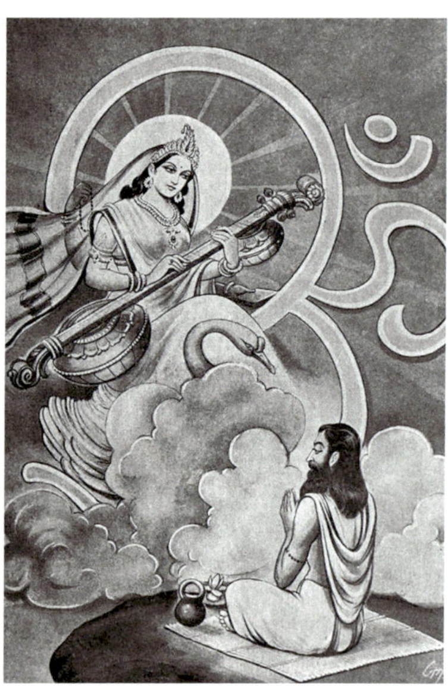

Angelomorphosis
Source: *Wikimedia Commons*.

Angelomorphosis

The wise old woman paced back and forth on the jaguar-skin carpet. 'O Princess, struggling to balance the demands of their careers, families, marriages and faiths, while ever striving to break the glass ceiling, women are often told that perfectionism is what holds them back. As one of the world's most powerful women writes, "Aiming for perfection causes frustration at best and paralysis at worst".[23] She embraces the motto *Done is better than perfect*, and encourages women to let go of unattainable standards. Indeed, my dear Ornament, perfection is impossible: there is no such thing as a perfect princess. But we must reach towards something even greater. Not perfection but angelomorphosis. The princess must strive to become the arched, perfectly groomed brow on the eyes of this world and the next. It's an unrealisable, infinite demand. But attempting to live up to the impossible divides us from ourselves, puts us opposite ourselves, and suddenly we can see our reflections, as in the glass. It's in the mirror that the angel is seen; we become what we behold. And as an apostle once said, "If men were angels, no government would be necessary"'.[24]

23
Sheryl Sandberg, *Lean In: Women, Work, and the Will to Lead* (New York: Knopf, 2013), 126. The COO of Facebook, Sandberg was №9 in Forbes' List of The World's 100 Most Powerful Women for 2014.

24
James Madison, under the pseudonym of Publius, arguing for a constitution that would establish a structure of checks and balances. Excerpt from 'The Federalist, №51' in *The New York Packet*, 8 February 1788.

'New motto: *New Nazareths in us*.[25] The angel is born not in the womb but in an epiphany, through vision. Existing first in the eye, it transfigures us. "I have attained to that which I beheld", spoke Rabi'a from the afterlife to her friends in their sleep'.

Your mind surely has a hundred wings, Highly Aged.
But how will I know when I see the angel?
What do they wear?

'"Do they dye their wings after Forever, tinting their haloes, aging zero without Time, those androgynous angels?"[26] It came to Louis Massignon wearing the phosphorescence of a fish.[27] For Ibn 'Arabi, the angel arrived as a woman. He was walking around the Ka'ba when he met a girl, "a divine initiatrix" with an astral aura, who, speaking with unwavering authority, revealed the secrets of love.[28] No woman more beautiful, more spiritual, more subtle, said Ibn 'Arabi, than this Nizam Ayn al-Shams, "Eye of the Sun". God is seen more perfectly in the form of a woman than a man, he declared As for the Ka'ba, it appeared to hover above the ground, lifting the skirts of its robe like a girl about to jump'.

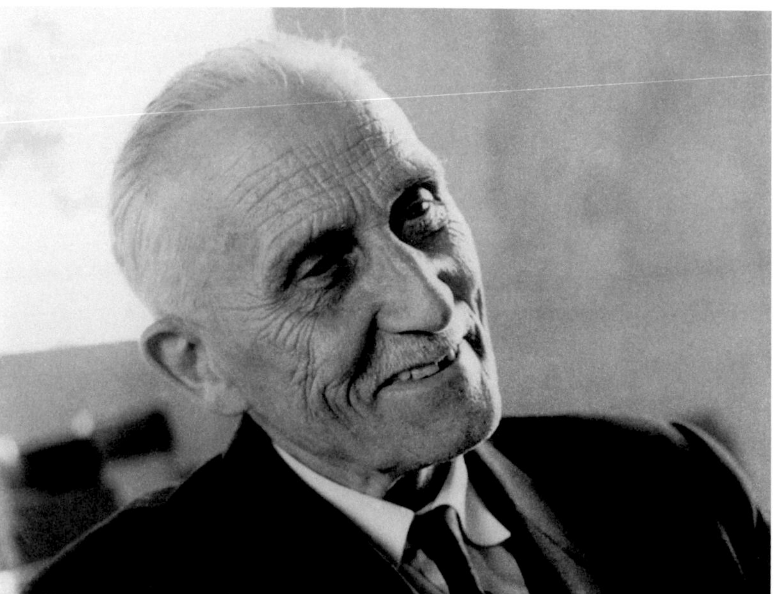

The French Orientalist scholar and Melkite priest **Louis Massignon** wrote to his pen-pal Thomas Merton on New Year's Eve, 1960: 'My case is not to be imitated; I made a duel with our Lord…'. Source: *henryanedechaponay.free.fr*

25
Gerard Manley Hopkins, 'The Blessed Virgin Compared to the Air We Breathe', "*God's Grandeur*" and *Other Poems* (New York: Dover Editions, 1995), 39.

26
From 'Angels' by Agha Shahid Ali (1949–2001). In *The Veiled Suite: The Collected Poems* (New York: W.W. Norton, 2009), 341.

27
'My inner mirror revealed Him to me', wrote Massignon in 'Visitation of the Stranger: Response to an Inquiry about God' (1955). In *Testimonies and Reflections. Essays of Louis Massignon*, ed. and trans. Herbert Mason (Notre Dame, IN: University of Notre Dame Press, 1989), 41.

28
In Henri Corbin, *Creative Imagination in the Sufism of Ibn 'Arabi*, trans. Ralph Manheim (London: Routledge, 1969).

O Highly Aged, "Night is about to throw meteors
at my blurred head"…[29] I fear I must retire to bed.

'Sleep well, my princess, more luminous than a thousand Pleiades. Remember, this is the wisdom that will bring you glory. As a friend once taught me,

> **"A person approaches her perfect nature,**
> **and becomes herself in the truest sense,**
> **by acceding at times to the angel within**
> **her – its flitting presence her only defence**
> **against perfection's petrifaction,**
> **suggests Avicenna's Celestial Ascent**
> **(pun intended), as subtraction leads**
> **her to more than she ever meant."**[30]

Princess Ornament-On-World and Highly Aged retreated to their beds. The whole realm was wrapped in a warm quilt of their splendour. The sky stretched out in his kaftan of cobalt and sequins. The earth put on her sleeping mask, the sun was off in a dream. Meanwhile, the moon summoned her cavalry, the evening dew, and stationed it on top of the flowers. Spurred by the whip of the wind, the fields of the kingdom galloped as they stood.'*

*

I uttered this discourse in the summer of 2014. It took me three sleepless weeks to compose. Taking breaks during the day, I went on walks in the city, allowing my blazing mind to rove. Princesses passed me in the streets, in pink tulle and tiaras, waving inert plastic wands. They ran ahead of their strollers. But over what will they rule? Their mothers, failing to balance the needs of their families and careers, turn to self-help literature, knowing that the state will not help them. But these books don't even have a clue as to what the 'self' is. I thought I could offer something better than their impotent advice. I selected my words carefully, stringing them together like pearls around the neck of an empress. I found the English language to be much like a spotted doe. In the evenings, caught in the light of my desk lamp, I drew her to me, though from time to time she was skittish and fled my grasp. I followed her tracks. Now that I have finished the piece, I present it to you as a gift, rolled up, a small patterned carpet with a bit of fringe. Here I end. A cool breeze rustles my skirt and dries the ink.

Der, der Worte redet verliert seine Seele,
Der Hörende gedeiht, macht stark seinen Körper.

Mówca duszę swą zasmuca,
Ten co słucha, odpoczywa i ciało swe syci.

[29] This line is from the Abbasid poet Abdullah ibn al-Mu'tazz, who ruled as caliph for one day and one night. In *Birds through a Ceiling of Alabaster*, ed. and trans. G.B.H. Wightman and A.Y. Al-Udhari (Baltimore: Penguin Books, 1975), 89. The image of the dew as cavalry is also his.

[30] Peter Cole, 'The Perfect State', *The Invention of Influence* (New York: New Directions, 2014), 88.

Shaggy or Shaved
THE SYMBOLISM OF HAIR AMONG PERSIAN QALANDAR SUFIS[1]

Lloyd Ridgeon

The Qalandars have usually been considered antinomian Sufis, a view that may have been perpetuated by their shocking appearance (the shaving of head hair, eyebrows, moustache and beard), that is, the so-called four shaves, *chahār-ẓarb*, which runs against the normative Islamic tradition. This paper briefly highlights the significance of hair in the Islamic tradition with reference to the sacred sources (the Qur'ān Ḥadīth and biographies of the Prophet). Subsequently the general Sufi perspective on hair is considered, and then the study focuses on the Qalandars. Following a brief investigation of the term, four seemingly different Qalandar explanations for the origins of the *chahār-ẓarb* are presented. Despite the apparent dissimilarity in these emic sources, it is argued that they hold significant parallels. An understanding of the contents of these stories reveals the Qalandars to be located firmly within a normative Sufi tradition; rather than having an unbounded, intoxicated and antinomian lifestyle, these stories suggest that the Qalandars were deeply attached to Qur'ānic and Islamic referents, and wished to uphold an ethic by which they were able to devote their focus to the divine.

The believers of many of the major religious traditions are frequently identified simply through the way their hair has been groomed, cut, shaved, coloured or left untouched. For example, the Jewish male often has distinctive ringlets, the Hindu ascetic sports long matted hair, the Christian monk boasts a tonsure, the Buddhist monk is completely shaven, and the Sikh has his hair

1

This paper first appeared in the *Journal of Iran and the Caucasus*, vol. 14, № 2 (2010): 233–63. I would like to thank Dr. David Shankland for reading an initial version, and for suggesting various ways in which it could be developed. I am also very grateful to Dr. Richard Gauvain, whose insights and recommendations shaped much of this paper. Any errors, misunderstandings or deficiencies, however, are mine alone.

collected beneath a turban. Hair is a distinguishing feature, a marker of difference over a whole range of classifying features such as belief, practice, social status, age, gender and ethnicity. Even in the contemporary secular West, when religion plays a less prominent role in society than in the premodern period, hair remains an important symbol of social aspirations. Social comments with hair have been made by hippies with long, unkempt hair in the 1960s, by Afro-Caribbeans with big afro-style hair in the 1970s, and by punk rockers with their mohicans in the late 1970s. The symbolic significance of hair is manifested in the present age within many societies.[2]

Hair is a topic rich with potential for interesting research, and many of the well-known contemporary ethnographic studies have tended to focus on Asian traditions.[3] In Islamicate traditions, hair has not attracted much scholarly attention,[4] although an associated topic, the *ḥijāb*, is one of the most controversial and sometimes acrimonious discussions in the contemporary period. While interest has surrounded the issue of female sexuality and hair (and purity) in the modern era,[5] it was male hair that resulted in some debate in the medieval period, within Sufi circles at least. This was because a group of Sufis engaged in a ritual of shaving the hair of the head, eyebrows, beard and moustache, the so-called four shaves, which made them instantly recognisable in society and set them apart from other Muslims. These individuals were known as *Qalandars*, a term that emerged as a literary trope in the tenth to the eleventh centuries.[6]

QUR'ĀN, ḤADĪTH AND SĪRA

The Qur'ān does not offer specific instructions to Muslims about how believers should grow or cut their hair. There are references to shaving the head at the end of the *hajj* pilgrimage at Mecca (2.196; 48.27), but it is in the *Ḥadīth* and *Sīra* literature that issues related to hair are considered in more detail. (The veracity of these reports is not of concern here, since most Muslims in the medieval period when the Qalandars appeared would have assessed these reports using their own methods to verify their historical authenticity.) That Muḥammad

2
On the recent '*Modesty and the Veil Festival*' in Iran, promoting suitable hairstyles for males, see *The Times* (6 July 2010): 31.

3
Edmund Leach, 'Magical Hair', *The Journal of the Royal Anthropological Institute of Great Britain and Ireland*, vol. 88, № 2 (1958): 147–64; Paul Hershman, '*Hair, Sex and Dirt*', Man, vol. 9, № 2 (1974): 274–98; G. Obeyesekere, *Medusa's Hair* (Chicago: University of Chicago Press, 1981); A. Hiltebeitel and B. Miller, eds., *Hair: Its Power and Meaning in Asian Culture* (Albany: State University of New York Press, 1998).

4
Exceptions include: I. Pfluger-Schindlbeck, 'On the Symbolism of Hair in Islamic Societies: An Analysis of Approaches', *Anthropology of the Middle East*, vol. 1, № 2 (2006): 72–88; and Carol Delaney, 'Untangling the Meanings of Hair in Turkish Society', *Anthropological Quarterly*, vol. 67, № 4 (1994): 159–72.

5
Julie Marcus, *A World of Difference: Islam and Gender Hierarchy in Turkey* (London: Allen & Unwin, 1992).

6
J. T. P. de Bruijn, 'The *Qalandariyyāt* in Persian Mystical Poetry, from Sanā'ī Onwards', in L. Lewisohn, ed., *The Legacy of Medieval Persian Sufism* (London: Khanaqah Nimatullahi Publishing, 1992), 75–86.

was a model for believers meant that his conduct and
his presentation provided the ideal to emulate. The *Sīra*
includes passages in which Muḥammad is described
as having hair that was neither 'too curly nor lank, but
definitely curly',[7] and tradition held that 'the plaits of
his hair were parted'.[8] Moreover, Ḥadīths confirm that
he was meticulous in grooming his hair,[9] and he is
reported to have said: 'He who has hair should honour
it'.[10] Muḥammad also gave recommendations for cutting
and clipping head hair, the moustache and beard before a
period of forty nights had elapsed.[11] There are indications
that Muḥammad was aware of the symbolic significance
that hair could have. The simple principle of belonging,
of insider and outsider, is apparent in several anecdotes.
For example, it is said that the Jews and Christians used to
let their hair fall down, while the heathens parted it, and
Muḥammad followed the ways of the People of the Book
on matters upon which he had no specific instructions from
God. So he used to let his hair fall down without parting it,
but subsequently he did part it (probably in the Medinan
period when relations between Muslims and the People of
the Book were less than harmonious).[12] In addition, it is
reported that Muḥammad used to clip his moustache, and
a Magian came to him and said: 'You ought to clip your
beard and allow your moustaches to grow', but Muḥammad
replied: 'My Lord commands me to clip the moustaches
and allow the beard to grow'.[13] The significance of all of
these reports is simply that Muḥammad enjoined Muslims
to pay suitable attention to their hair, ensuring that it was
clean, orderly and of a relatively short length. In addition,
moustaches and beards were to be grown, but facial hair
was to be kept neat and tidy. This was the model, or pattern,
for believers to emulate.

More than this, there are indications that the early Muslims
believed that Muḥammad's head hair possessed *baraka*,
or a form of holy power. There are traditions that relate
how his hair was carefully collected after it was cut
or shaved and used as an amulet.[14] Moreover, it is also
related that, 'When the Prophet had his beard shaven and
his companions surrounded him, they never suffered a
single hair to fall to the ground but seized them as good
omens or for a blessing. And since his Excellency had his
hair cut only at the time of pilgrimage, this had become
sunna'.[15] The traditional association of hair with power
may be linked to the custom of cutting the newborn's first
hair ('aqīqa), and this may be connected with both the idea

7
Ibn Hishā, *The Life of Muhammad*, trans. Alfred Guillaume (Oxford: Oxford University Press, 1955), 725–26.

8
Annemarie Schimmel, *And Muhammad is His Messenger* (Chapel Hill: University of North Carolina Press, 1985), 34.

9
Muhammad Ibn Ismail Al-Bukhari, *The Translation of the Meanings of Sahih Al-Bukhari*, trans. Muhammad Muhsin Khan (Lahore: Kazi Publications, 1986), 7.745.

10
Abu Dawud, Sunan, Book 33, *On Combing the Hair* (*Kitāb Tarajjul*), №4151. See: http://www.scribd.com/doc/33710880/Sunan-Abu-Dawud-Book-33-Combing-the-Hair-Kitab-Tarajjul/ (accessed 5 November 2014).

11
Ibid.

12
William Muir, *The Life of Mahomet and History of Islam to the Era of the Hegira*, vol. 6 (London: n.p., 1861), 331; Ibn Taymiyya, 'Iqtiḍā al-ṣirāt al-mustaqīm', Riyadh, vol. 1 (1991): 413, 416, 420–21.

13
Muir, ibid., 332.

14
Samuel Zwemer, 'Hairs of the Prophet', *Ignace Goldziher Memorial Volume*, Part 1, eds. S. Löwinger and J. Somogyi (Budapest: n.p., 1948): 50.

15
Ibid.

كۆپ سۆز لەپتىن بىلىن تالىغ بولىدۇ. كىشى تاڭلاپ بىلىن كىسىنىڭ بېشى كېتىدۇ.

of controlling and sharing this power. The ʿaqīqa ritual involved the weighing of the cut hair and the equivalent weight (in silver or gold) was donated in alms, and a sheep was also sacrificed and the meat donated to the needy.[16]

The Qur'ān has very little to say about hair, although Schimmel notes that there is a mention of the forelock (in 96.15–16) and, indeed, the portrayal of the forelock (nāṣīya) is negative, suggesting that it held a power that required some control: 'And yet, indeed, if he does not desist. We shall drag him by the forelock. By the lying, the sinful forelock'.[17] Schimmel adds that in the Islamic tradition, grasping someone by the forelock was 'to hold his most power-laden part, that is, to overcome him completely'.[18] The power of hair may have something to do with the realisation that hair is a liminal material, that is to say, it is dead and has no sensation, yet it is somehow powerful enough to grow, one of the indications of life.[19]

Interpreting the power of hair has resulted in different perspectives, ranging from linkages with the holy (as in the baraka associated with Muḥammad's hair) to something more base and animalistic. Schimmel argued that it is due to the hair's power that Muslim men are not supposed to enter a sacred place with the head uncovered.[20] Thus, a fez, turban or cap is worn with a small prayer cap underneath. On the other hand, a possible conceptual link between hair and animals (and irrational, nonhuman behaviour) is evident in early Islamic texts, such as the report of Wahb b. Munabbih (d. 14) who narrated the travels of Dhu al-Qarnayn to the mythical creatures of Gog and Magog, which, among other animalistic features (claws and big sharp teeth), were hairy. Their big hairy ears were used as clothes, and males and females would 'have sex whenever they met, like beasts'.[21]

It is evident that the symbolism of hair in the Islamicate traditions contains a wealth of meanings, and this essay focuses solely on one aspect, namely the Qalandar perspective. However, to fully appreciate the significance of hair within the Qalandar worldview, it is necessary to investigate very briefly the general Sufi position.

16
Th. W. Juynboll and J. Pedersen, 'Akika', *Encyclopaedia of Islam 2*, ed. H.A.R. Gibb, vol. I (London: Luzak, 1960): 337; Ibn Rushd, *Bidāyat al-Mujtahid wa Nihāyat al-Muqtaṣid* (*The Distinguished Jurist's Primer*), trans. Imran Nyazee, vol. I (Reading: Garnet, 2006): 560–62; Schimmel, *And Muhammad is His Messenger*, 181.

17
The forelock is also mentioned in 11.56.

18
Schimmel, *And Muhammad is His Messenger*, 181.

19
On the symbolic value of the forelock in the Yezidi ritual, see Garnik S. Asatrian, 'The Holy Brotherhood: The Yezidi Religious Institution of the "Brother" and the "Sister" of the Next World', *Iran and Caucasus*, vols. 3–4 (Boston: Brill, 1999–2000): 85ff.

20
Schimmel, *And Muhammad is His Messenger*, 94.

21
Brannon Wheeler, *Prophets in the Qu'ran* (New York: Continuim, 2002), 234.

THE SUFI PERSPECTIVE

The Sufi tradition of the medieval period contains much material relating to hair, but it seems that the Sufis grew their beards and moustaches, and cut their hair at regular intervals. That the celebrated Persian mystic Jalāl al-Dīn Rūmī (d. 274) sported hair, moustache and beard, is supported in an anecdote contained in Shams al-Dīn Aḥmad Aflākī's hagiography of the great poet, in which he instructs the barber to cut his facial hair in such a way that only enough remained to tell the difference between a man and woman. Interestingly, Aflākī continued:

> Another day he [Rūmī] said, 'I am jealous of the qalandars because they have no beard'. And he recited the following tradition: It is a man's good fortune if he has a thin beard because the beard is an adornment for a man and if it is large he becomes conceited, and that is a form of perdition. And he said: 'An abundant beard is pleasing to the Sufis, but by the time a Sufi has combed out his beard, a knower of God had already reached God'.[22]

Rūmī's warnings about nurturing pride by paying attention to facial hair are reflected in a number of other cases.[23] For example, the celebrated Sufi, Abū Ḥafṣ 'Umar Suhrawardī (d. 234), instructed trainees in the Sufi-futuwwat associations that mushroomed in Persian- and Turkish-speaking lands between the thirteenth and sixteenth centuries AD[24] not to fiddle with their moustaches or beards when in the presence of their master, yet the trainee should possess at all times a comb so that he may groom his moustache and beard.[25] Some of these Sufi-futuwwat associations restricted entry to those whose appearance conformed to the ideal male image. For example, a Persian *futuwwat-nāma* states:

> There are other people too for whom futuwwat is impermissible because they have no beard. This is because the Prophet said: 'No futuwwat, no man'. First, [God] gave futuwwat to Adam. When the Truth brought Adam and Eve from the hiding of nonexistence to existence there was no beard on his face, and they say that Eve did not respect him,

22

Shams al-Dīn Aḥmad Aflākī, *The Feats of the Knowers of God (Manāqeb al-ʿārefīn)*, trans. John O'Kane (Leiden: Brill, 2002), 284.

23

See also the story in *'Aṭṭār's Manṭiq al-Ṭayr* about the old man who loved his beard very much, but did not enjoy spiritual ecstasy. He asked Moses the reason for this, and the Prophet was told by God that the old man had not attained a high level of spiritual insight because of the attention he paid to his beard. On hearing this, the old man started to tear out his beard, but Gabriel indicated to Moses that this reaction was just as bad, because it indicated that the old man was still thinking about his beard. The primary purpose of the spiritual life is God and not those things that orientate the individual towards the divine. Peter Avery, *The Speech of the Birds* (Cambridge: The Islamic Texts Society, 1998), 265–66.

24

For these Sufi-futuwwat associations, see Lloyd Ridgeon, *Morals and Mysticism in Persian Sufism: A History of Sufi-futuwwat* (London: Routledge, 2010), 61–91. Briefly, however, the Sufi-futuwwat organisations were urban groups of males who had their own forms of ritual initiation and clothing, and engaged in forms of Sufi activity, such as the *samāʿ* and dhikr. Such groups appear to have been focused on those who did not desire to engage in Sufi activity on a full-time basis.

25

M. Ṣarrāf, ed., *Rasāʾel-e javānmardān* (Tehran: n.p., 1991), 145, 162.

nor was she afraid. Adam complained,
'Oh God! Eve does not respect me'. God Most
High granted Adam a beard, and when Eve saw
Adam's blessed beard, fear and wonder fell into
her heart, and after that without saying anything,
she had such modesty before Adam that they say
she never spoke a word to his face, and she never
smiled in front of his beard.[26]

That Sufis were very conscious of hair may be linked to
their perception of God in the mundane world, especially
in beautiful faces.[27] In Sufi Persian poetry, the face of
the Beloved (God) was framed, hidden or highlighted
by the locks or tresses. Such a focus is worthy of lengthy
consideration, for if Islamicate tradition is weak in
iconography or painting, it certainly compensates in
its poetry. The amount of Sufi verse in both Arabic and
Persian languages testifies to a tradition that spiritually
visualised God in an anthropomorphic fashion. The trope
of the flowing tresses of the Beloved was one of the most
popular found in this tradition, perhaps because of the
ambivalence or multivocality of its message. On the one
hand the tress (*zulf*) of the Beloved brings raptures to the
lover, and yet the same tress conceals His face.[28] This is an
example of the hide-and-seek played by lovers, but which
was utilised by the Sufis to demonstrate the manifest and
nonmanifest dimension (or immanence and transcendence)
of God. As Rūmī says: 'When I passed beyond my
intellect, I seized the end of His tresses / Now I am caught,
captured by His curls; The Banner of Thy tresses veils
Thy Beauty / Otherwise Thy light would shine forth'.[29]

These descriptions of the Beloved stand in contrast
to the appearance of the Sufi, some of whom appeared
to have shaved their heads, as indicated by Kāshī
(who lived in the fourteenth century), who commented
that shaving the head (*ḥulq-e sar*) was the custom in
Sufism but not in futuwwat.[30] A number of famous
medieval Sufis, including Majd al-Dīn Baghdādī (d. 209)
and Yaḥyā bin Aḥmad Bākharzī (d. ca. 1335–6), have left
sufficient evidence in their writings to indicate that shaving
the head in the wider Sufi tradition was not the exception.

26
Afshārī and M. Madāyenī,
eds., (1381), *Čahārdah resāle
dar bāb-i fotowwat wa aṣnāf*
(Tehran: n.p., 2002), 90–91.

27
The *shāhid* (or witness) is
the individual who presents the
lover with the proof of God's
manifestation. The famous Sufi,
Ibn 'Arabī (d. 240), recollected
his sentiments about the beautiful
Iranian woman from Isfahan,
Niẓām, in his *Tarjumān al-
ashwāq*: 'Every time I mention
a name it is her I am naming.
Every time I refer to an abode
it is her abode I am describing',
and he adds: 'in composing these
verses my allusions throughout
were to divine inspirations and
spiritual revelations'. See Claude
Addas, *The Quest for the Red
Sulphur* (Cambridge: Islamic
Texts Society, 1993), 209.

28
The *zulf* was utilised as a
metaphor by poets writing in
Persian at a very early stage in
the history of Persian poetry.
It appears in the works of Rūdakī
(d. ca. 941), Anvarī (d. 189) and
Khāqānī (d. 199) and it was also
adopted by Sufi poets such as
Sanā'ī (d. 131) and Rūmī. See
Dehkhodā (1373), 'Zulf', *Loyat-
nāme*, vol. 8 (Tehran, n.p., 1994),
11357–60.

29
Rūmī (1363), *Dīvān-i Šams*,
3rd ed., ed. B. Forūzānfar
(Tehran: n.p., 1982), 14951,
21768.

30
Ṣarrāf, *Rasā'el-e
javānmardān*, 15.

THE QALANDARS

Although the practice of shaving the head seems to have been common among the Sufis, the Qalandars took the shaving of hair to an extreme, as their custom of the *chahār-żarb* gave them a distinctive appearance. Whereas the shaved head of the Sufi was no doubt concealed by a turban or head covering,[31] the Qalandar was readily identified as he would have had no beard, moustache or eyebrows. The unusual appearance of the Qalandars must have seemed appropriate for individuals whose image in Persian literature from the tenth century onwards was antinomian and nonconformist. The term *Qalandar* was used by Persian poets as a trope to refer to a dissolute and destitute individual who cared little for social etiquette or the laws of the Sharī'a.[32]

The following quatrain is one of the first uses of the term, and it comes from the middle of the twelfth century when Ibn Munawwar wrote a biography of Abū Sa'īd ibn abi'l Khayr (967–1049)   thus, it is possible that the term was in currency as early as the tenth century:

> I had tuppence,
>> but was one penny short,
> Two pitchers of wine I bought,
>> a trifle short.
> On my lute the high string,
>> but the low strings are gone,
> So don't tell me of
>> the qalandar's woes.[33]

Aḥmad Ghazālī (d. 126) offered more on the person who became known as a Qalandar, and linked this clearly with recognisable Sufi terminology:

> This is the lane of blame,
>> the field of annihilation;
> This is the street where gamblers
>> bet everything in one go.
> The courage of a qalandar,
>> clothed in rags is needed
> To pass through in bold
>> and fearless manner[34]

31
Many Iranians associate Qalandars with Rūmī's story in the *Mathnawī* about a parrot and a bald dervish. In this story, the parrot's head feathers have fallen out following an altercation with its owner, and the bird subsequently refuses to speak until it sees a dervish in a woollen garment with a bald (or shaved?) head. However, there is no evidence in the text that Rūmī's intention was to portray a Qalandar dervish. See: Rūmī, *The Mathnawī of Jalalu'ddin Rumi*, ed. R. A. Nicholson (Leiden; London: Cambridge University Press, 1925–40), 347–61.

32
Katherine Pratt Ewing, *Arguing Sainthood* (Durham; London: Duke University Press, 1997), 230–52. A recent study has offered two possibilities for the origin of the term *Qalandar*, and both express the idea that it was a location rather than a person. See M. Shafī'ī-Kadkanī (1386), *Qalandariyya dar tārīx*, (Tehran: n.p., 2007): 3749. The first is that the word is derived from *Kā-langar*, which means a place, such as a lodge or a *khānaqāh*. The second is that the word comes from *kālanjar*, meaning the black fort in Hindi, because the word appeared in Persian for the first time when Maḥmūd of Ghaza was attacking India in the early eleventh century. The first usages of the word indicate that Qalandar was a place where the marginalised, the roughs and outcasts congregated, and those who frequented the Qalandar were termed *Qalandarī*. Soon these terms were adopted by some Sufis and men of letters to designate a place where spiritual truths were discovered.

33
Slightly adapted translation from O'Kane's translation in *The Feats of the Knowers of God* (Manāqeb al-'ārefīn), 153.

34
J. T. P. de Bruijn, *Persian Sufi Poetry* (Richmond: Curzon, 1997), 74.

Dinlemek kulak için bir zevktir;
Çok söz söylemekte fayda yoktur.

ولكن لا خير في كثرة الكلام

الإصغاء متعة للأذن

Listening provides pleasure to the ear,
but there is no profit in too much speaking.

'Ayn al-Quḍāt Hamadānī (d. 131) cited approvingly
a quatrain of Yūsuf 'Amarī:

> **In the alley of taverns [there is no
> difference between] dervish and shah.
> In the path of unity [there is no difference
> between] obedience and sin. Before the
> Throne [of God, there is no difference
> between] the sun and moon. [And there
> is no difference if] a qalandar's cheek is
> black or white.**[35]

Similar ideas of wine-drinking individuals frequenting
disreputable places and engaging in illicit practices were
expressed by Sanā'ī (d. 131), and included references
to spiritual leaders of the Qalandar rite, a *mi'rāj* into
the heavens and drinking in taverns. Verses such as
those cited, and other references, are best understood
as 'originally daring imagery, derived perhaps from
secular poetry, [which developed] into items of a set of
symbolic allegories'.[36] But it was in the thirteenth century
that the Qalandar movement seems to have emerged as a
social phenomenon, and gave expression to the idea of life
copying art (or literature).

The appearance of the Qalandars at this historical juncture
may well be related to the increasing appeal of Sufism
among the masses, and the acceptance by leading Sufis
of the participation by the general public in certain Sufi
rituals, permitting them some dispensations or relaxation
of the Sufis' normally exacting rules and requirements.
It was perhaps in conjunction with this that structured Sufi
brotherhoods began to emerge in the twelfth century, a
feature of which was a degree of order, formalisation and
centralisation.[37] It is possible, therefore, that the very early
Qalandar movement was an attempt to revive a rigorous
and ascetic spiritual lifestyle, as opposed to the perceived
weakened yet centralised and rigid Sufi life.[38] The origins
of the movement lie with two individuals native to Iran,
Quṭb al-Dīn Ḥaydar (d. ca. 1200) and Jamāl al-Dīn Sāwī
(d. ca. 1232–3). The information that has been passed down
about these two Qalandars should be treated with a degree
of caution because the sources were written at least a
century after the end of their lives.[39]

From its origins in the medieval period, groups of
Qalandars spread across Islamic lands, and diversity

35
'Ayn al-Quḍāt, *Hamadānī* (1373),
ed. 'Afīf 'Osayrān Tamhīdat
(Tehran: n.p.,
1994), 228.

36
J. T. P. de Bruijn, 'The
Qalandariyyāt in Persian
Mystical Poetry, from Sanā'ī
Onwards', *The Legacy of
Medieval Persian Sufism*,
ed. L. Lewisohn (London:
Khaniqahi-Nimatullahi
Publications, 1992), 7586.
Slightly adapted translation
from O'Kane in Aflākī's
*The Feats of the Knowers
of God*, 153.

37
One of the great proponents of
this kind of Sufism was Shaykh
Abū Ḥafṣ 'Umar Suhrawardī,
and it is not surprising that he
was a vehement opponent of
the Qalandar movement. See
Karamustafa, *God's Unruly
Friends*, 34.

38
See the introduction to the
futuwwat-nāma of Shaykh Abū
Ḥafṣ 'Umar Suhrawardī in Lloyd
Ridgeon, *Javānmardī: A Sufi
Code of Honour* (Edinburgh:
Edinburgh University Press,
2011); Karamustafa, *God's
Unruly Friends*, 2538.

39
Information on Quṭb al-Dīn
Ḥaydar is found in *Khayr al-
majālis*, which was compiled
after 1353, while the details
of Jamāl al-Dīn Sāwī are in
a versified Persian biography
of him by Khaṭīb Fārisī (born
1297–8). See Karamustafa,
God's Unruly Friends, 3949.

of ritual related to the *chahār-ẓarb* appeared among the various denominations of Qalandars.[40] Qalandars were known under different names, including *Abdāls*, *Jāmīs*, *Shams-i Tabrīzis* and *Bektāshīs* in Ottoman territories, the *Jawālaqīyya* and *Ḥaydarīyya* in Persian-speaking lands, the *Jalālīyya* and *Madārīyya* in India, and the *Naqshbandī* Qalandars who seem to have existed in Central Asia.[41] By the late medieval period and into the seventeenth and eighteenth centuries, the Qalandars continued to be associated with an antinomian lifestyle, which did not conform to the *Sharī'a*. One Russian subject visiting Isfahan during the mid-seventeenth century testified to the 'deviancy' of Qalandar life:

'[The Qalandars] went barefoot and naked, wearing only a sheepskin with the fur outwards flung over their shoulders. On their heads they put hideous caps, in their hands they carried sticks and spears and axes, and in their ears they stuck big crystal stones. Their appearance was terrible, as though mad and evil. By day they would walk around the Maydān-i Shāh and bazaar, and would eat and drink little, at night they would drink wine and fornicate'.[42]

QALANDAR EXPLANATIONS FOR THE ORIGIN OF SHAVING

In this section four different versions for the origin of the shave will be presented. The first is based on the accounts related to the two individuals (Quṭb al-Dīn Ḥaydar and Jamāl al-Dīn Sāwī) who are associated with the first appearance of the Qalandars in the medieval period. This version is then followed by other Qalandar – or Qalandar-inspired – accounts, which I have ordered on the basis of the chronology of individuals mentioned in the texts (Adam, Muḥammad and Ḥusayn), rather than the age of the texts themselves.

40
See the introduction to the *futuwwat-nāma* of Shaykh Abū Ḥafṣ Umar Suhrawardī (Ridgeon, *Morals and Mysticism in Persian Sufism*; Karamustafa, *God's Unruly Friends*, 2538). The literature in English on the Qalandars is very limited. Among works that are worth investigating are S. Digby, 'Qalandar Related Groups: Elements of Social Deviance in the Religious Life of the Delhi Sultanate of the Thirteenth and Fourteenth Centuries', *Islam in Asia*, ed. Yohannan Friedman, vol. I, (Jerusalem: Magnes Press, 1984): 87–98; Gunnar Jarring, *Dervish and Qalandar: Texts from Kashghar* (Stockholm: Almqvist & Wiksell International, 1987); Karamustafa, *God's Unruly Friends*; in Persian, see Zarrīnkūb 1990: 359–79; Shafī'ī-Kadkanī, *Qalandariyya dar tārīx*: 3479.

41
For these groups, see Afshārī and Mīr'ābedīnī, *Čahārdah resāle dar bāb-i fotowwat wa aṣnāf*, 54–63; cf. also Karamustafa, *God's Unruly Friends*, 70–78.

42
Cited in Mehdi Keyvani, *Artisans and Guild Life in the Later Safavid Period: contributions to the social-economic history of Persia* (Berlin: Klaus Schwartz, 1982), 54.

I. QUṬB AL-DĪN ḤAYDAR

Quṭb al-Dīn Ḥaydar seems to have spent all of his life around the region of Zawa in Khurasan. The story of his life is simple: it consists of him ascending a mountain as a youth, and never completely returning to everyday existence. He agreed to see his parents provided that they moved to the foot of the mountain, but otherwise his existence was one of seclusion. In these circumstances he was free to distance himself from the dictates of the *Sharī'a*, and the sources describe how he used only leaves to cover his body and would eat what nature provided for him. The association with leaves perhaps suggested to authors at a later stage that it was Quṭb al-Dīn who was responsible for discovering how to use cannabis leaves as an intoxicant, which was a practice that came to be associated with Qalandars.[43] He was also known for his ascetic practices, which were designed to control his carnal soul (*nafs*), and his followers subsequently designed various iron implements to perform this function, both physically and symbolically. Such iron implements included collars, bracelets, belts and rings – some of which were placed around the genitals.[44] Another feature of this early Qalandar ascetic was a prototype of the *chahār-ẓarb*, which involved the burning or scorching of the beard, but leaving the moustache to grow.[45] This practice reflected that of the pre-Islamic Zoroastrians and contrasted with the model provided by Muḥammad, according to the *ḥadīth* cited previously.[46] It can only be speculated that Quṭb al-Dīn Ḥaydar's practice was a specific challenge to a tradition which he felt had become petrified and had lost its original spiritual content.

Jamāl al-Dīn Sāwī appears to have been a bookish person as a young man, but he adopted the practice of travelling, which was not that unusual in Sufi circles. However, in Damascus he came across an ascetic who was naked except for a covering of leaves, and was sitting motionless on a grave. Jamāl al-Dīn Sāwī was to follow this example, which to him was a manifestation of the Sufi axiom 'die before you die'.[47] To these practices he added his own: the four shaves (the eyebrows, head, moustache and beard) and the four *takbīrs* (a verbal utterance of 'Praise be to God'), which is usually said when someone dies. Despite his attempts to live a reclusive life, Jamāl al-Dīn soon became surrounded by a small clique of followers,

43
Karamustafa, *God's Unruly Friends*, 44–46. One of the first to associate Quṭb al-Dīn Ḥaydar with *hashish* was the Egyptian scholar Maqrīzī (d. 442). See M. Shafī'ī Kadkanī (1386), *Qalandariyya dar tārīx* (Tehran, n.p. 2007): 222.

44
It does not appear that Quṭb al-Dīn Ḥaydar had been celibate all of his life as he is known to have had a wife and children. See: Kadkanī, *Qalandariyya dar tārīx*: 218. For the use of iron bracelets, necklaces and other implements, see ibid., 220.

46
Muir, *The Life of Mahomet and History of Islam to the Era of the Hegira*, 332.

45
Ibid., 225. There were a number of Qalandar groups in the Ottoman Empire whose individuals let their moustaches grow. See Karamustafa, *Sufism: The Formative Period*, 65–84.

47
This is a ḥadīth that was commonly cited by Sufis. It is contained in B. Forūzānfar, ed. (1334), *Aḥādīth-e Mathnavī* (Tehran: Čāpḫāna-i Dānišgāh, 1955): № 352.

and this social interaction may have forced him to
moderate his behaviour somewhat, so that he began to
wear a coarse sackcloth garment, and allowed his followers
to eat the food donated by others.[48] But these are also the
essential features of later Qalandar lifestyles: seclusion,
renunciation, travelling and rejection of society. This kind
of lifestyle may have been directed at negating the value
of existing forms of worship and Islam, or at least those
that appeared stagnant and spiritually redundant. Another
interesting aspect about Jamāl al-Dīn Sāwī concerns
two possible origins for the *chahār-ẓarb*.[49] The first,
summarised above, simply describes how Jamāl al-Dīn
Sāwī came under the influence of an ascetic called Jalāl
Darguzīnī, and as a result, Jamāl al-Dīn Sāwī shaved his
face and beard and began to sit motionless in graveyards,
facing Mecca, with no food. The second tradition relates
how Jamāl al-Dīn Sāwī was constantly bothered by a
certain woman who had fallen in love with him. Having
been tricked into the woman's house, he managed to
escape by shaving off his head hair, moustache, beard
and eyebrows.[50] Subsequently Jamāl al-Dīn Sāwī adopted
a life of asceticism.[51]

The shock factor of these kinds of hairless individuals
must have been considerable in the medieval Middle East
when the normative style was to emulate the Prophet
Muhammad. Their appearance must have caused a mix
of wonder, astonishment, fear and outright antipathy,
and Julia Kristeva's observation about the abject being
edged with the sublime could not be more apposite.[52]
The Qalandars' rejection of conventional norms, their
supposed association with the roughs and hoodlums,
and their tolerance of 'non-Islamic' behaviour cast them
as the abject members of society who could instil horror
and fear into the hearts of those who beheld them.[53]

II. ADAM'S CLOSE SHAVE

There is evidence that the Qalandars and those within
the *futuwwat* tradition (mentioned above) linked the
shaving of the head with the Prophet Adam. In particular,
one Qalandar text states that the shave took place after
Adam repented, having been thrown out of heaven and
landing on a mountain in Sri Lanka.[54] He was, of course,
remorseful for disobeying God's command, which in the

48
For more details of the main
disciples of Jamāl al-Dīn
Sāwī, see Shafīʿī-Kadkanī,
Qalandariyya dar tārīx: 236–62.

49
One influence on the origin of
the 'four shaves' may be found
in the Buddhist tradition.
Buddhist monks shave their
heads to manifest their celibate
status (although contemporary
Zen monks in Japan may marry).
Nevertheless, it appears that there
were many Buddhist centres
around Central Asia and parts of
Eastern Iran in the 13th century.
It has been claimed that 'Iran
must have been full of Buddhist
temples – we hear of them only
when they were destroyed in
1295–96.' See: A. Bausani,
'Religion under the Mongols',
in *Cambridge History of Iran*,
vol. 5 (Cambridge: Cambridge
University Press, 1968), 541.
It is not possible within the
confines of this article to
develop this argument further.

51
Ibn Baṭṭūṭa, *The Travels
of Ibn Battuta*, vol. I, trans.
H. A. R. Gibb (New Delhi:
Munshiram Manoharlal,
1993), 38.

50
The shaving of the eyebrows is
particularly interesting, if only
for the similarity of the Persian
word for eyebrow (*abrū*) with
the word *ābrū* meaning honour,
which – due to a secondary
folk-etymological reference –
is perceived as composed of *āb*
(water) and *rū* (face). (As kindly
pointed out to me by Prof.
G. Asatrian, āb, in this compound
means rather 'splendour', being
just a homonym of *āb* 'water').
It is speculative, but perhaps the
connection between the Qalandar
(who made no claim of upholding
the honour, *ābrū*, and reputation
of normative Islam, and who
shaved off his eyebrows, *abrū*)
was made by villagers who
witnessed the Qalandars pass by
on their wandering through the
regions of Iran and beyond.

52
Julia Kristeva, *Powers of
Horror: An Essay on Abjection*
(New York: Columbia University
Press, 1982), 11.

53
'Aṭṭār's story of the Arab being
'accosted' by Qalandar dervishes
is a good example of how the
Qalandars were used as a literary
trope to express such fascination.
See Avery, *The Speech of the
Birds*, 307–9.

54
Afshārī, and Mīrʿābedīnī,
*Čahārdah resāle dar bāb-i
fotowwat wa aṣnāf*, 161, 169–70.

كىشى كېرەكلىك سۆزىنى سۆزلەيدۇ، يوشۇرماپ.
كىشى سۆزلەشى ئۈچۈن ئۇنىڭغا سوئال بېرىش لازىم.
سوئال بېرىلمىسە سۆزلىرىنى يۇشۇرۇشى چوقۇم ساقلىنىش لازىم.

Qur'ān is an order not to eat of the tree (2.34). As a result of eating from the tree he becomes aware of his sexuality: 'When they tasted of the tree, their private parts became visible to them, and they started to cover themselves with the leaves of Paradise' (7.20). The connection between nakedness, sexuality, repentance and the shave is sufficiently clear not to require further elaboration.

Another Adam story, which appears in two *futuwwat* treatises, is suggestive of such a linkage.[55] (Although the basic story is the same, there are very important differences, which are highlighted in the footnotes). According to this myth, when Adam was in heaven he had no hair on him (*mū bar andām nadāsht*). After he ate the wheat, he was cast out of heaven and came to a mountain in Sri Lanka.[56] After some time God accepted the repentance of Adam, 'the chosen one' (*Ādam-i ṣafī*),[57] but he commanded Gabriel to tell Adam that he must not disobey His command again. On seeing Gabriel, Adam was informed that Eve was in Mecca, so the Prophet set off to be reunited with her. Eve did not recognise Adam because of the incredibly long hair that had grown from him, and exclaimed 'This is not my Adam! Adam was a hairless person (*ṣafī*),[58] but this Adam has hair on him!'[59] His hair had grown to about seventy metres (*haftād gaz*) in length and his beard was forty metres.[60] Adam lamented and said, 'Oh God! She does not accept me'. Finally Gabriel came to shave Adam's head.[61]

III. EMULATING MUḤAMMAD

Qalandar treatises (such as chapter two of the Qalandar text included in the Appendix of this article, pp. 151–54) and those in the *futuwwat* tradition of the barbers often cite the Qur'ānic verse 48.27: 'God has fulfilled His prophet's vision in truth. You shall enter the sacred mosque, if God wishes, in security, your heads shaved and your hair cut short, without fear'. This verse was supposedly revealed after the Battle of Uhud when Muḥammad was in a position to safely perform the ḥajj to the Ka'ba, which included the ritual shaving and cutting short of the hair. This Qur'ānic citation and origin is elaborated within a Qalandar treatise from the Safavid period in which Gabriel

55
The first of these appears in Afshārī, 'Qalandar nāma-ye Arbāb al-ṭarīq', 73–88. The second is in Afshārī and Madāyenī, *Čahārdah resāle dar bāb-i fotowwat wa aṣnāf*, 241–45.

56
The Qur'ān speaks of Adam eating from the tree, and the Islamic Persian tradition describes how he ate of wheat (gandum).

57
An honorific name given to Adam. Many of the Prophets were given honorific names, such as Muḥammad, the beloved of God (*ḥabīb Allāh*). This sentence only appears in Afshārī and Madāyenī, *Čahārdah resāle dar bāb-i fotowwat wa aṣnāf*, 242.

58
The word *ṣāf* (here in the form of *ṣāfī*) literally means 'pure, smooth, clear'.

59
Afshārī, 'Qalandar nāma-ye Arbāb al-ṭarīq', 81.

60
Afshārī and Madāyinī, *Čahārdah resāle dar bāb-i fotowwat wa aṣnāf*, 242.

61
The Ḥadīth literature tells a different story. Ubayy Ka'b (a companion of the Prophet) reports Muḥammad saying that before he sinned, Adam had 'a lot of hair on his head like the top of a palm tree.' See: Wheeler, *Prophets in the Qu'ran*, 25. Tabarī states: 'When Adam fell he brushed his head on heaven and thus became bald, and passed on baldness to his children.' Ibid., 27.

Der Mensch spricht das Nötige und verbirgt es nicht.
Damit der Mensch redet, muss man ihm Fragen stellen.
Wenn ihm keine Frage gestellt wird,
So muss er seine Worte verstecken.

Człowiek mówi tylko prawdę, niczego nie skrywa.
Lecz, aby rozmawiać, trzeba go zapytać.
Gdy jest się niepytanym, słowy należy skrywać.

is instructed by God to shave Muḥammad's head.[62] The treatise states that the Prophet's hairs were so valuable that God forgave a thousand sinners with each of them. Moreover, when Gabriel had finished shaving and cutting short the Prophet's hair, Muḥammad's companions remarked that not a single hair had fallen to the floor. Gabriel explained that the Prophet had 30,332 head hairs; 30 had fallen to the ground, and he had left them there. The rest he had given to the angels and the houris; 10,000 of the hairs were for Muḥammad and his children; the angels had taken the rest to heaven so that the Carriers of the Throne and the Angels in Proximity could make scent from them.[63] God took pity on them through the blessing (baraka) of Muḥammad's hair, which the angels kissed and rubbed on their eyes and cheeks.[64]

IV. IN REMEMBRANCE OF ḤUSAYN

Yet another explanation for the origin of the shave is contained in another Qalandar treatise in which the purpose appears simply as an attempt to link the origins of the shave with the Shī'ite version of Islam.[65] The following is a translation from the beginning of the treatise:

Know that the place was Karbala where Imām Ḥusyan – peace be upon him – and a group of Shī'ites and lovers were captured by Yazid, curses upon him. It was the tenth day of the month of 'Ashūrā, and all the lovers sat before His Excellency, Imām Ḥusyan, who was in deep thought. Suddenly Imām Ḥusyan raised his head and said: 'Friends! It is blessed (mubārak).' They replied: 'Oh Imām! What is blessed?' And Imām Ḥusyan said: 'The rank of martyrdom (daraja-yi shahādat), for tomorrow will be our final day'. So, seventy-two people said: 'Oh Imām Ḥusyan! There are many foreigners and hypocrites, but we number just a few. We desire that they recognise us tomorrow among all the dead, and they distinguish a client (mawālī) from a foreigner'. So, therefore, those among the foremost of the seventy-two shaved their heads (tarāsh kardand), and this has been the reason for shaving…

62
This treatise is found in Afshārī and Mīr'ābedīnī, *Čahārdah resāle dar bāb-i fotowwat wa aṣnāf*: 79–213. The particular passage is found on pages 144–45.

63
Carriers of the Throne are mentioned in the Qur'ān, 40.7. Angels in Proximity, Al-muqarrabū, a Qur'ānic term, see, for example, 83.21, 83.28.

64
A very similar story is related in a *futuwwat-nāma* for barbers (dated at 1890), which is collected in a group of treatises outlining the customs and beliefs of Khāsār dervishes (who are supposed to have inherited many Qalandar beliefs). See Afshārī 'Qalandar nāma-ye Arbāb al-ṭarīq', 81–82.

65
Ibid., 90–94. Although the treatise is anonymous and does not mention the word *Qalandar*, it discusses Qalandar symbolism, such as the *chahār-ẓarb*, the implements for shaving, and specific items of clothing, leaving little doubt that it was composed by a Qalandar dervish.

But if someone has the four shaves (*chahār-zarb*), it is necessary that he yields to absolute annihilation, and leaves behind all worldly attachments and becomes a solitary and single lover in the path of love, and he must obliterate these human acts, names and habits, and the invitation of 'die before you die' is given to him in order that he reaches the station of the *abdāl*…[66]

They often ask the wayfarer: 'What is the meaning of the four shaves?' Say: 'The meaning of shaving the beard is that we do not bow down to anything other than the Truth and Reality, and we put aside the adornments of the world. And the meaning of shaving the moustache is that we do not instigate our lips to lie, back-bite, slander or annoy people. The meaning of shaving the head is that we make a stand and put ourselves in the station of nonexistence. And the meaning of shaving the eyebrow is that we leave behind duality, and we see and know everything as one'.

The editor of the text believes that it was probably written during the Safavid period between the sixteenth and eighteenth centuries. The Safavids transformed the denominational map of Iran (which at the time was still a majority Sunni area) by making Shī'ism the official creed of the state. In addition, the Safavid monarchs, despite their own emergence from a Sufi-esque movement, quickly realised that in order to rule Iran it was necessary to promote a more rational and less emotional or ecstatic spirituality, which stood in contrast to the Sufi movement. As a result, the Safavids adopted various policies that aimed to belittle the role and influence of Sufism, particularly the more established and sedentary Sufi orders.[67] The Qalandars, although clearly of a Sufi nature, were not geographically located in a specific area that was affiliated to the tomb of their founder, and so it seems that they were able to avoid the Sufi persecution of the Safavid state. It may also be the case that the Shī'ism of the Qalandars, epitomised in the quote above, permitted them to operate more comfortably in Iran than other orders, which were of a Sunni origin. Therefore, the symbolism of the *chahār-ẓarb* developed in new ways; it gave denominational security to the Qalandars, and it also retained its tendency to signify the ethical high ground and renunciation.

66
It is unclear whether *abdāl* refers to a specific rank of dervish among the Qalandars, or whether this refers to the generally recognised Sufi understanding of a group of individuals known as *abdāl* (substitutes) who were a part of a spiritual hierarchy of 'saints' who had always existed in the world and as one passed away another took his place.

67
S. A. Arjomand, 'Religious Extremism (*Ghuluww*), Ṣūfism and Sunnism in Safavid Iran: 1501–1722', *Journal of Asian History*, vol. 15, № 1 (1981): 1–35; Ridgeon, *Morals and Mysticism in Persian Sufism*, 123–65.

COMMENTARY ON
THE FOUR EMIC SOURCES

The symbolism of hair has been the source of much
controversy among anthropologists. One of the most
important theories was that of Edmund Leach, whose
investigation of the Indian tradition of ascetics led him
to accept the argument that the head is a symbol for the
phallus and the hair represents semen. He argued that,
'An astonishingly high proportion of the ethnographic
evidence fits the following pattern in a quite obvious way.
In ritual situations: long hair = unrestrained sexuality;
close shaven head = celibacy'.[68] A third category,
matted hair, which is grown without concern, 'means
total detachment from the sexual passions'.[69] Leach's
connection between head hair and sexuality has been
accepted by a number of leading anthropologists, including
Obeyesekere;[70] others, however, most notably Hallpike,[71]
reject the subconscious relationship between the head
and phallus, hair and semen, hair-cutting and castration,
and long hair and unrestrained sexuality, short hair and
restricted sexuality, and close-shaven hair and celibacy.[72]
Instead Hallpike argues that long hair is symbolic of being
outside of society (witches, intellectuals and hippies), and
cutting (and by extension shaving) symbolises reentering
society, or living under a particular disciplinary regime
within society (soldiers and convicts).[73]

In many Islamic contexts it would appear that, for males,
hair on the head or the face is symbolically connected to
sexuality. Moussa[74] notes that: 'The respect with which
the moustache is regarded seems to be common among
the people of the Middle East whatever their ethnic or
religious origin may be. It is a social custom, associated
with the belief that the moustache is a symbol of virility
and masculinity, in societies where the male reigns
supreme. Among many people of the Middle East,
it is a grave matter to swear by one's moustache. It is
like testifying under oath in the Western world'.[75]

The connection between sexuality and hair in some of the
Qalandar 'myths' relating to the origins of the *chahār-ẓarb*
is not difficult to identify. This is particularly the case with
the story of Jamāl al-Dīn Sāwī, whose original act (if the
source is to be believed) seems to have been an individual,
psychological response to personal anguish. Subsequent

68
Leach, 'Magical Hair': 154.

69
Ibid.: 156.

70
Gananath Obeyesekere,
Medusa's Hair (Chicago:
Chicago University Press,
1981).

71
C. R. Hallpike, 'Social Hair',
Man, vol. 4, № 2 (1969): 256–64.

72
Ibid.: 257.

73
Ibid.: 261.

74
Matti Moussa, *Extremist Shiites*
(New York: Syracuse University
Press, 1988), 254.

75
The contemporary significance
of the moustache in Turkey is
contained in Yumul, 'Scenes
of Masculinity from Turkey'.
Arnus Yumul, *Zeitschrift fur
Turkeistudien*, 1 (1999), 107–117.

143

Qalandars formed small groups or communities, and, therefore, the *chahār-ẓarb* also served as an identity marker or communicative symbol. Thus the primary significance of the *chahār-ẓarb* may not necessarily have been related to the psychological state of the actor, that is to say, it may not always have symbolised the desire to remain chaste, but it reflected an amalgamation of other attributes and associations, such as extreme asceticism and the rejection of the more ossified forms of Islamic spirituality. It is important to note that much of the Qalandar literature does not discuss celibacy in a detailed fashion, but merely mentions the requirement to abandon lust and sexual gratification.[76] The absence of thorough discussions on celibacy does not mean that Qalandars enjoyed free licence to engage in sexual acts. The use of iron implements around the genitals of Ḥaydarī Qalandars, in addition to the general lifestyle of poverty, mendicancy and otherworldliness, militated against marriage and sexual relations.[77]

That the *chahār-ẓarb* was in some way connected with celibacy may be argued with reference to the idea that the Qalandars lived the spiritual ideal contained within the *ḥadīth* cited previously, 'Die before you die'. In effect, the Qalandar, in shaving his head, performed a ritual of spiritual rebirth, and became once more as innocent as a child before his father (God). Children, of course, are chaste, have no facial hair and usually have very little head hair. As adult/child, dead/alive, the Qalandar occupied a very unusual space; however, this state resembles the liminal status that was discussed by Victor Turner as a circumstance that is betwixt and between, located somehow in the middle of sacred and profane dimensions.[78] Turner also observed that, in a liminal state, 'neophytes are likened to or treated as embryos, newborn infants or sucklings by symbolic means, which varies from culture to culture'.[79] Liminality also involves a degree of structural 'invisibility' as the neophyte falls between two distinct structures, in which it may be possible for the subject to be physically invisible.[80] Indeed, the Qalandars were associated with an itinerant lifestyle,[81] and this too contributed to their invisibility, as did the shaving of the head, which made them anonymous to outsiders (just as the huge piles of corpses from Nazi concentration camps lacked elements of individuality, which had been shaved away with their hair). Yet invisibility, anonymity and selflessness are the kind of spiritual attributes to which

76
A good example of this is the rejection of sexual gratification in the first Qalandar treatise included in Mīrʿābedīnī and Afshārī, *Čahārdah resāle dar bāb-i fotowwat wa aṣnāf*, 134, in which there is a list of ten stations in the *ṭarīqat* for the Gnostics. The sixth station is abandoning pleasure and lust (*tark-i lidhat wa shahvat kardan*).

77
It is worth noting Karamustafa's observation that the detractors of the Qalandars accused them of sodomy and zoophilia. While he disregards much of this kind of criticism, Karamustafa considers the possibility of Qalandars observing celibacy, which did not exclude unproductive forms of sexual activity. See: Ahmet Karamustafa, *God's Unruly Friends* (Oxford: One World, 2006), 20–21.

78
Victor Turner, 'Betwixt and Between: The Liminal Period in *Rites de Passage*' in *Forest of Symbols* (London: Cornel University Press, 1972), 93–111. Although Turner's work was specifically orientated to rites of passage in which the subject moved from one state to a second state (the liminal) and then moved back and was reintegrated into society, the Qalandars never completed the final stage of reintegration. They lived permanently in the liminal stage.

80
Ibid., 95.

79
Ibid., 96.

81
Travelling in search of knowledge was also a general recommendation within the wider Sufi tradition. See, for example, Hujwiri, of *Al Hujwiri*, trans. R.A Nicholson (London: n.p., 1911), 345–47. The Qalandars must also have remained sedentary for periods, as there is much evidence of Qalandar lodges (*langar* and *takiya*). See Shafiʿī-Kadkanī, *Qalandariyya dar tārīx*, 260–62, 278–79; Ridgeon, *Morals and Mysticism in Persian Sufism*, 138–39; Kiyīnī, *Tārīx-e xāneqāh dar Irān*: 248–49.

the ideal Sufi and Qalandar aspired. The adult/child, alive/dead, visible/invisible, secular/profane Qalandar in the liminal state was clearly a potentially dangerous subject, and herein provides yet another reason for the shaved head: a symbolic marker for separating himself from society's norms and orientating himself towards the divine within a new social community of Qalandars.

Sexuality is also apparent in the Adam story. While the brief story may merely be a very simple play on the similarity of the Persian words 'the chosen one' (*ṣafī*) and 'hairless' (*ṣāfī*), it is also possible that Qalandars understood that Adam's disobedience and subsequent realisation of his nakedness were somehow represented by his long hair, which necessitated its shaving. With his hair shaved and beard trimmed, Eve recognised Adam, and his repentance was finally complete. It is also significant that the treatise states that Adam had no hair in heaven; that is, he was childlike, innocent and unaware of sexuality. His disobedience in eating from the tree symbolised his coming of age and the awareness of sexuality. It was, of course, the disobedience that caused Adam's difficulty, because on earth he did not remain ignorant of his sexuality; rather, he fathered several children. The shave, however, was a symbolic reminder of his primordial nature that did not involve the knowledge of sexuality, which for some Sufis created an obstacle for paying complete and utter attention to God.[82]

Sexuality is also present within the Muḥammadan myth of the origin of the *chahār-ẓarb*. Although this message in the Muḥammadan story appears as a simple justification of the shave to emulate the Prophet's practice, the Qalandars would also have been aware of the larger context of the Qur'ān (verse 48.27) and Islamic tradition, which connects the shave to the *ḥajj* and its rituals, including specific rulings about sexual activity. The tradition of shaving at the pilgrimage seems to be linked to sexuality, for Muslims refrain from sexual activity during the period of the *ḥajj* when men let their head hair and beards grow. Grooming the hair would imply that the object of their thoughts was not God alone. It is after the performance of the *ḥajj* rituals that men may cut their hair and shave, and this represents a return to sexuality, or at least the conventions and laws associated with controlled Islamic sexual practice.[83] The Qalandars adopted the shave as a practice that was not specific to the *ḥajj*, but was relevant at all times; that

82
For the sake of presenting a comprehensive survey of the Adam stories, it should be noted that in the same *futuwwat* treatise that describes Adam as having no hair in heaven, another origin for the shave is presented, though it does not seem to hold any explicit relation to sexuality. In this myth, Adam was very tall, which conforms to the *ḥadīth* portrayal of Adam (Wheeler, *Prophets in the Qu'ran*, 31), and the heat of the sun caused him some discomfort. As a result, God commanded Gabriel to brush Adam's head with his wing. The spot where Gabriel's feathers touched Adam's head made the latter bald. However, Adam wondered whether there was something wrong with him, since one part of his head had hair and another part was bald. Gabriel confirmed there was nothing the matter, but he shaved Adam's head so that it would feel the same all over. See: Afshārī and Madāyenī, *Čahārdah resāle dar bāb-i fotowwat wa aṣnāf*: 243.

83
Delaney, 'Untangling the Meanings of Hair in Turkish Society': 167.

فَالَّتِي يَكُونُ لَهَا رَجُلٌ وَرُبَّمَا يَلِدَانِ تَوْأَمَانِ

Dişi için bir erkek koca olur;
Eğer doğarsa bunlardan iki çocuk doğar.

The female takes one male as her husband,
but she may give birth to two male children.

is to say, it represented the interior, or *bāṭin*, message of the Prophet. Although the texts do not say so, it may be speculated that this shave was symbolic of a kind of 'greater *jihād*'. Indeed, the connection is not as speculative as may be assumed, as the greater *jihād ḥadīth* was uttered after the Battle of Uhud (when verse 48.27 was revealed).

Verse 48.27, which serves as a 'myth' in which the sacred nature of Muḥammad's hair is discussed, is used to justify the Qalandar tradition, and as mentioned above, it appears in a number of *futuwwat-nāmas* for barbers. The significance of this requires some explanation, especially as the majority of *futuwwat-nāmas* (or those works which are contained in the genre of 'occupational treatises') that were composed in Persian contain details related to the barbers' trade. The relative abundance of such texts may be related to the Zoroastrian belief, which was widespread in pre-Islamic Iran, that anything – such as hair, teeth or blood – which became detached from the body, was impure. As a result, barbers were considered with some suspicion and their profession was regarded as contemptible.[84] It is worth speculating whether the legacy of this Zoroastrian belief resulted in the restrictions that were included in the *Futuwwat nāma-yi Nāṣirī* (written in the late thirteenth century), which included a list of twelve trades, the members of which were prohibited from joining the *futuwwat* organisations.[85] One of these trades was that of the barber or masseur (*dallāk*). Although the Islamic aversion to nakedness may account for this prohibition, the Zoroastrian influence may well have contributed to the distaste among Muslims in the medieval period. What is indisputable, however, is the number of treatises dealing with aspects of the barbers' trade, from shaving to the utensils that were used (such as the razor, the whetstone and the mirror).[86] The prohibition of barbers joining *futuwwat* organisations may have resulted in the barbers composing their occupational literature in an attempt to legitimise the profession.

The intriguing point to note is that there are many similarities between the literature of the Qalandars and the occupational literature of the barbers. Both display a particular interest in the ethic of *futuwwat*, include sections on shaving the head and its mythic origins, and discuss the tools of the barbers' trade. Given the suspicions surrounding the ritually impure profession of the barber on the one hand, and given that the Qalandars supposedly

84
Ibid., 73.

85
A. Golpenārlī (1378), *Fotovvat dar keshvar-hā-ye eslāmī* (Tehran: n.p., 1999), 162.

86
As Afshārī notes: 'It is worthy of attention that among the handwritten treatises that the followers of *futuwwat* have left – in particular the treatises from the Safavid period – more than any other trade, the barbers and bath-attendants are praised and honoured'. Afshārī edited six treatises related to the barber's trade and included them in the work cited above. See Afshārī, 'Qalandar nāma-ye Arbāb al-ṭarīq', 73.

paid scant attention to such considerations, perhaps even desiring to court notoriety (especially through their shocking appearance), it is tempting to speculate a link between the two groups. Could it be the case that Qalandars may even have worked as barbers at times in the premodern period? The point that needs to be highlighted is that, on the basis of such Qalandar-*futuwwat* literature, the explanation to legitimise shaving through Islamic referents, in particular the Qur'ān and Muḥammad, is explicit. Implicit, however, is the connection of verse 48.27 with the *ḥajj* rituals and laws pertaining to permitted sexual activity. That the Qalandars lived in a permanent state of chastity located them symbolically at the Ka'ba, performing the *ḥajj*, in the presence of God.[87]

Hair functioning as a symbol of sexuality, and the *chahār-ẓarb* representing a commitment of celibacy, does not seem to work in all cases. This is nowhere more apparent than in the original myth that discusses the events at Karbala and the followers of Ḥusayn who wished to be identified with his cause. However, it is common that the meanings that individuals perceive in symbols change; indeed, they are frequently multivocal. Such new symbolic meaning of hair offered by the Qalandars is a good example of the 'invention of tradition', to use a much-used expression.[88] Conspicuously absent from the Karbala origins of the *chahār-ẓarb* is anything that can be equated with sexuality; however, this does not necessarily invalidate the anthropological theory that equates shaving with celibacy. The relationship of hair, celibacy and the Qalandars is wrapped up in the concept of the 'condensed symbol', which is a symbol that is 'so powerful that it encapsulates all the diverse aspects of the symbolised'.[89] That is to say, even though the Qalandar treatise may speak primarily of denominational origins, performing the *chahār-ẓarb* implicitly links the Qalandar to a lifestyle of asceticism; the terms used in the Karbala origins myth are nonexistence and forsaking the adornments of the world (including, perhaps, women and young men). In addition, as mentioned above, the very lifestyle of the Qalandar (poverty and mendicancy) would have made difficult the normal sexual relationship between a man and wife. The ideal of celibacy was contained within the condensed symbol of the *chahār-ẓarb*. This theory works, according to Olivelle,[90] through the theory of displacement, which 'occurs when the unconscious substitutes the entity X for the entity Y, thus permitting

87
The importance of Islamic and Qur'ānic referents should not be underestimated in the highly ritualised Qalandar performance of the *chahār-ẓarb*. One Qalandar treatise gives a specific order to the shaves, which start with the head, and is performed with the recitation of *Hadīth* and Qur'ānic verses (including 48.27). This is followed by the shaving of the beard, then the moustache and finally the eyebrows. The Qur'ānic verse to be recited when the eyebrows are shaved is 53.9: 'Coming within two bows' length or closer', which is traditionally understood as a reference to Gabriel's descent before Muḥammad. That the eyebrows are shaped like two bows offered the Qalandars a symbolic reminder of the possibility of Gabriel descending before their own eyes to provide divine illumination. Moreover, once the ritual of the *chahār-ẓarb* was completed, associated rituals commenced, including offering praise for the Shī'ite Imāms and receiving certain garments, including a cloak (*kisvat*) and head covering (*tāj*). This Qalandar treatise is included in Shafī'ī-Kadkanī, *Qalandariyya dar tārīx*, 414–20.

88
E. Hobsbawm and T. Ranger eds., *The Invention of Tradition* (Cambridge, Cambridge University Press, 1983).

89
P. Olivelle, 'Hair and Society: Social Significance of Hair in South Asian traditions', in *Hair*, eds. A. Hiltebeitel and B. Miller (Albany, State University of New York, 1998), 40–41.

90
Ibid., 37.

individuals at the conscious level to speak about and to manipulate X, which at a deeper level are statements about and the manipulation of Y'. Thus, the hair displaces the penis as the locus of sexuality, just as the discussion of the events at Karbala displaces the ideal of celibacy. In this discussion of Karbala, the condensed symbolism of the shave includes familiar Sufi themes, such as the refusal to worship anything other than God; in other words, the focus is on unity (*tawḥīd*). Thus, the beard is considered an adornment (as described previously by Rūmī), which must be shaven so that the Qalandar may focus on unity.

Likewise, it is necessary to remove the duality of the two eyebrows, so that the Qalandar may see and know one. This form of understanding that posits an ontological unity between God and the believer was problematic for many Shīʿite clerics, but it was relatively standard among Sufi circles.

CONCLUSION

In this paper, I have attempted to provide some coherence to four seemingly different emic discussions relating to the origins of the *chahār-ẓarb*. Three of the examples can be linked relatively easily to sexual themes, and seem to fit within the kind of arguments offered by psychologists and anthropologists, such as Leach. Yet the changing content of three of these narratives ensured that the message remained pertinent; the different stories relating to the *chahār-ẓarb* reflect the adage of 'old wine in new bottles'. The fourth case in this paper is more problematic, and only if the theory of displacement is used can it be associated with any theory about sexuality. The problem with the theory of displacement, however, is that it may be used to reduce any form of symbolism to overarching psychological theory.[91]

However, the theories of shaven hair = celibacy and shaven = social control do not contradict each other, especially when they are applied to the Qalandars. It should be noted firstly that concern with sexuality in the Sufi context should also be linked with a range of attributes that are also connected with sexuality.

91
The hair/sexuality association has been questioned. Hallpike rejected the subconscious relationship between the head = phallus, hair = semen, hair cutting = castration, and long hair = unrestrained sexuality, short hair = restricted sexuality, and close shaven hair = celibacy. Instead, he argued that long hair is symbolic of being outside of society (witches, intellectuals and hippies), and cutting (and by extension, shaving) symbolises re-entering society, or living under a particular disciplinary regime within society (soldiers, convicts, etc.). See: Hallpike, 'Social Hair': 261.

Rampant sexuality was obviously not encouraged by the Sufis; rather than 'strutting around like a peacock', the Sufi was encouraged to be humble and focus his energies on controlling the *nafs*. This meant that one-upmanship, the predominance of one male over another and the attempt to attract females by belittling the competition was something that would not have occurred to the genuine Sufi. Thus, the *chahār-ẓarb* was symbolic of a denial of sexuality and a range of associated behavioural traits that were considered reprehensible. At the same time, the *chahār-ẓarb* was also symbolic of the Qalandar separating himself from what might be termed society, yet he still lived within a 'particular disciplinary regime,[92] that is to say, the specific conventions of the Qalandar group, with all its inherited traditions and unique ritual performance.

Finally, it is worth pointing out that not all Qalandars performed the *chahār-ẓarb*. As early as the fifteenth century, there is a suggestion of this in the following verse by the celebrated Persian poet Ḥāfiẓ:[93]

**Here arc a thousand points finer than a hair,
Not everyone who shaves his head understands
what it is to be a Qalandar[94]**

This verse does not allude to actual Qalandars with head hair, but, rather Ḥāfiẓ argues that the spiritual dimension of being a Qalandar transcends the shaving of the head. The once antinomian Qalandars had lost their shock factor, and a new form of antinomianism was necessary to convey the spiritual message. The literary trope of the Qalandar, as discussed in a previous section, depicted an individual who rose above hypocrisy and the ossified conventions of society and religion that distracted the individual from God. However, Ḥāfiẓ, like all great poets, was a step ahead of his time, and dared to think the unthought.

A Qalandar treatise entitled *Arbāb al-ṭarīq* ('Lords of the Way') includes a chapter – Chapter Two, given in the Appendix following – which illustrates that the *chahār-ẓarb* was not always a clear indication of being a Qalandar.[95] This text, composed in the seventeenth century during the reign of 'Abd al-'Azīz Khān in Bukhara (r. 1645–81),[96] states that even though Muḥammad grew his hair from his ears to his shoulder, there are some who shave their heads (that is, the experienced wayfarer, whereas the

92
Ibid.: 260.

93
Ibid.: 348.

94
See Avery, *The Speech of the Birds*, 232.

96
For this ruler and his times, see Robert McChesney in *EIr.*, vol. 5 (1992): 188ff.

95
This treatise must be accepted as a Qalandar text, as the author says that it is about Qalandarism and the rituals that are usually associated with the Qalandars. The edited Persian text appears in Afshārī, 'Qalandar nāma-ye Arbāb al-ṭarīq' (1381) in *Pažūheŝ-hā-ye Irānshināsī*, vol. 13, ed. Iraj-e Afshār (n.d.), 155–59.

inexperienced let their hair grow). The author proceeds to explain that it is possible that an individual can be attracted or pulled towards God, to become enraptured and lose his free will, and in such a condition all concern for shaving his hair vanishes. In the terminology of the Sufis he is known as a *majdhūb*. Since the *majdhūb* is with God, the concern for symbolically presenting himself as celibate, as an ascetic, or as devoted to God, has no meaning. Such an individual inevitably ends up with entangled hair that is not controlled or groomed in any fashion.

The existence of long-haired lovers with ungroomed locks does not contradict the general perspective, which considers that individuals of this group should refrain from sexual activity. Leach argues that long, unkempt, ungroomed, matted hair is symbolic of a 'total detachment' of sexual interest.[97] And Olivelle is of the opinion that those who shaved their hair separated themselves from society since this act was symbolic of the denial of sexual maturity, and denial in an adult placed him outside social structures. He continues by claiming that leaving the hair uncontrolled is symbolic in a similar way. Thus, in some Asian societies, those involved in mourning rituals and menstruating women have long, unkempt hair, and distance themselves temporarily from society.[98] However, it seems from the Qalandar treatise *Arbāb al-ṭarīq* that the Qalandar was permanently separated from society, whether he shaved his head, involuntarily let his hair grow, or even if both took place. Thus, the ideal Qalandar, with shaggy hair or shaven head, lived a celibate life, separated from society in a liminal state, within a community of like-minded companions.

97
Leach, 'Magical Hair': 156.

98
Olivelle, 'Hair and Society: Social Significance of Hair in South Asian traditions': 39. It is interesting to note that in his ethnographic work on hair in the Punjab, Hershman offers the following categories for Hindu men: at the 'profane' level, the Hindu male cuts his hair; at the 'sacred' level, the Hindu male shaves his head; at the 'divine' level, the Hindu male has matted hair and becomes as God. See Hershman, 'Hair, Sex and Dirt': 279.

APPENDIX: Chapter Two of *Arbāb al-ṭarīq*[99]

Know, truthful seeker, that letting the hair grow from the ears to the shoulder is the attribute of His Excellency, God's peace and greetings upon him. More than this is forbidden. Shaving is also the custom (*sunnat*), but only for the experienced (*muntahā*) not the novice (*mubtadā*). This is because letting the hair grow is the method and the choice of the Abdāliyya who have drowned in the illustrious ocean and have been slashed (*mustahlak*) by the razor blade of majesty of the divine unity (*tīgh-i jalāl-i aḥadiyyat*), and it is not for those who in the ranks of 'they are like cattle'[100] [who] are busy with [drinking] the water and [grazing on] the pasture of this world, and despite this habit they speak the discourses and the circumstances of shaykh-hood, and talk of being a dervish. They are among the liars, and the noble verse *they are even more misguided*[101] will be their attribute. In other words, letting the hair grow is good for the person who is not aware of his own hair.

> **Whoever is aware [even]**
> **a little bit (*sar-i mū*)**
> **is not Majnūn.[102]**
> **If he takes pleasure in**
> **all the chains, then he**
> **makes a false claim.**

Know that among the stations of this group (*ṭī'ifa*), there is a station that is called the station of the *abdāl*, which is the station of enrapture and [divine] insanity (*maqām-i jadhb wa junūn*). One must know how many people are within this station, and what is the [mystical] state (*ḥīl*) of each person: the enraptured engaged in wayfaring (*majdhūb-i sālik*)[103] or the wayfarer-enraptured (*sālik-i majdhūb*), or the enraptured who is not wayfaring (*majdhūb-i ghayr-i sālik*).

The enraptured engaged in wayfaring is the person that the Truth most Glorious and High calls to Himself. The Sultan commands the rapture, which alights in the throne of the servant's heart, and [the servant] spends some time in that situation. Since he has been completely released from the affairs of the world, he steps out in the path of wayfaring, which is an expression for the knowledge of commanding [the good] and forbidding [the evil]. Then it is permissible for the enraptured engaged in wayfaring to let the hair grow because he has no free will, until he comes into the service of an eminent spiritual guide who guides him on the path of wayfaring. Having head hair is forbidden for him when he is engaged in wayfaring, and [so he] shaves the head because the commentators on the method of wayfaring have offered guidance for the seekers on [the basis of] the contents of this glorious verse: 'God has fulfilled His Prophet's vision in truth. You shall enter the sacred mosque, if God wishes, in security, your heads shaved and your hair cut short, without fear'.[104] And so it is necessary for the *ḥājīs* to shave their heads after [the rituals] of running between Ṣafā and Marwa.[105] It is necessary for such a wayfarer to pay attention when encountering a *pīr*, for he is like the Ka'ba.[106]

> **A body in pain discovered**
> **a soul in your alley;**
> **The forsaken heart discovered**
> **the eternal treasure.**

99
Afshārī, 'Qalandar nāma-ye Arbāb al-ṭarīq', 155–59.

100
Ibid., 7.179.

101
Ibid., 7.179.

102
Majnūn is the devoted 'madman' who was besotted with Layla. Madmen were often placed in chains, which in poetry were symbolic of the strands of hair.

103
Karamustafa argues that the concept of the enraptured individual appears to have emerged in Sufi thought and practice from the 11th century onwards. See A. Karamustafa, *Sufism: The Formative Period* (Edinburgh: Edinburgh University Press, 2007), 150.

104
Afshārī, 'Qalandar nāma-ye Arbāb al-ṭarīq', 48.27.

105
These are the two hills that are situated on the course of the pilgrimage around Mecca, between which pilgrims traverse in the course of the ritual performance.

106
In other words, just as the *ḥajj* makes the Ka'ba the object of his pilgrimage, so should the Qalandar pay particular attention to the *pīr*, making him the object of such concentrated attention.

The wayfarer enraptured is the person who was engaged in wayfaring from the beginning until the time that the raptures of the divine dominate him as a result of much ascetic discipline and worship. And the soldiers (*shahna*) of love seized the collar of his soul and dragged it off in the alleys and markets, as Mawlawī has said:

> **Whoever is our friend**
> **involves himself in**
> **ignominy.**
> **Whoever associates with**
> **an ignominious person**
> **becomes like him in**
> **the end.**

The growing of the hair of the wayfarer in this station comes about involuntarily. And the enraptured who is not wayfaring is he who is in the level of love from the beginning to the end, and [in] this level is the attribute of majesty (*ṣifat-i jalāl*) because he could burn the world with a glance or turn it into a flower garden. Such actions are not the result of his free will. [Such a person] has the attribute of entangled hair and it is the sign of love that casts a shadow upon his head.

> **The entangled hair on**
> **my head is worthless,**
> **It is the shadow of the wealth**
> **of love that I possess.**

But there is also the wayfarer who is not enraptured, [and such individuals] include ascetics, worshippers and the pious. Abandoning the way of the practice of His Excellency is a major sin for this group, which is the intention of commanding the good and forbidding the evil. Therefore, their way is by praying more than the five [prescribed] times for prayer. Examples include prayers repeated at night and the prayers recited with *tasbīḥ* beads and others, which they have considered obligatory. So renouncing one of these acts will be a major sin for this group, and growing the hair is not a command according to this group. So, it has become clear that growing the hair is specific for the lovers and the gnostics and is not suitable for the ascetics and worshippers.

Oh dervish! Know that there are two kinds of attraction: of fire (*nārī*) and of light (*nūrī*). [Attraction] by fire is a burner of the soul, and [attraction] by light is an illuminator of faith. One must flee from the individual enraptured in fire, and one must mingle with the individual enraptured in light, because distress is increased through fire [but] gnosis is yielded through light. So, it is clear that the intention of [rapture] through light is the enraptured wayfarer, and [the intention of rapture] through fire is the enraptured who is not a wayfarer.

Oh dervish! Know that there are two kinds of enrapture through fire: majestic (*jalālī*) and essential (*dhātī*). If [enrapture] through fire is majestic, then the [enrapture] is through love (*'ishqī*). Its sign is that whenever the lover becomes absorbed (*maghrūq*) in conceiving or imagining the beloved, it is such a fashion that he fancies that any voice or call that comes to anyone in the world from the beloved (*maḥbūb*) is for his sake. They have said that Majnūn was following Layla's camel. Layla had a dog called Ram. She called the dog to her, using that name, but Majnūn imagined that she called him 'Ram'. In other words, he stood [to attention] in his place, and stayed there for a while. He spoke about Layla's eyes to the fawns of the meadows. The purpose of his standing to attention was [to manifest] his resolution.

Oh dervish! If you boast about being an *abdāl*, you must fasten the belt of constancy through worship, and you must not turn the head of obedience from the essential, required commanding the good and [you must] be God-wary of the prohibitions that have been forgotten. And if you are in such a way [that is, an *abdāl*, then] the Truth – Glorious and Most High – is a lover of you just as Layla was a lover of Majnūn.

Now listen to the description of the essential [attraction] by fire. Know that Iblis was created through essential fire and his task is to deceive the seekers in the first stage of seeking through [his] perverse whispering. For example, wonderful colours and strange forms appear in their sight, like oceans of fire, or like flourishing and abundant gardens, the form of a gathering of shaykhs, and delivering good news to them from the unseen world. When [the seekers] see these colours, corrupt desires take shape in them, and they speak of unveiling and inspiration, and they suppose that it is a sign of attraction and intoxication. This station is the station of satans. Oh dervish! It is necessary to avoid [the individuals] of that group who divulge things about these stations in order not to become influenced by their filth.

Sit seldom with the evil,
    for the wrong associate
Will defile you [even] if you
    are pure.
Despite its immensity, the sun
Is made to vanish behind
    a speck of a cloud.

Know, oh truthful seeker, [that] just as there are two kinds of [enrapture] by fire, there are also two kinds [of enrapture] by light: the light of majesty and the light of beauty. Love appears from the light of majesty, and manifestations of perfect vision come from the light of beauty. And the light of majesty causes spiritual endeavour, spiritual disputation, enthusiasm and tasting to appear, while the light of beauty makes spiritual witnessing, intimacy, stability and proximity appear. The station of love belongs to the person who is manifested in the light of majesty, while the rank of gnosis belongs to whoever is manifested in the light of beauty. Know that the people of poverty are clad in both of these attributes, both the lover and beloved.

In addition, it should not be concealed that the difference between the light of beauty and the light of majesty is that the light of majesty is metaphorical while the light of beauty is real.

O dervish! [If] in this path a tiny speck is a veil – [so consider] the head hair! This path is thinner than a hair and service to the *pīr* in the proper fashion is sharper than a sword.

Know, oh truthful seeker, that a head hair has been considered worthy for three *abdāls*: His Excellency Shāh Naqshband,[107] Sayyid Burhān al-Dīn Qalandar[108] and Pādshāh Ḥusayn Qalandar.[109] At the start of seeking most of the servants have grown their hair, and they have cut it when wayfaring.

If they ask for the origin [of these beliefs associated with] head hair, answer that it is etiquette (*adab*), and the top of a head hair is service, and the bottom of a head hair is the hair of sincerity.

107
A reference to Bahā' al-Dīn Naqshband (1318–89).

108
The identity of this individual is unknown to me.

109
The identity of this individual is unknown to me.

Know that the purpose of this
discussion is guidance for the seekers
and wayfarers of the path so that they
do not step out of the prophetic *Sharī'at*
and engage in ascetic discipline:

> **Etiquette is a hat**
> **of divine light,**
> **Place it on your**
> **head and wander**
> **wherever you wish.**
> **The Prophet said:**
> **Etiquette is a command**
> **of God, the Most High.**

بنكگنكی ناو اﻣﻨﻠﻖ قارنی توریسا نوکرزدك باتندو ناو ووقۇب نورزنی سامر نتب باتندو. بيهۇ دە سوزرگكە

Hat das Volk den Bauch gesättigt, liegt es da wie ein Ochse,
Mit ungehörigen Worten mästet es sich selbst.

Gdy prosty lud naje się, leży jak bydło,
Zabawia się czczą gadaniną i tuczy swe ciała.

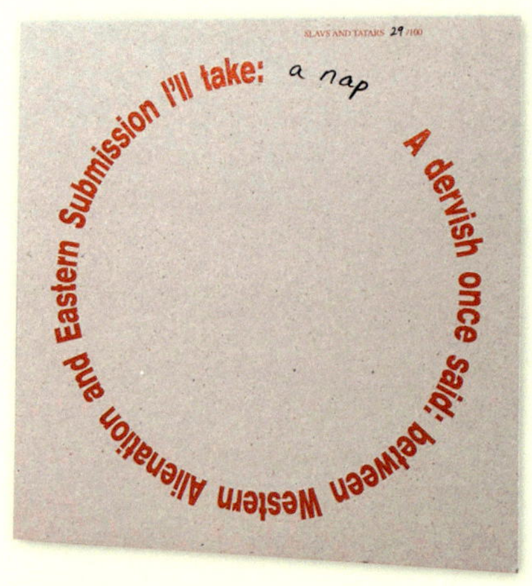

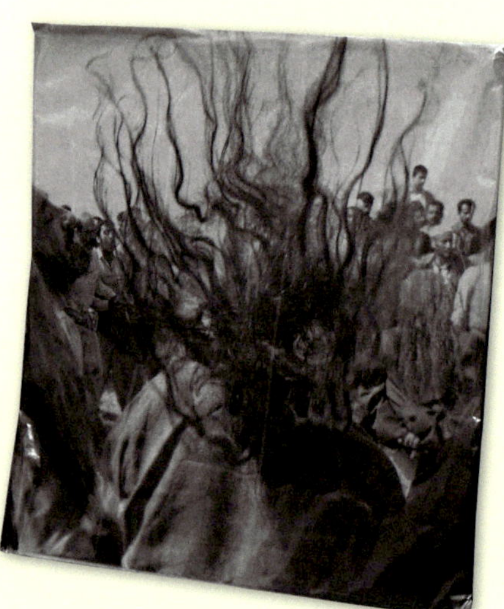

Between 79.89.09
Screen-print with handwritten
word unique to each edition.
The cover slip *(bottom)*
features a photograph of
a Qaderi Kurdish dervish
by Kaveh Golestan. Offset
print on slipcase, 26 × 26 cm,
edition of 100, signed and
numbered, 2009.

Echo Translation

David Crowley

In his book *La voix au cinéma* (*The Voice in Cinema*), Michel Chion coined the word *acousmêtre* to describe a character that can be heard but not seen on screen. Rather than nail down his term with a comprehensive definition, Chion introduces his readers to various kinds of disembodied voices in the cinema. They include the 'complete acousmêtre, the one who is not-yet seen, but who remains liable to appear in the visual field at any moment'; the 'already visualized acousmêtre' – like a character who becomes a temporary narrator to explain an on-screen flashback; and, perhaps its most familiar kind, the 'commentator-acousmêtre', the disengaged speaker who provides a voice-over, 'but never shows himself [and] who has no personal stake in the image'.[1] The acousmêtre seems to derive special powers by eschewing visibility: these are 'the ability to be everywhere, to see all, to know all, and to have complete power. In other words: ubiquity, panopticism, omniscience, and omnipotence'.[2] When the acousmêtre acquires a body, it seems to lose authority, even if – as in the case of the Wizard of Oz in the 1939 Hollywood movie – this power was never more than a matter of the faith of others.

Disembodied, the acousmêtre cannot occupy a clearly demarcated place. Chion writes that it 'must, even if only slightly, have *one foot in the image*, in the space of the film; he must haunt the borderlands that are neither the interior of the filmic stage nor the proscenium', thereby bringing about 'disequilibrium and tension'.[3] Alfred Hitchcock's *Psycho* (1960) provides Chion with numerous examples of how the uncanny, haunting qualities of the acousmêtre can be summoned to produce dramatic effects. Norman Bates's mother is foremost an offscreen voice, while her body is little more than an evanescent shadow flickering in and out of sight. When, at the end of the movie, and after a police psychiatrist has diagnosed Bates's condition, we see Norman sitting in a holding cell; it is his invisible

1
Michel Chion, *The Voice in Cinema*, ed. and trans. Claudia Gorbman (New York: Columbia University Press, 1999), 21.

2
Ibid., 24.

3
Ibid., 24.

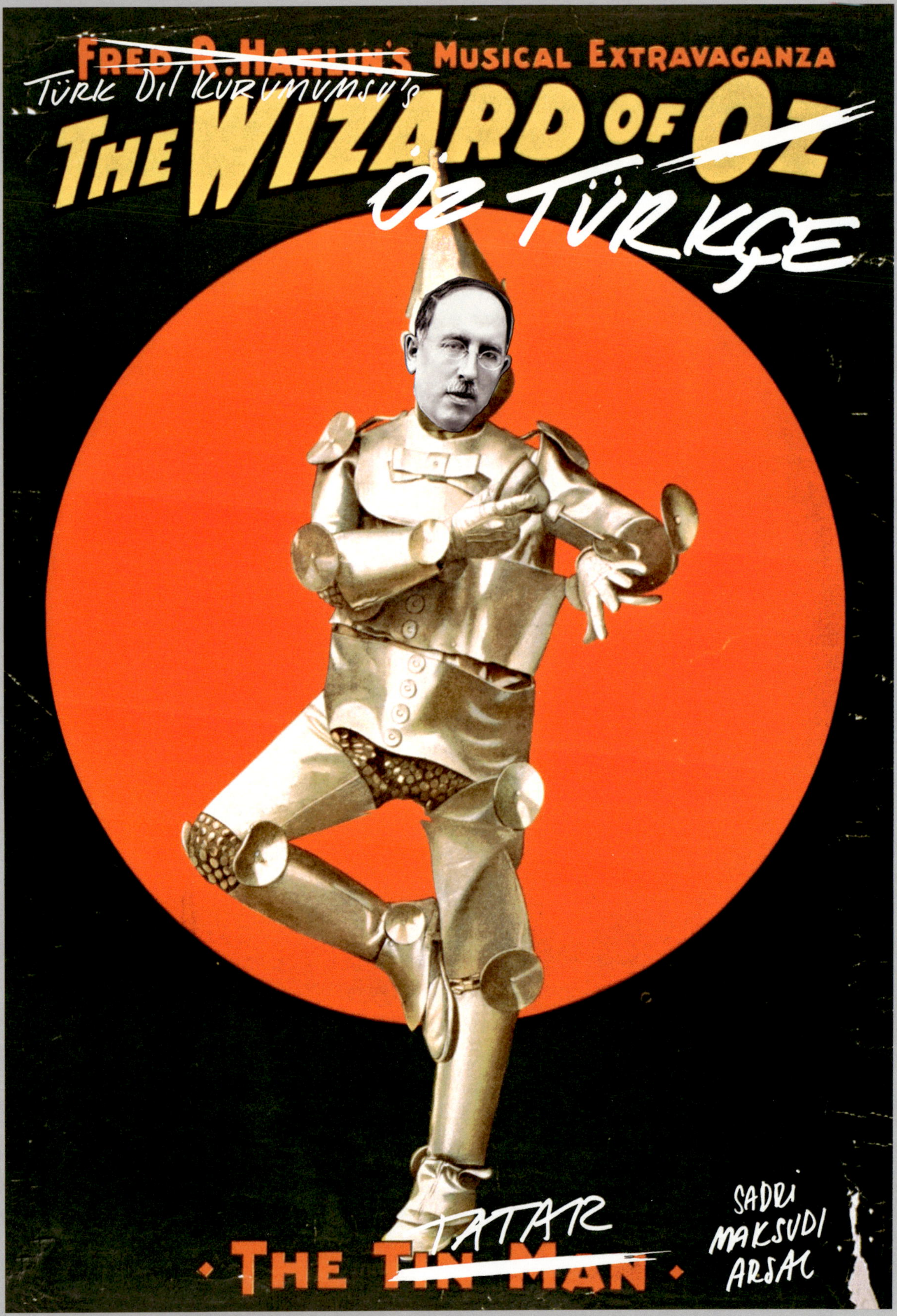

FRED R. HAMLIN's MUSICAL EXTRAVAGANZA
TÜRK DİL KURUMUMSU's
THE WIZARD OF OZ
ÖZ TÜRKÇE
TATAR
THE TIN MAN
SADRİ
MAKSUDİ
ARSAL

mother who speaks. 'When we hear the voice over Norman's face', writes Chion, 'his mouth is closed, as if to suggest possession by spirits or ventriloquism'.[4] This, according to Chion, is the 'triumph of the acousmêtre'.

4
Ibid., 149.

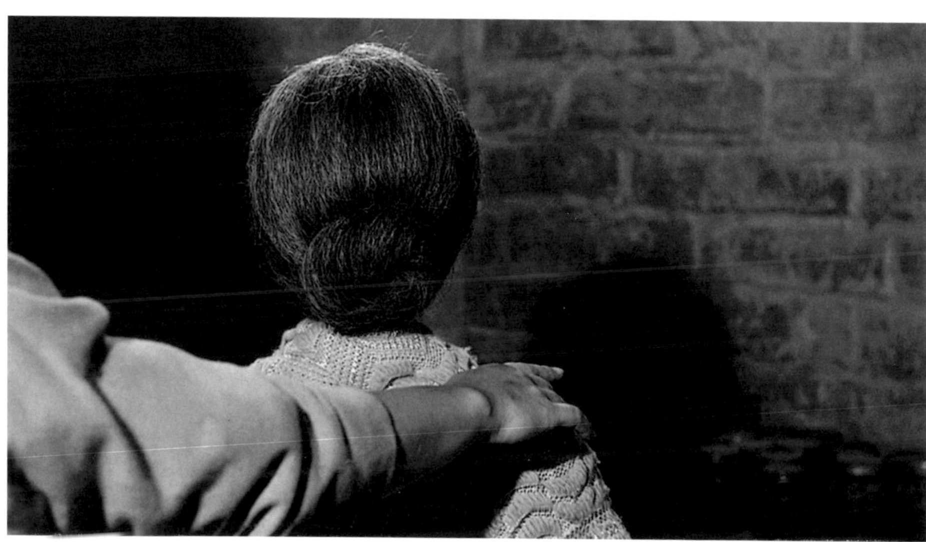

Norman Bates's mother in **Psycho,** the 1960 thriller by Alfred Hitchcock. Courtesy *Universal Pictures*.

Audiences watching Hitchcock's film in the People's Republic of Poland, when it was first screened on television there in 1980, heard a second, unique acousmatic voice, that of a translator. A single voice delivered the words of all the characters on screen. Both the actors and translator were audible, although the Polish voice was louder and followed a second or less later. The acousmatic voice of Norman's mother which seemed to have buried itself in his body was now, almost certainly, voiced by a man. Hitchcock's trashy Freudianism was undone by this act of gender reassignment.

Audiences in Poland – like those in the People's Republic of Bulgaria and the Soviet Union (where *Psycho* was not shown) – were developing viewing habits which still shape the ways in which people like to watch foreign films and broadcasts today. The practices of subtitling and synchronised dubbing by using a cast of voice actors which dominate film translation elsewhere in the world were too costly. Instead, a single – or sometimes multiple – voice-over translation was imposed over the original soundtrack of imported films and other foreign footage. In Russia this technique is known by various names, including *perevod Gavrilova* (Gavrilov translation, after one of the technique's practitioners). The Poles call the voice-over translator a *Szeptanka* (whisperer) or a *Lektor Filmowy* (film reader).

Preferred by television broadcasters, voice-over translation is largely scripted, recorded and added in postproduction today, but its origins in Eastern Europe can be traced to *live* acts of translation in the cinema, first of 'trophy films' which had been looted from Germany at the end of the Second World War (including prints of movies by the Allies) and then of a handful of imported films which were shown under

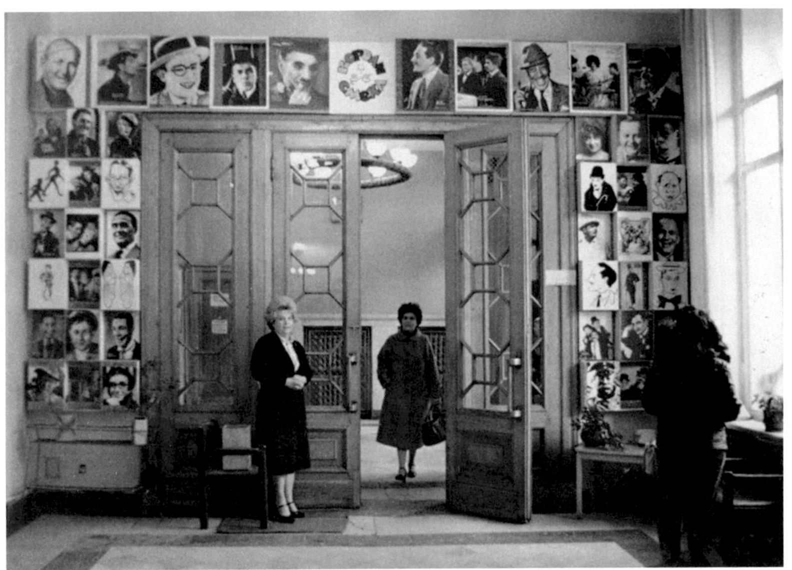

Interior of **Illusion Cinema,** opened in 1966 by the Directorate State Film Fund. Source: *gosfilmofond.ru*

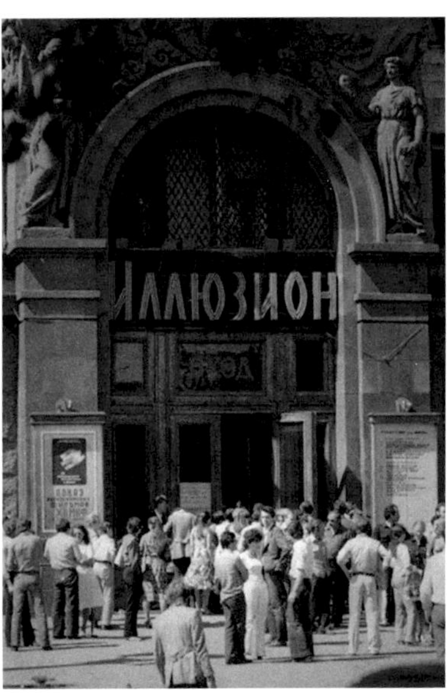

Illusion Cinema,
outside view of the façade.
Source: *gosfilmofond.ru*

licence in the Eastern Bloc from the late 1950s on. The appearance of films made in the West might be taken as a sign of the political 'thaw', particularly in relatively liberal Poland – the Film Repertoire Council (Filmowa Rada Repertuarowa) established there in 1957 set out to achieve a tactical even balance of films from the two Cold War blocs.[5] Nevertheless, Soviet film censors remained wary of the influence of Western films on local audiences, cutting politically 'incorrect' scenes and censoring images of drug use and sexuality.

5
Marek Haltof, *Polish National Cinema* (Oxford & New York: Berghahn, 2002), 78.

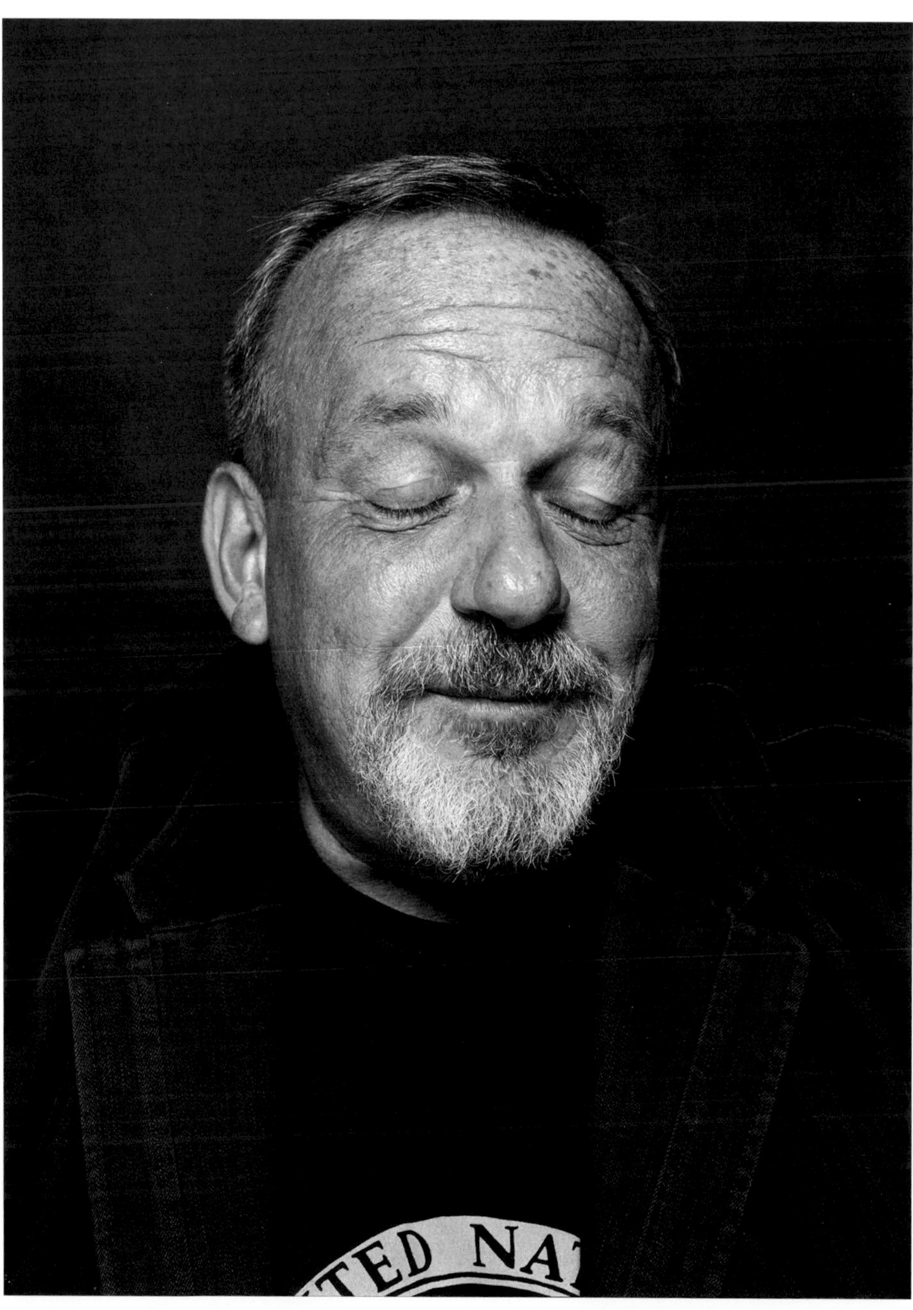

Andrei Yurevich Gavrilov has dubbed an endless number of English, French and Japanese films on video, beginning in the 1980s. Like many an outstanding career, his as a 'lektor' was down to a fortuitous mishap: a translator hadn't shown up for a series of screenings for Soviet bosses and a desperate boss grabbed Andrei to fill his place. Photo by Ivan Kaydash.

In the Soviet Union occasional film festivals and a few specialist cinemas were rare places where audiences could see international films which had not been approved for wide distribution. The Illusion Cinema – which opened in Moscow in 1966 – was one such place. It was the official theatre of Gosfilmofond, the State Film Archive, and a key venue for the Moscow International Film Festival.

**Der Wissende Mann achtet den Besitz gering,
Mit Wissen nährt er die Seele.**

Ciała uczonych starzeją się i niszczeją,
Lecz radują się wiedzą i sycą nią swe dusze.

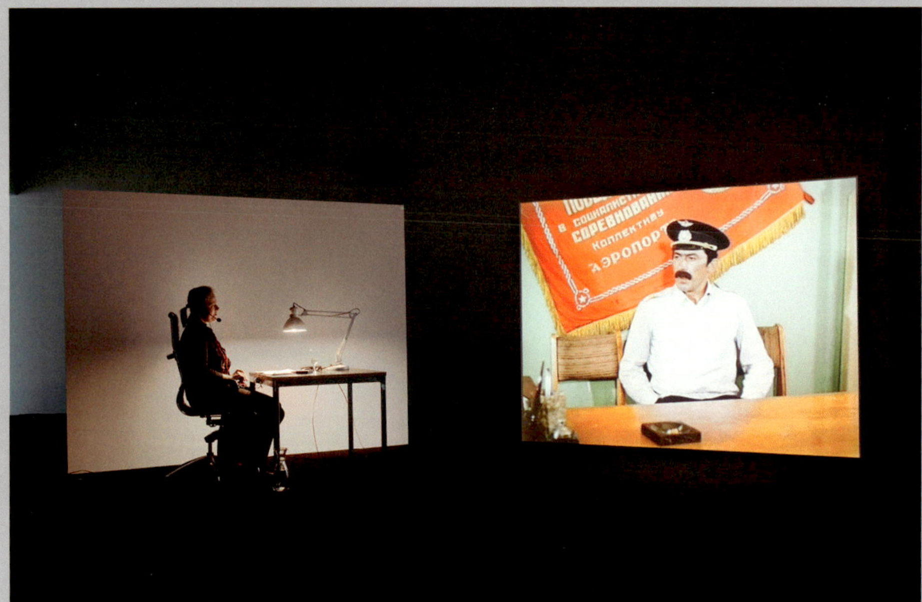

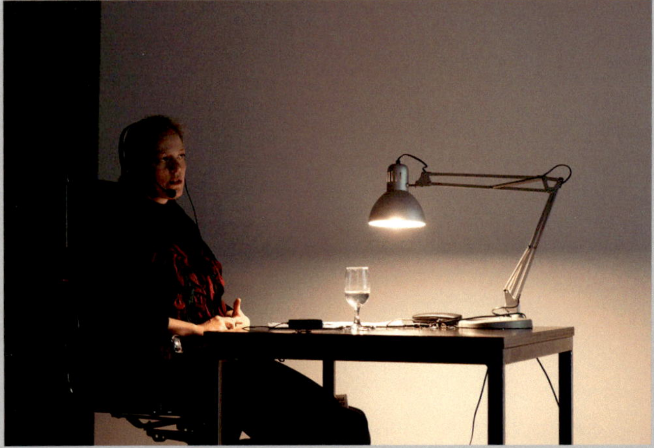

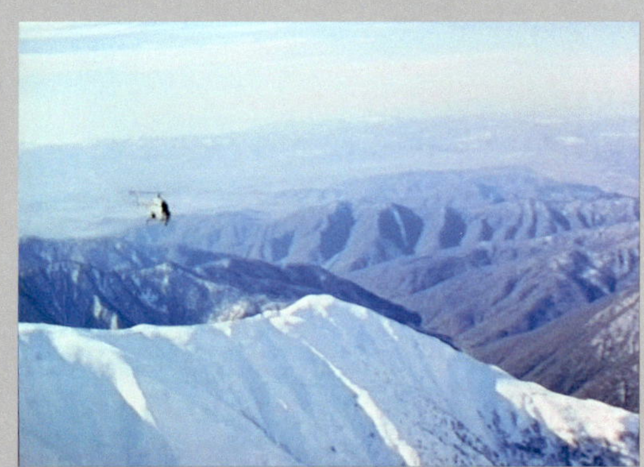

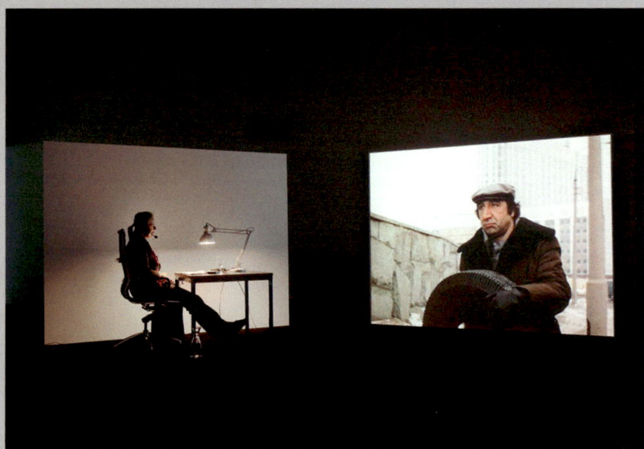

Mimino (Мимино), Soviet Union, 1977.
Written by Revaz Gabriadze, Viktoriya Tokareva
and Georgiy Daneliya. Directed by Georgiy
Daneliya. Screening with live translation into
German. Kunsthalle Zürich.

Bilgili kişiler vücutlarını yıpratır;
Bilgi ile avunur ve ruhlarını semirtir.

أهل العلم ينّهكون أجسادهم، وبها يفتنون أرواحهم.

**The wise, on the other hand,
let their bodies grow thin and fatten their souls,
taking pleasure in wisdom.**

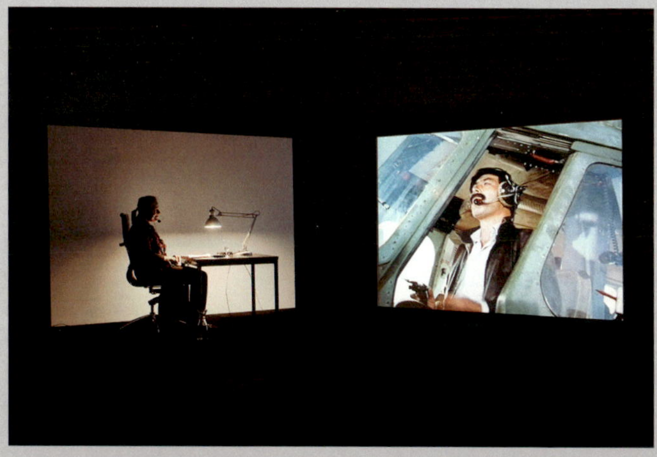

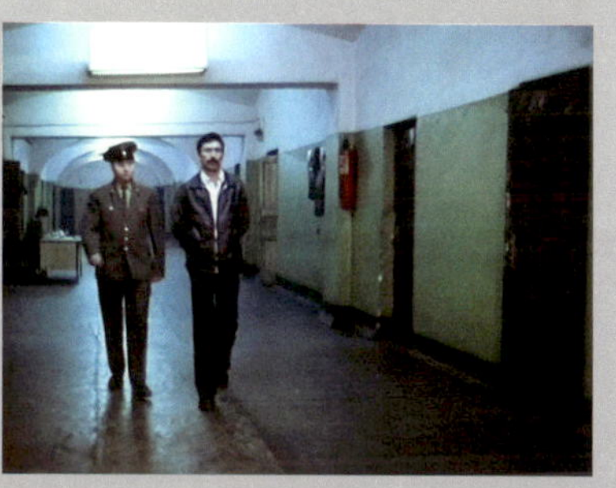

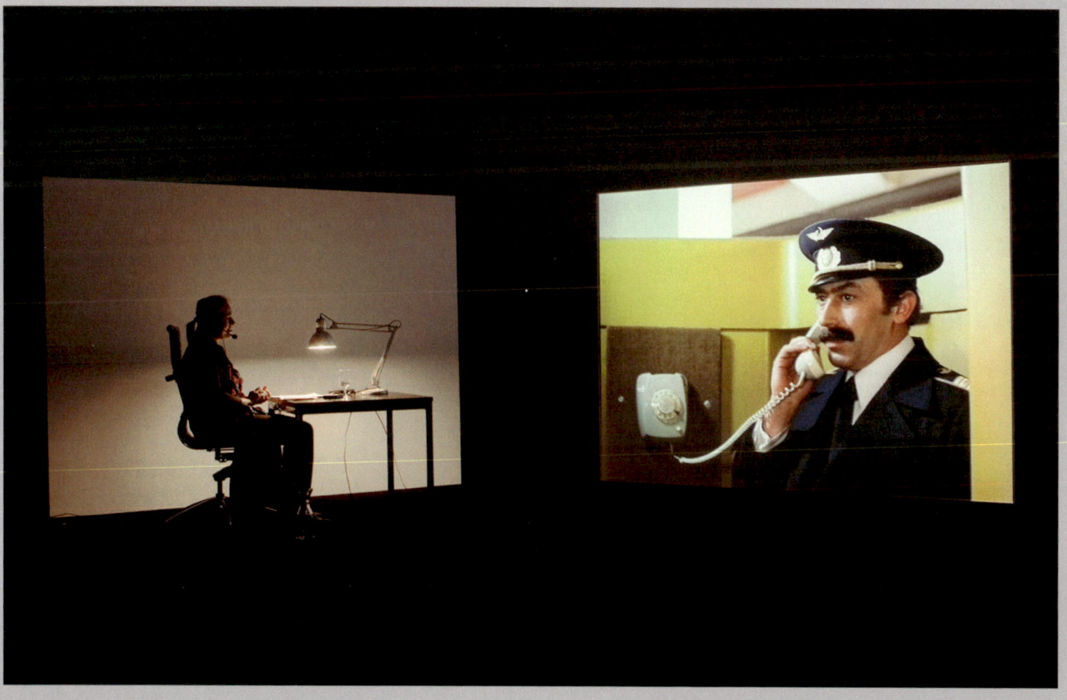

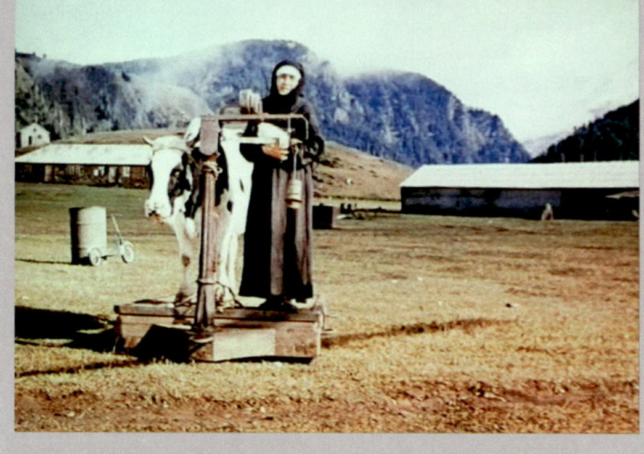

Curated by Julia Moritz, Slavs and Tatars' film programme at the Kunsthalle Zürich featured **live translators or 'lektors' during screenings.** Used for films in Poland and Russia and elsewhere primarily for news segments, the simultaneous playback of two distinct audio tracks, aka Gavrilov translation, makes for an uncanny experience, one where hermeneutics and affect mingle profanely. Photos by Basil Stücheli.

Was der Besitz bietet, das dringt durch die Kehle ein,
Die Seele, das wahre Wort, dringt durch das Ohr ein.

To co jest udziałem ciała, przechodzi przez gardło,
A to co udziałem duszy, to prawdziwe słowa przez uszy wchodzące.

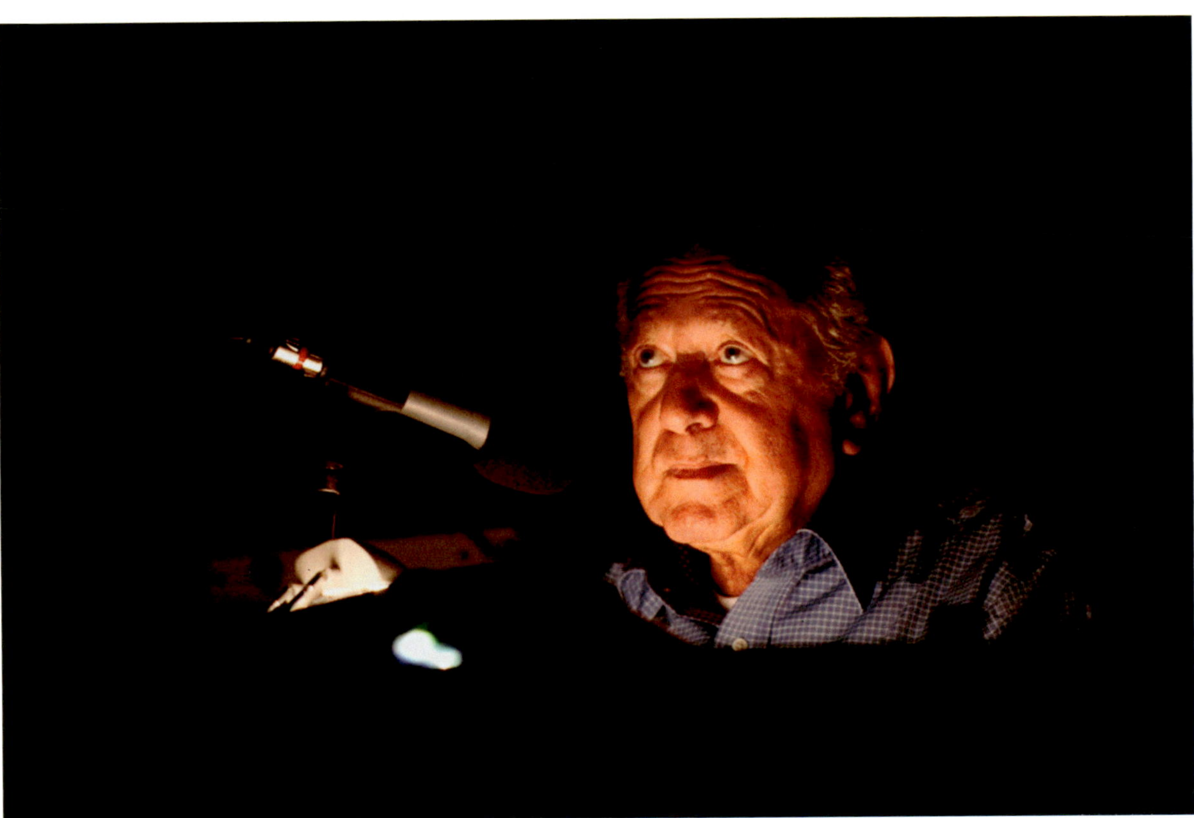

Henryk Pijanowski of the more esoteric faction of 'lektors.' Source: *kocanblog.blogspot.de*

Early screenings there included *Gone with the Wind* (1939), the Japanese arthouse classic *The Naked Island* (1960), directed by Kaneto Shindō, and the 1963 Oscar-winning Italian comedy, *Yesterday, Today and Tomorrow*, starring Sophia Loren.[6] To support its international programme, the Illusion Cinema trained and employed a cadre of professional translators who operated from a special booth equipped with microphones and headphones, as well as lecturers who introduced the repertoire to the public. And when prints were sent to film festivals in the Soviet republics they would often be accompanied by a professional translator from the Illusion Cinema.

Translation and interpretation were exercises in ideological alignment. Just as sexual scenes might be cut by the censors, vulgarity and slang would be suppressed by the translator at the microphone. The translators did not necessarily need to speak the original language of the film: often they would translate from the English, French or German subtitles which accompanied an imported title. Occasionally

6
Gone with the Wind, dir. Victor Fleming, prod. David O. Selznick (Los Angeles: Selznick International Pictures); *The Naked Island*, prod. Eisaku Matsuura and Kaneto Shindō (Tokyo: Kindai Eiga Kyokai); *Yesterday, Today and Tomorrow*, dir. Vittorio De Sica, prod. Carlo Ponti (Rome: Compagnia Cinematografica Champion, Les Films Concordia).

a foreign film would arrive without subtitles or any other kind of textual aids and so the translator would make a stab at interpretation. The spontaneous and even improvisational aspect of translation was, however, muted by repetition – a translator might relay the same film many times in a day and, in the case of the most popular films like *Casablanca* (1942),[7] many hundreds of times in a career. Nevertheless, the Illusion's translators saw themselves as performers of a particular genre of live performance. Irina Razlogova has interviewed a number of them. One, Grigory Libergal, who worked at the Moscow cinema from its opening until the 1980s, recalled:

> When you are watching a film with a simultaneous translation, you, the viewer, have to clearly hear the original soundtrack of the film. If the translator is a master of his craft, he will not 'dominate' the screen, speak on top of the actors. If he is a virtuoso, if he can feel the balance between the film proper and his own voice, after several minutes the spectator in the theatre will forget about the translator, feeling that he himself can understand English, French or Japanese.[8]

Whilst Razlogova's interviewees emphasise character and even artistry as valuable qualities, the ideal, as Libergal stresses, was for the translator to be 'out of mind'. Henryk Pijanowski, a veteran lektor in Poland, suggests that the words should disappear too: 'Mastery of film translation is when the lektor strives to read so that the listener does not hear a thing'.[9] According to this *doxa*, the lektor's voice seeks to bury itself in the mind of the listener, to become like thought. All on-screen words – whether titles, close-ups of text, dialogue, voice-over narration, or on-screen addresses to the viewer – are his. Moreover, they are unified by tone, colour and timbre. Intonation is to be steady and consistent, even when the original on-screen dialogue is delivered at a high emotional pitch; fast-paced exchanges are compressed by judicious editing by the lektor; and those points where speech breaks down – like screams and moans – are left alone, as is singing (though lyrics are often relayed in monotone). This professional voice is never embarrassed by what appears on screen, or doubts the action. Nor does it listen to itself.

7
Dir. Michael Curtiz, prod. Hal B. Wallis (Burbank: Warner Bros.).

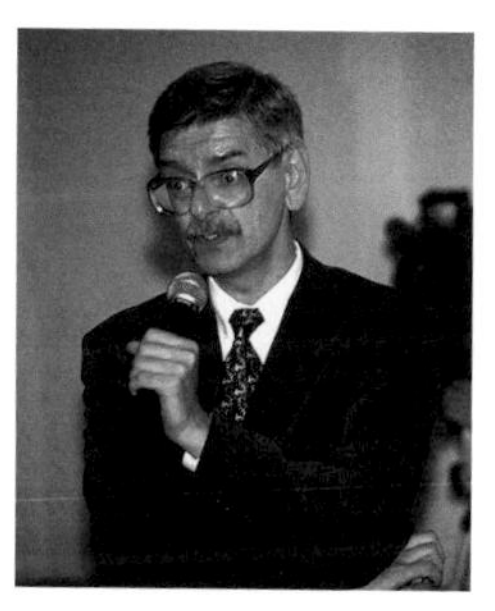

A producer of over 30 documentaries, **Grigory Libergal** first made a name for himself as a simultaneous translator or lektor for films at the Illusion Cinema in the last 1960s and 1970s. Copyright *Séance Magazine Archives*.

8
Grigory Libergal, cited by Elena Razlogova in 'Listening to the Inaudible Foreign. Simultaneous Translators and Soviet Experience of Foreign Cinema', in Lilya Kaganovsky and Masha Salazkina, eds., *Sound, Speech, Music in Soviet and Post-Soviet Cinema* (Bloomington, IN: Indiana University Press, 2014), 169. Razlogova's translation.

9
Henryk Pijanowski, interviewed in *Zawód Lektor* (*Profession Lektor*), a television programme (prod. and dir. Michał Jeczeń) for TVP1, 2006.

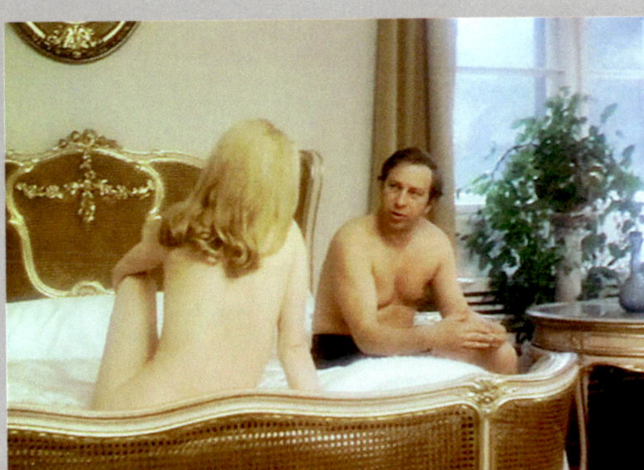

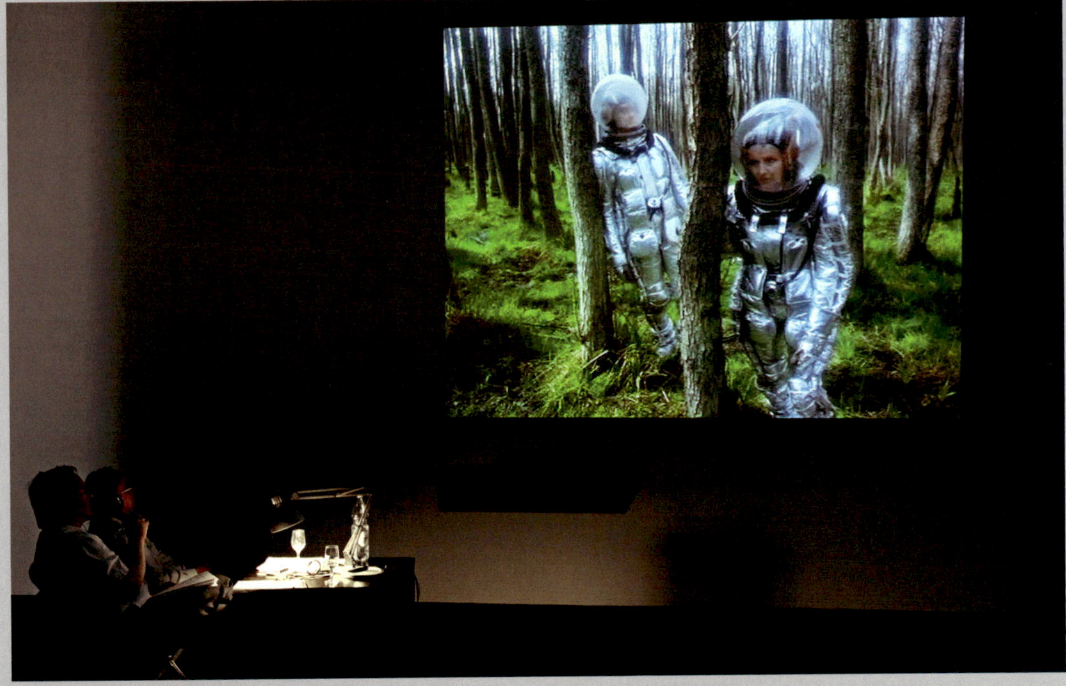

بِه! المعلومة لها علامتان؛
وبهما يكون الإنسان محظوظًا.

Bak bilginin iki alameti vardır;
Bu iki şey ile insan bahtiyar olur.

Controlling these two things – the tongue and the throat – is the hallmark of wisdom, and reddens a man's cheeks.

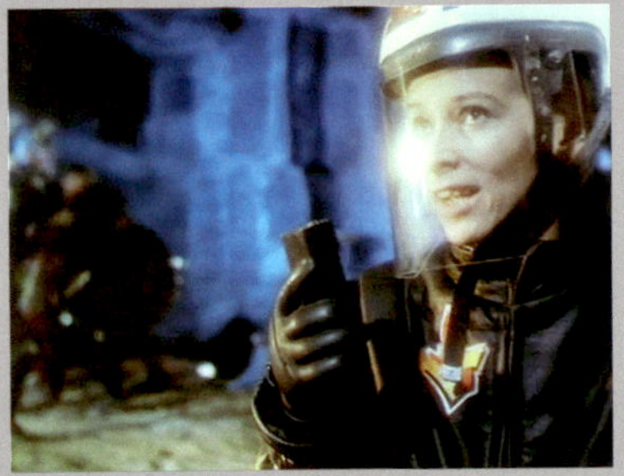

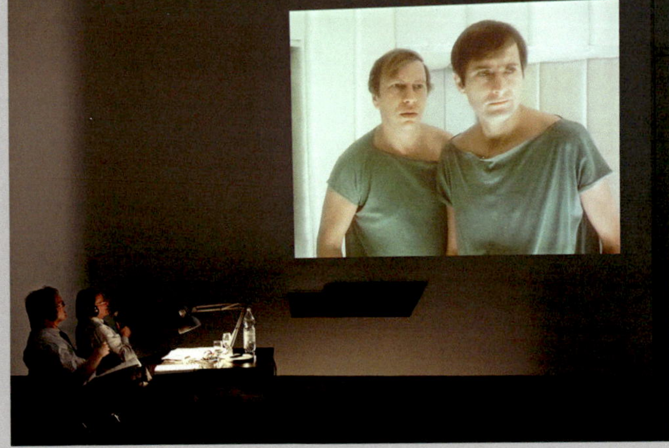

Sex Mission (Seksmisja), Poland, 1984.
Written and directed by Juliusz Machulski.
Screening with live translation into German.
Kunsthalle Zürich.

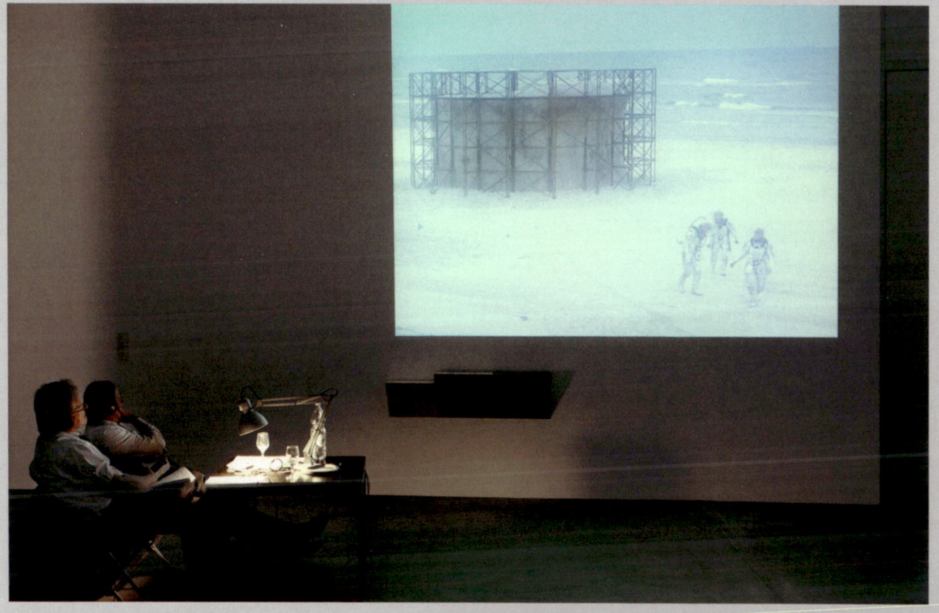

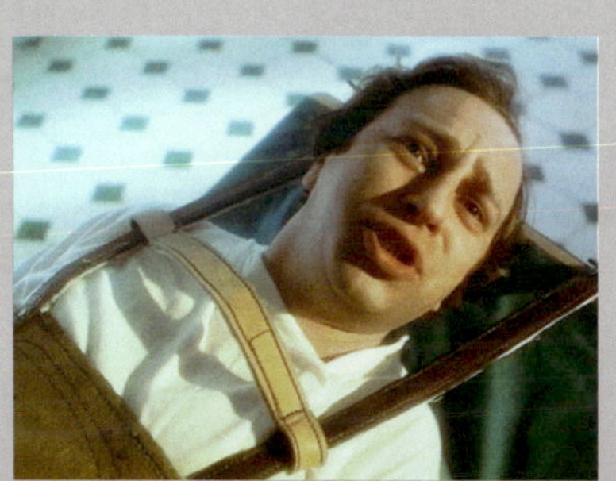

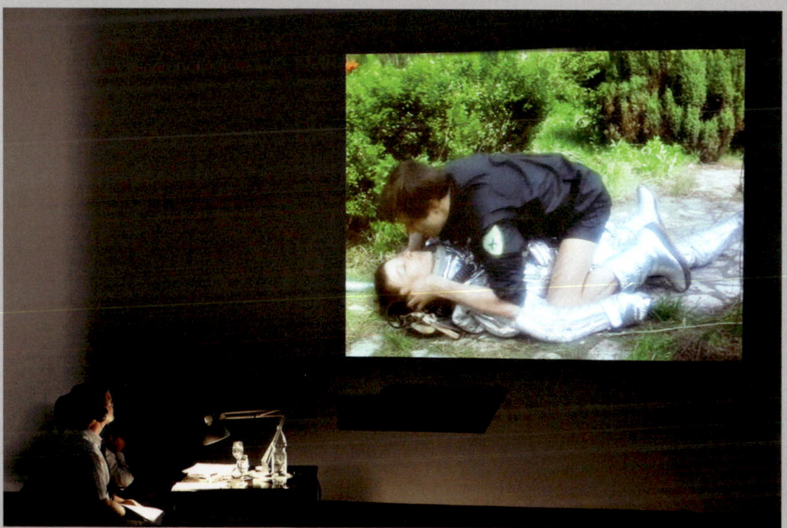

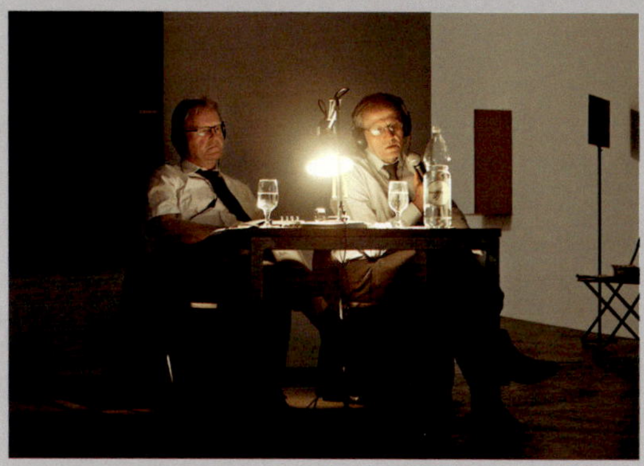

بۇ نىڭ بىرى تىل، بىرى بوغۇزدۇر. بۇ ئىككىسىنى ياخشى باشقۇر الىسا دېرىدىك ياخشى تېگىدۇ.

Das eine ist die Zunge, das andere die Kehle,
Hält man beide im Zaum, so ist der Gewinn gross.

Jeden to język, a drugi – gardło,
Gdy człowiek oba posiada, dużą ma z nich korzyść.

A World in Your Ear

Voice-over translation would seem to be akin to the better-known and more widespread practice of dubbing or what is sometimes called 'voice replacement'. But the practices differ in crucial ways. In dubbing, for instance, the aim of the vocal actor is to present the illusion of synchronised speech by overlaying his or her voice over that of another. Gender and age should match, as should the sound with the movement of lips (at least in countries like Germany where the imperative to sync sound with image overrides the requirement of fidelity to the script).[10] By contrast, a lektor uses delay to distinguish his voice from those of the actors on screen: his words follow theirs.

The popularity of voice-over translation in Poland may well be a product of the poor reputation of dubbing, particularly in the 1950s when it was still the dominant way of translating foreign films. In 1955, *Film* magazine gathered the opinions of Polish viewers of René Clair's French production *Les Belles de nuit* (*Beauties of the Night*) (1952) and Slátan Dudow's East German *Stärker als die Nacht* (*Stronger than the Night*) (1954): 'The dubbing in *Stronger than the Night*', according to one, 'was primitive, and completely embarrasses the filmmakers with errors and awkwardness. The actors on the screen open their mouths, and there is silence. This lasts for a while until we hear a Polish voice…the same effect is also found in the scene depicting a clandestine meeting by the river when the mouths of those gathered is met by annoying silence on the screen – like a silent film'.[11] Even when the dubbing was well synchronised, other cavils were raised. 'I cannot accept the convention that the Frenchman on screen speaks Polish. This is something unnatural…' remarked one viewer of the Clair film.[12] Unnaturalness is a familiar complaint in the history of sound dubbing (Antonin Artaud characterised dubbing as a form of possession and Jorge Luis Borges said that it produces monsters).[13] But the erasure of foreignness might well have been unwelcome too. Unlike dubbing (but like subtitling), voice-over translation allows for foreign words and accents to be audible, and, as such, for difference to persist. During the Cold War, the gap between the original voice and its translation was also the gap between East and West, or, for that matter, between East and East. In hearing Gérard Philipe or Gina Lollobrigida's voices in *Les Belles de nuit*, audiences were able to enjoy a little of the

---

10
On national differences in the approach to dubbing, see K. J. Donnelly, *Occult Aesthetics: Synchronization in Sound Film* (Oxford: Oxford University Press, 2014).

11
Cited in Czesław Michałski, 'O dubbing dobrze i źle' in *Film*, vol. 50 (1955): 3.

12
Ibid.

13
See Michail Yampolsky, 'Voice Devoured: Artaud and Borges on Dubbing', trans. Larry P. Joseph, *October*, vol. 64 (Spring 1993): 57–77.

Bunlardan biri dil, biri de boğazdır; insan bu ikisine hakim olursa çok fayda görür.

أحدهما اللسان والآخر مجرى الطعام، فإن أحكم الإنسان عليهما فإنه يلقى فوائد كثيرة.

One is the tongue, the other is the throat, he who keeps both in check, stands to profit much.

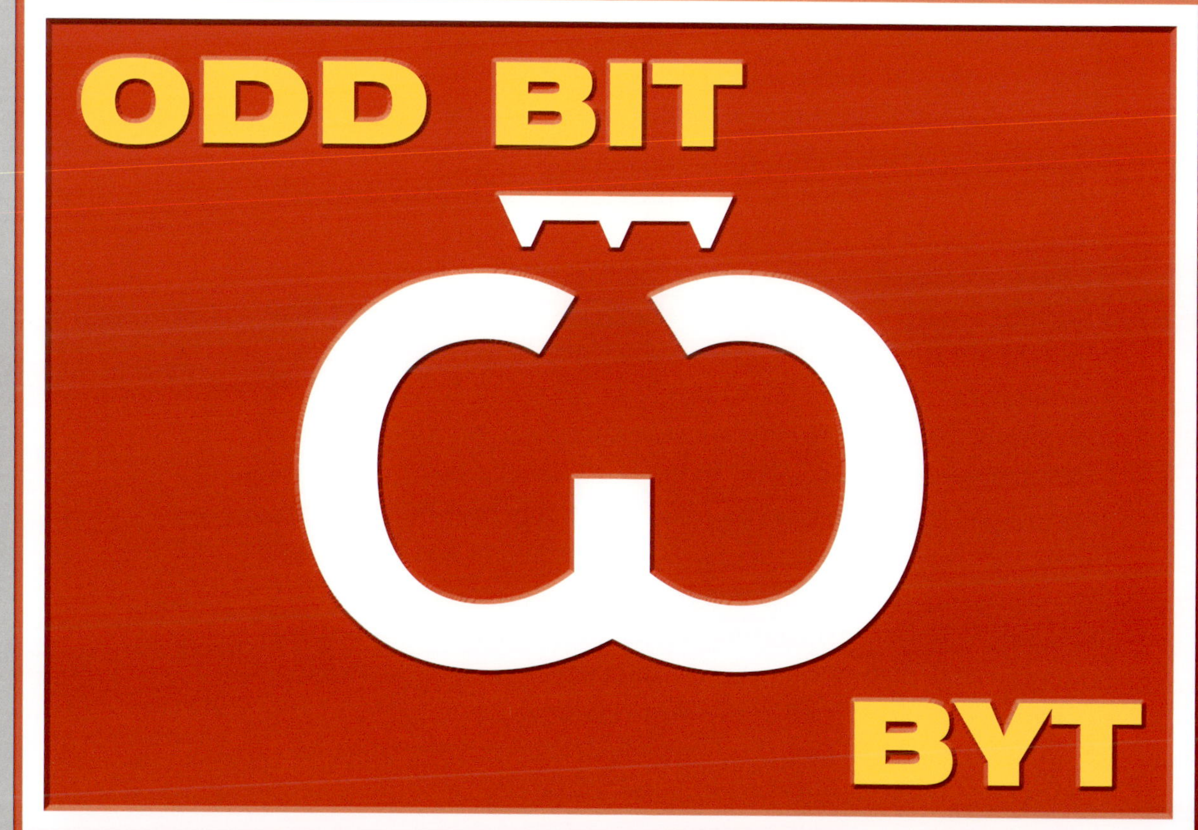

JĘZZERS
JĘZYK!

ODD BIT
BYT

internationalism which the Soviet Bloc proclaimed so loudly in its propaganda but denied its citizens in life. Whether this was a wish for solidarity with working classes around the world or a desire to satisfy what Czesław Miłosz once called the 'hunger for strangeness' in the grey world of state socialism is hard to know.[14]

Another difference between dubbing and voice-over narration is the fact that the lektor assumes responsibility for delivering all words heard or seen on screen. To contain this proliferating polyphony, the 'best' voice-over is transparent, unobtrusive, lacking corporeality. This tendency was amplified when voice-over translation was imported into the expanding field of television broadcasting in Eastern Europe in the 1970s. Post-sync recording means that the infelicities of live translation are ironed out. Close-micing, producing a very 'dry' sound with little reverberation, erases all traces of the space of the studio. Offering clear definition, close-micing also lifts the voice out of the space of the film. So close, this voice seems to be inside the ear. It is always there, always on, even, it seems, when the lektor is not speaking.

Almost always male, transmitted over the airwaves, and having the capacity to speak for all and to translate every language, the voice of the lektor might seem to have the powers that Chion ascribes to the acousmêtre. But, unlike the narrator of movies, newsreels or documentaries, the lektor does not provide expert explanations of events, or insight into the inner thoughts of the characters on screen. He has no capacity for reflection or hindsight. His is, seemingly, an automatic voice, only triggered by the words of others. Rather than being the voice of God, the lektor is a servant of the speaker. His humble status is perhaps revealed by the 'first' voice-over translator in the Soviet world, Ivan Bolshakov, chairman of the Committee on Cinematography of the USSR. In the 1940s Bolshakov would arrange daily private screenings for the generalissimo in his private cinema. These were both moments of private entertainment and, at the same time, a meetings of the most important film censorship board in the USSR.[15] Stalin's displeasure would mean that a film would not be acquired for distribution. According to eyewitnesses, he was a particularly active viewer, delivering a running report of the ideological merits and failings of each film – a dictator's commentary. He had a

14
Czesław Miłosz, *The Captive Mind* (Harmondsworth: Penguin, 1980), 69.

15
Grigory Mariamov, *Kremlevskii tsenzo:. Stalin smotrit kino* (*The Kremlin Censor: Stalin Watches the Cinema*) (Moscow: Kinotsentr, 1992).

taste for cowboy movies as well as the films of Spencer Tracy and Clark Gable but, according to Nikita Khrushchev, would also 'curse them, giving them an ideological evaluation'.[16] A canny retainer, Bolshakov would usually arrange for a choice of films to be available at each screening to improve Stalin's mood. This introduced a new problem – the prints of the films were not subtitled and so Bolshakov had to be

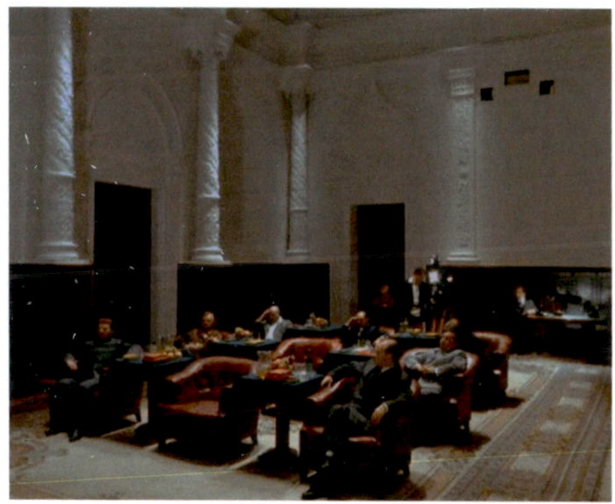

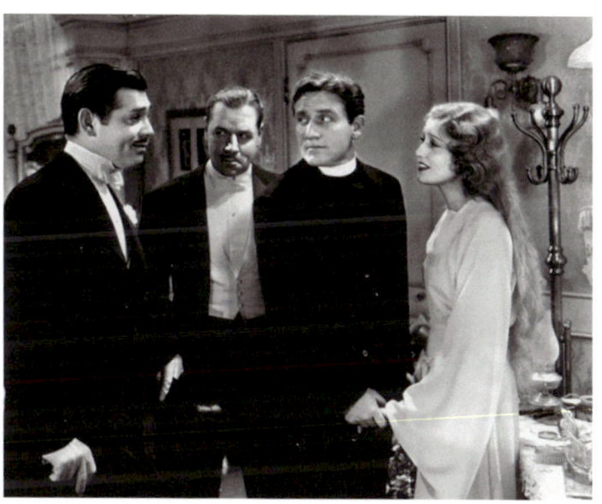

Clark Gable (far left) and *Spencer Tracy* (3rd left) with Jeannette Macdonald in *San Francisco*, a 1936 musical drama directed by W. S. Van Dyke (with a helping hand from D. W. Griffith).

A captive audience, **Stalin's Film Screening Room** from the movie *Inner Circle* (1991). The projector breaks down, causing Stalin to become furious with his cinema minister and projectionist, Ivan Bolshakov. Courtesy *Columbia Pictures*.

ready to give his mercurial master an extempore translation of the dialogue on the spot. Speaking only faltering English, Bolshakov would prepare by spending hours with interpreters learning the story and lines. Even then, he struggled to keep up with the plot and dialogue of the many films he'd put at Stalin's command. Stalin apparently enjoyed the deep discomfort felt by his subaltern. Such anecdotes are often relayed by Stalin's biographers to illustrate his volatile and malevolent character; nevertheless, Bolshakov was a wily operator, successfully extending his role to become the first minister of cinematography in 1946.

Abusive Translations

Like many things in Eastern Europe, voice-over translation may have originated at the command of authority but it eluded the control of the state. In the 1980s unlicenced copies of Western films began to be made on video cassettes and traded (their illegal origins often confirmed by the legend 'For Preview Purposes Only' across the screen). These were

16
Nikita Krushchev, cited by Sergei Khrushchev, ed., *Memoirs of Nikita Khrushchev: Volume 2: Reformer, 1945–1964*, (Philadelphia, PA: Penn State University Press, 2006), 115.

Bilgilinin boğazına ve diline hakim olması gerekir;
Boğazını ve dilini gözeten bilgililer gereklidir.

موضع الكلام سرٌّ، ولكن ينبغي ذكر واحد منها فقط
ينقسم الكلام إلى عشرة

The wise man has power over throat and tongue,
he who guards tongue and throat is full of knowledge.

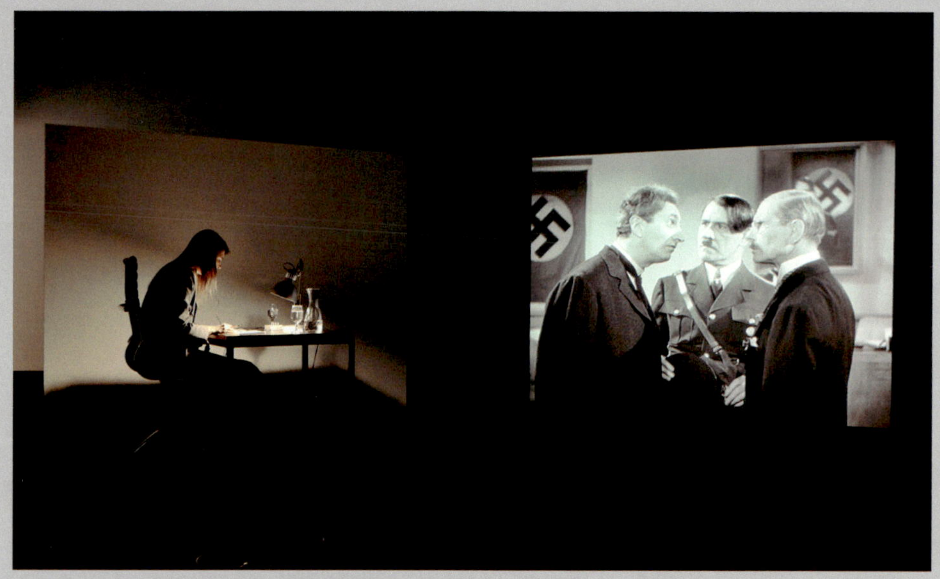

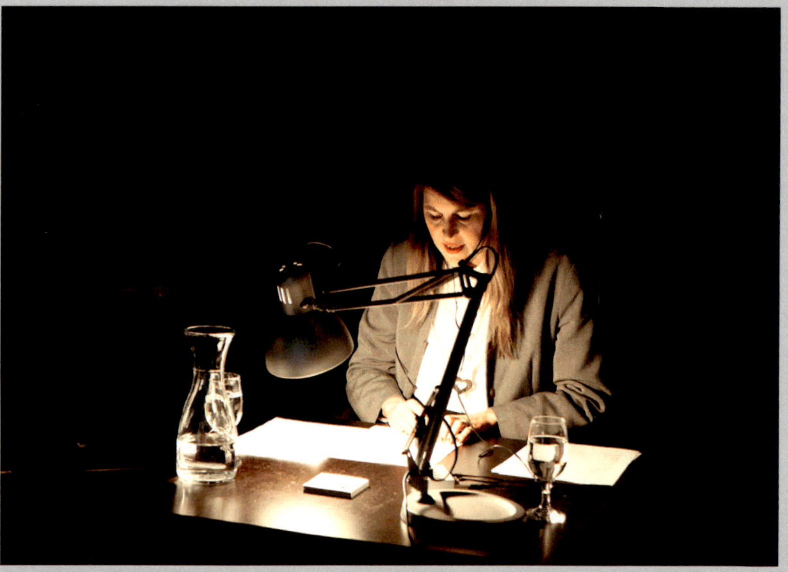

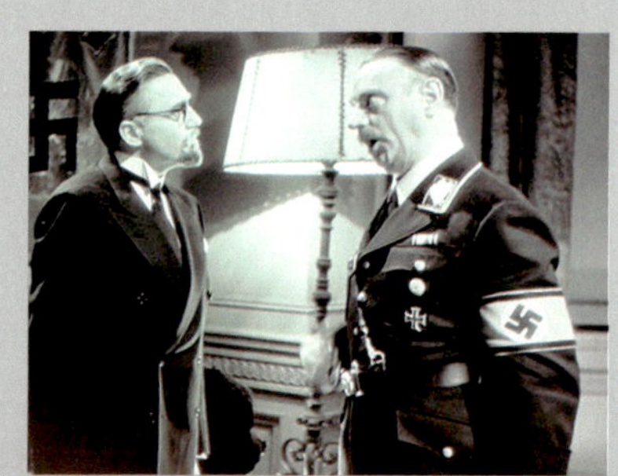

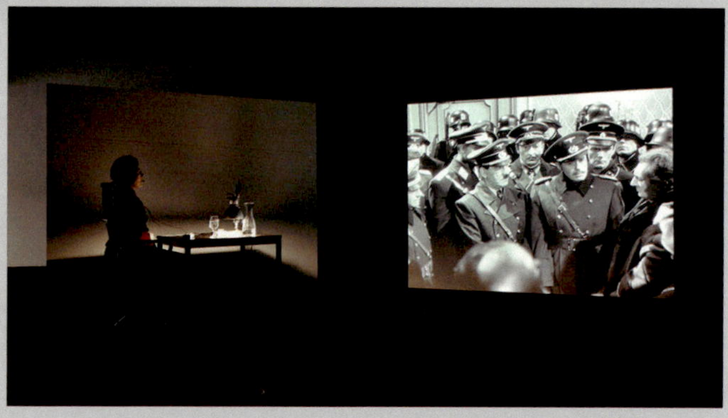

Des Wortes Ursprung ist ein Geheimnis,
Zehnfach ist der Gewinn des Wortes,
Auch wenn man nur eines spricht.

Tajemnicą jest, gdzie przebywa słowo,
Słowo ją dzieli, lecz ktoś musi je wypowiedzieć.

To Be or Not to Be, United States, 1942.
Written by Melchior Lengyel (original story) and
Edwin Justus Mayer (screenplay). Directed by
Ernst Lubitsch. Screening with live translation
into Swiss German. Kunsthalle Zürich.

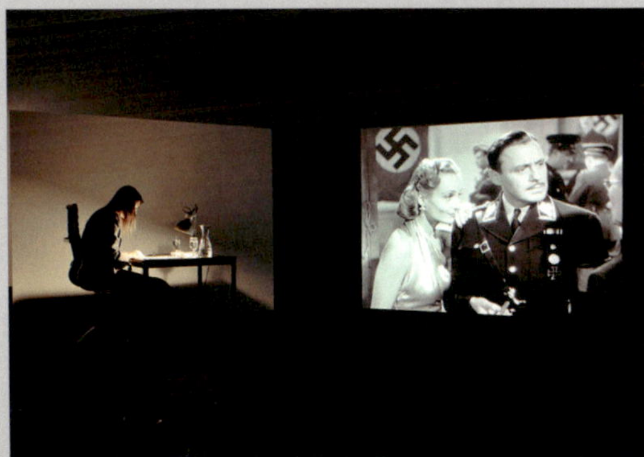

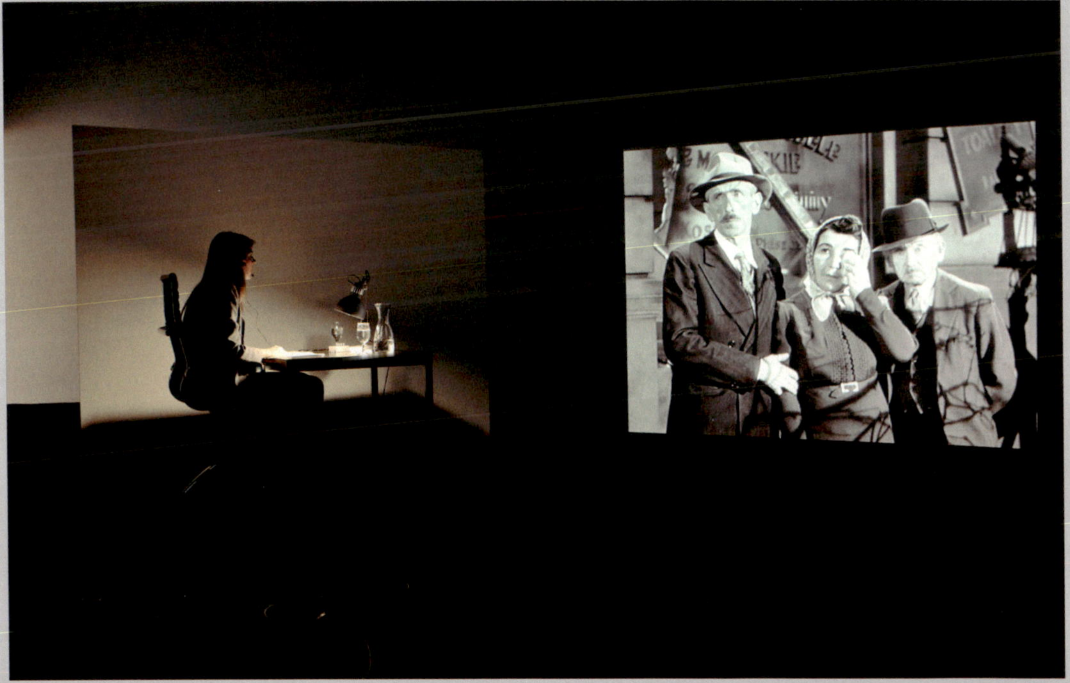

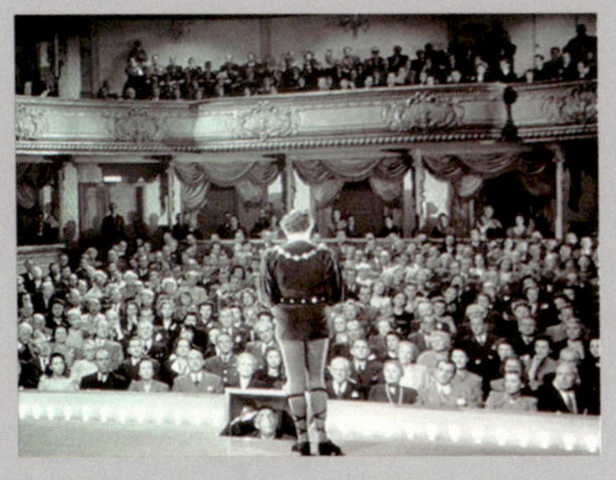

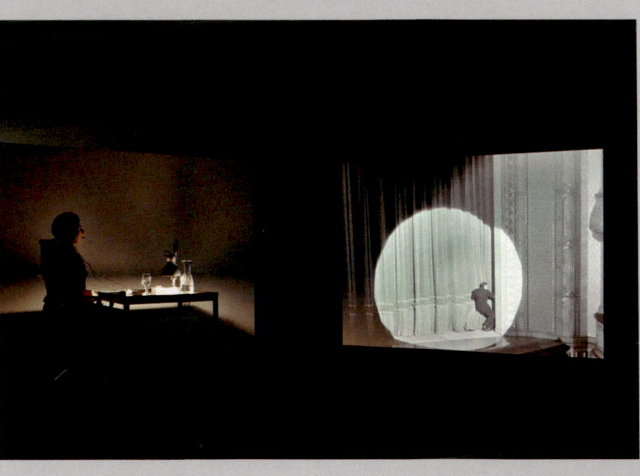

The source of the speech is the inmost heart.
The shares of speech are ten: only one of these ought to be spoken,

ينقسم الكلام إلى عشرة وواحدة منها هي التي تقال، والتسعة الباقية ممنوعة.

Sözün yeri sırdır;
Söz ona bölünür, fakat biri söylenmelidir.

accompanied by voice-over translations provided by amateurs, many of whom were academics or professional translators who had benefited from language training. Leonid Veniaminovich Volodarskii recalls the process:

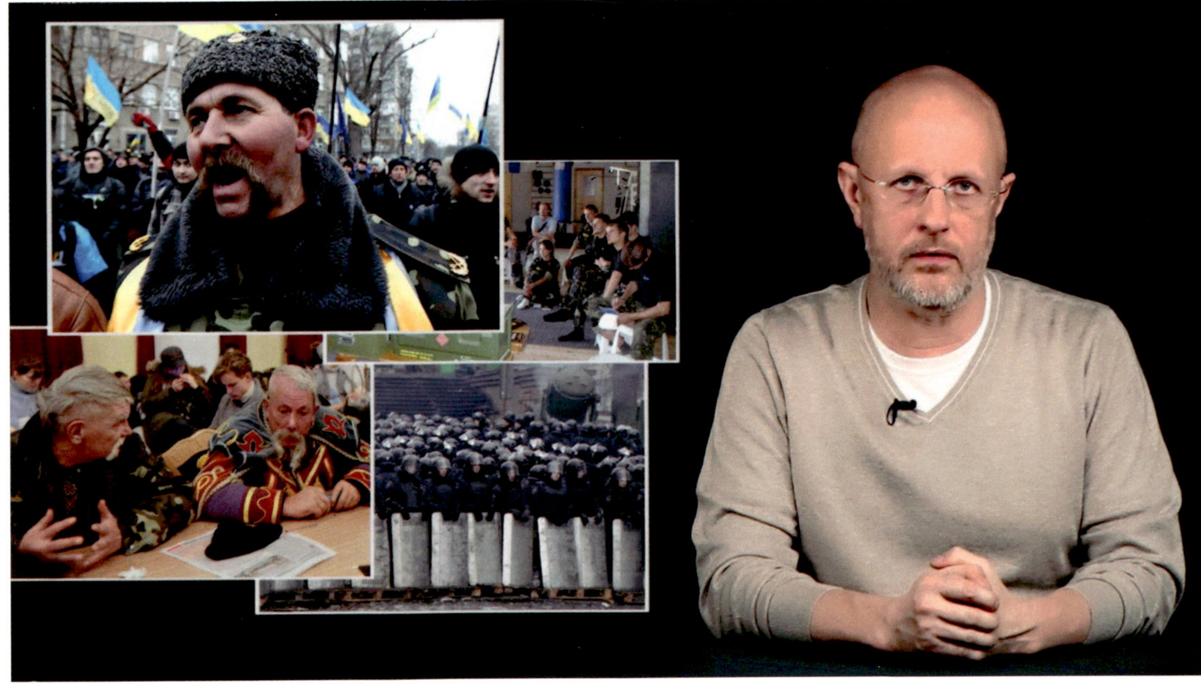

Dmitry Puckhov (aka Goblin), in his *Goblin News*. Source: *oper.ru*

Everything was done using two VCRs, sitting on your knees, basically. One of them had to be stereo. You stuck the original [VHS cassette] into one VCR, a blank VHS cassette into the other VCR, and a mic into this other VCR, too. I translated simultaneously, and my voice was recorded by the second VCR. Then some techie – I'm strictly not technically minded – made a master tape of my voice-over. From that point on, it was 'Full speed ahead!' – multiple copies were made, and the voice-over hit the popular masses.[17]

Often idiosyncratic, these translations departed from the script in ways that appeal to both their viewers and to scholars of translation. One, Alexander Burak, stresses the fact that such translations were

17
Volodarskii, cited by Alexander Burak, 'Some Like it Hot – Goblin-Style: "Ozhivliazh" in Russian Film Translations', in *Russian Language Journal*, vol. 61 (2011): 7. Burak's translation.

made without a great deal of preparation: often long passages of slang or idiomatic phrases would elude the translator and so he would have to improvise (an unintended echo of Bolshakov's performances for Stalin).[18] Even skilled translators might well enhance the original with local colloquialisms and vivid profanities in an effort to capture what they believed to be the colour of the original. The creative translator of Martin Scorsese's *Mean Streets* (1973) replaced New York's street slang with that of Warsaw's Praga district in a pirate version on sale in Poland in the early '90s. Widely acclaimed as the master of the genre in Russia, Dmitry Puckhov (aka Goblin), who acquired his English in the '80s on a two-year course at the Dzerzhinsky Police House of Culture and by translating rock lyrics at home, achieved success and some degree of notoriety for his voice-over translations, which far exceed the principle of fidelity. In rescripting imported thrillers and crime films such as *Pulp Fiction* (1994), Puckhov incorporated the full force of Russian expletives as well as an urgent, highly distinctive tone of voice. These devices, he claims, capture the gritty qualities of

18
Ibid.

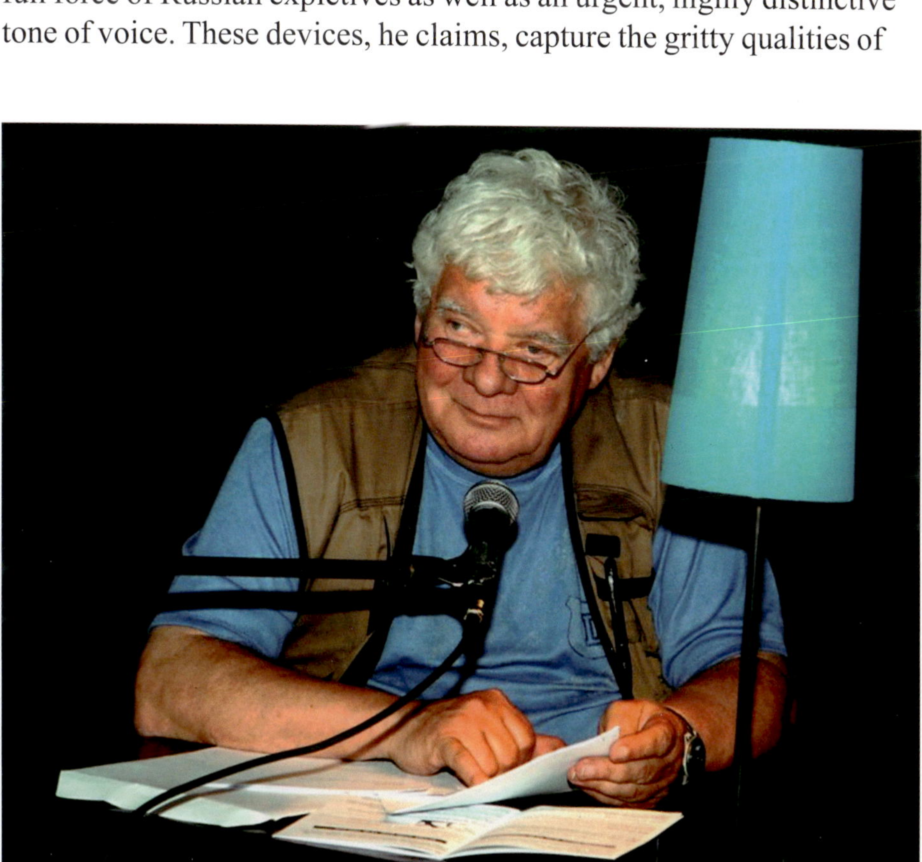

Polish *Pulp Fiction* lektor, **Tomasz Knapik.** Source: *kocanblog.blogspot.de*

the original films far more effectively than the pious, literary-minded cultural approach to translation promoted by the film studios.[19] His reputation, however, owes more to his comic voice-over translations of the first two *Lord of the Rings* films made in the early 2000s, which relocate Middle-earth to contemporary Russia. The principal characters were given comic Russified names:[20] Frodo Baggins became Fedor Mikhailovich Sumkin (a derivative of the Russian word sumka, or bag); the Ranger, Aragorn, was renamed Agronom (farm worker); Legolas became Logovaz, after the Russian car company responsible for Ladas. Puckhov also introduced new elements into the soundscape: courtly dancing at Bilbo Baggins's birthday party, for instance, is accompanied by a well-known techno track by Ruki Vverh! (Hands Up!). Woven through the voice-over narration are what remain topical themes relating to the rampant advance of capitalism in the country. The search story becomes something like a crime drama set in the Russian underworld. The tone is set from the outset when the main character,

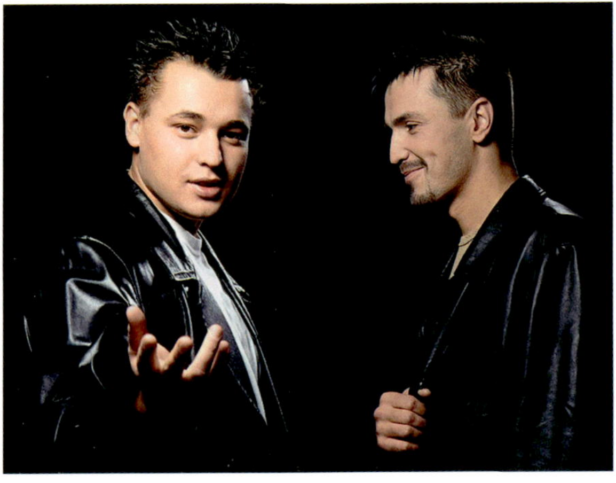

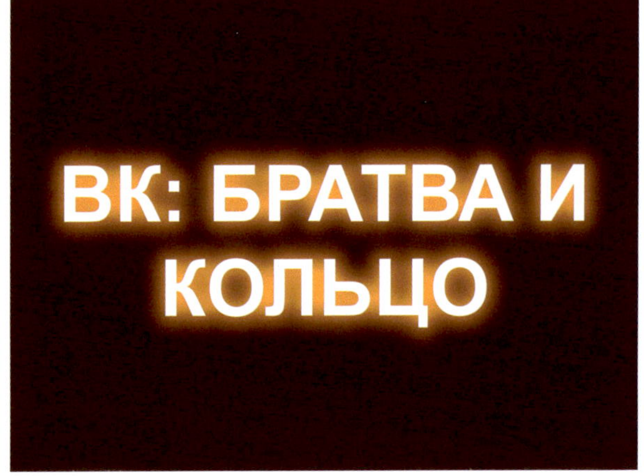

Ruki Vverh! (Hands Up!), a '90s 'technopop' duo from Russia who couldn't have anticipated the travesty of justice their name would evoke 20 years later in street riots across the United States, after the events in Ferguson, MO. Source: *topdesktop.org*

just returned to Middle-earth after years of wandering, announces: 'The world is not much changed – people steal as before. MacDonald's have cropped up everywhere – it is funny I don't see them here'. In effect, Puckhov's versions of *Lord of the Rings* are social satires which function as what Abé Mark Nornes calls 'abusive translations' – acts of rescripting which 'tamper with language usage and freely ignore or change much of the source text'. What Nornes calls 'abuse' has a

19
Carl Shreck, 'Goblin Makes the Case against Demonising Expletives', *St. Petersburg Times* (29 July 2003), http://sptimes.ru/index.php?action_id=2&story_id=10583 (accessed 20 October 2014).

20
Natalia Rulyova, 'Piracy and Narrative Games: Dmitry Puchkov's Translations of "The Lord of the Rings"', in *Slavic and East European Journal*, vol. 49, №4 (Winter 2005), 625–638.

Властелин Колец (*The Lord of the Rings*), the dubbed Russian version, with in-movie music by Russian pop artists. Puchkov's 'funny translations' are parodies of awkward translations presented at the Russian movie market, where characters speak quite differently from how they spoke in the original films. The Russian title translates *LotR: The Fellas* (Mob) *and the Ring* (the word *Fellas* is a common idiom for the Russian mob, and mobsters specifically – roughly equivalent to the use of 'the boys' in an old American mob film.

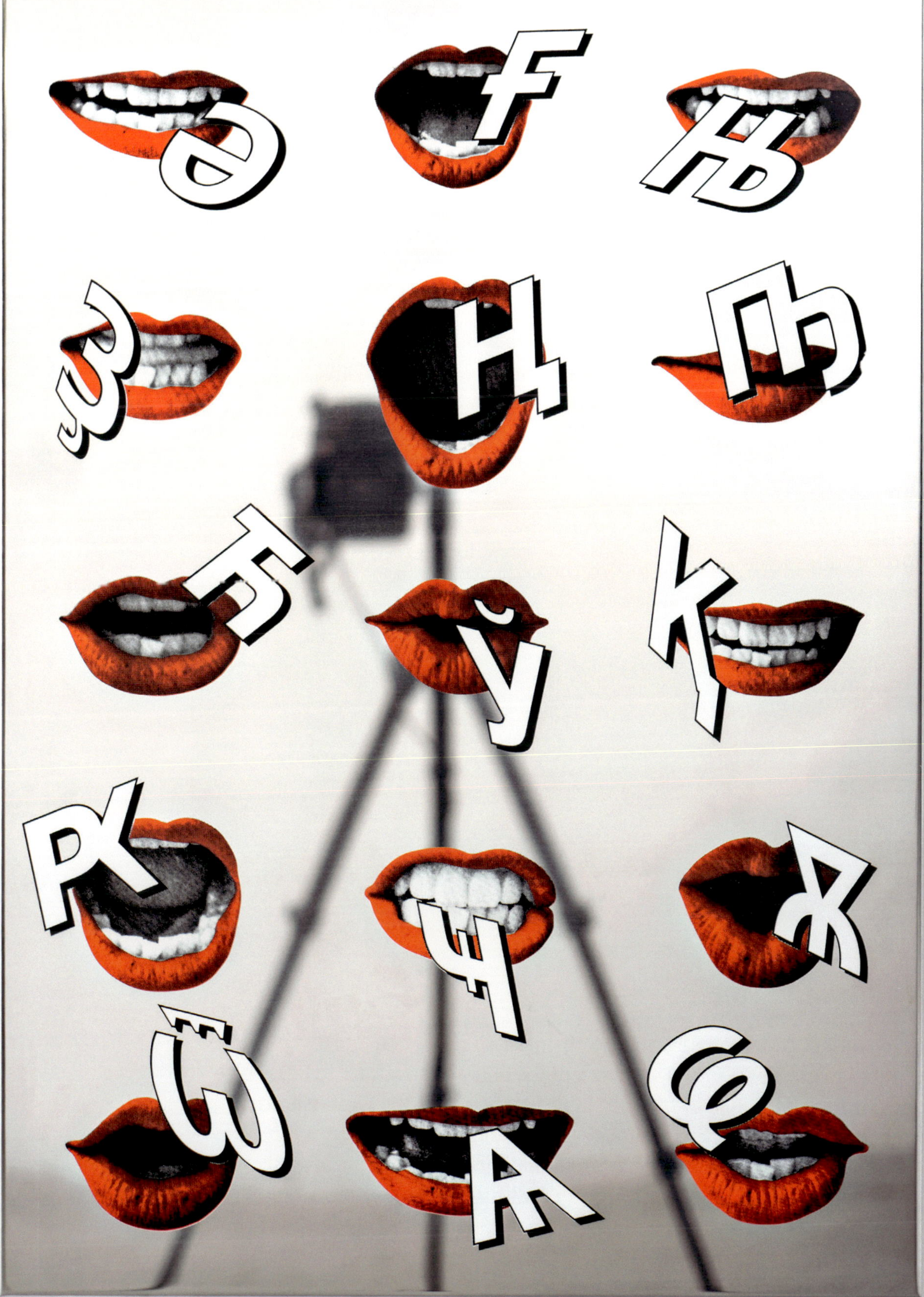

positive value when it 'helps inject a palpable sense of the foreign'.[21] Freely available for download, Russian viewers would play Puckhov's translations over imported films. As Vlad Strukov notes, 'the sound of the original Hollywood movie becomes secondary as the movie is now meant to accompany the "translation" and not the other way around, as one would expect'.[22]

Deeply engrained listening habits mean that voice-over translation continues to be the way in which Poles and Russians prefer to watch broadcasts of foreign material (though subtitling is on the rise in cinemas). As K.I. Donnelly notes, 'it is conventional and thus naturalistic in its own way'.[23] But the attachment to the phenomenon runs deeper than that. In Poland and Russia today, considerable

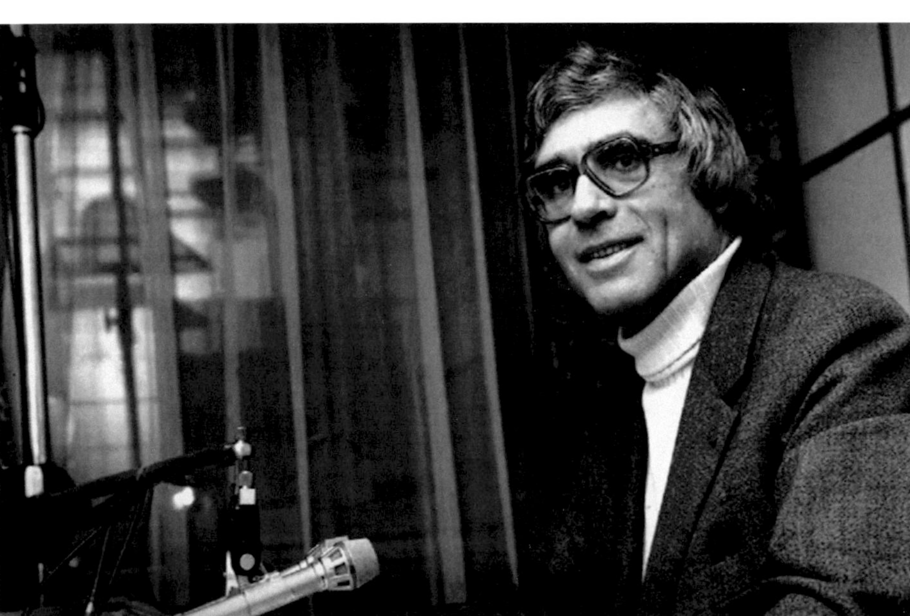

Lucjan Szołajski Source: *kocanblog.blogspot.de*

nostalgia attaches to the early translators of these black market releases (and in marked contradistinction to the characterisation of voice-over narration by Polish film critics in the early 1990s as an unwelcome hangover from the Soviet Bloc). The extent of the audiences for these illegally traded copies was so great that their voices are still well known, instantly and comfortingly familiar.[24] Figures who would have once needed to mask their activities with anonymity have become

21
Abé Mark Nornes, *Cinema Babel. Translating Global Cinema* (Minneapolis, MN: University of Minnesota Press, 2007), 179.

22
Vlad Strukov, 'Translated by Goblin: Global Challenge and Local Response in Post-Soviet Translations of Hollywood Films', in Brian James Baer and John Benjamin, eds., *Contexts, Subtexts and Pretexts: Literary Translation in Eastern Europe and Russia* (Amsterdam: John Benjamins Publishing, 2011), 242.

23
Donnelly, op. cit., 178.

24
When Lucjan Szołajski died in Warsaw in June 2013, numerous obituaries recorded the fact that he had provided voice-over translation for more than 20,000 films and television series over forty years.

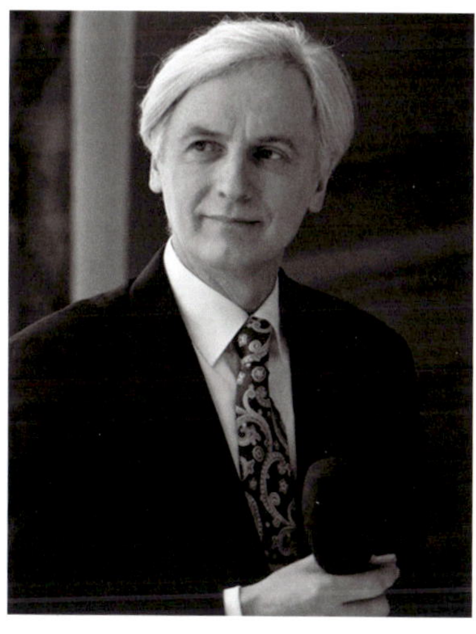

Władysław Frączak Source: *eravhs.fora.pl*

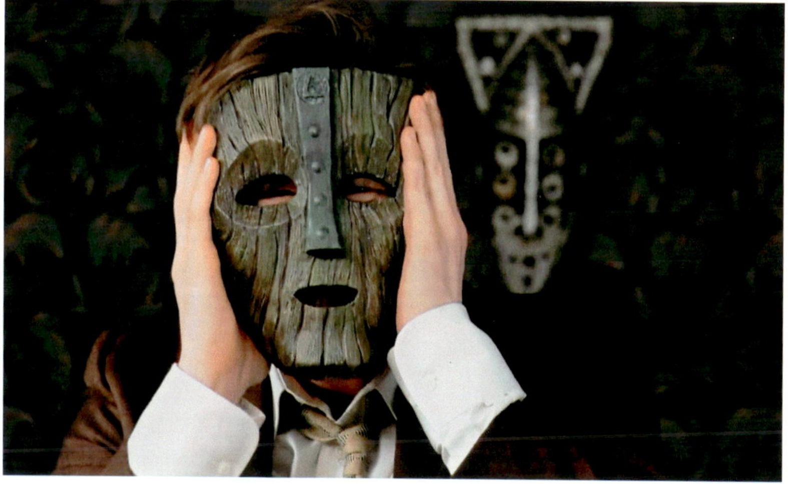

Jim Carrey in **The Mask.** Courtesy *New Line Cinema.*

minor celebrities. Of Władysław Frączak, for instance, one online fan in Poland wrote in 2011, 'This lektor stood out when I watched my first American film on VHS – *The Mask* with Jim Carrey. I can listen to him even when the film is hopeless'.[25] This listener was drawn to Frączak's idiolect. That the voice-over technique is known in Russia by the name of one of its chief practitioners, Andrei Gavrilov, who began his work in the '80s moonlighting from his work as a journalist in the European section of TASS news agency, is itself evidence of recognition. Many now work in the mainstream media today. In recent years, the best-known in Russia, Puckhov, has developed a career as an online political commentator (his *Goblin News* sometimes accompanied, by a neat table-turn, with English subtitles). Increasingly visible and often valued for the vocal idiosyncrasies that they brought to the act of translation, these once-acousmatic voices have now acquired names and visibility.

Being visible and credited as the owner of a voice is a benefit of post-communism: it chimes with the principles of the freedom of speech, accountability and ownership which have been claimed as rights by opponents of the Soviet Bloc. Bylines are an aspect of professionalisation too. Others include representation by agents and the construction of commercial 'voice banks'. Lektors in Poland now ply their trade as 'voice-over artists' for advertising and radio. And when they provide voice-over translations, they usually read scripts translated by others. Professional codes and standards – like those articulated by Libergal and Pijanowski above – have been set down.

25
As cited in Emil Sowiński, 'Subiektywny ranking lektorów filmowych' ('Subjective ranking of film lektors') (20 September 2011), http://emil.ozorkow. net/2011/09/subiektywny-ranking-lektorow-filmowych/ (accessed 1 July 2014).

Der Vorteil des Wortes ist gross,
Spricht man zur rechten Zeit, erhöht es den Sklaven.

Gdy używa się słów w odpowiednim czasie,
To i niewolnika słowo może wynieść.

Expansion of the profession has also provided opportunities for a small number of women. But what, one might wonder, has been lost in these developments? Chion – the chief celebrant of the voice in the cinema – calls the process by which the acousmêtre acquires

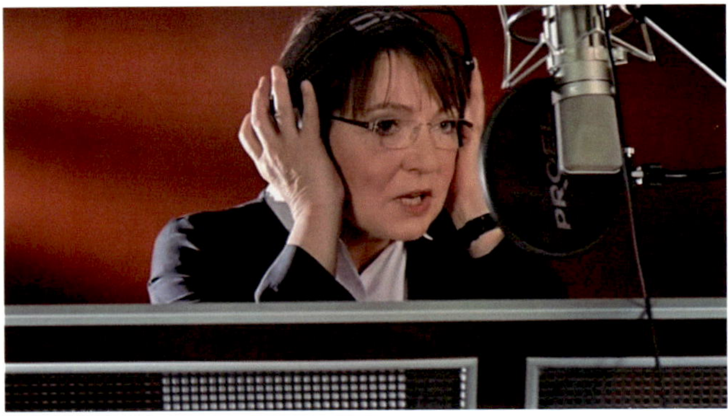

Krystyna Czubówna Source: *youtube.com/watch?v=2b09IKIUFrQ*

a body 'de-acousmatization'. 'Embodying the voice', he writes of fantasy, thriller and gangster movies which feature powerful shadowy kingpins, 'is a sort of symbolic act, dooming the acousmêtre to the fate of ordinary mortals. De-acousmatization roots the acousmêtre to a place and says, "here is your body, you'll be there, and not elsewhere"'.[26] Brought down to earth, the acousmêtre is deprived of its off-screen panopticism and omnipotence. The voice of the lektor in Eastern Europe has however never occupied this all-knowing, all-seeing realm. Instead, it spoke from the shadows, always echoing another, more authoritative voice. The gap between these two voices was the space in which sometimes fretful, occasionally improvised and, at times, 'abusive' translations could be heard.

26
Chion, op. cit., 27–8.

BIBLIOGRAPHY

Abbas, Ihsan, ed. *'Ahd-i Ardashīr*. Translated by Sayyid Muhammad 'Ali Imam Shushtari. Tehran: Anjuman Athar Milli, 1969.

Abé, Mark Nornes. *Cinema Babel Translating Global Cinema*. Minneapolis: University of Minnesota Press, 2007.

'Aflākī, Shams al-Dīn Aḥmad. *The Feats of the Knowers of God (Manāqeb al-'ārefīn)*. Translated by John O'Kane. Leiden: Brill Publications, 2002.

Amirsoleimani, Soheila, 'Of This World and the Next: Metaphors and Meanings in the Qābūs-nāmah'. *Iranian Studies*, vol. 35, № 1/3 (Winter–Summer 2002): 1–22.

Amanat, Abbas. 'The Downfall of Mīrzā Taqī Khān Amīr Kabīr and the Problem of Ministerial Authority in Qājār Iran'. *International Journal of Middle East Studies*, vol. 23, № 4 (November 1991): 577–99.

Aruzi, Nizami. *Chahar Maqala* (Four Discourses). London: Cambridge University Press, 1921.

al-A'ur, Sami Salman, ed. *Sirr al-asrār: al-siyāsa wa al-firāsa fī tadbīr al-ri'āsa lī al-Arisṭuṭālīs*. Beirut: Dar al-'Ulum al-'Arabiya, 1995.

'Awfi, Muḥammad. *Jawāmi al-hikāyāt*. Edited by Muḥammad Ramezani. Tehran: Kulalih Khavar, 1956.

Badawi, 'Abd al-Rahman, ed. *Sirr al-asrār: al-usūl al-Yūnāniya lī al-naẓariyāt al-siyāsiya fī al-Islām*. Cairo: Maktaba al-Nahda al-Misriya, 1954.

Bastug, Susan. 'Tribe, Confederation and State among Altaic Nomads of the Asian Steppes'. *Rethinking Central Asia: Non-Eurocentric Studies in History, Social Structure and Identity*. Edited by Korkut A. Ertürk. Reading: Ithaca Press, 1999.

Blaydes, Lisa, Justin Grimmer and Alison McQueen. 'Mirrors for Princes and Sultans: Advice on the Art of Governance in the Medieval Christian and Islamic Worlds'. Paper presented at the annual meeting of the American Political Science Association, Chicago IL, August 2013.

Boroujerdi, Mehrzad (ed.). *Mirror for the Muslim Prince: Islam and the Theory of Statecraft*. Syracuse: Syracuse University Press, 2013.

Brown, Alison. 'Philosophy and Religion in Machiavelli'. *The Cambridge Companion to Machiavelli*. Edited by John M. Najemy. Cambridge: Cambridge University Press, 2010.

Brown, Norman Oliver. *The Challenge of Islam: the Prophetic Tradition*. Berkeley: New Pacific Press, 2009.

al-Bukhari, Muhammad Ibn Ismail. *The Translation of the Meanings of Sahih Al-Bukhari*. Translated by Muhammad Muhsin Khan. Lahore: Kazi Publications, 1986.

Burak, Alexander. 'Some Like it Hot – Goblin-Style: "Ozhivliazh" in Russian Film Translations'. *Russian Language Journal*, vol. 61 (2011): 5–31.

Calmard, Jean. 'Le Chiîsme imamite en Iran à l'époque seldjoukide d'après le Kitāb al-Naqḍ'. *Le Monde Iranien et l'Islam 1*. Edited by Jean Aubin. Paris: Minard, 1971.

Carson, Anne. *Decreation.* New York: Vintage, 2006.

Chaumont, Marie Louise. 'Callisthenes'. *Encyclopaedia Iranica Online* (December 1990). See: http://www.iranicaonline.org/articles/callisthenes-the-name-of-a-greek-historian-of-the-period-of-alexander-the-great-q/ (accessed 23 October 2014).

Cherewatuk, Karen. 'Speculum Matris: Duoda's Manual'. *Florilegium* 10 (1988-91): 49–64.

Chion, Michel. *The Voice in Cinema.* Edited and translated by Claudia Gorbman. New York: Columbia University Press, 1999.

Cioran, E. M. 'The Book of Delusions'. Translated by Camelia Elias. *Hyperion,* vol. 5, № 1 (May 2010).

Cole, Peter. *The Invention of Influence.* New York: New Directions, 2014.

Corbin, Henri. *Creative Imagination in the Sufism of Ibn 'Arabi.* Translated by Ralph Manheim. London: Routledge, 1969.

Critchley, Simon. *The Faith of the Faithless: Experiments in Political Theology.* New York: Verso, 2012.

Dakhlia, Jocelyne. 'Les Miroirs des princes islamiques: une modernité sourde?'. *Annales HSS,* № 5 (September – October 2002): 1191–206.

Dankoff, Robert A. 'Kashgari on the Tribal and Kinship Organization of the Turks'. *Archivum Ottomanicum,* vol. 4 (1972): 23–43.
—. 'Qarakhanid Literature and the Beginnings of Turco-Islamic Culture'. *Central Asian Monuments.* Edited by Hasan B. Paksoy. İstanbul (1992): 73–80.
—. *From Mahmud Kaşgari to Evliya Çelebi.* The Isis Press, Istanbul 2008.

Darling, Linda T. '"Do Justice, Do Justice, For That is Paradise": Middle Eastern Advice for Indian Muslim Rulers'. *Comparative Studies of South Asia, Africa and the Middle East,* vol. 22, № 1 & 2 (2002): 3–19.

Dawood, Abdel Hakim Hassan Omar Muhammed. 'A Comparative Study of Arabic and Persian Mirrors for Princes from the Second to the Sixth Century'. Ph.D. diss.,University of London, 1965.

Delaney, Carol. 'Untangling the Meanings of Hair in Turkish Society'. *Anthropological Quarterly,* vol. 67, № 4 (1994): 159–72.

de Weese, Devin. *Islamiztion and native religion in the Golden Horde: Baba Tükles and conversion to Islam in historical and epic tradition.* University Park: The Pennsylvania State University Press, 1994.

Dhuoda. *Handbook for William. A Carolingian Woman's Counsel for Her Son.* Translated by Carol Neel. Lincoln: University of Nebraska Press, 1991.

Digby, S. 'Qalandar Related Groups: Elements of Social Deviance in the Religious Life of the Delhi Sultanate of the Thirteenth and Fourteenth Centuries'. *Islam in Asia,* edited by Yohanan Friedman, vol. 1. Jerusalem: Magnes Press, 1984.

Doniger, Wendy. *The Hindus: An Alternative History.* Oxford: Oxford University Press, 2010.

Donnelly, K. J. *Occult Aesthetics: Synchronization in Sound Film.* Oxford: Oxford University Press, 2014.

El-Hibri, Tayeb. *Reinterpreting Islamic Historiography: Hārūn al-Rashīd and the Narrative of the 'Abbāsid Caliphate.* Cambridge: Cambridge University Press, 1999.

Ewing, Katherine Pratt. *Arguing Sainthood: Modernity, Psychoanalysis, and Islam.* Durham: Duke University Press, 1997.

Faroqhi, Suraiya. *Another Mirror for Princes: The Public Image of the Ottoman Sultans and its Reception.* Istanbul: The Isis Press, 2008.

Ferster, Judith. *Fictions of Advice: The Literature and Politics of Counsel in Late Medieval England.* Philadelphia: University of Pennsylvania Press, 1996.

Forster, Regula and Neguin Yavari, eds. *Global Medieval: Mirrors for Princes Reconsidered.* Cambridge: Harvard University Press; ILEX Foundation, 2015.

Fouchécour, Charles-Henri de. Moralia: *Les notions morales dans la littérature persane du 3e/9 e siècle au 7 e/13 e siècle.* Paris: Editions Recherche sur les civilisations, 1986.

Ghazali. *Ghazali's Book of Counsel for Kings: Nashihat Al Muluk.* Translated by F.R.C. Bagley and edited by Jalal Huma'i. London: Oxford University Press, 1964.

Gnoli, Gherhardo. 'Farr(ah)'. *Encyclopaedia Iranica Online* (December 1999); www.iranicaonline.org (accessed 22 October 2014).

Goethe, Johann Wolfgang von. *West-Eastern Divan.* Translated by Edward Dowden. London: JM Dent & Sons Ltd, 1914.

Gray, Vivienne J. *Xenophon's Mirror of Princes: Reading the Reflections.* New York: Oxford University Press, 2011.

Grignaschi, Mario. 'La diffusion du *Secretum secretorum* (*Sirr al asrār*) dans l'Europe occidentale'. *Archives d'histoire doctrinale et littéraire du Môyen Age,* vol. 47 (1980): 7–70.

Haghighat, S. Sadegh. 'In the Name of God: Persian Mirrors for Princes. Pre-Islamic and Islamic Mirrors Compared'. Paper presented at Freie Universität, Berlin, November 2012.

Ḥājib, Yūsuf Khāss. *Wisdom of Royal Glory (Kutadgu Bilig): A Turko-Islamic Mirror for Princes.* Translated by Robert Dankoff. Chicago: University of Chicago Press, 1983.

Hiltebeitel, A., and B. Miller. *Hair: Its Power and Meaning in Asian Culture.* Albany: State University of New York Press, 1998.

Hopkins, Gerard Manley. *Selected Poetry.* Edited by Catherine Philips. Oxford: Oxford University Press, 2008.

Hyder, Qurratulain. *River of Fire.* New York: New Directions, 2003.

Ibn al-Jawzī, Abū al-Faraj 'Abd al-Rahmān b. 'Alī. *Al-Muntaẓam fi tā'rikh al-mulūk wa al-'umam,* vol. 9. Hyderabad: Osmania, 1940.

Ibn al-Muqaffa', 'Abdallāh. *Āthār Ibn al-Muqaffa'.* Beirut: Dār al-Kutub al-'Ilmīya, 1989.

Jarring, Gunnar. *Dervish and Qalandar: Texts from Kashghar.* Stockholm: Almqvist and Wiksell, 1987.

Juynboll, Th., and J. Pedersen. 'Akika'. *Encyclopaedia of Islam 2,* vol. 1. Edited by H.A.R. Gibb. London: Luzak, 1960.

Kai Iskandar Kā'Ās, Ibn. *A Mirror for Princes: The Qabus Nama.* Translated by Reuben Levy. E.P. Dutton (1951): 288.

Karamustafa, Ahmet. God's Unruly Friends: dervish groups in the Islamic later middle period, 1200-1550. Oxford: One World, 2006.

—. Sufism: The Formative Period. Edinbugh: Edinbugh University Press, 2007.

Kāshgharī, Maḥmūd. *Dīwān lughāt at-Turk, Compendium of the Turkic Dialects*. Edited by Robert Dankoff. Cambridge: Harvard University Printing Office, 1982.

Keyvani, Mehdi. *Artisans and Guild Life in the Later Safavid Period: contributions to the social-economic history of Persia*. Berlin: Klaus Schwarz, 1982.

Kivelson, Valerie, 'Patrolling the Boundaries: Witchcraft Accusations and Household Strife in Seventeenth-Century Muscovy'. *Harvard Ukrainian Studies*, vol. 19 (1995): 302–323.

Lambton, A.K.S. 'Justice in the Medieval Theory of Kingship'. *Studia Islamica*, № 17 (1962): 91–119.

—. 'Islamic Mirrors for Princes'. *Theory and Practice in Medieval Persian Government*, VI (1980): 419–442.

—. "Early Timurid Theories of State: Ḥāfiẓ Abrū and Niẓām-al-Dīn Šāmī'. *Bulletin d'Études Orientales* 30 (1978): 1–9.

—. 'The Dilemma of Government in Islamic Persia: The "Siyāsat-nāma" of Niẓām al-Mulk'. *Iran*, vol. 22 (1984): 55–66.

—. 'Quis custodiet custodes: Some Reflections on the Persian Theory of Government: I'. *Studia Islamica*, № 5 (1956): 125–148.

Larson, Laurence Marcellus, ed. and trans. *The King's Mirror*. New York: Twayne Publishers and The American-Scandinavian Foundation, 1972.

Lester, K. Born. 'The specula principis of the Carolingian Renaissance'. *Revue belge de philologie et d'histoire*, Tome 12 fasc.3 (1933): 583–612.

Loewen, Arley. 'Proper Conduct (Adab) Is Everything: The Futuwwat-nāmah-i Sulṭānī of Husayn Va'iz-i Kashifi'. Iranian Studies, vol. 36, № 4 (December 2003): 543–570.

Machiavelli, Niccolò. *The Prince*. Translated by George Bull. New York: Penguin, 2003.

—. *The Prince*. Translated by Daniel Donno. New York: Bantam Classics, 1984.

Manzalaoui, Mahmoud, ed. *Secretum Secretorum, Nine English Versions*. Oxford: Oxford University Press, 1977.

Marcus, Julie. *A World of Difference: Islam and Gender Hierarchy in Turkey*. London: Allen & Unwin, 1992.

Marlow, Louise. 'A Samanid Work of Counsel and Commentary: The Naṣīḥat al-Mulūk of Pseudo-Māwardī'. *Iran*, vol. 45 (2007): 181–192.

—. *Hierarchy and egalitarianism in Islamic thought*. Cambridge: Cambridge University Press, 1997.

Massignon, Louis. 'Time in Islamic Thought', Ralph Manheim, trans. *Man and Time: Papers from the Eranos Yearbooks*. Edited by Joseph Campbell. Princeton: Princeton University Press, 1973.

McDermott, Rachel Fell. *Singing to the Goddess: Poems to Kali and Uma from Bengal*. Oxford: Oxford University Press, 2001.

Meens, Rob. 'Politics, mirrors of princes and the Bible: sins, kings and the well-being of the realm'. *Early Medieval Europe*, vol. 7, Issue 3 (November 1998): 345–357.

Milani, Abbas. 'Amir-Abbas Hoveyda', *Encyclopaedia Iranica Online*, (March 2012) http://www.iranicaonline.org/articles/hoveyda-amir-abbas/ (accessed 23 October 2014).

al-Mulk, Nizam, *The Book of Government or Rules for Kings: The Siyasat-nama.* Translated by Hubert Darke. London: Routledge and Paul, 1960.

—. *The Book of Government or Rules for Kings.* Edited and translated by Hubert Darke. New York: Routledge and Kegan Paul, 1978.

Olivelle, Patrick. *Pañctantra: The Book of India's Folk Wisdom.* Oxford: Oxford University Press, 1997.

Perkins, Nicholas. *Hoccleve's 'Regiment of Princes': Counsel and Constraint.* Cambridge: D. S. Brewer, 2001.

Pollard, Lisa. *Nurturing the Nation: The Family Politics of Modernizing, Colonizing, and Liberating Egypt, 1805–1923.* Berkeley: University of California Press, 2005.

Porete, Marguerite. *The Mirror of Simple Souls.* Translated by Edmund Colledge, Judith Grant and J. C. Marler. Indiana: Notre Dame Press, 1999.

Pouncy, Carolyn Johnston. 'The Origins of the Domostroi: A Study in Manuscript History'. *Russian Review*, vol. 46, № 4 (October 1987): 357–373.

Pouncy, Carolyn Johnston, ed. *The Domostroi: Rules for Russian Households in the Time of Ivan the Terrible.* Ithaca: Cornell University Press, 1994.

Rajgopal, Arvind. *Politics after Television: Hindu Nationalism and the Reshaping of Public in India.* Cambridge: Cambridge University Press, 2001.

Rangarajan, L. N., ed. *The Arthashastra.* New Dehli: Penguin Books, 1992.

Razlogova, Elena. 'Listening to the Inaudible Foreign: Simultaneous Translators and Soviet Experience of Foreign Cinema'. *Sound, Speech, Music in Soviet and Post-Soviet Cinema.* Edited by Lilya Kaganovsky and Masha Salazkina. Bloomington: Indiana University Press, 2014.

Ridgeon, Lloyd. *Morals and Mysticism in Persian Sufism: A History of Sufi-futuwwat.* London: Routledge, 2010.

—. *Jawānmardī: A Sufi Code of Honour.* Edinburgh: Edinburgh University, 2011.

Rogin, Michael. 'Kiss Me Deadly: Communism, Motherhood, and Cold War Movies'. *Representations*, № 6. (1984).

Rulyova, Natalia. 'Piracy and Narrative Games: Dmitry Puchkov's Translations of "The Lord of the Rings"'. *The Slavic and East European Journal*, vol. 49, № 4 (Winter 2005): 625–38.

Rūmī, Jalāl al-Dīn. *The Mathnawī of Jalalu'ddin Rumi.* Edited by R. A. Nicholson. Lahore: Sang-e-Meel Publications, 2004.

Ryan, W.F. 'Alchemy, Magic, Poisons and the Virtues of Stones in the Old Russian *Secretum Secretorum*'. *Ambix*, vol. 31, Part I (March, 1990): 46–54.

Sandberg, Sheryl. *Lean In: Women, Work, and the Will to Lead.* New York: Alfred A. Knopf, 2013.

Sani, Muhammad Baqir Najmi. *Advice on the Art of Governance: An Indo-Islamic Mirror for Princes (Mau'izahi Jahangiri).* Translated by Sajida Sultana Alvi. Albany: State University of New York Press, 1989.

Sanneh, Lamin. 'Religion and Politics: Third World Perspectives on a Comparative Religious Theme'. *Daedalus*, vol. 120, № 3, Religion and Politics (Summer 1991): 203–218.

Scanlon, Larry. *Narrative, Authority and Power: The Medieval Exemplum and the Chaucerian Tradition*. Cambridge: Cambridge University Press, 1994.

Schamiloglu, Uli. 'The Umdet ul-ahbar and the Turkic Narrative Sources for the Golden Horde and the Later Golden Horde'. *Central Asian Monuments* Edited by Hasan B. Paksoy. İstanbul 1992.

Selby, Martha Ann. *Grow Long, Blessed Night: Love Poems from Classical India*. New York: Oxford University Press, 2000.

Shahid Ali, Agha. *The Veiled Suite: The Collected Poems*. New York: W.W. Norton, 2009.

Shushud, H.L. 'The Masters of Wisdom of Central Asia'. *Systematics*, vol. 6, № 4 (March, 1969).

Smith, Margaret. *Rabi'a the Mystic and Her Fellow Saints in Islam*. Cambridge: Cambridge University Press, 1928.

Sneath, David. *The Headless State: Aristocratic Orders, Kinship Society, and Misrepresentations of Nomadic Inner Asia*. New York: Columbia University Press, 2007.

Steele, Robert, ed. *Opera hactenus inedita Rogeri Baconi*, vol. 5. Oxford: Clarendon, 1920.

Strohm, Paul. *Politique: Languages of Statecraft between Chaucer and Shakespeare*. Notre Dame: University of Notre Dame Press, 2005.

Strukov, Vlad. 'Translated by Goblin: Global Challenge and Local Response in Post-Soviet Translations of Hollywood Films'. *Contexts, Subtexts and Pretexts: Literary Translation in Eastern Europe and Russia*. Edited by Brian James Baer and John Benjamin. Amsterdam: John Benjamins Publishing, 2011.

al-Subkī, Taqī al-Dīn. *Ṭabaqāt al-Shāfi'iyya al-kubrā'*, vol. 5. Edited by M. M. Tanahi and A. M. al-Hulw. Cairo: 'Isa al-Babi al-Halabi, 1968.

Tansar. *Letter of Tansar*. Translated by M. Boyce. Instituto Italiano Per Il Medio Ed Estremo Oriente, Rome 1968.

Thyrêt, Isolde. *Between God and Tsar: Religious Symbolism and the Royal Women of Muscovite Russia*. Illinois: Northern Illinois University Press, 2001.

al-Udhari, A. Y. and G. B. H. Wightman, eds. and trans. *Birds through a Ceiling of Alabaster: Three Abbasid Poets*. Baltimore: Penguin Books, 1975.

Van Bladel, Kevin. 'The Iranian Characteristics and Forged Greek Attributions in the Arabic Sirr al-asrār (Secret of Secrets)'. *Mélanges de l'Université Saint-Joseph*, № 57 (2004): 151–72.

van den Boorn, G. P. F., ed. and trans. *The Duties of the Vizier: Civil Administration in the Early New Kingdom*. London: Kegan Paul International, 1988.

Wylie, Philip. *Generation of Vipers*. New York: Holt, Rinehart and Winston, 1955.

Yampolsky, Michal. 'Voice Devoured: Artaud and Borges on Dubbing'. *October*, vol. 64 (Spring 1993): 57–77.

Yavari, Neguin. 'Polysemous Texts and Reductionist Readings, Women and Heresy in the Siyar al-Muluk of Niẓām al-Mulk'. *Views From the Edge: Essays in Honor of Richard W. Bulliet*. Edited by Negiun Yavari et al. New York: Columbia University Press for the Middle East Institute, 2004.

—. 'Mirrors for Prince sor Hall of Mirrors? Nizam al-Mulks Siyar al-muluk Reconsidered'. Al-Masaq, vol. 20, № 1 (March 2008): 47–69

—. *Advice for the Sultan: Prophetic Voices and Secular Politics in Medieval Islam*. New York: Oxford University Press, 2014.

Yumul, Arus. 'Scenes of Masculinity from Turkey'. *Zeitschrift für Türkeistudien*, vol. 12, № 1 (1999): 107–17.

Anthony Downey, Editor

Anthony Downey is an academic, writer and editor. Recent and forthcoming publications include *Art and Politics Now* (2014), *Uncommon Grounds: New Media and Critical Practices in North Africa and the Middle East* (2014), *The Future of a Promise: Contemporary Art from the Arab World* (2011) and *Dissonant Archives: Contemporary Visual Culture and Contested Narratives in the Middle East* (forthcoming, 2015). He is the director of the master's programme in contemporary art at Sotheby's Institute of Art, London and editor-in-chief of Ibraaz (www.ibraaz.org), a research and publishing platform for contemporary visual culture in the Middle East and North Africa. He is currently editing *Future Imperfect: Building Institutions through Practice across the Maghreb and Middle East* (forthcoming, 2016) and conducting research for a book on the poetics and politics of narrative and visual rhetoric in contemporary art (forthcoming, 2017).

Maya Allison

Maya Allison is the founding director and chief curator of the Art Gallery at New York University Abu Dhabi, which opened in fall of 2014 on the Saadiyat Island campus. She relocated to Abu Dhabi from the US. Previously she held positions as curator at Brown University's Bell Gallery, program director of the annual new media festival *Pixilerations* and director of the 5 Traverse Gallery and at The RISD Museum (Rhode Island School of Design) she was interim head of the contemporary art department. She holds an MFA from Columbia University, a BA in art history from Reed College and was awarded a research fellowship on contemporary curatorial practices at Brown University's Center for Public Humanities.

Beatrix Ruf

Beatrix Ruf is the director of the Stedelijk Museum Amsterdam. From September 2001 to October 2014 she headed the Kunsthalle Zürich as director and chief curator. In 2012 she completed the aquisition, remodelling and extension of the Kunsthalle Zürich building at the Löwenbräu art building in Zürich. In 2008 Ruf co-curated the Yokohama Triennial and in 2006 she curated the Tate Triennial for Tate Britain, London. Ruf had been director/curator of the Kunsthaus Glarus from 1998 to 2001 and curator at the Kunstmuseum of the Canton of Thurgau between 1994 and 1998. She serves as a board member and expert on numerous commissions, among others, the Ringier collection, the Schweizerische Graphische Gesellschaft (SGG), JRP|Ringier, the Cultural Advisory board of CERN, Geneva and the Board of Trustees of the Museum Ludwig, MuMok. Ruf has curated exhibitions, written essays and published catalogues on a wide range of contemporary artists.

Neguin Yavari

Neguin Yavari studied international economics and history at Georgetown University and medieval history at Columbia University. Political thought in the medieval period, with an emphasis on transitions from medieval to early modern, is among the key foci of her research. Her latest book on the rhetoric of advice in medieval political thought, *Advice for the Sultan: Prophetic Voices and Secular Politics in Medieval Islam* (New York: Oxford University Press; London: Hurst, 2014), is a comparative study of European and Islamic mirrors for princes and their resonances in the construction of political language in the modern period, especially in the Islamic world. The subjects of her forthcoming study, *Global Medieval: Mirrors for Princes Reconsidered*, coedited with Regula Forster (2015), include mirrors for princes across political and spatial divides and possibilities for theorising transnational and global – both *avant la lettre*, perhaps – political thought. She is currently preparing a modern biography of Nizām al-Mulk, the great eleventh-century vizier.

Manan Ahmed Asif

Manan Ahmed Asif is assistant professor in the Department of History at Columbia University where he teaches a survey course on South Asia. He is interested in the relationship between text, space and narrative. His work on Arab military campaigns in coastal Sind and Gujarat in the eighth century traces a *longue durée* history of contestations over origins and conquests at varied points in South Asian history. His areas of specialisation include the political and cultural history of Islam in South and Southeast Asia, frontier spaces and the city in medieval South Asia, imperial and colonial historiography and philology. He is involved in digital humanities projects, especially with visualising space in medieval texts and textualising medieval and early modern maps.

Anna Della Subin

Anna Della Subin writes about sleepwalkers, grave worship, animal rights in Cairo, mummies, imperial Ethiopian court etiquette, visions of the flood, thirteenth-century occulists, occultists, Catullus and Amaru, Albert Cossery, Shah Rukh Khan, pilgrimages, Dr. Death's childhood, dreams of 9/11, 300-year naps, cricket, men becoming gods and gods becoming men. Her essays have appeared in the *London Review of Books*, *The New York Times*, *Harper's*, *BOMB*, *The Millions*, *The White Review*, *Jadaliyya* and *The Paris Review Daily*, among other publications. She is a contributing editor at the Middle East arts and culture magazine *Bidoun*. She studied philosophy and classics at the University of Chicago and the history of religion at Harvard University.

Lloyd Ridgeon

Lloyd Ridgeon is reader in Islamic Studies at the University of Glasgow. His main area of research is medieval Persian Sufism, but he also engages in studies of modern Iranian society and culture. In 2014 he was chosen to be the editor of

the *British Journal of Middle Eastern Studies*. His books include *Jawanmardi: A Sufi Code of Honour* (2011), *Morals and Mysticism in Persian Sufism: A History of Futuwwat in Iran* (2010), *Sufi Castigator: Ahmad Kasravi and the Iranian Sufi Tradition* (2006), *Persian Metaphysics and Mysticism* (2002) and *Aziz Nasafi* (1998). He has also edited a number of works, including the four-volume collection of essays in Routledge's Critical Concepts Series entitled *Sufism* (2008), *Islamic Interpretations of Christianity* (2011), *Religion and Politics in Modern Iran* (2005), *Iranian Intellectuals: 1997–2007* (2008) and *Shi'-i Islam and Identity* (2012). His most recent edited volume is *The Cambridge Companion to Sufism* (2014).

David Crowley

David Crowley is a professor in the School of Humanities at the Royal College of Art, London, where he runs the Critical Writing in Art & Design MA. He has a specialist interest in the art and design histories of Eastern Europe under communist rule. He is the author of various books, including *National Style and Nation-State: Design in Poland from the Vernacular Revival to the International Style* (1992) and *Warsaw* (2003), and coeditor with Susan Reid of the three volumes: *Socialism and Style: Material Culture in Post-war Eastern Europe* (2000), *Socialist Spaces: Sites of Everyday Life in the Eastern Bloc* (2003) and *Pleasures in Socialism: Leisure and Luxury in the Eastern Bloc* (2010). He writes regularly for the art and design press. Crowley also curates exhibitions, including *Cold War Modern* at the Victoria and Albert Museum, London, in 2008–9; *The Power of Fantasy: Modern and Contemporary Art from Poland* at BOZAR, Brussels, in 2011; and *Sounding the Body Electric: Experimental Art and Music in Eastern Europe 1957–1984* at Muzeum Sztuki, Łódź, in 2012 and Calvert 22, London, in 2013.

Der Dichter schmückt die Sprache mit schönen Wörtern
Und erhellt ihr Gesicht. Worte reihte er an Worte und sagte:

Poeta, co pięknymi słowy zdobi swój język
W ten sposób wypowiedział słowa:

The poet embellishes his speech with pretty words and lightens their face.
Words he strung together and said:

Dilini güzel sözle süsleyen ve onun yüzünü açan şair,
Bu vadide şöyle bir söz söylemiştir:

الشاعر الذي يزخرف الكلام ويفتح وجه الجمال
يقول هذا الكلام في هذا الميدان:

This book is part of *Mirrors for Princes*, a cycle of research and production by the art collective Slavs and Tatars, published on the occasion of their eponymous exhibition at NYU Abu Dhabi Art Gallery, 1 Mar–31 May 2015.

Collaborating venues
Kunsthalle Zürich, Zurich, Switzerland 30 Aug–9 Nov 2014

Galerie für Zeitgenössische Kunst Leipzig, Leipzig, Germany 15 Nov 2014–3 Mar 2015

Collective Gallery, Edinburgh, Scotland, United Kingdom 17 April–12 July 2015

Institute of Modern Art, Brisbane, Australia 24 Oct–19 Dec 2015

Blaffer Art Museum, University of Houston, Texas, United States 16 Jan–19 Mar 2016

First published by
NYU Abu Dhabi
Art Gallery
and JRP|Ringier

© 2015 Slavs and Tatars, the authors, NYU Abu Dhabi Art Gallery, and JRP|Ringier. All rights reserved.

Editor
Anthony Downey, Ibraaz (www.ibraaz.org)
Project Manager
Nour K Sacranie, Ibraaz
Designer
Stan de Natris, Slavs and Tatars
Design Assistant
Davide Giorgetta
Production Manager
Dustin Cosentino
Copy Editing
Liz Allen, Miles Champion
Proofreading
Fran Carlen
Image Researcher
Sarah al Dabaghy
Assistant Image Researchers
Sophie Arni, Agustina Zegers
Lithographer
Tadeusz Mirosz
Research
Mara Goldwyn
Kutadgu Bilig adaptation
Rüştü Asyalı and Reşit Rahmeti Arat (Turkish), Ulrich Gerhardt and Wilhelm Radloff (German), Tadeusz Majda (Polish), Yusuf Yavuzcan (Arabic)

NYU Abu Dhabi Art Gallery
Saadiyat Island,
PO Box 129188
Abu Dhabi, UAE

JRP|Ringier
Kunstverlag AG
Limmatstrasse 270
CH-8005 Zürich, Switzerland

Distribution
Austria and Germany
Vice Versa Distribution GmbH
Immanuelkirchstrasse 12
D-10405 Berlin, Germany
info@vice-versa-distribution.com

France
Les presses du réel
35 rue Colson
F-21000 Dijon, France
info@lespressesdureel.com

Switzerland
AVA Verlagsauslieferung AG
Centralweg 16
CH-8910 Affoltern a. Albis,
Switzerland
verlagsservice@ava.ch

United Arab Emirates
NYU Abu Dhabi Art Gallery
Saadiyat Island,
Building A4, Room 007
PO Box 129188
Abu Dhabi, UAE
nyuad.artgallery@nyu.edu

United Kingdom and other European countries
Cornerhouse Publications
70 Oxford Street
Manchester M1 5NH,
England, United Kingdom
publications@cornerhouse.org

USA, Canada, Asia, and Australia
ARTBOOK | D.A.P.
155 Sixth Avenue, 2nd Floor
New York, NY 10013, USA
orders@dapinc.com

The artists, authors and publishers gratefully acknowledge permission granted to reproduce the copyrighted material in this book. Every effort has been made to trace copyright holders and to obtain their permission for the use of copyrighted material. The publishers apologise for any errors or omissions and would be grateful if notified of any corrections that should be incorporated in future reprints or editions of this publication.

ISBN 978-3-03764-407-2

Printed and bound by
Medialis Offsetdruck GmbH, Berlin, Germany
Printed on
LuxoArt Samt, 150g/m²
LuxusCard, 300g/m²
MultiArt Silk, 130g/m²
Fonts
Arial Narrow
Helvetica Neue
Sh Times Modern
Times New Roman
Print run
2,000 copies

The following pages feature works by Slavs and Tatars:

p.69, 121: *Nations,* 2007.
pp.68–69, 74–75, 82–83, 96–97, 110–111, 120–121: *Behind Reason,* mimeograph prints, various sizes, 2012.
p.111: *In the Name of God,* 2013.
p.156: *The Wizard of öz Türkçe,* offset print, 48.6 × 69.5 cm, 2014. Untitled Art, Miami, curated by onestar press.
p.167: *Jęzzers Język, Odbyt,* from *The Tranny Tease,* sketches, 2015.
p.175: *Larry nixed, trachea trixed,* screen-print, 70 × 50 cm, 2015. Photo courtesy Raster Gallery.

The research for this publication has been generously supported by the Kamel Lazaar Foundation. www.kamellazaarfoundation.org

Slavs and Tatars
and the publishers
would like to thank

Muhamed Al-Khalil, Maya Allison, Sophie Arni, Anlam Arslanoğlu and the Istanbul Modern team, İlker Aytürk, Çelenk Bafra, Hilary Ballon, Nabil Baradey, Ildiko Beller-Hann, Rahel Blättler, Zlata Borůvková, Devon Britt-Darby, Aileen Burns, Evan Camfield, Siobhan Carroll, Contemporary Art Organisations Australia, Rahila Dawut, Lisan Dierkx, Joanna Domańska, Rebecka Domig, Adi Eberhard, Abdu Khayum Emin, Sam Faix, Reindert Falkenberg, Galeria Arsenał, Ulrich Gerhardt, Kate Gray, Patrick Hällzon, Imam Husan, Otto Kakhidze,

Kunsthalle Zürich is regularly supported by: Stadt Zürich Kultur, Kanton Zürich Fachstelle Kultur, Zürcher Kantonalbank – Partner of Kunsthalle Zürich, LUMA Foundation.

Bana Kattan, Julia Kurz and the GfZK team, Laura Latman, Johan Lundh, Titus Maderlechner, Anastasia Marukhina, Laura Metzler, Julia Moritz, Dr. Arend Oetker, onestar press, Attila Panczel, Krzysztof Pyda, Arts Queensland, Raster, Dilnur Reyhan, Beatrix Ruf, Claudia Schmuckli, Mark Swislocki, The Third Line, Tudajim, Gayane Umerova, Visual Arts and Craft Strategy, Visual Arts Board of the Australia Council for the Arts, Abdurishid Yakup, Thierry Zarcone, Agustina Zegers, Kraupa-Tuskany Zeidler, Franciska Zólyom.

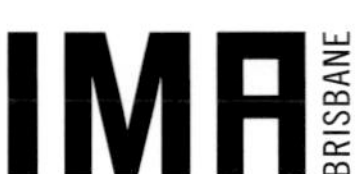

jrp|ringier

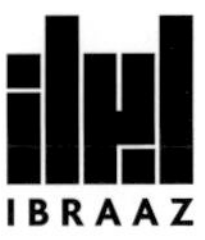

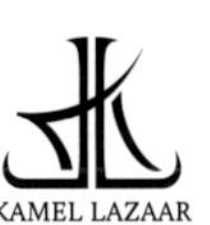

Sözü güzel ve iyice düşünerek söyle ve kısa kes.
Ancak sorulduğunda söyle ve kısa kes.

قل الكلام الجميل بعد التفكير و عند السؤال.
الجيد

Consider well and then respond;
Be not prolix – that is uncouth.

Słuchaj cierpliwe, mało mów
Mów rozważnie, upiększaj je wiedzą innym.

Çok dinle, fakat az konuş;
Sözü akıl ile söyle, bilgi ile süsle.

Höre viel, aber sprich nicht viel!
Sprich mit Verstand und mit Wissen!'

اسمع كثيراً وتكلم قليلاً وزينه بالمعرفة.
قل الكلام بعقل وزينه بالمعرفة

Listen much, speak to the point,
And string your words with pearls of truth.

Gerekli sözü büyüklerden dinlemeli ve
Ona göre hareket etmeleri için küçüklere söylemeli.

Von den Grossen muss man die notwendigen Worte hören,
Den Kleinen muss man sie geben, damit sie sich danach richten.

ينبغي للصغار أن يستمع الكلام من الكبار.

Słów prawdy słuchać należy od możnych,
Postępować należy zgodnie z nimi i przekazywać je maluczkim.

One ought to listen to the wise, then speak to the ignorant;
hear the speech of superiors, and report it to inferiors;

Çok dinlemeli fakat sözü birer birer söylemeli;
Bilgili hakim bana böyle dedi.

Viele Worte muss man hören, aber nur zu einem Wort sprechen,
So hat es mir der wissende Weise gesagt.

ينبغي قول الكثير من الأصغار، و الكلام شيئاً فشيئاً قال لي الحاكم العالم.

Słuchać należy wiele, lecz mówić niewiele,
Uczony i mędrzec tak rzekli:

hearken to many words, and utter few –
thus have the sages instructed me.

Çok söylemekle bilge olmaz kişi;
Çok dinlemekle bilge bulur başköşeyi.

Wer da viel spricht, ist kein weiser Mann,
Vor vielen wird der Weise das Haupt am Ehrenplatze sein.

فبالكلام الكثير لا يصبح الشخص حكيماً، و بالاستماع الكثير يصبح ملك الحكماء.

A man does not become wise by speaking much;
but by listening much the wise man gains the seat of honour.

Człowiek nie staję się uczonym jeśli wiele mówi,
Słuchając wiele uczony dostąpi zaszczytnego miejsca.

İnsan, dilsiz de olsa bilgili olabilir;
Fakat sağır olursa bilgiyi elde edemez.

Wenn der Mensch stumm ist, kann er auch Wissen haben,
Wenn er aber taub ist, erlangt er das Wissen nicht.

يمكن للإنسان أن يكون عالماً حتى لو كان أبكم، لكن الأصم لا يستطيع الحصول على المعلومات.

A man can learn even if he is mute;
but if he is deaf he has no access to wisdom.

Nawet niemowa może być uczonym,
Lecz głuchy wiedzy nie zdobędzie.

Wenn man mit der Zunge nicht spricht,
Bleibt das Wissen liegen.

Jeśli człowiek się nie wysłowi, to wiedzy nie ujawni.

Dil ile söylenmezse bilgi öylece kalır.

تىلى سۆز كۆرسىكىدا بولمايدۇ، مەختەلىدىغان ياخشى تەرىپى نۇرغۇن بار.

If one fails to speak altogether, then wisdom is left in the dark.

و المعلومة تبقى في مكانها ما لم يخبر بها اللسان.

Die Zunge darf man nicht immer schelten,
Man muss sie auch loben.
Manches ist an den Worten zu loben, manches zu schelten.

سۆزرنىڭمۇ مەختىلىدىغان ۋە ھەم سۆكۈلىدىغان تەرەپلىرى بار.

Języka nie powinno się wyłącznie ganić, lecz także go wychwalać.
Wszak ma on wiele zalet, jak i wad.

و المعلومة تبقى في مكانها ما لم يخبر بها اللسان.

Dile yalnız sövmek olmaz, övülecek tarafı da çoktur;
Sözün de övülecek ve sövülecek tarafları vardır.

It is not meet to curse the tongue,
for it has many praiseworthy qualities as well as faults.

لا ينبغي نَخ اللسان دائماً، فقد جوانب تستحق الذم و الثناء.

ساناسىز تىرىك جانلىق ساغ جۇ داننىڭ ھەممىسى مادح تىل بىلەن گۇۋاھلىق بېرىدۇ

Bütün canlılar, bütün bu sayısız yaratıklar
Tanrı'nın birliğine dil ile şehadet getirir.

Wszyscy ludzie i niezliczone stworzenia,
Oni wszyscy dają świadectwo Jedynemu Bogu.

Alle Geschöpfe, die zahllos vielen,
Geben Zeugnis mit Worten von dem einen Gott.

All the countless crowds of living things bear witness to the one God.

ۋۇجۇدى بارلىق خالايىقچە خالىق بىر تىلى بىلەن مەختەيدۇ.

Tanrı yüz binlerce mahluku yarattı;
Onların hepsi de Tanrı'yı dilleriyle över.

He created myriads of creatures,
and all sing God's praises with their tongues.

خلق مئات الالاف من المخلوقات
و جميعهم يحمدون الله باللسان.

Er hat geschaffen die zehntausend Geschöpfe,
Mit der Zunge loben sie Gott in reiner Weise.

Bóg stworzył mnogie stworzenia,
I wszyscy swymi językami chwalą Boga.

كىشى نۇ جۇن كېرەك نەرسە بىرى تىل بىلەن سۆزى

Vücut sahibi kişiye gereken şeylerden
Biri dil ve söz, biri de gönüldür.

ما يحتاجه صاحب البدن و البيان و الشيء هو القلب.

Dem begüterten Mann sind diese Dinge nötig,
Das mit der Zunge gesprochene Wort und das Herz.

The prosperous man has need of these things,
the word spoken by the tongue and the heart.

Człowiekowi, by żyć potrzebne są:
Język, słowa i serce.

تىلنى كۆڭۈل ۋە تىللى تۈغرا سۆز ئۈچۈن يوغان بار ئىتقان. سۆزى تەتلۇر تۇتتا كىرگۈشكە سەكجەز بولسۇ.

Tanrı gönlü ve dili doğru söz için yarattı;
Sözü eğri olanları zorla ateşe atarlar.

خلق القلب و اللسان من أجل كلمة الحق،
الذين يحرفون الكلام يُلقون في النار قهراً.

Zunge und Herz hat Er geschaffen für gerechte Worte,
Sind die Worte ungerecht, so erzittert der Mensch vor Furcht.

Bóg stworzył serce i język dla prostych słów,
Tych, co łamią słowa, siłą wrzucają do ognia.

Tongue and heart did He create for just words,
Are these words unjust, so man must tremble with fear.

توغرا سۆز تۈنى سۆزلەنسە پايدىسى كۆپتۇر. ئەگرى تىلغى سۆز ئەيب جۇ جىرايدۇ.

Söz doğru söylenirse faydası çoktur.
Eğri söz daima ayıplanır.

و البيان لو قورنت كثيرة عند يقال بشكل داتى. و الكلام الباطل يُنح دائماً.

Spricht er gerechte Worte, so hat er viel Vorteil davon,
Spricht er Ungerechtes, so erntet er nur Schimpf.

Z prostych słów jest wielka korzyść,
Złamane słowa zawsze hańbią.

If he speaks just words, so he will benefit greatly,
should these words be unjust, so will he only reap insults.

I

Doğru söylenecekse dilin kımıldasın;
Sözün eğriyse onu gizlemelisin.

Sprichst du gerecht, so möge Deine Zunge sich bewegen!
Sind aber Deine Worte ungerecht, so verbirg dich!

So let your tongue bring forth your words if they are straight;
but if they are crooked, then keep them hidden.

Chcąc wyrazić się prosto, poruszaj językiem,
Jeśli słowa twe są kręte, ukryj je.

II

Konuşmayan kişiye dilsiz derler;
Çok söyleyenin adıysa geveze başıdır.

Spricht er mit seiner Zunge nicht,
So wird der Mensch stumm genannt.
Spricht er aber viel, so wird er des Irrtums bezichtigt.

When a man fails to speak altogether, people call him 'dumb',
but if he talks too much, they call him 'chatterbox'.

Człowieka mało mówiącego zwą niemową,
A na rozgadanego mówią – gaduła.

III

Kişinin itibarsızı geveze olandır;
Kişinin itibarlısı cömert olandır.

Das schlechteste beim Menschen ist sein Irrtum.
Das ehrenvollste beim Menschen ist aber seine Wahrhaftigkeit.

And the chatterer is the meanest of men,
while the noblest is the generous giver.

Człowiek nie mający poważania to gadatliwy.
Zaś poważany człowiek to - dzielny.

IV

Misk ve bilgi birbirine benzer;
İnsan bunları yanında gizli tutamaz.

Moschus und Wissen sind einander ähnlich,
Man kann sie nicht lange haben und verbergen,

Musk and wisdom are of the same sort:
neither one can be kept hidden.

Piżmo i wiedza są do siebie podobne,
Nie można ich utrzymać w tajemnicy.

V

Miski gizlersen, kokusundan belli olur;
Bilgiyi saklarsan dili ayarlamasından belli olur.

Verbirgst du den Moschus, so verrät ihn sein Geruch,
Verbirgst du das Wissen, bringt es die Sprache ans Licht.

If you try to hide musk, its scent gives it away;
and if you conceal wisdom, it nevertheless continues to regulate your tongue.

Schowasz piżmo, to i tak je zdradzi zapach,
Wiedzę ukryjesz, ujawni ją język.

VI

Takva sahibi insan ne der, dinle;
Ey boğazının kulu, bu söze göre hareket et.

Höre den Worten der gottesfürchtigen Menschen zu
Und handele nach diesen Worten,
Du Sklave Deines eigenen Rachens.

Listen to the words of God-fearing people and take action according to these words,
you, slave to your own throat.

Posłuchaj, co mówi pustelnik/asceta,
O, sługo gardła, postępuj wedle tych słów!